NAOKI URASAWA'S

20th CENTURY BOYS

Naoki Urasawa's
20th Century Boys
Volume 10

VIZ Signature Edition

STORY AND ART BY NAOKI URASAWA

20 SEIKI SHONEN 10 by Naoki URASAWA/Studio Nuts
© 2002 Naoki URASAWA/Studio Nuts
With the cooperation of Takashi NAGASAKI
All rights reserved. Original Japanese
edition published in 2002 by Shogakukan Inc., Tokyo.

English Adaptation/Akemi Wegmüller
Touch-up Art & Lettering/Freeman Wong
Cover & Interior Design/Sam Elzway
Editor/Kit Fox

VP, Production/Alvin Lu
VP, Sales & Product Marketing/Gonzalo Ferreyra
VP, Creative/Linda Espinosa
Publisher/Hyoe Narita

Printed in the U.S.A.

Published by VIZ Media, LLC
P.O. Box 77010
San Francisco, CA 94107

10 9 8 7 6 5 4 3 2 1
First printing, August 2010

VIZ SIGNATURE
www.vizsignature.com

www.viz.com

NAOKI URASAWA'S
20th CENTURY BOYS

VOL 10
THE FACELESS BOY

Story & Art by

NAOKI URASAWA

With the cooperation of

Takashi NAGASAKI

PROFILES

NAOKI URASAWA'S 20th CENTURY BOYS

Kanna has begun mobilizing the Neo Tokyo underworld as she prepares to take on the powerful enigma known only as the Friend. Meanwhile, Koizumi Kyoko is being followed. Who is the strange man that now makes his presence known? It's 2014 and the future of the planet is about to be decided!

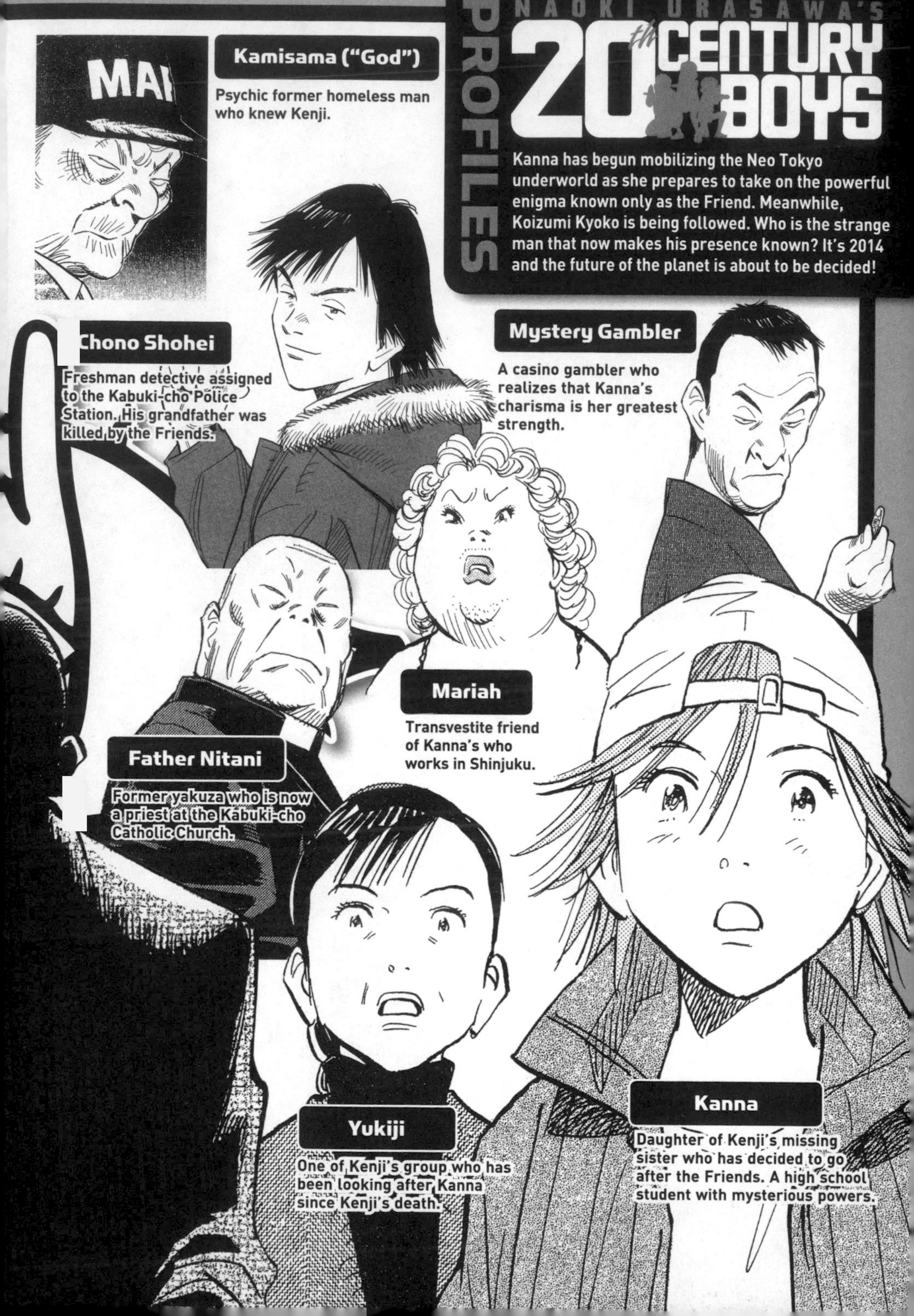
MA

Kamisama ("God")

Psychic former homeless man who knew Kenji.

Chono Shohei

Freshman detective assigned to the Kabuki-cho Police Station. His grandfather was killed by the Friends.

Mystery Gambler

A casino gambler who realizes that Kanna's charisma is her greatest strength.

Mariah

Transvestite friend of Kanna's who works in Shinjuku.

Father Nitani

Former yakuza who is now a priest at the Kabuki-cho Catholic Church.

Kanna

Daughter of Kenji's missing sister who has decided to go after the Friends. A high school student with mysterious powers.

Yukiji

One of Kenji's group who has been looking after Kanna since Kenji's death.

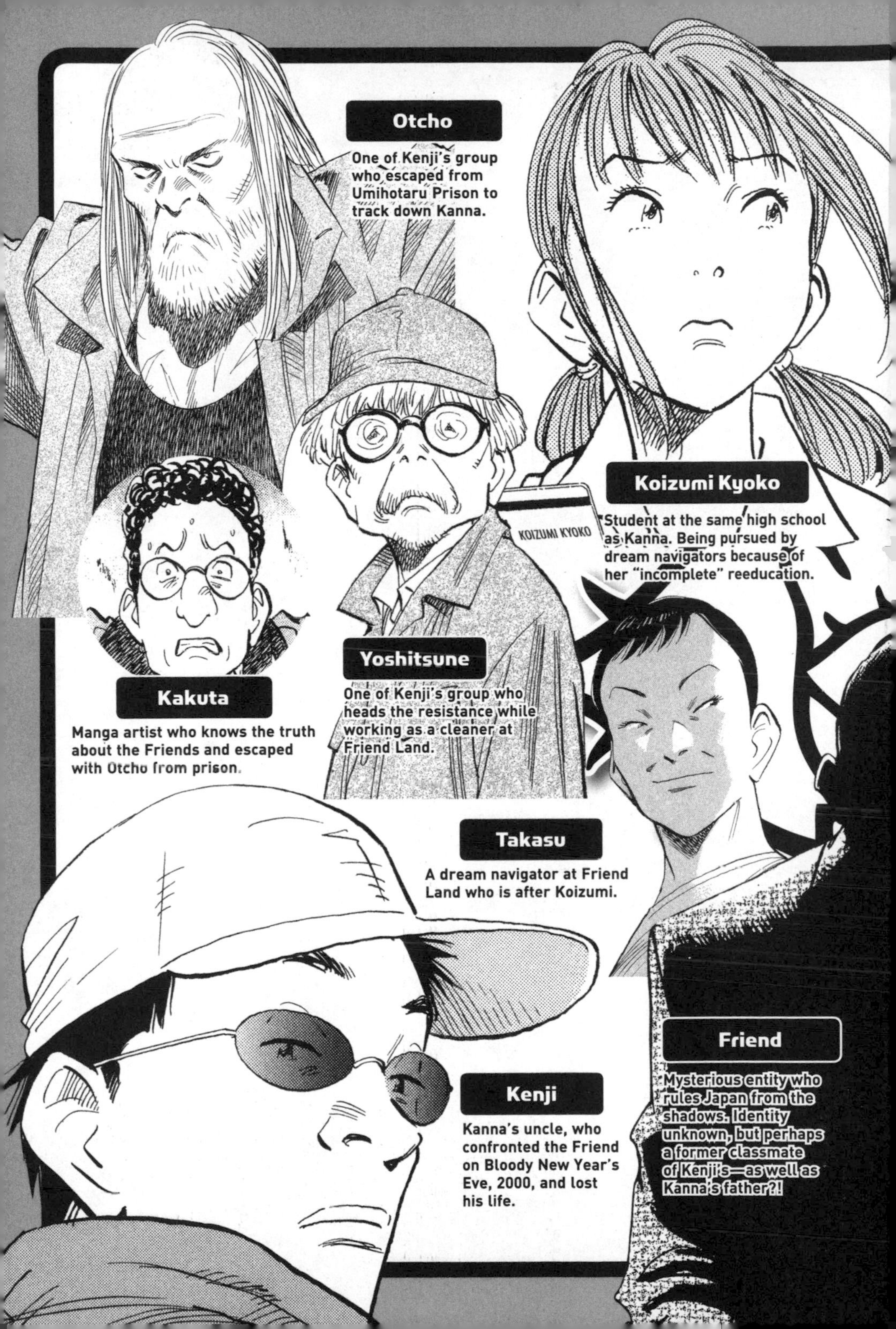

Otcho
One of Kenji's group who escaped from Umihotaru Prison to track down Kanna.
Koizumi Kyoko
KOIZUMI KYOKO
Student at the same high school as Kanna. Being pursued by dream navigators because of her "incomplete" reeducation.
Kakuta
Manga artist who knows the truth about the Friends and escaped with Otcho from prison.
Yoshitsune
One of Kenji's group who heads the resistance while working as a cleaner at Friend Land.
Takasu
A dream navigator at Friend Land who is after Koizumi.
Friend
Mysterious entity who rules Japan from the shadows. Identity unknown, but perhaps a former classmate of Kenji's—as well as Kanna's father?!
Kenji
Kanna's uncle, who confronted the Friend on Bloody New Year's Eve, 2000, and lost his life.

CONTENTS

VOL 10
THE FACELESS BOY

NAOKI
URASAWA'S

20th CENTURY BOYS

Chapter 1 Truce

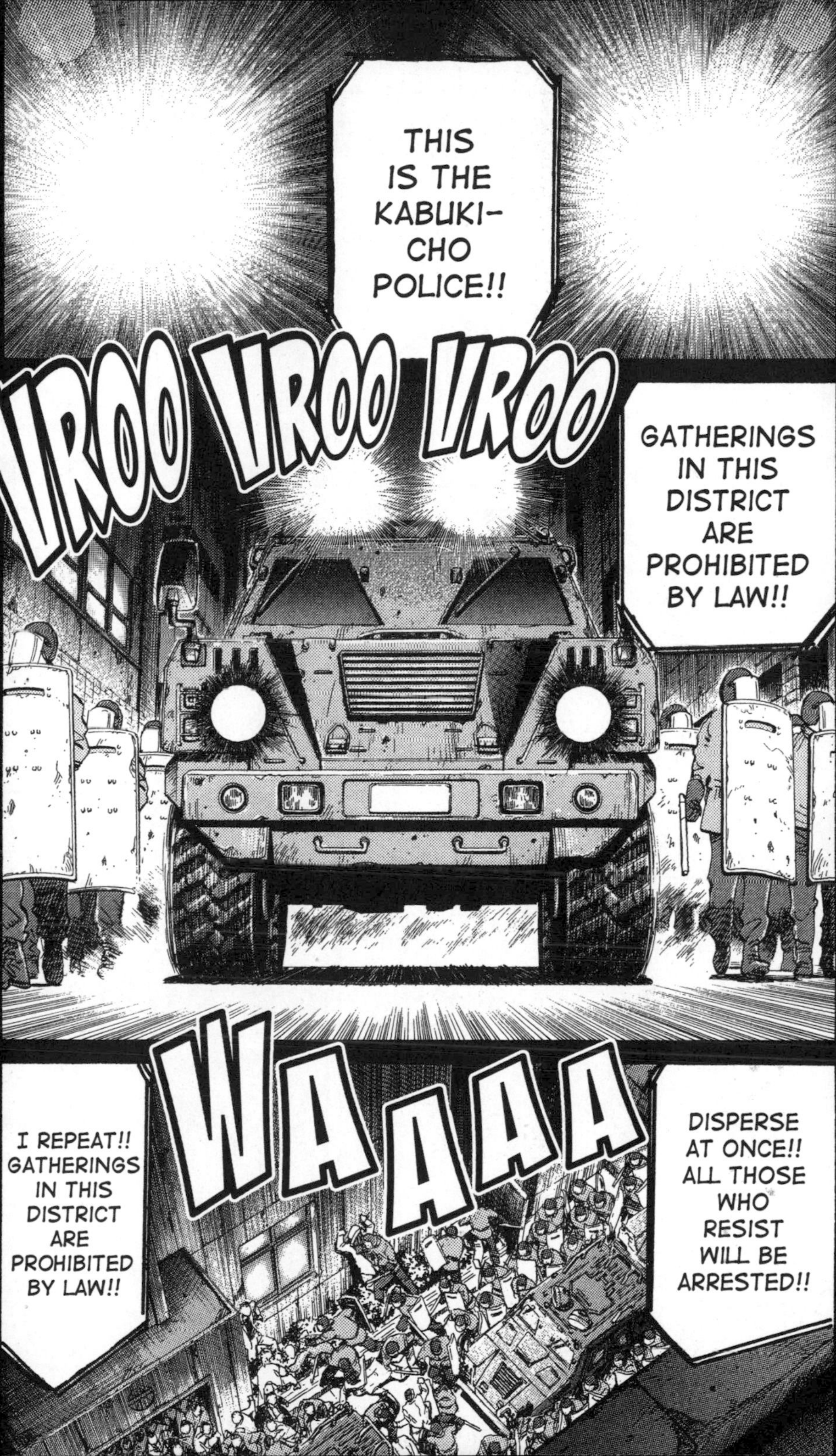
THIS IS THE KABUKI-CHO POLICE!!
GATHERINGS IN THIS DISTRICT ARE PROHIBITED BY LAW!!
VROO VROO VROO
DISPERSE AT ONCE!! ALL THOSE WHO RESIST WILL BE ARRESTED!!
WAAAA
I REPEAT!! GATHERINGS IN THIS DISTRICT ARE PROHIBITED BY LAW!!

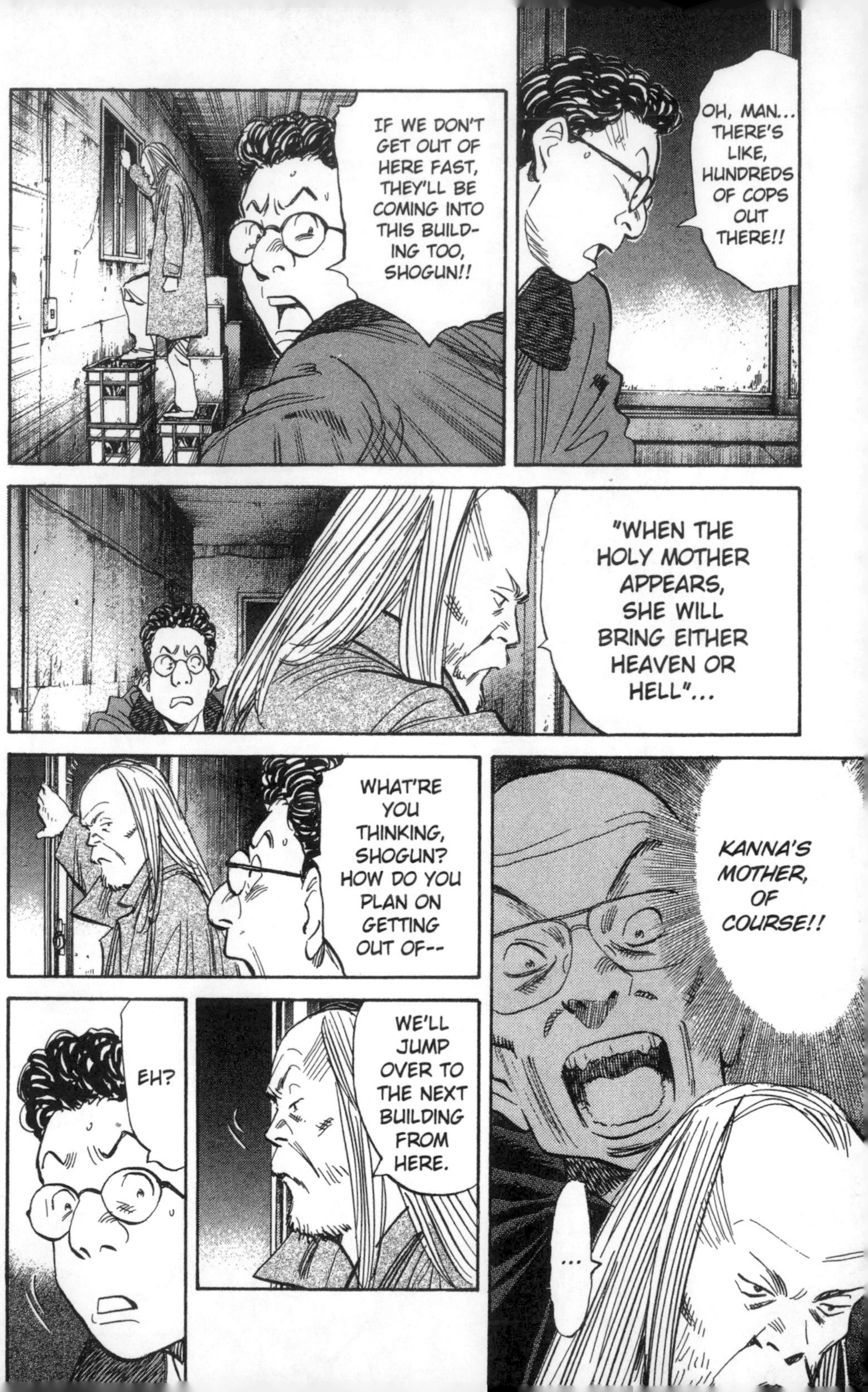
OH, MAN... THERE'S LIKE, HUNDREDS OF COPS OUT THERE!!
IF WE DON'T GET OUT OF HERE FAST, THEY'LL BE COMING INTO THIS BUILD-ING TOO, SHOGUN!!
"WHEN THE HOLY MOTHER APPEARS, SHE WILL BRING EITHER HEAVEN OR HELL"...
KANNA'S MOTHER, OF COURSE!!
...
WHAT'RE YOU THINKING, SHOGUN? HOW DO YOU PLAN ON GETTING OUT OF--
WE'LL JUMP OVER TO THE NEXT BUILDING FROM HERE.
EH?

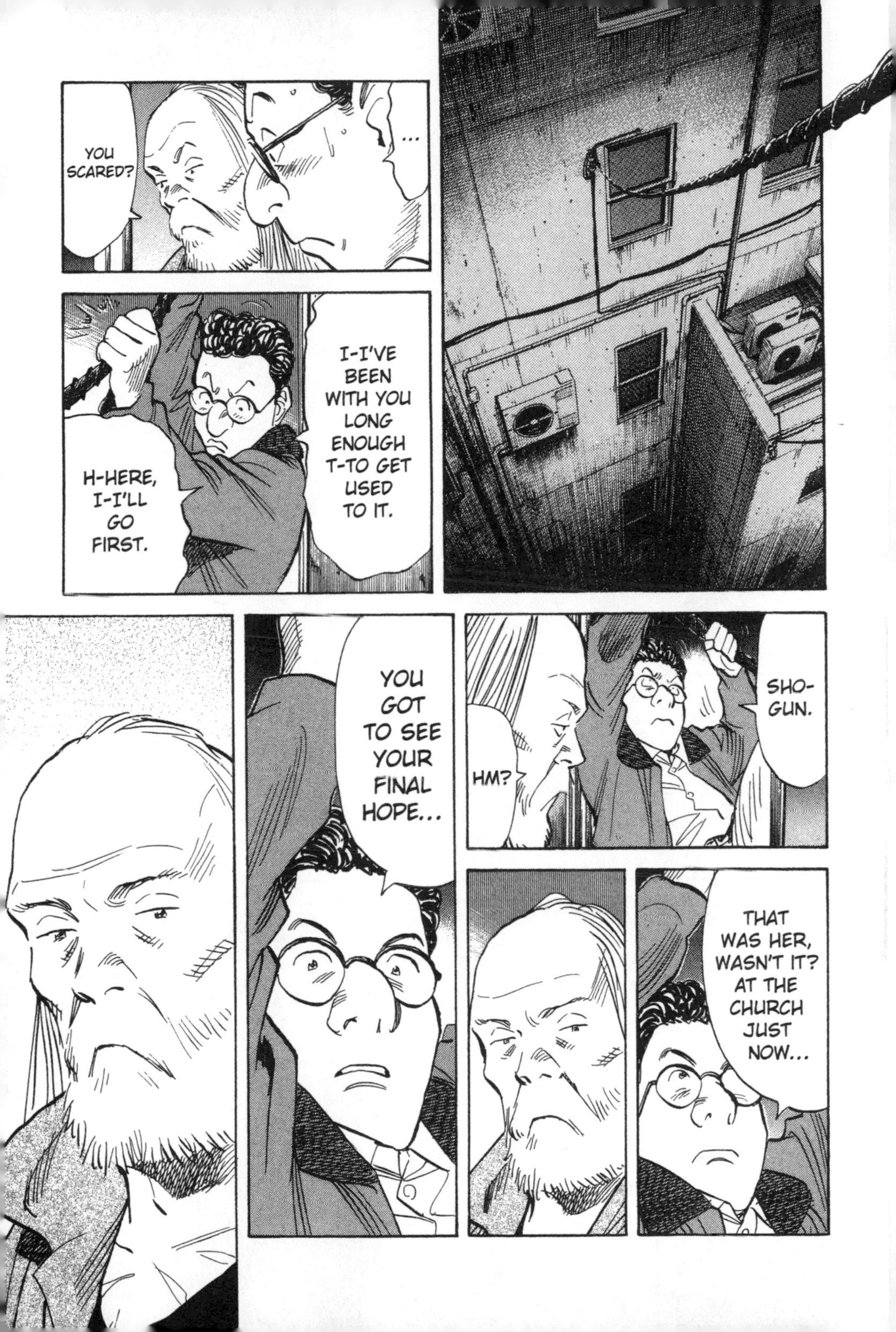
...
YOU SCARED?
I-I'VE BEEN WITH YOU LONG ENOUGH T-TO GET USED TO IT.
H-HERE, I-I'LL GO FIRST.
SHO-GUN.
HM?
THAT WAS HER, WASN'T IT? AT THE CHURCH JUST NOW...
YOU GOT TO SEE YOUR FINAL HOPE...

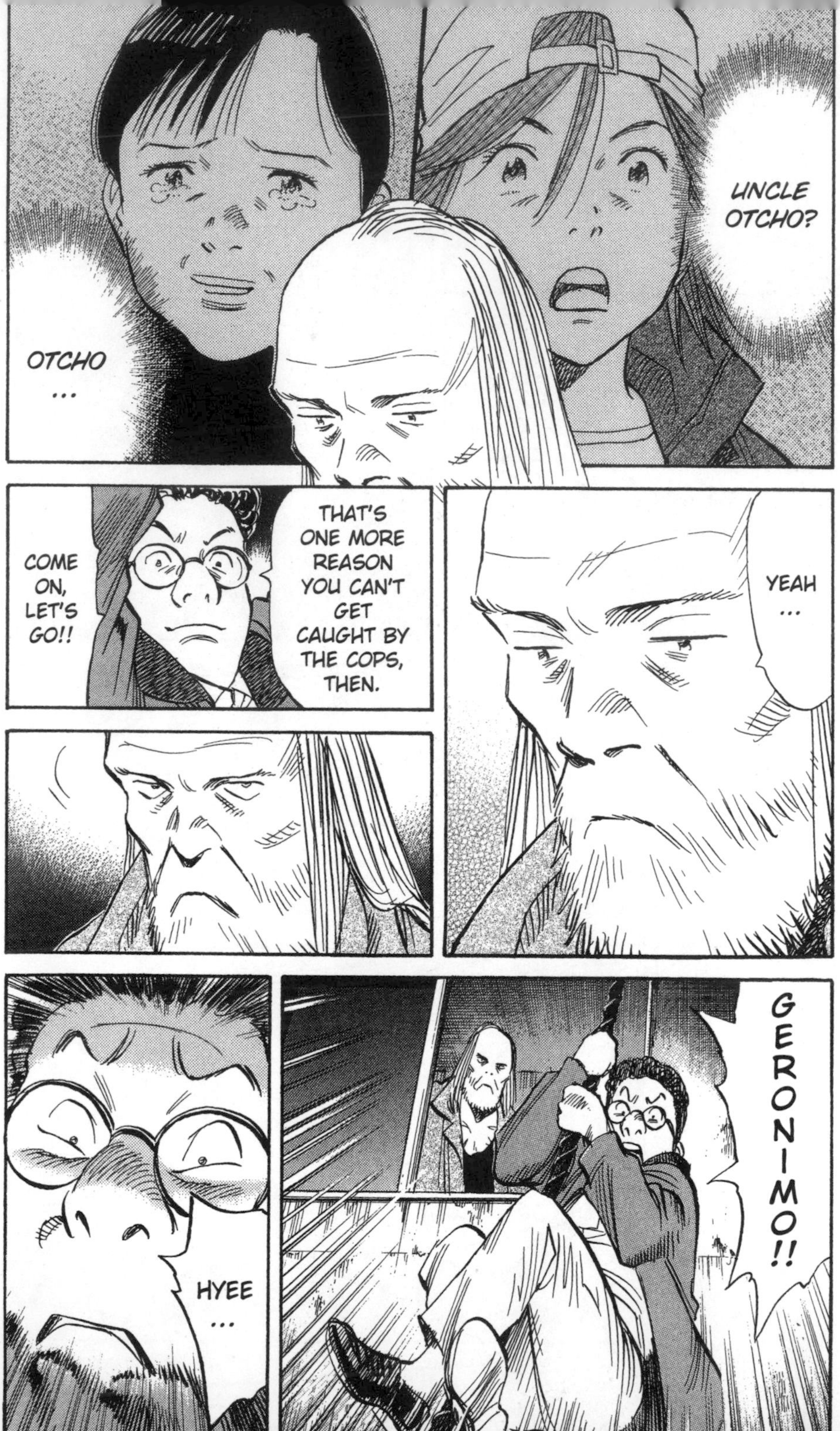
UNCLE OTCHO?
OTCHO ...
YEAH ...
THAT'S ONE MORE REASON YOU CAN'T GET CAUGHT BY THE COPS, THEN.
COME ON, LET'S GO!!
GERONIMO!!
HYEE ...

Chapter 1 Truce

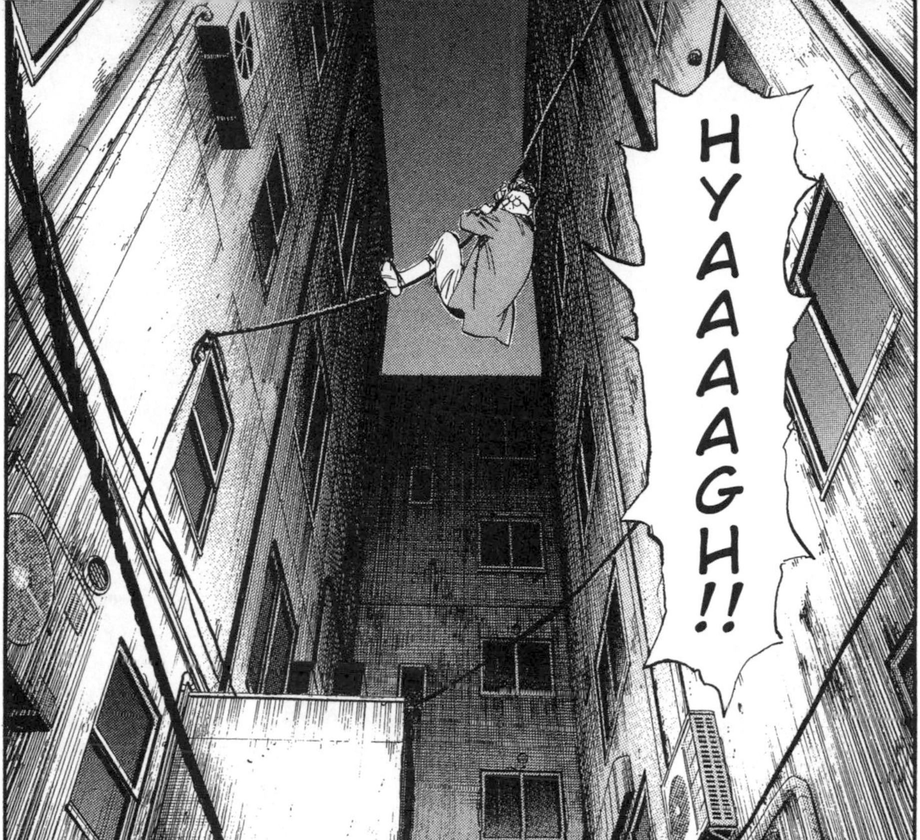
HYAAAAAGH!!

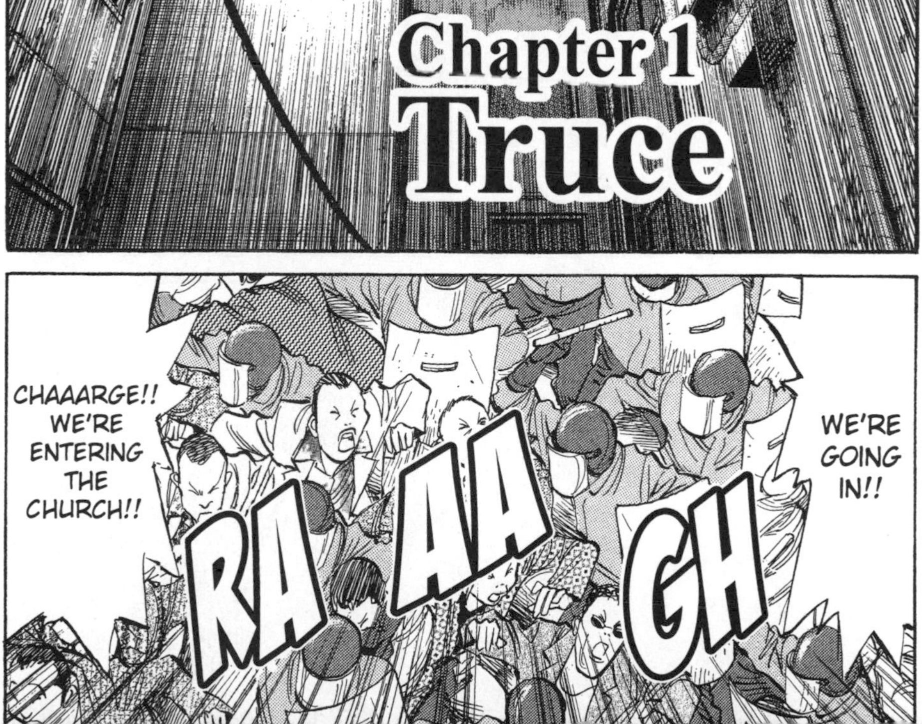
WE'RE GOING IN!!
CHAAARGE!! WE'RE ENTERING THE CHURCH!!
RA AA GH

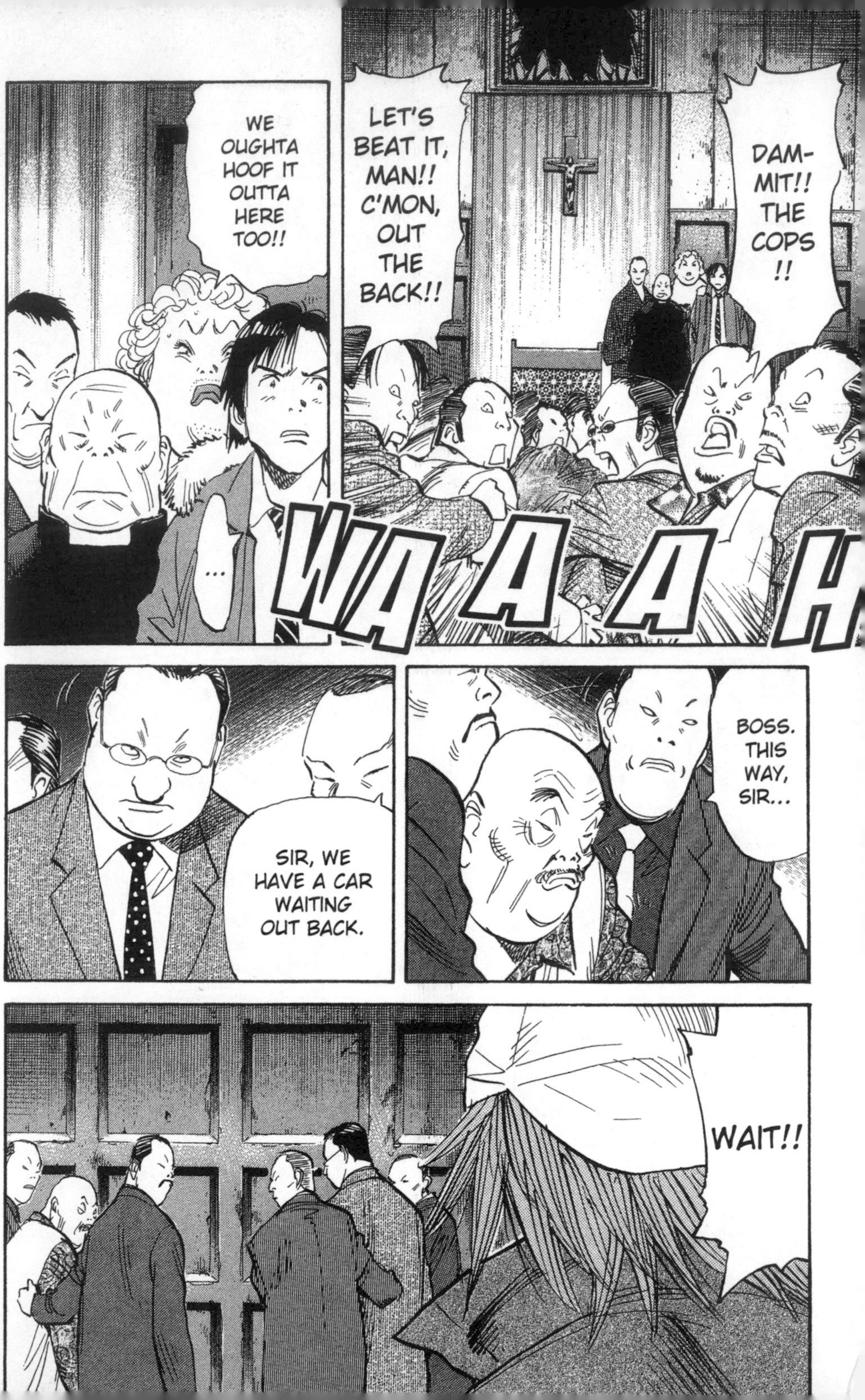
DAM-MIT!! THE COPS !!
LET'S BEAT IT, MAN!! C'MON, OUT THE BACK!!
WAAAH
WE OUGHTA HOOF IT OUTTA HERE TOO!!
...
BOSS. THIS WAY, SIR...
SIR, WE HAVE A CAR WAITING OUT BACK.
WAIT!!

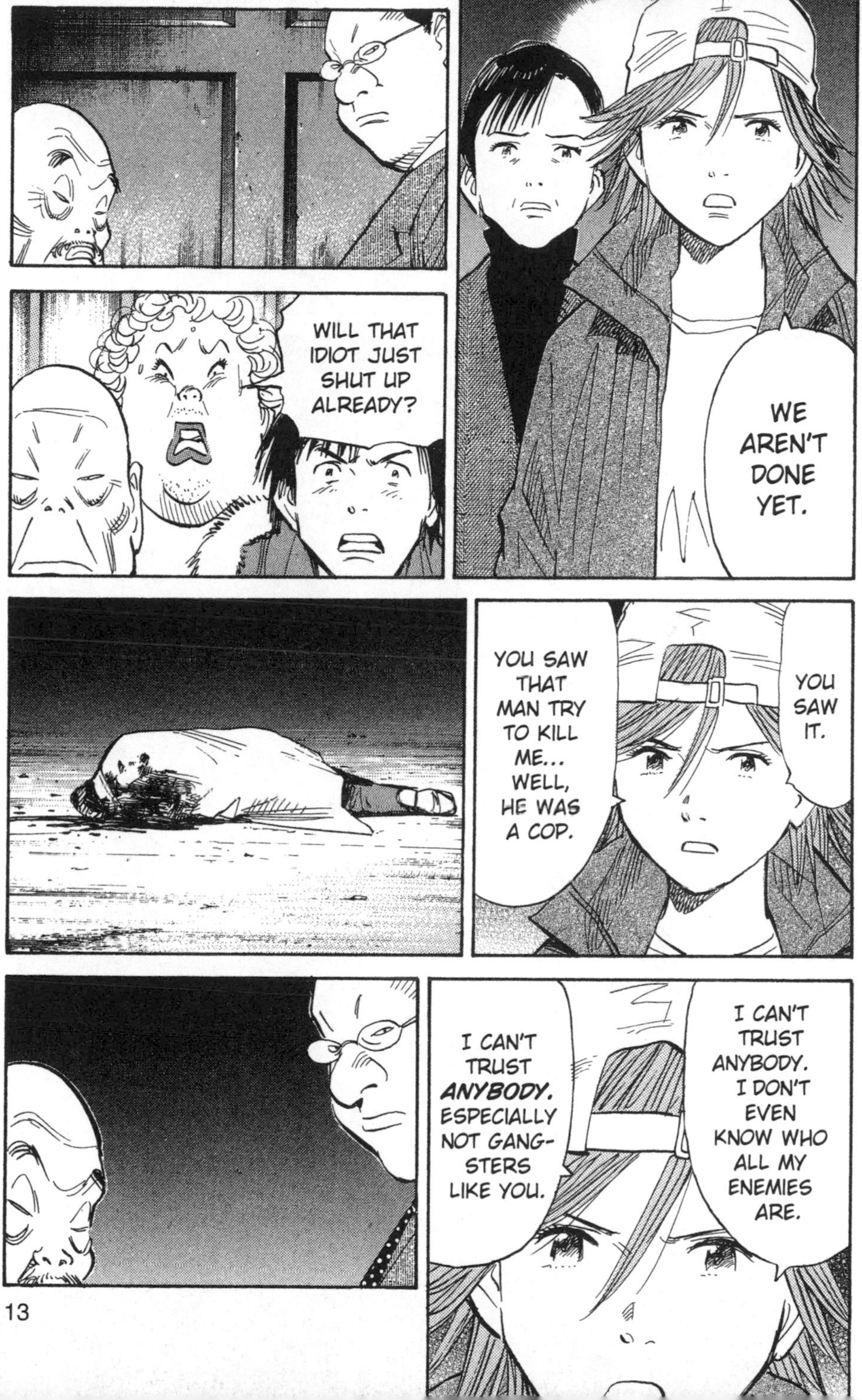
WE AREN'T DONE YET.
WILL THAT IDIOT JUST SHUT UP ALREADY?
YOU SAW IT.
YOU SAW THAT MAN TRY TO KILL ME... WELL, HE WAS A COP.
I CAN'T TRUST ANYBODY. I DON'T EVEN KNOW WHO ALL MY ENEMIES ARE.
I CAN'T TRUST **ANYBODY.** ESPECIALLY NOT GANGSTERS LIKE YOU.

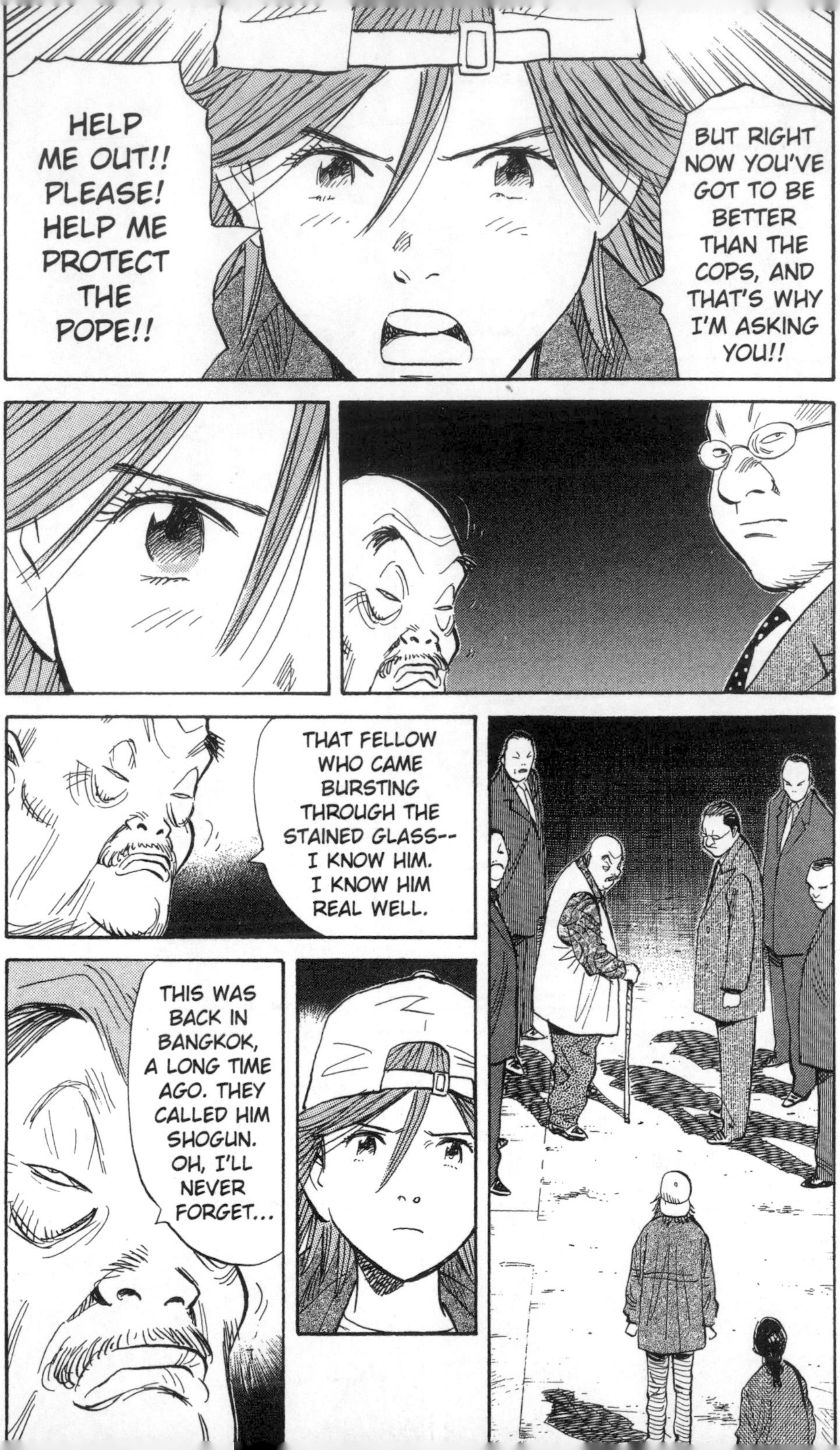
BUT RIGHT NOW YOU'VE GOT TO BE BETTER THAN THE COPS, AND THAT'S WHY I'M ASKING YOU!!
HELP ME OUT!! PLEASE! HELP ME PROTECT THE POPE!!
THAT FELLOW WHO CAME BURSTING THROUGH THE STAINED GLASS-- I KNOW HIM. I KNOW HIM REAL WELL.
THIS WAS BACK IN BANGKOK, A LONG TIME AGO. THEY CALLED HIM SHOGUN. OH, I'LL NEVER FORGET...

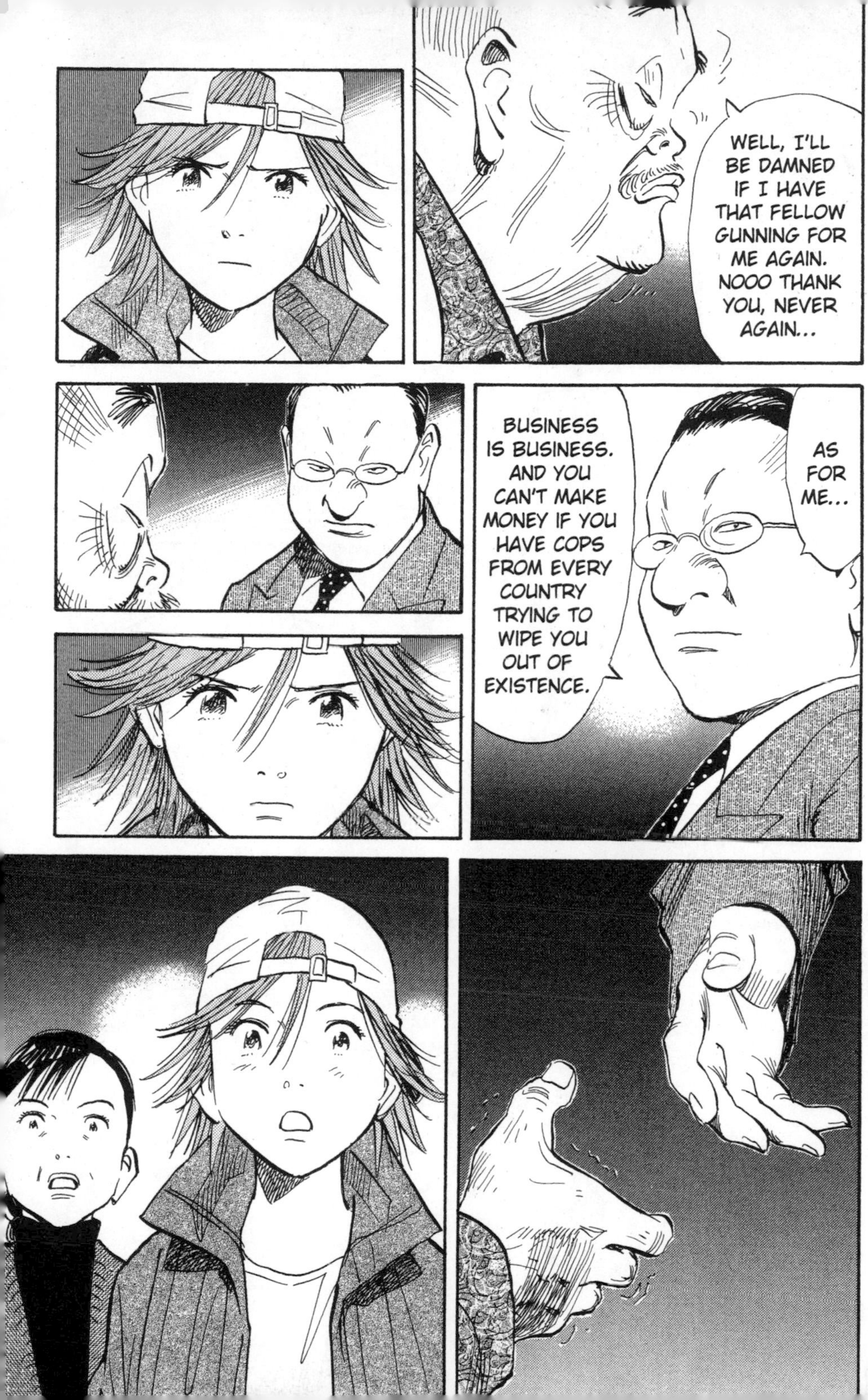
WELL, I'LL BE DAMNED IF I HAVE THAT FELLOW GUNNING FOR ME AGAIN. NOOO THANK YOU, NEVER AGAIN...
AS FOR ME...
BUSINESS IS BUSINESS. AND YOU CAN'T MAKE MONEY IF YOU HAVE COPS FROM EVERY COUNTRY TRYING TO WIPE YOU OUT OF EXISTENCE.

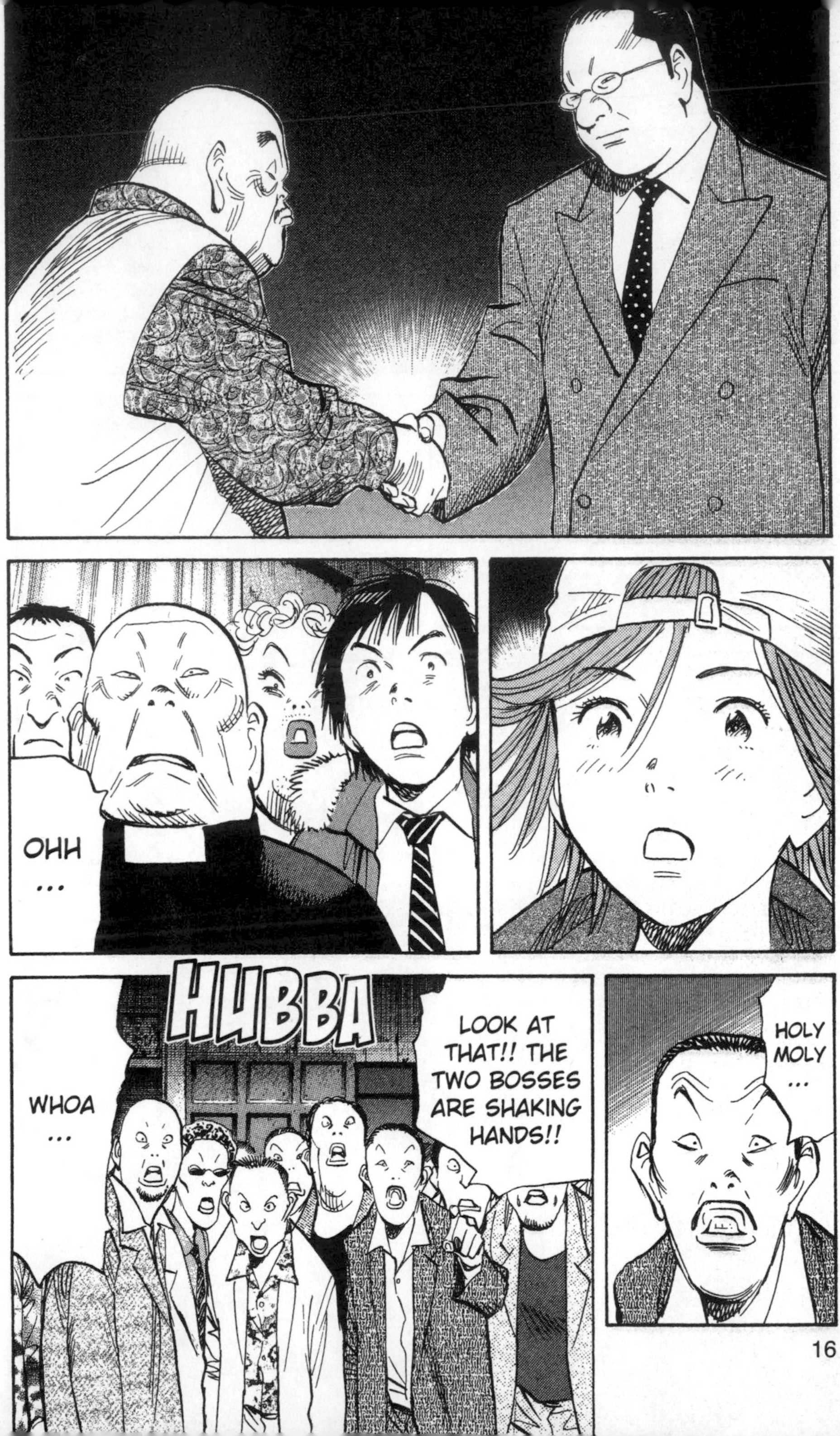
OHH ...
HOLY MOLY ...
LOOK AT THAT!! THE TWO BOSSES ARE SHAKING HANDS!!
HUBBA
WHOA ...

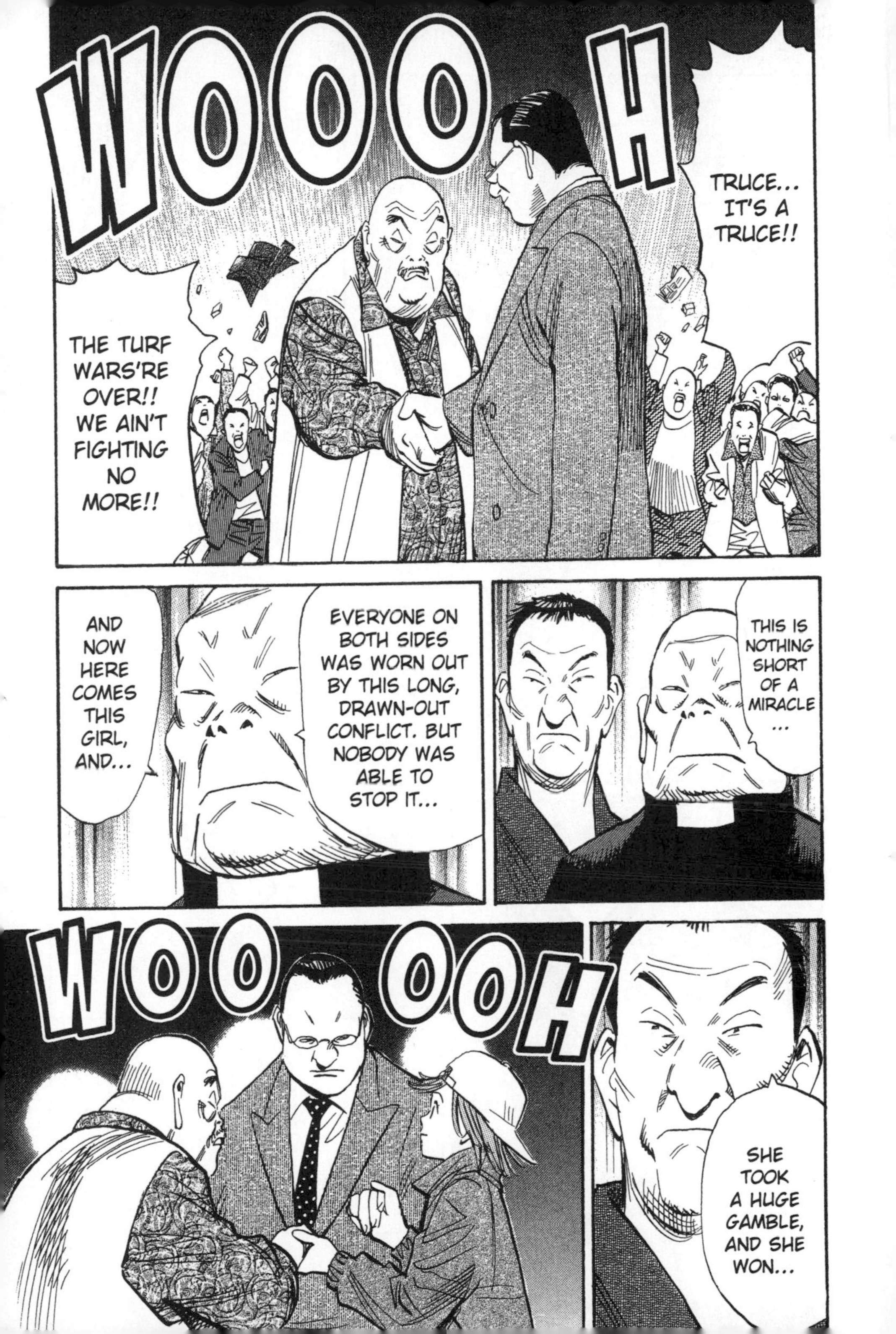
WOOOH
TRUCE... IT'S A TRUCE!!
THE TURF WARS'RE OVER!! WE AIN'T FIGHTING NO MORE!!
THIS IS NOTHING SHORT OF A MIRACLE...
EVERYONE ON BOTH SIDES WAS WORN OUT BY THIS LONG, DRAWN-OUT CONFLICT. BUT NOBODY WAS ABLE TO STOP IT...
AND NOW HERE COMES THIS GIRL, AND...
SHE TOOK A HUGE GAMBLE, AND SHE WON...
WOOOOH

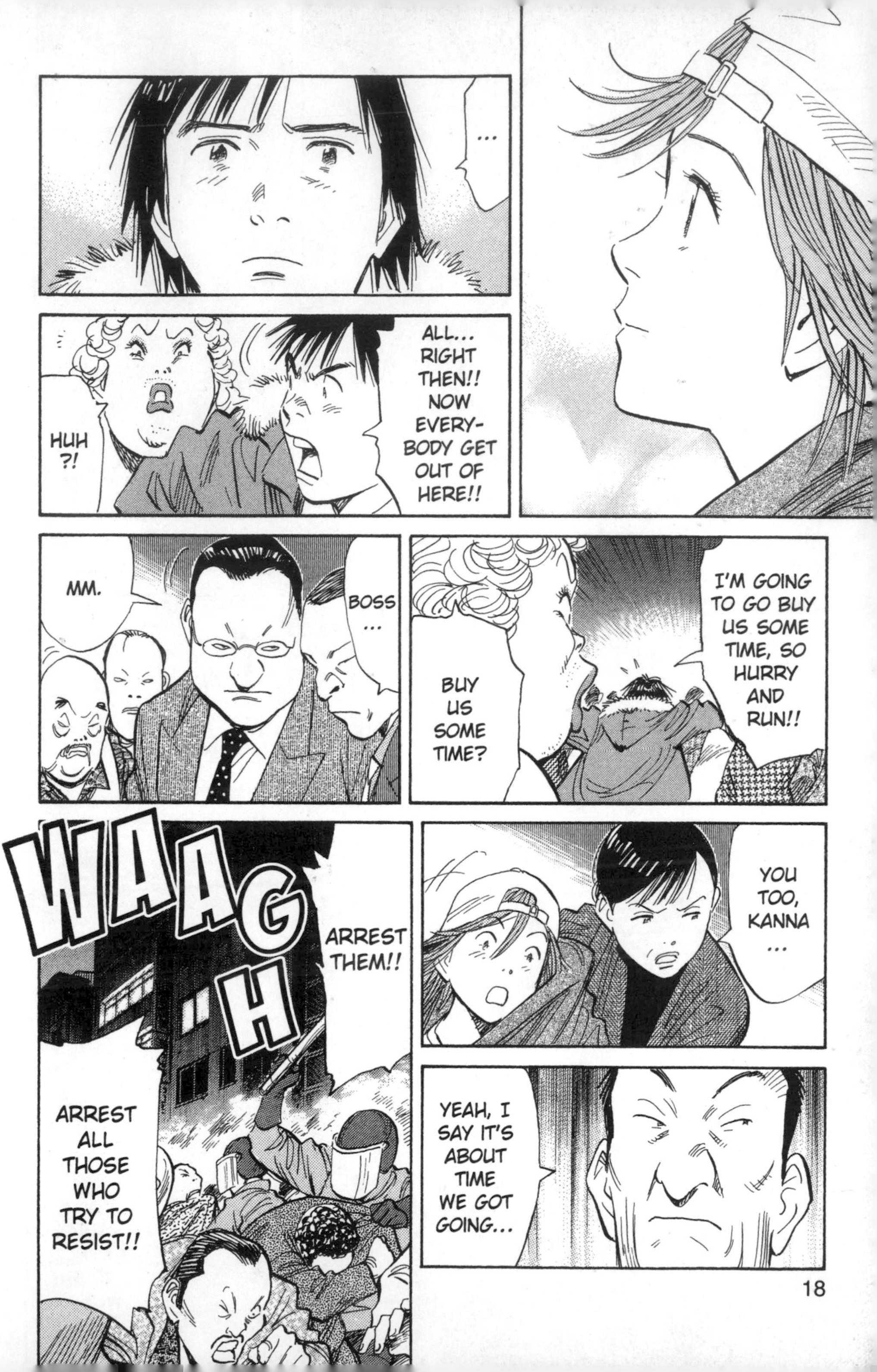
...
ALL... RIGHT THEN!! NOW EVERY-BODY GET OUT OF HERE!!
HUH ?!
I'M GOING TO GO BUY US SOME TIME, SO HURRY AND RUN!!
BUY US SOME TIME?
BOSS ...
MM.
YOU TOO, KANNA ...
YEAH, I SAY IT'S ABOUT TIME WE GOT GOING...
WAAGH
ARREST THEM!!
ARREST ALL THOSE WHO TRY TO RESIST!!

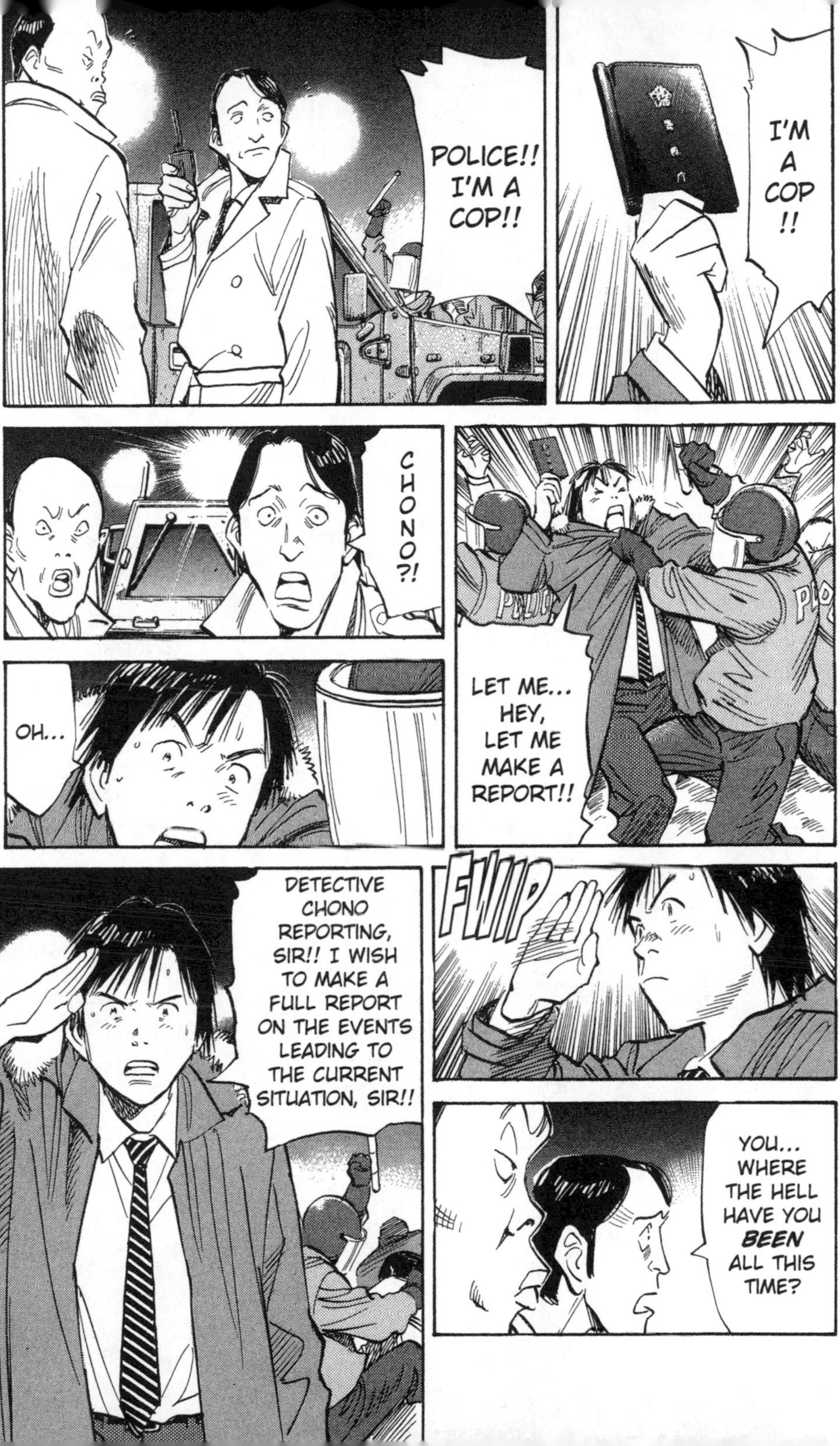
I'M A COP!!
POLICE!! I'M A COP!!
LET ME... HEY, LET ME MAKE A REPORT!!
CHONO?!
OH...
FWIP
YOU... WHERE THE HELL HAVE YOU ***BEEN*** ALL THIS TIME?
DETECTIVE CHONO REPORTING, SIR!! I WISH TO MAKE A FULL REPORT ON THE EVENTS LEADING TO THE CURRENT SITUATION, SIR!!

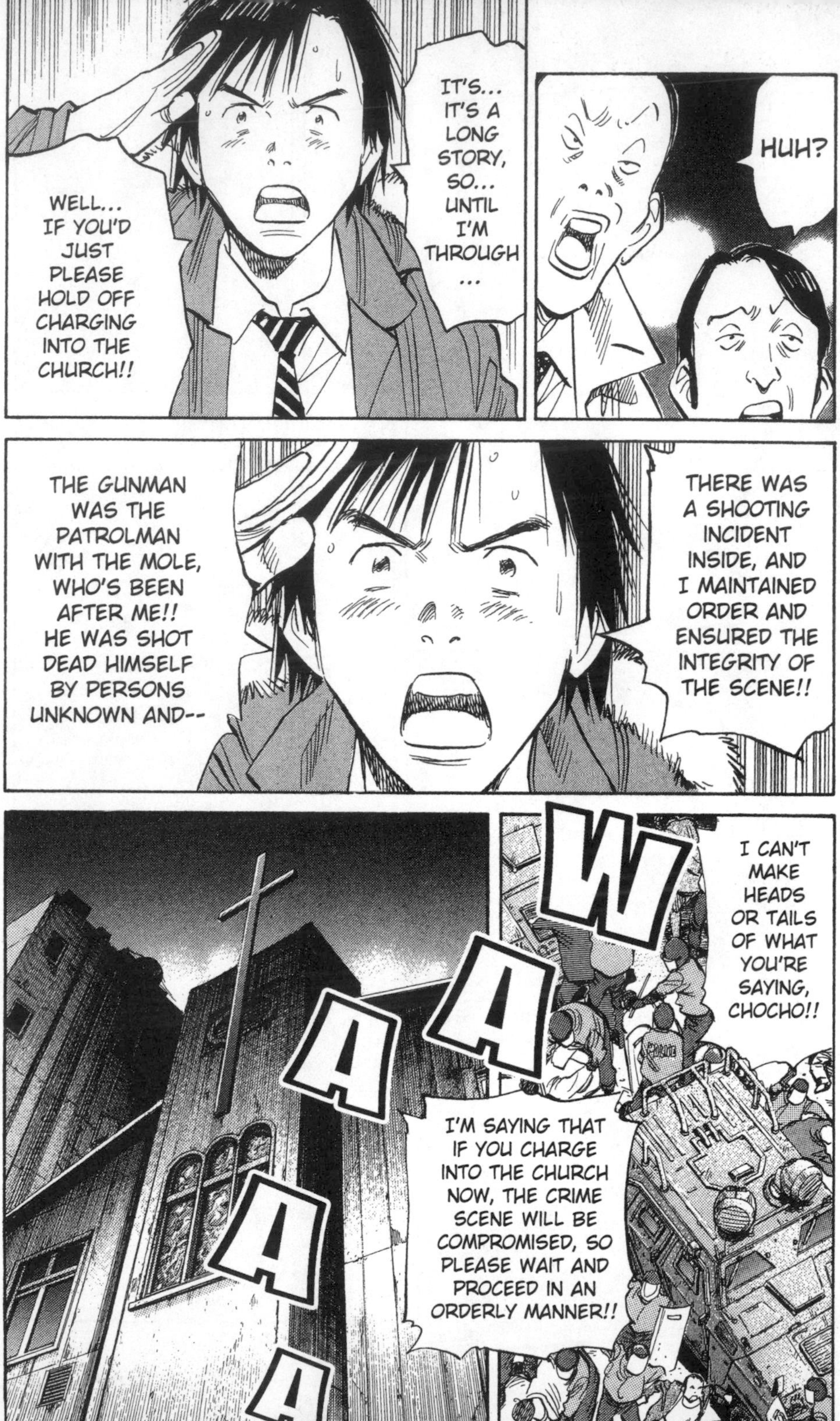
HUH?
IT'S... IT'S A LONG STORY, SO... UNTIL I'M THROUGH...
WELL... IF YOU'D JUST PLEASE HOLD OFF CHARGING INTO THE CHURCH!!
THERE WAS A SHOOTING INCIDENT INSIDE, AND I MAINTAINED ORDER AND ENSURED THE INTEGRITY OF THE SCENE!!
THE GUNMAN WAS THE PATROLMAN WITH THE MOLE, WHO'S BEEN AFTER ME!! HE WAS SHOT DEAD HIMSELF BY PERSONS UNKNOWN AND--
I CAN'T MAKE HEADS OR TAILS OF WHAT YOU'RE SAYING, CHOCHO!!
I'M SAYING THAT IF YOU CHARGE INTO THE CHURCH NOW, THE CRIME SCENE WILL BE COMPROMISED, SO PLEASE WAIT AND PROCEED IN AN ORDERLY MANNER!!
WAAAAA

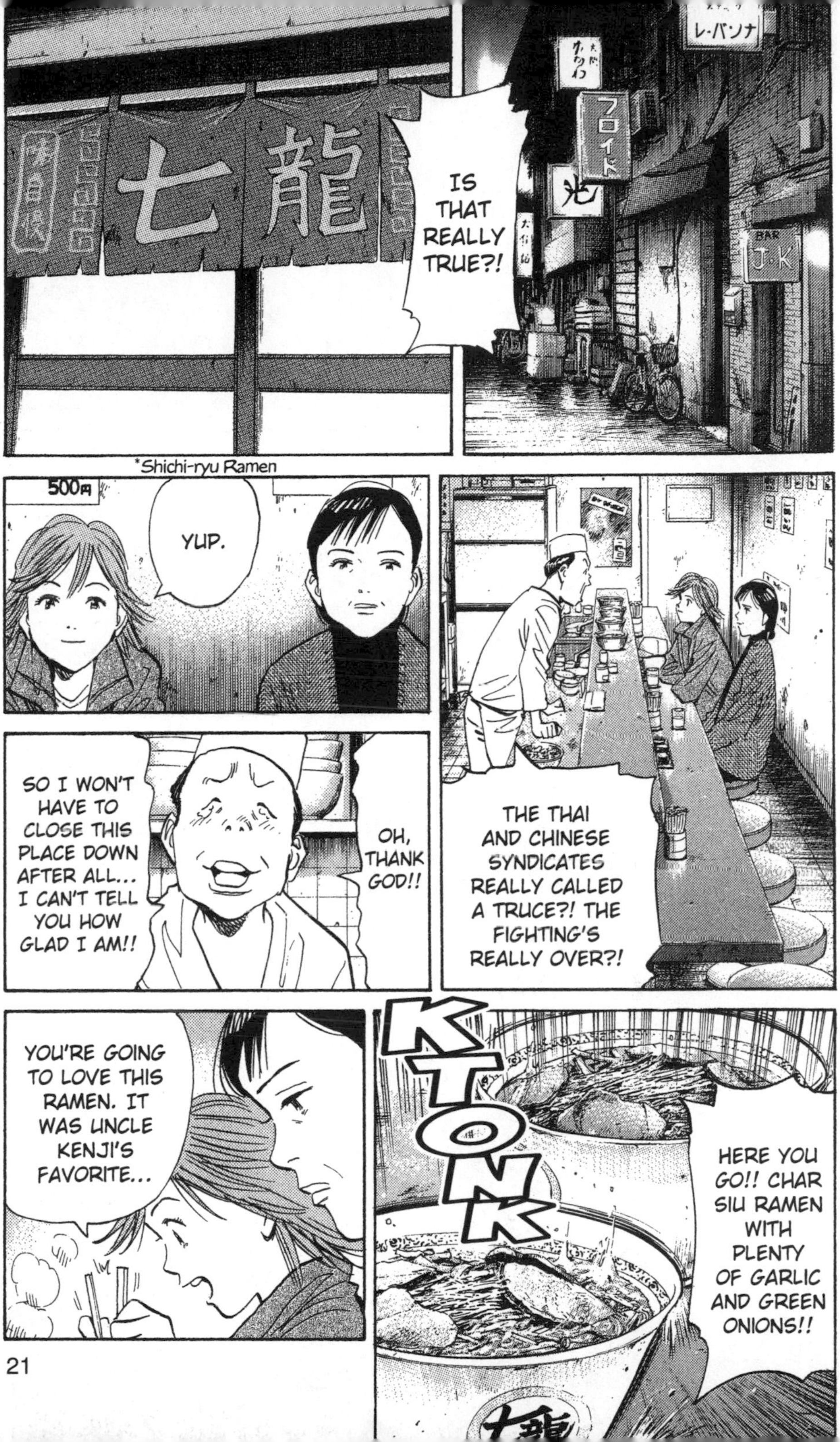
IS THAT REALLY TRUE?!
七龍
*Shichi-ryu Ramen
500円
YUP.
THE THAI AND CHINESE SYNDICATES REALLY CALLED A TRUCE?! THE FIGHTING'S REALLY OVER?!
OH, THANK GOD!!
SO I WON'T HAVE TO CLOSE THIS PLACE DOWN AFTER ALL... I CAN'T TELL YOU HOW GLAD I AM!!
KTONK
HERE YOU GO!! CHAR SIU RAMEN WITH PLENTY OF GARLIC AND GREEN ONIONS!!
YOU'RE GOING TO LOVE THIS RAMEN. IT WAS UNCLE KENJI'S FAVORITE...

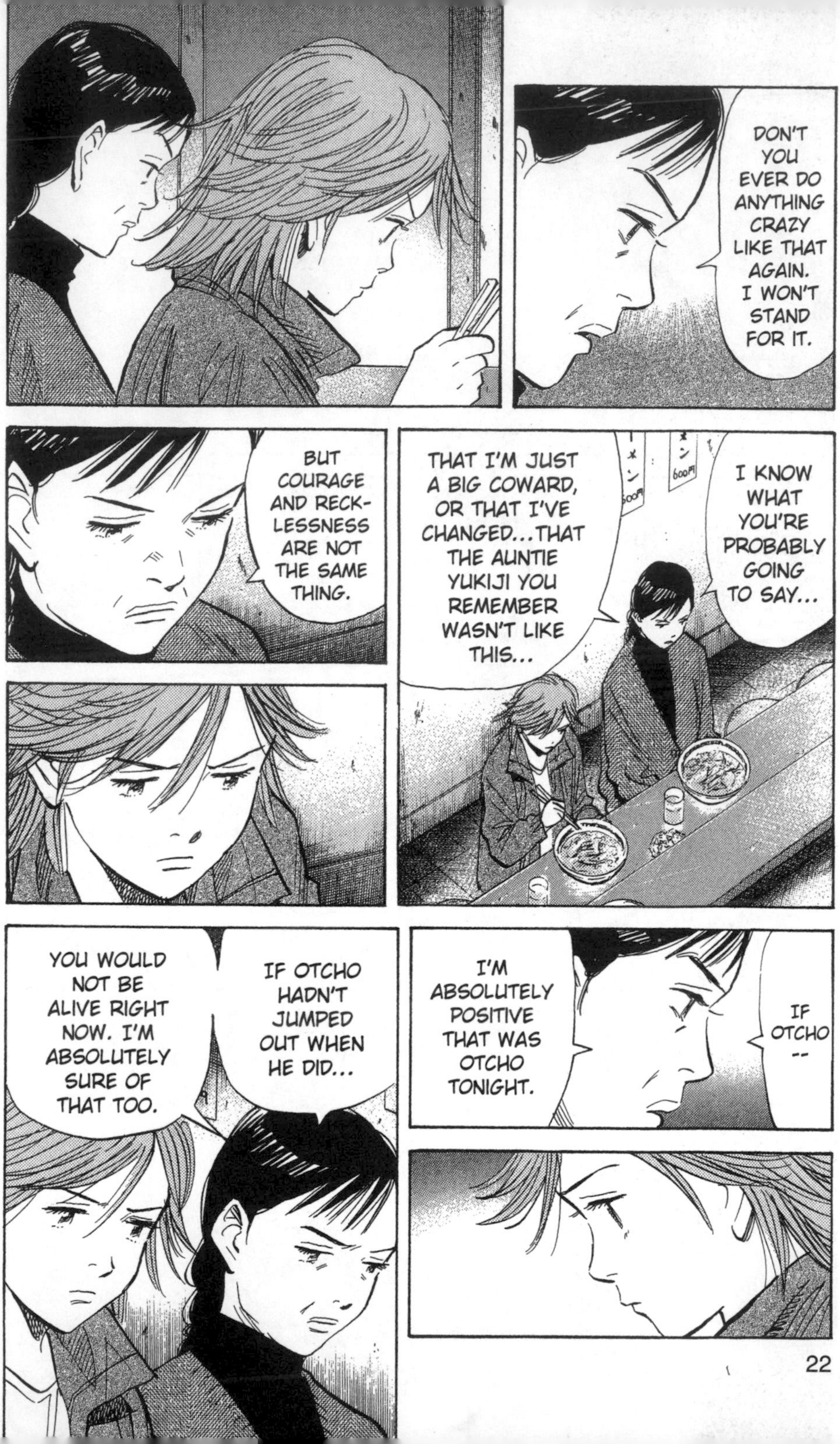
DON'T YOU EVER DO ANYTHING CRAZY LIKE THAT AGAIN. I WON'T STAND FOR IT.
I KNOW WHAT YOU'RE PROBABLY GOING TO SAY...
THAT I'M JUST A BIG COWARD, OR THAT I'VE CHANGED...THAT THE AUNTIE YUKIJI YOU REMEMBER WASN'T LIKE THIS...
BUT COURAGE AND RECK-LESSNESS ARE NOT THE SAME THING.
IF OTCHO --
I'M ABSOLUTELY POSITIVE THAT WAS OTCHO TONIGHT.
IF OTCHO HADN'T JUMPED OUT WHEN HE DID...
YOU WOULD NOT BE ALIVE RIGHT NOW. I'M ABSOLUTELY SURE OF THAT TOO.

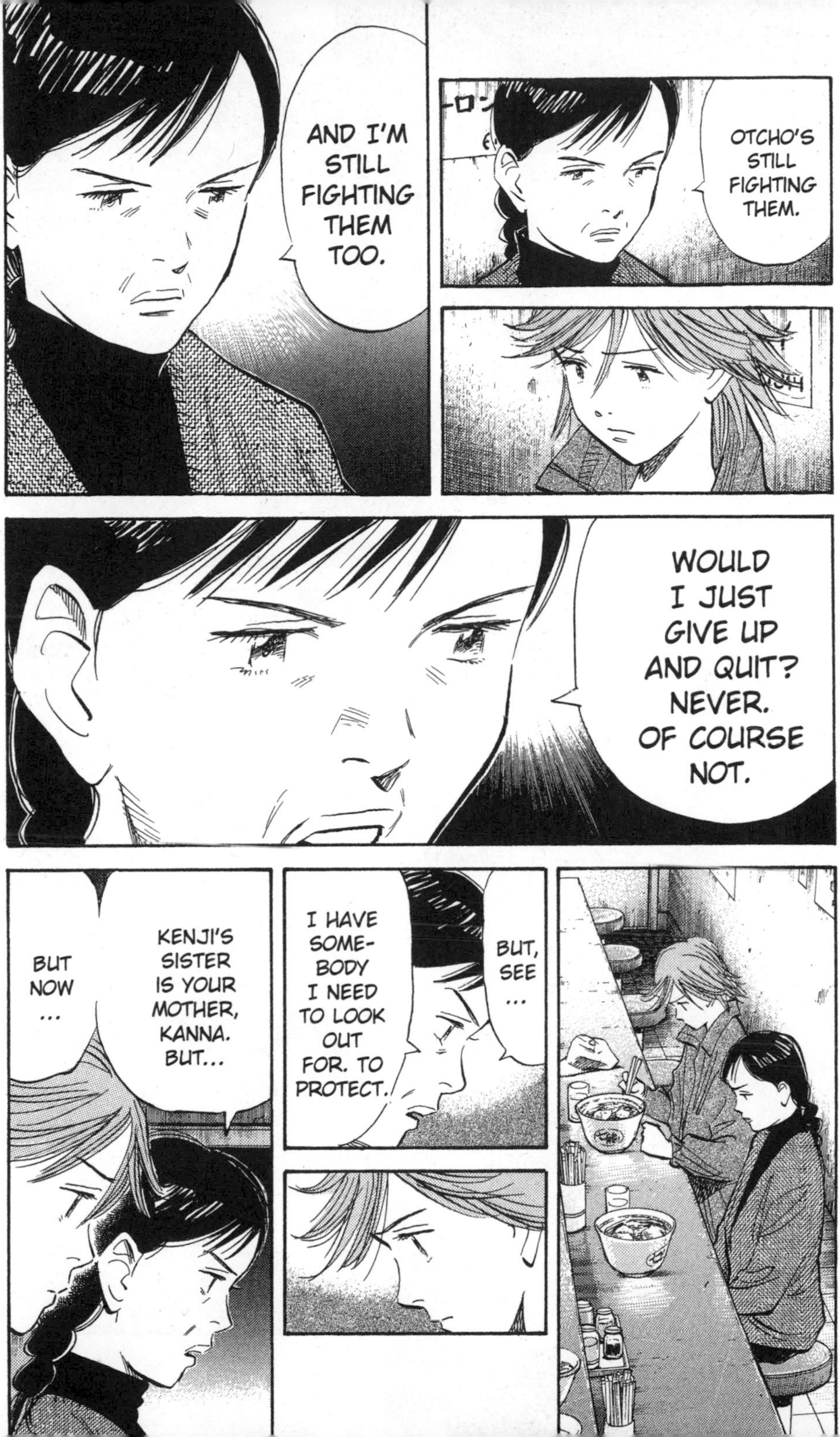
OTCHO'S STILL FIGHTING THEM.
AND I'M STILL FIGHTING THEM TOO.
WOULD I JUST GIVE UP AND QUIT? NEVER. OF COURSE NOT.
BUT, SEE ...
I HAVE SOME-BODY I NEED TO LOOK OUT FOR. TO PROTECT.
KENJI'S SISTER IS YOUR MOTHER, KANNA. BUT...
BUT NOW ...

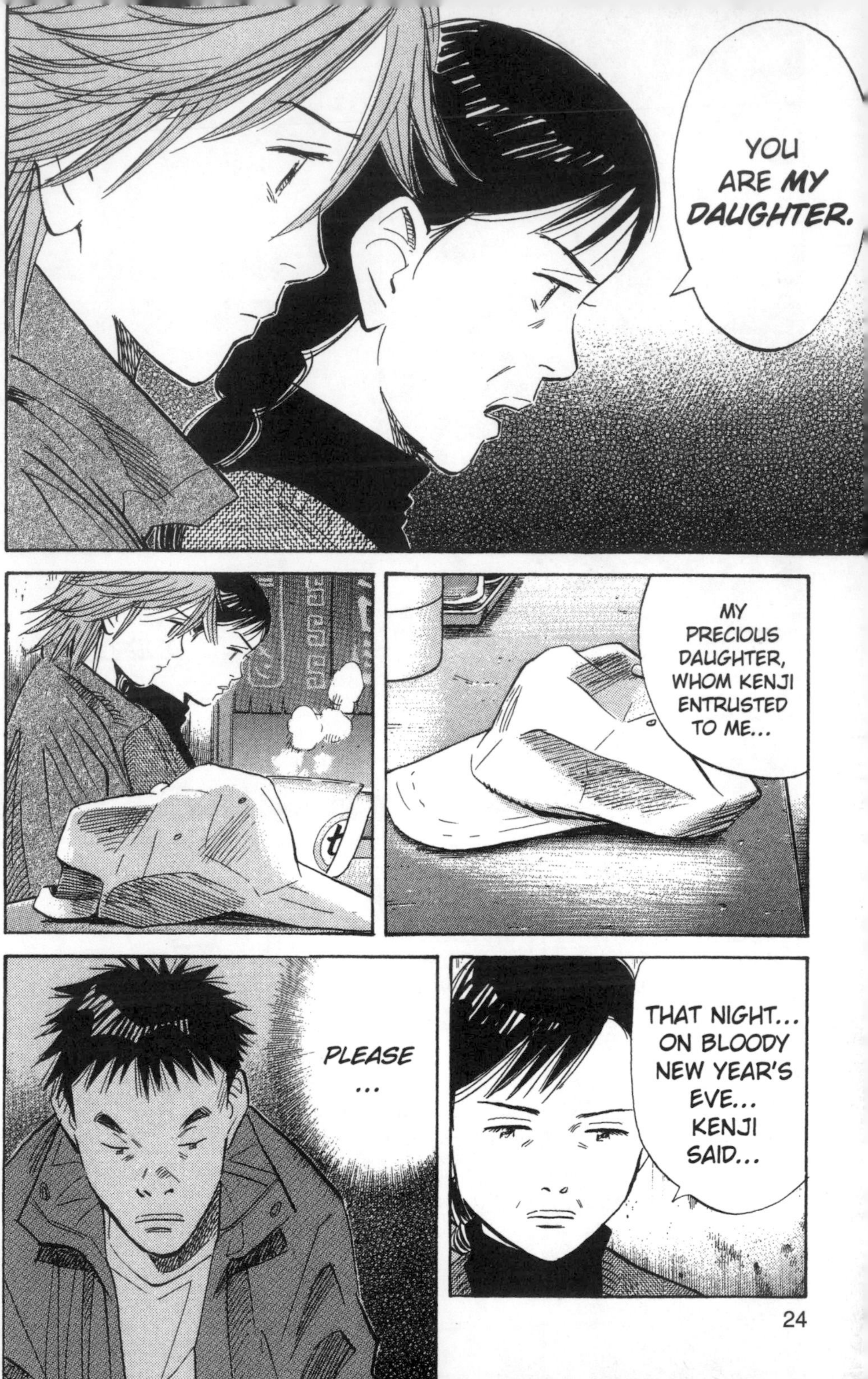
YOU ARE **MY DAUGHTER.**
MY PRECIOUS DAUGHTER, WHOM KENJI ENTRUSTED TO ME...
THAT NIGHT... ON BLOODY NEW YEAR'S EVE... KENJI SAID...
PLEASE ...

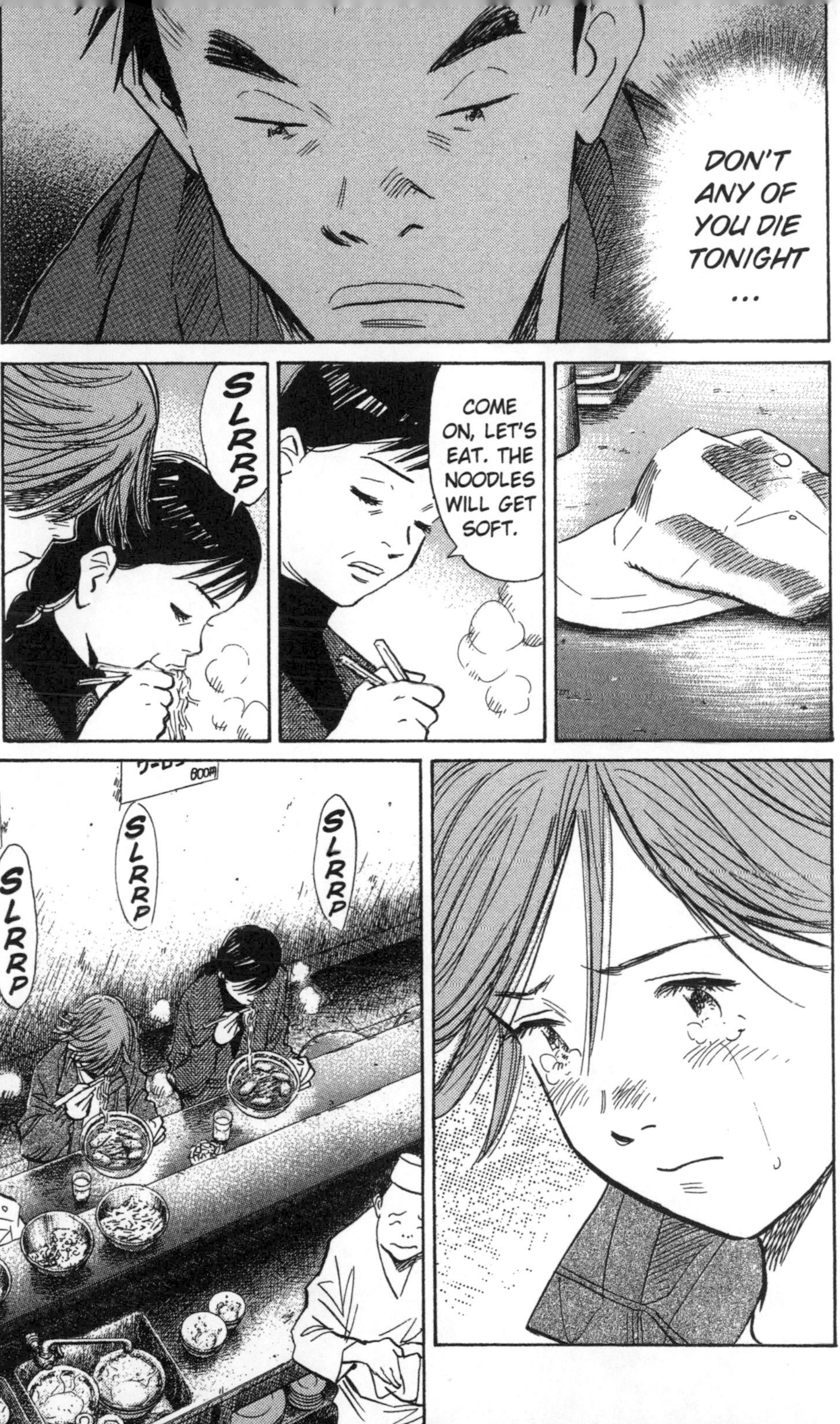
DON'T ANY OF YOU DIE TONIGHT ...
COME ON, LET'S EAT. THE NOODLES WILL GET SOFT.
SLRRP
800円
500円
SLRRP
SLRRP
SLRRP

Chapter 2 Crossroads

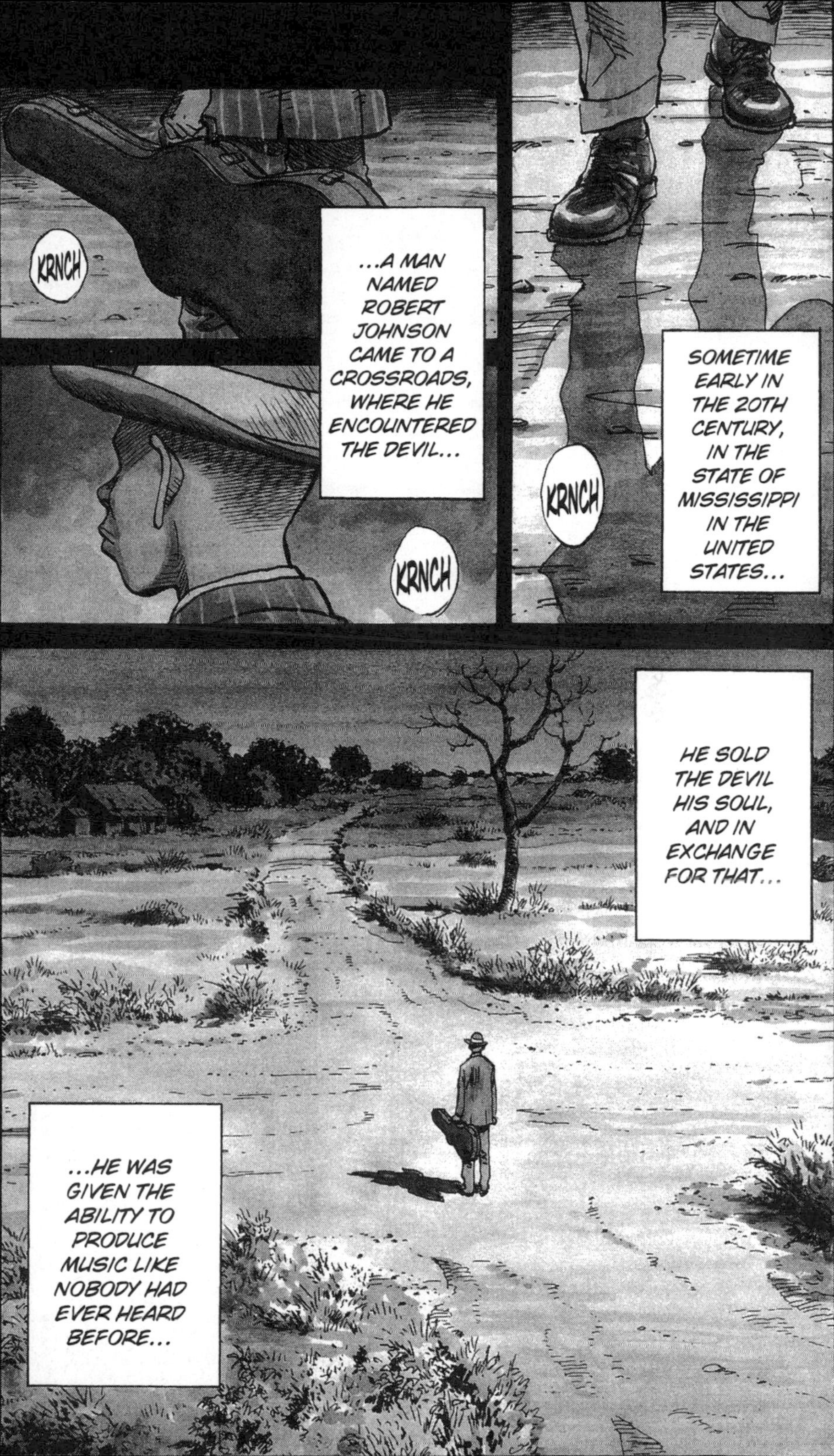
SOMETIME EARLY IN THE 20TH CENTURY, IN THE STATE OF MISSISSIPPI IN THE UNITED STATES…
KRNCH
KRNCH
…A MAN NAMED ROBERT JOHNSON CAME TO A CROSSROADS, WHERE HE ENCOUNTERED THE DEVIL…
KRNCH
HE SOLD THE DEVIL HIS SOUL, AND IN EXCHANGE FOR THAT…
…HE WAS GIVEN THE ABILITY TO PRODUCE MUSIC LIKE NOBODY HAD EVER HEARD BEFORE…

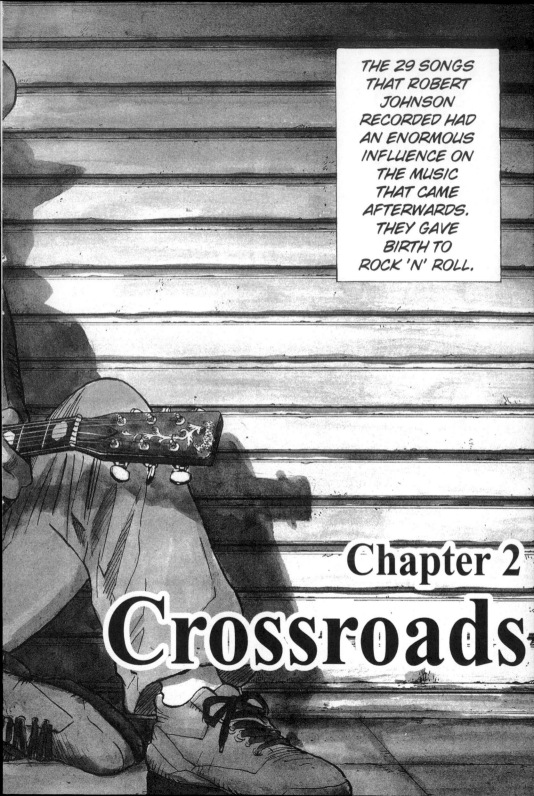

THE 29 SONGS
THAT ROBERT
JOHNSON
RECORDED HAD
AN ENORMOUS
INFLUENCE ON
THE MUSIC
THAT CAME
AFTERWARDS.
THEY GAVE
BIRTH TO
ROCK 'N' ROLL.

Chapter 2
Crossroads

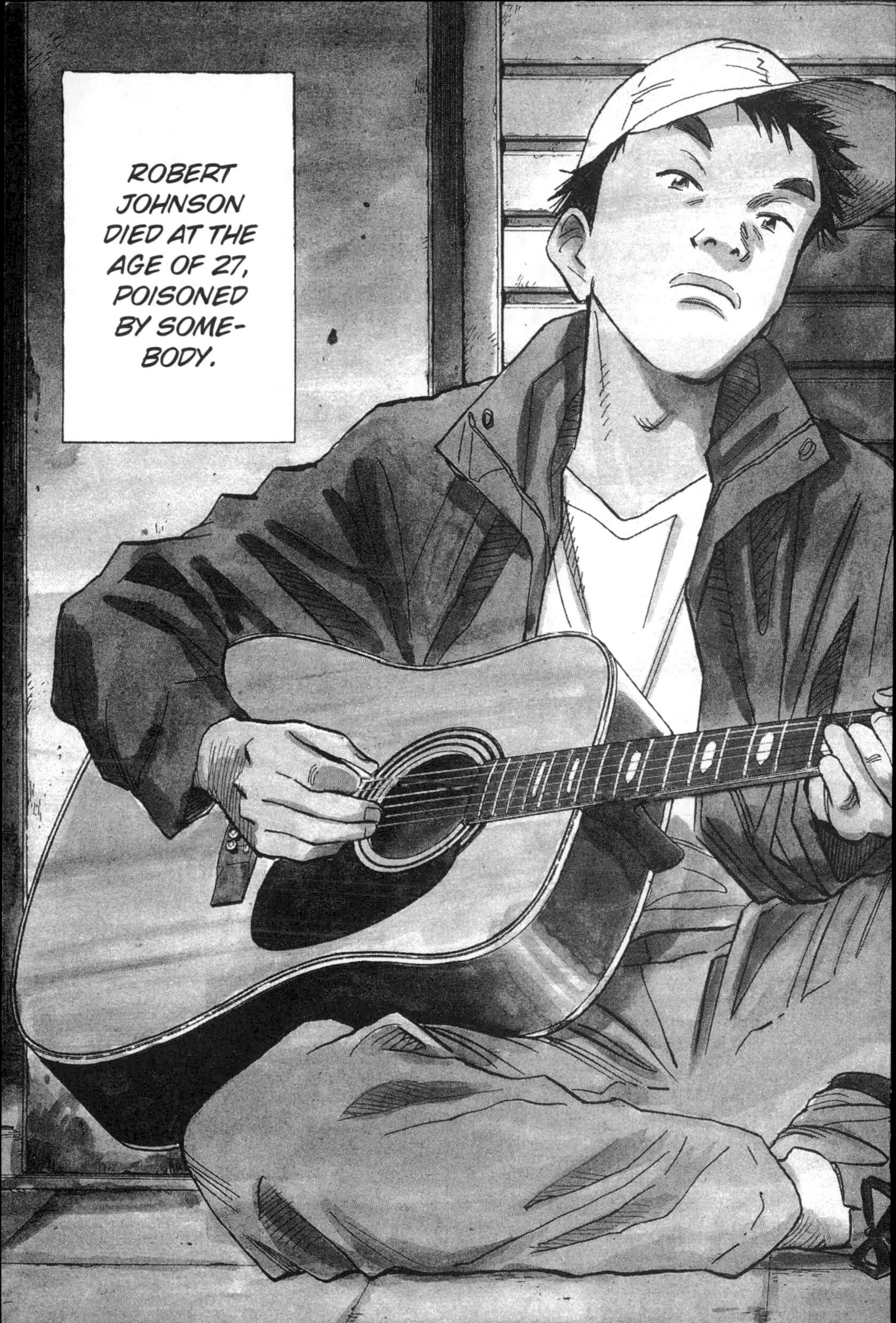
ROBERT JOHNSON DIED AT THE AGE OF 27, POISONED BY SOME-BODY.

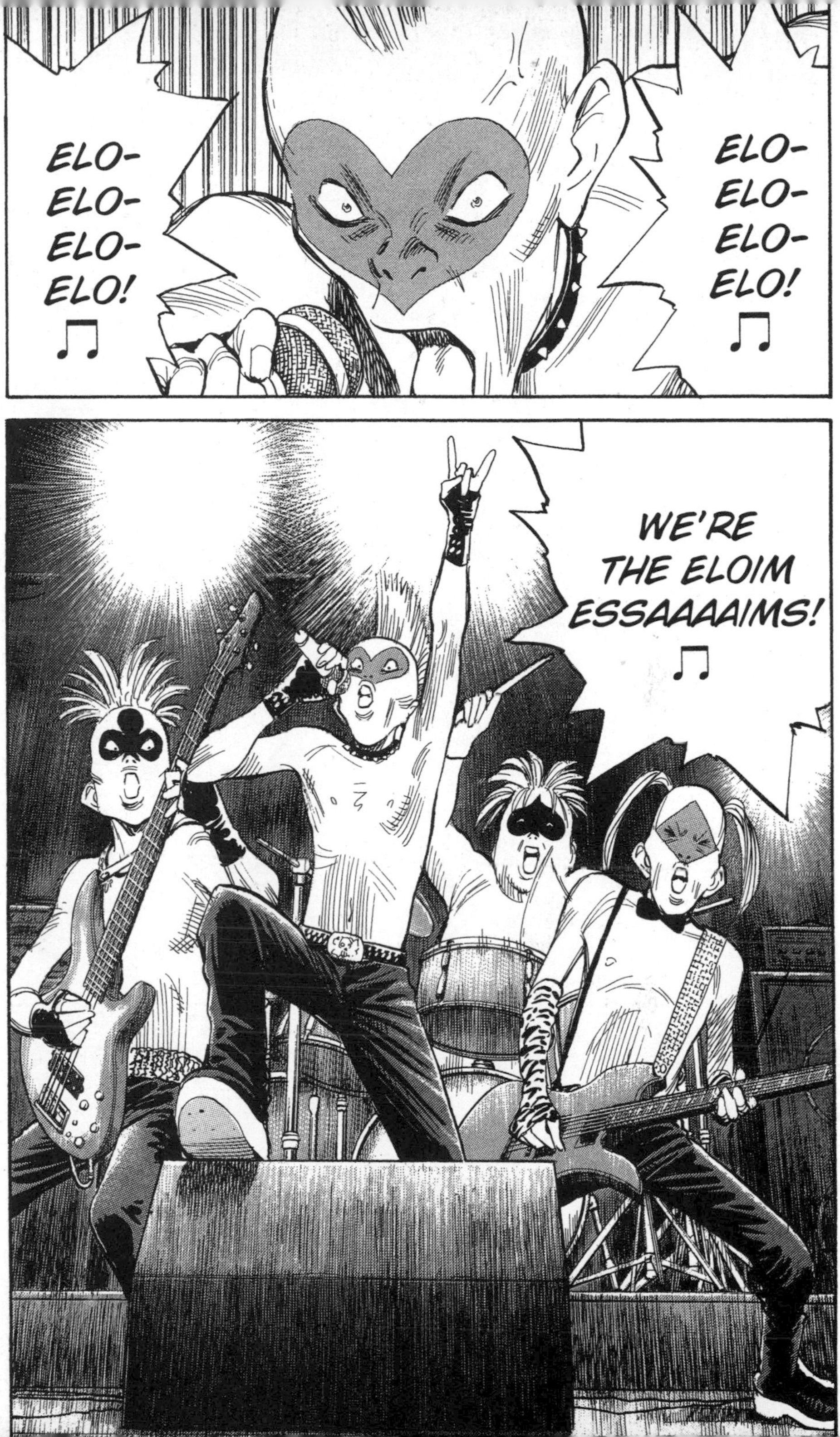
ELO-
ELO-
ELO-
ELO! ♫
ELO-
ELO-
ELO-
ELO! ♫
WE'RE
THE ELOIM
ESSAAAAIMS! ♫

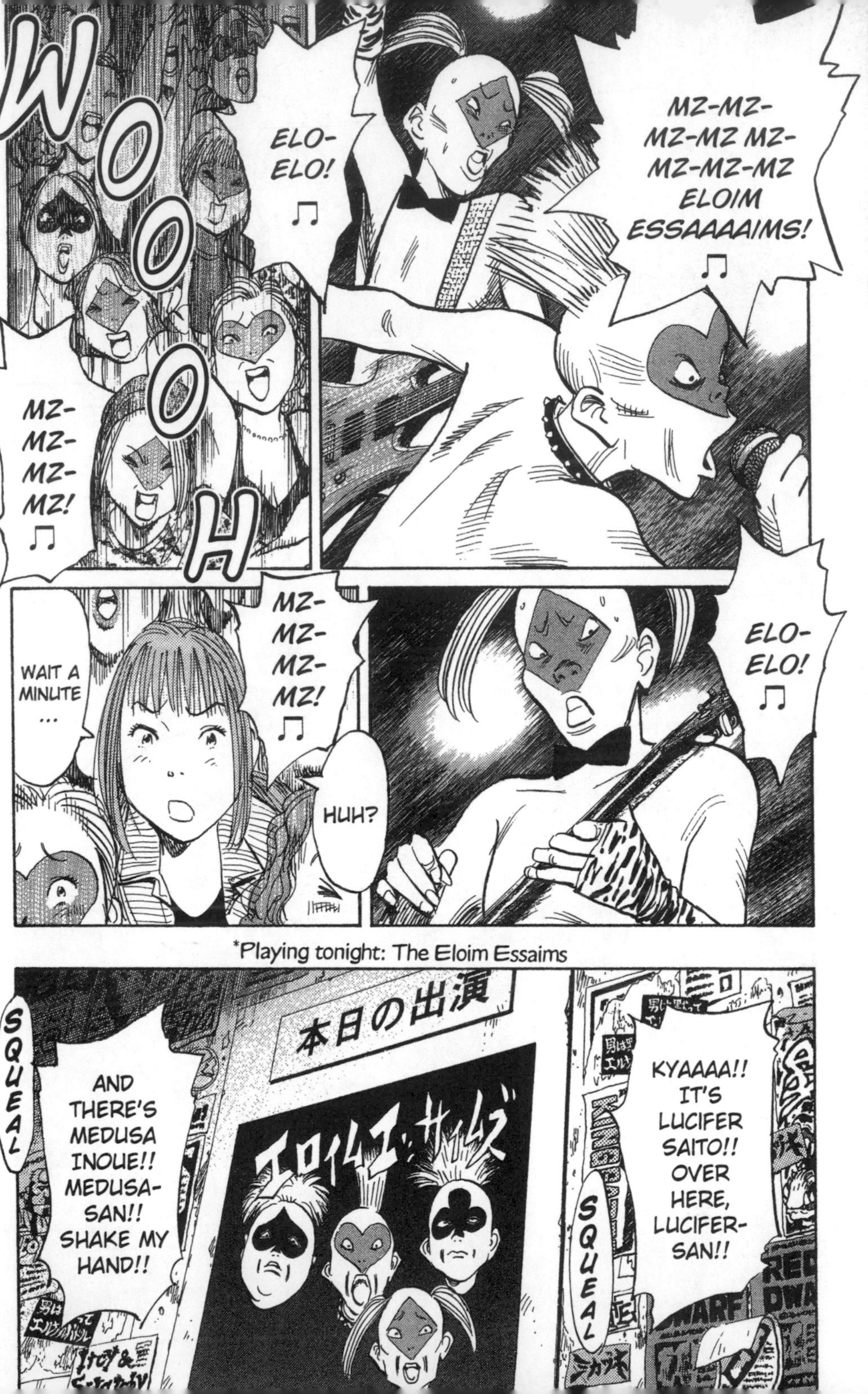
ELO-ELO! ♫
MZ-MZ-MZ-MZ MZ-MZ-MZ-MZ ELOIM ESSAAAAIMS! ♫
WOOOOH
MZ-MZ-MZ-MZ! ♫
ELO-ELO! ♫
MZ-MZ-MZ-MZ! ♫
WAIT A MINUTE ...
HUH?
*Playing tonight: The Eloim Essaims
KYAAAA!! IT'S LUCIFER SAITO!! OVER HERE, LUCIFER-SAN!!
SQUEAL
本日の出演
エロイムエッサイムズ
SQUEAL
AND THERE'S MEDUSA INOUE!! MEDUSA-SAN!! SHAKE MY HAND!!

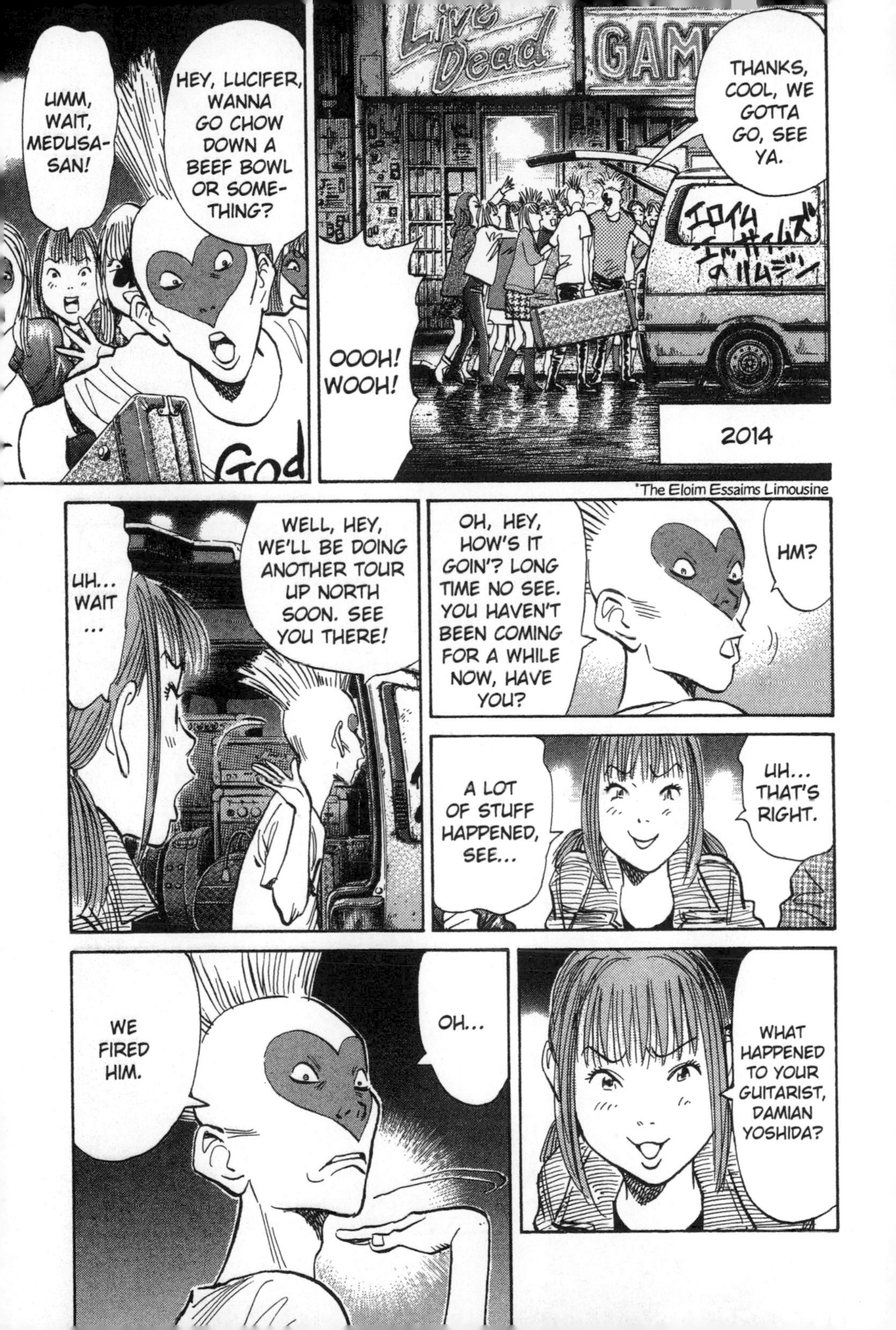
Live Dead
GAME
THANKS, COOL, WE GOTTA GO, SEE YA.
OOOH! WOOH!
2014
HEY, LUCIFER, WANNA GO CHOW DOWN A BEEF BOWL OR SOMETHING?
UMM, WAIT, MEDUSA-SAN!
God
HM?
OH, HEY, HOW'S IT GOIN'? LONG TIME NO SEE. YOU HAVEN'T BEEN COMING FOR A WHILE NOW, HAVE YOU?
UH... THAT'S RIGHT.
A LOT OF STUFF HAPPENED, SEE...
WELL, HEY, WE'LL BE DOING ANOTHER TOUR UP NORTH SOON. SEE YOU THERE!
UH... WAIT ...
WHAT HAPPENED TO YOUR GUITARIST, DAMIAN YOSHIDA?
OH...
WE FIRED HIM.

*The Eloim Essaims Limousine

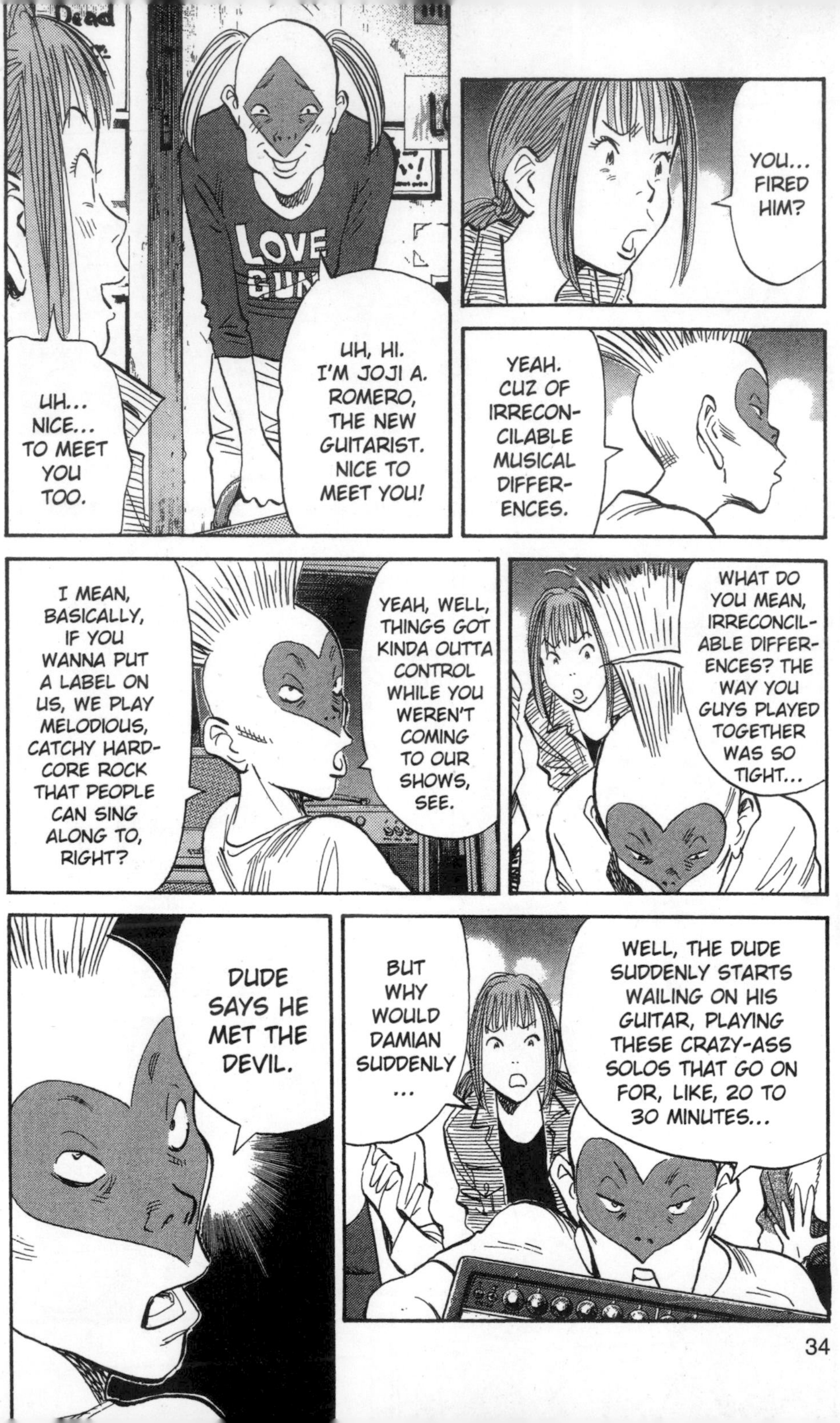
YOU... FIRED HIM?
YEAH. CUZ OF IRRECON-CILABLE MUSICAL DIFFER-ENCES.
UH, HI. I'M JOJI A. ROMERO, THE NEW GUITARIST. NICE TO MEET YOU!
UH... NICE... TO MEET YOU TOO.
WHAT DO YOU MEAN, IRRECONCIL-ABLE DIFFER-ENCES? THE WAY YOU GUYS PLAYED TOGETHER WAS SO TIGHT...
YEAH, WELL, THINGS GOT KINDA OUTTA CONTROL WHILE YOU WEREN'T COMING TO OUR SHOWS, SEE.
I MEAN, BASICALLY, IF YOU WANNA PUT A LABEL ON US, WE PLAY MELODIOUS, CATCHY HARD-CORE ROCK THAT PEOPLE CAN SING ALONG TO, RIGHT?
WELL, THE DUDE SUDDENLY STARTS WAILING ON HIS GUITAR, PLAYING THESE CRAZY-ASS SOLOS THAT GO ON FOR, LIKE, 20 TO 30 MINUTES...
BUT WHY WOULD DAMIAN SUDDENLY ...
DUDE SAYS HE MET THE DEVIL.

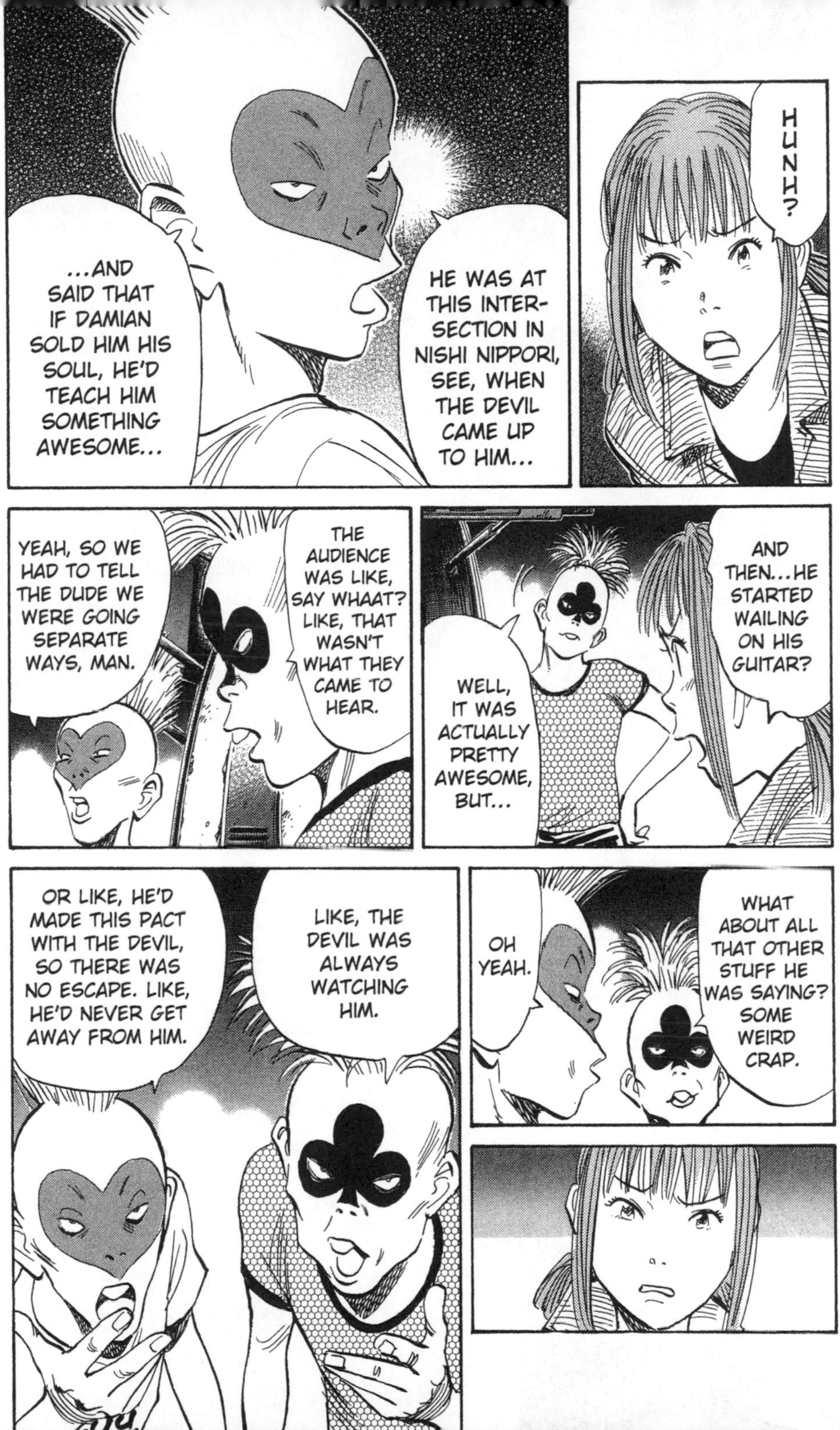
HUNH?
HE WAS AT THIS INTER-SECTION IN NISHI NIPPORI, SEE, WHEN THE DEVIL CAME UP TO HIM...
...AND SAID THAT IF DAMIAN SOLD HIM HIS SOUL, HE'D TEACH HIM SOMETHING AWESOME...
AND THEN...HE STARTED WAILING ON HIS GUITAR?
WELL, IT WAS ACTUALLY PRETTY AWESOME, BUT...
THE AUDIENCE WAS LIKE, SAY WHAAT? LIKE, THAT WASN'T WHAT THEY CAME TO HEAR.
YEAH, SO WE HAD TO TELL THE DUDE WE WERE GOING SEPARATE WAYS, MAN.
WHAT ABOUT ALL THAT OTHER STUFF HE WAS SAYING? SOME WEIRD CRAP.
OH YEAH.
LIKE, THE DEVIL WAS ALWAYS WATCHING HIM.
OR LIKE, HE'D MADE THIS PACT WITH THE DEVIL, SO THERE WAS NO ESCAPE. LIKE, HE'D NEVER GET AWAY FROM HIM.

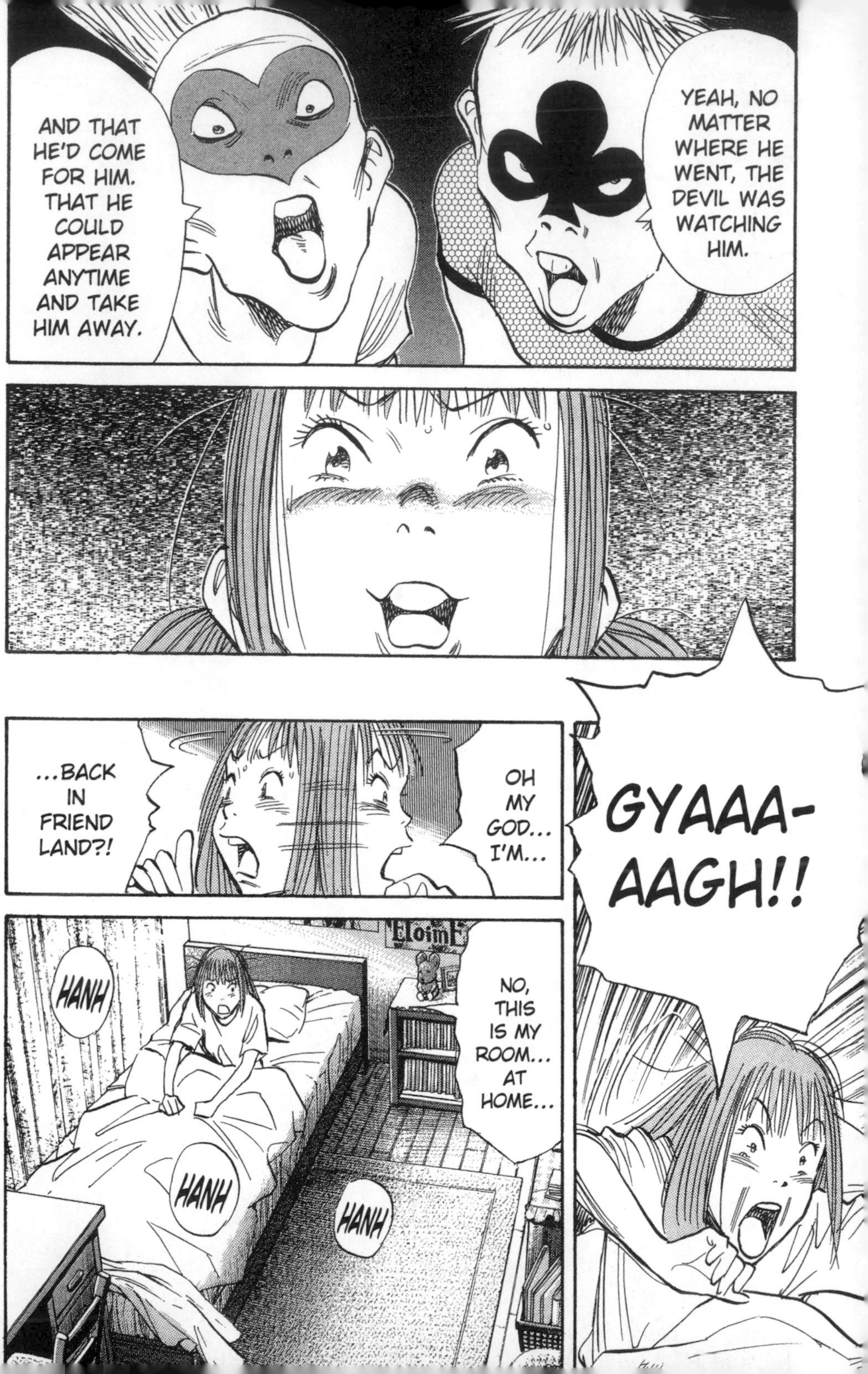
YEAH, NO MATTER WHERE HE WENT, THE DEVIL WAS WATCHING HIM.
AND THAT HE'D COME FOR HIM. THAT HE COULD APPEAR ANYTIME AND TAKE HIM AWAY.
GYAAA-AAGH!!
OH MY GOD... I'M...
...BACK IN FRIEND LAND?!
NO, THIS IS MY ROOM... AT HOME...
HANH
HANH
HANH

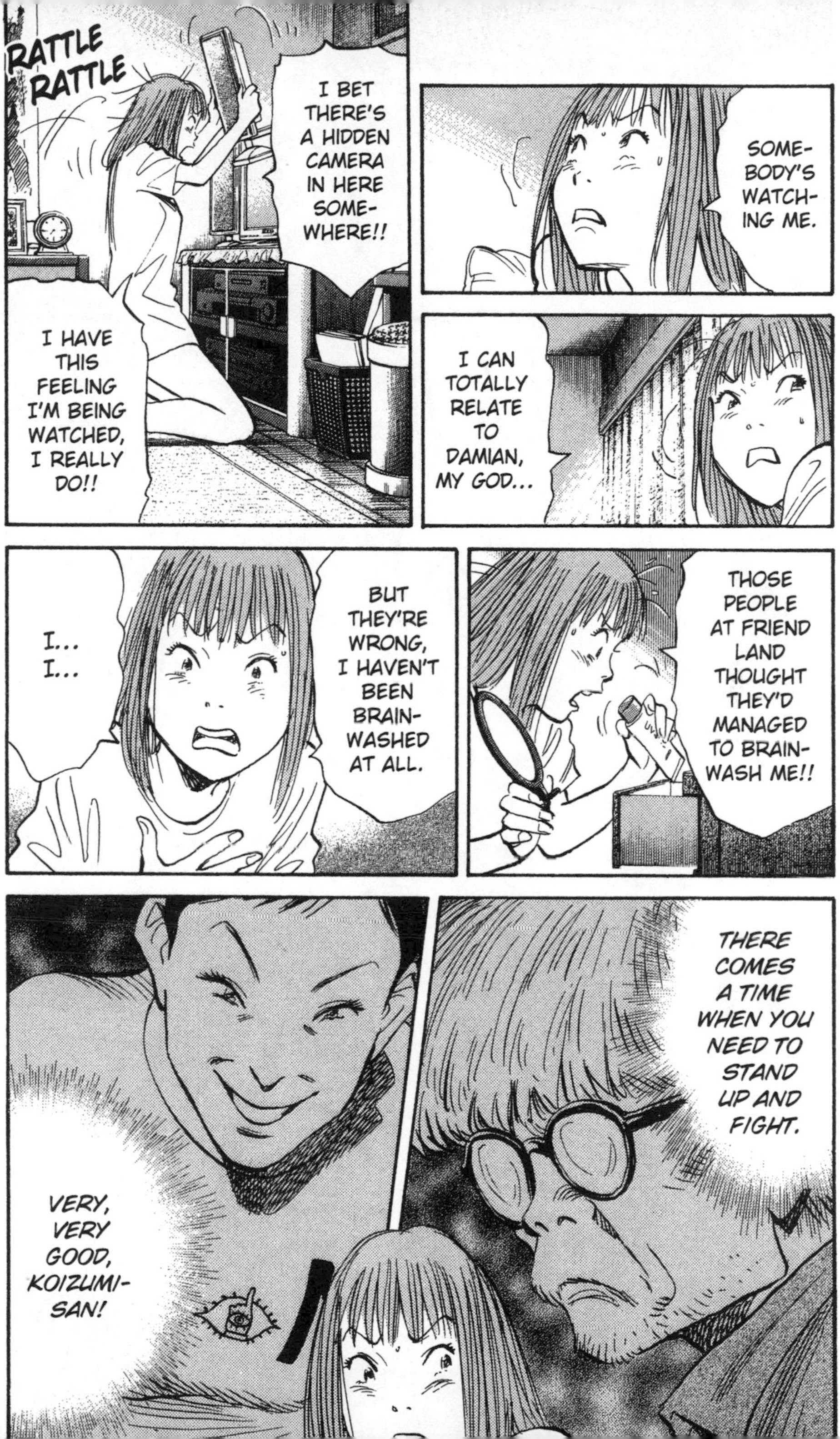
SOME-BODY'S WATCH-ING ME.
I CAN TOTALLY RELATE TO DAMIAN, MY GOD...
RATTLE RATTLE
I BET THERE'S A HIDDEN CAMERA IN HERE SOME-WHERE!!
I HAVE THIS FEELING I'M BEING WATCHED, I REALLY DO!!
THOSE PEOPLE AT FRIEND LAND THOUGHT THEY'D MANAGED TO BRAIN-WASH ME!!
BUT THEY'RE WRONG, I HAVEN'T BEEN BRAIN-WASHED AT ALL.
I... I...
THERE COMES A TIME WHEN YOU NEED TO STAND UP AND FIGHT.
VERY, VERY GOOD, KOIZUMI-SAN!

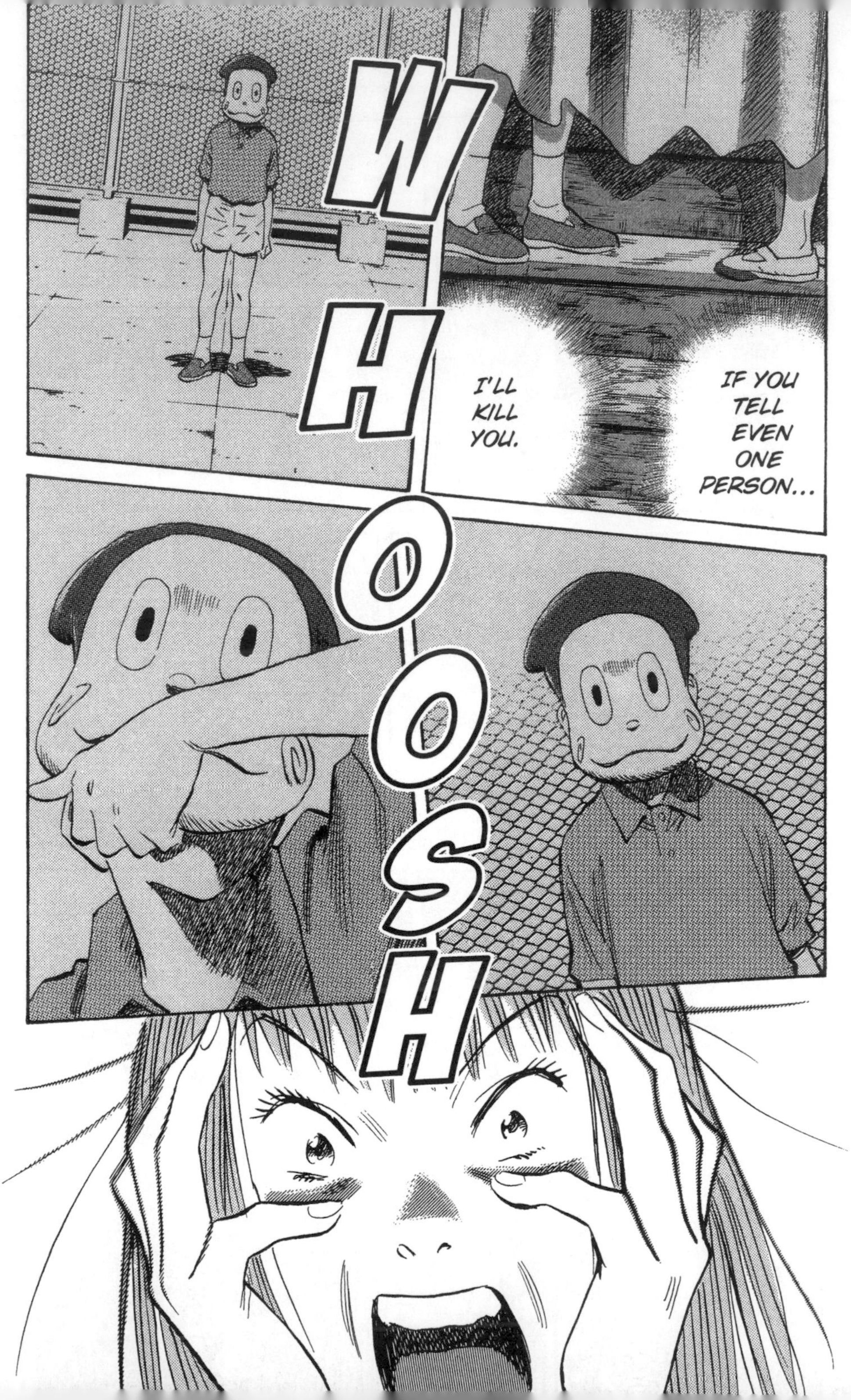
IF YOU TELL EVEN ONE PERSON...
I'LL KILL YOU.
WHOOSH

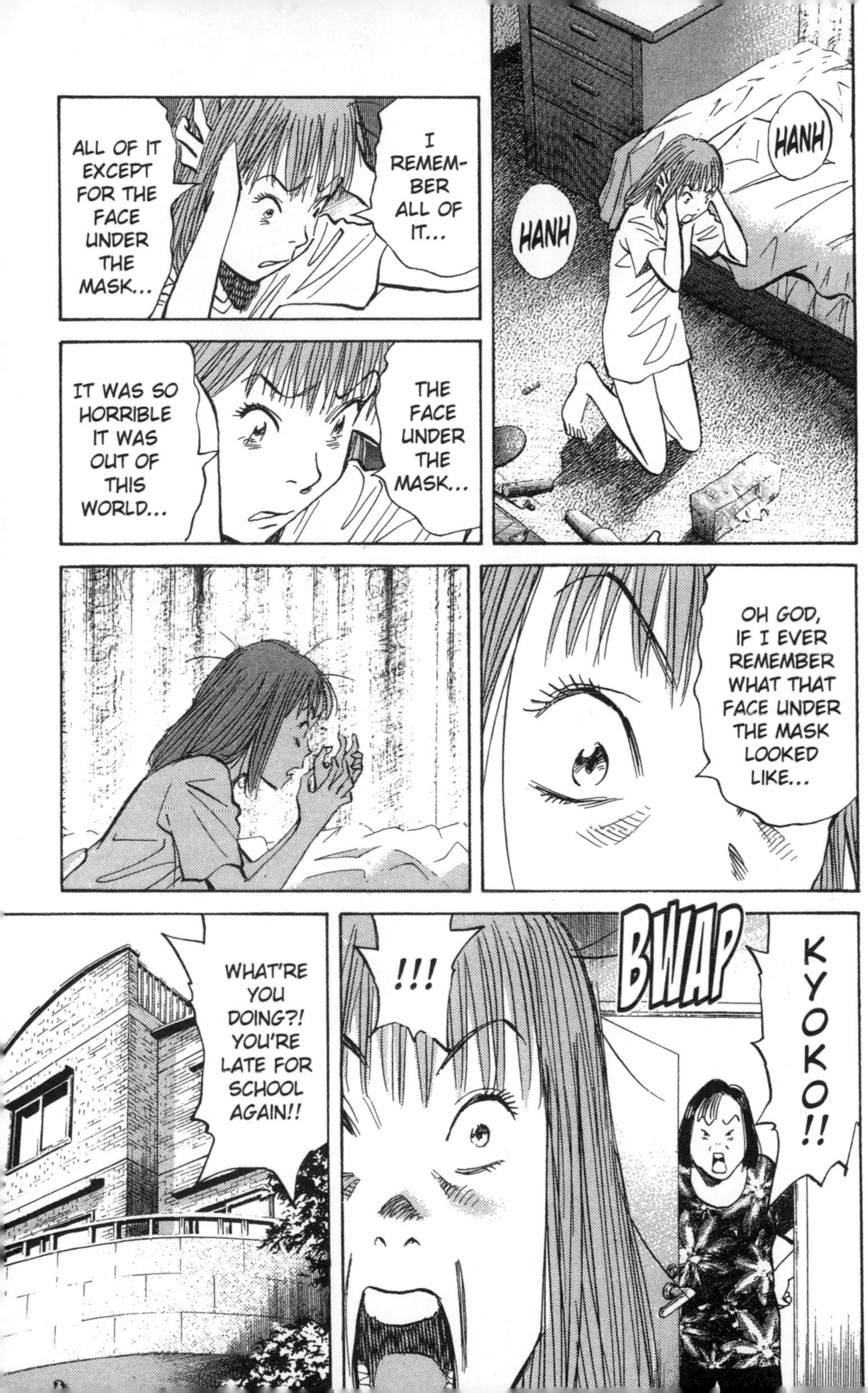
HANH
HANH
I REMEMBER ALL OF IT...
ALL OF IT EXCEPT FOR THE FACE UNDER THE MASK...
THE FACE UNDER THE MASK...
IT WAS SO HORRIBLE IT WAS OUT OF THIS WORLD...
OH GOD, IF I EVER REMEMBER WHAT THAT FACE UNDER THE MASK LOOKED LIKE...
KYOKO!!
BWAP
!!!
WHAT'RE YOU DOING?! YOU'RE LATE FOR SCHOOL AGAIN!!

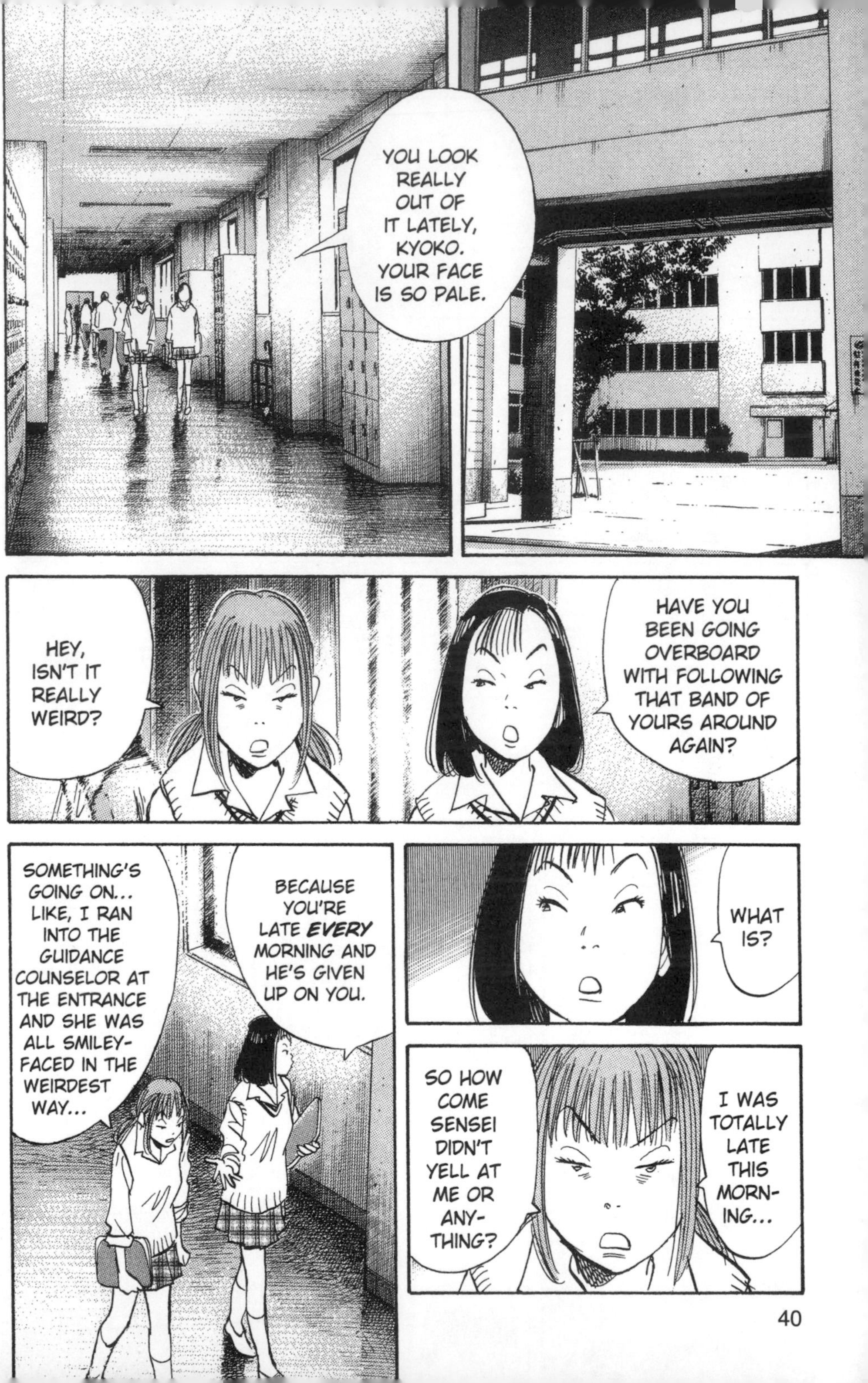
YOU LOOK REALLY OUT OF IT LATELY, KYOKO. YOUR FACE IS SO PALE.
HAVE YOU BEEN GOING OVERBOARD WITH FOLLOWING THAT BAND OF YOURS AROUND AGAIN?
HEY, ISN'T IT REALLY WEIRD?
WHAT IS?
I WAS TOTALLY LATE THIS MORN-ING...
SO HOW COME SENSEI DIDN'T YELL AT ME OR ANY-THING?
BECAUSE YOU'RE LATE ***EVERY*** MORNING AND HE'S GIVEN UP ON YOU.
SOMETHING'S GOING ON... LIKE, I RAN INTO THE GUIDANCE COUNSELOR AT THE ENTRANCE AND SHE WAS ALL SMILEY-FACED IN THE WEIRDEST WAY...

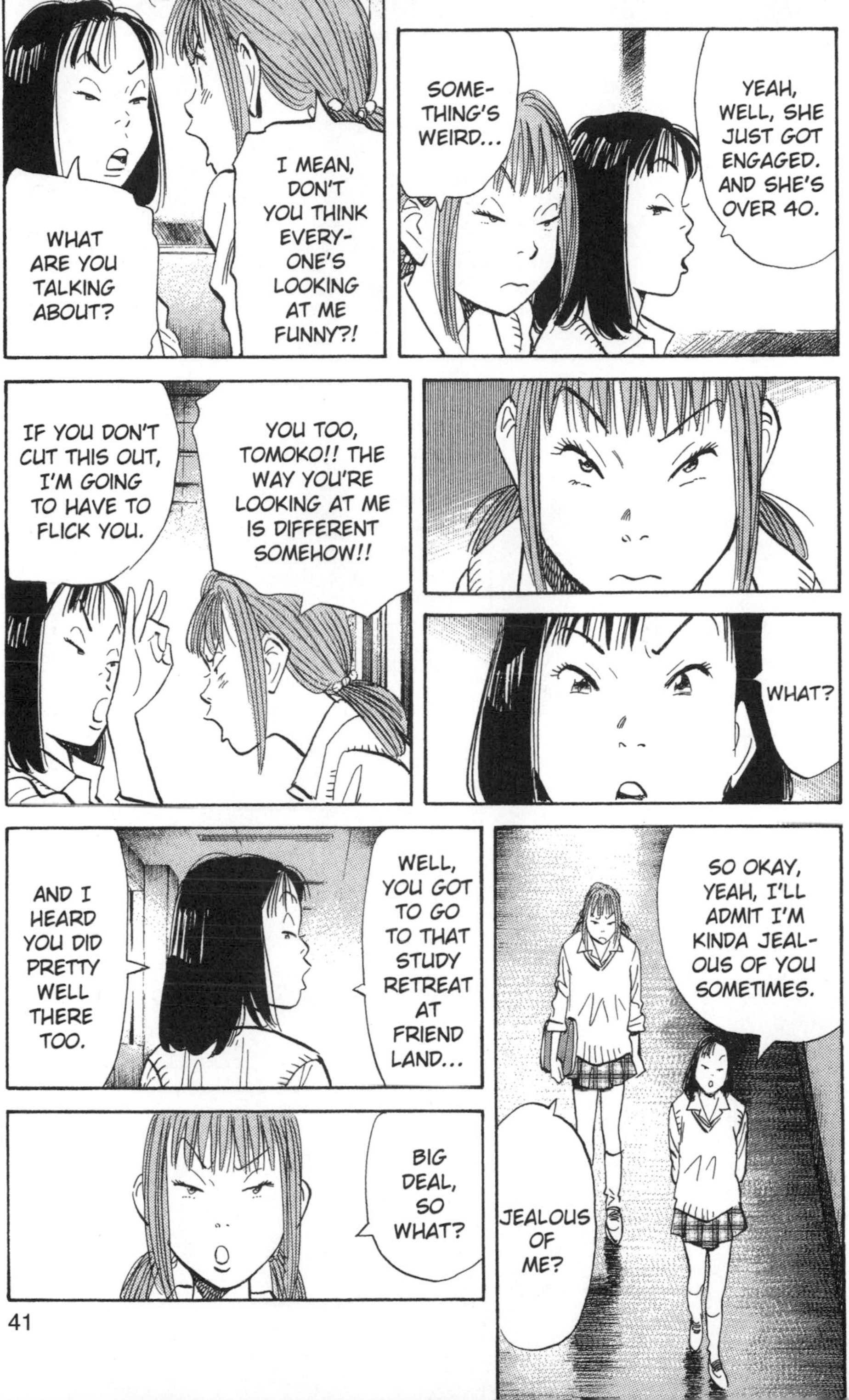
YEAH, WELL, SHE JUST GOT ENGAGED. AND SHE'S OVER 40.
SOME-THING'S WEIRD...
I MEAN, DON'T YOU THINK EVERY-ONE'S LOOKING AT ME FUNNY?!
WHAT ARE YOU TALKING ABOUT?
WHAT?
YOU TOO, TOMOKO!! THE WAY YOU'RE LOOKING AT ME IS DIFFERENT SOMEHOW!!
IF YOU DON'T CUT THIS OUT, I'M GOING TO HAVE TO FLICK YOU.
SO OKAY, YEAH, I'LL ADMIT I'M KINDA JEAL-OUS OF YOU SOMETIMES.
JEALOUS OF ME?
WELL, YOU GOT TO GO TO THAT STUDY RETREAT AT FRIEND LAND...
AND I HEARD YOU DID PRETTY WELL THERE TOO.
BIG DEAL, SO WHAT?

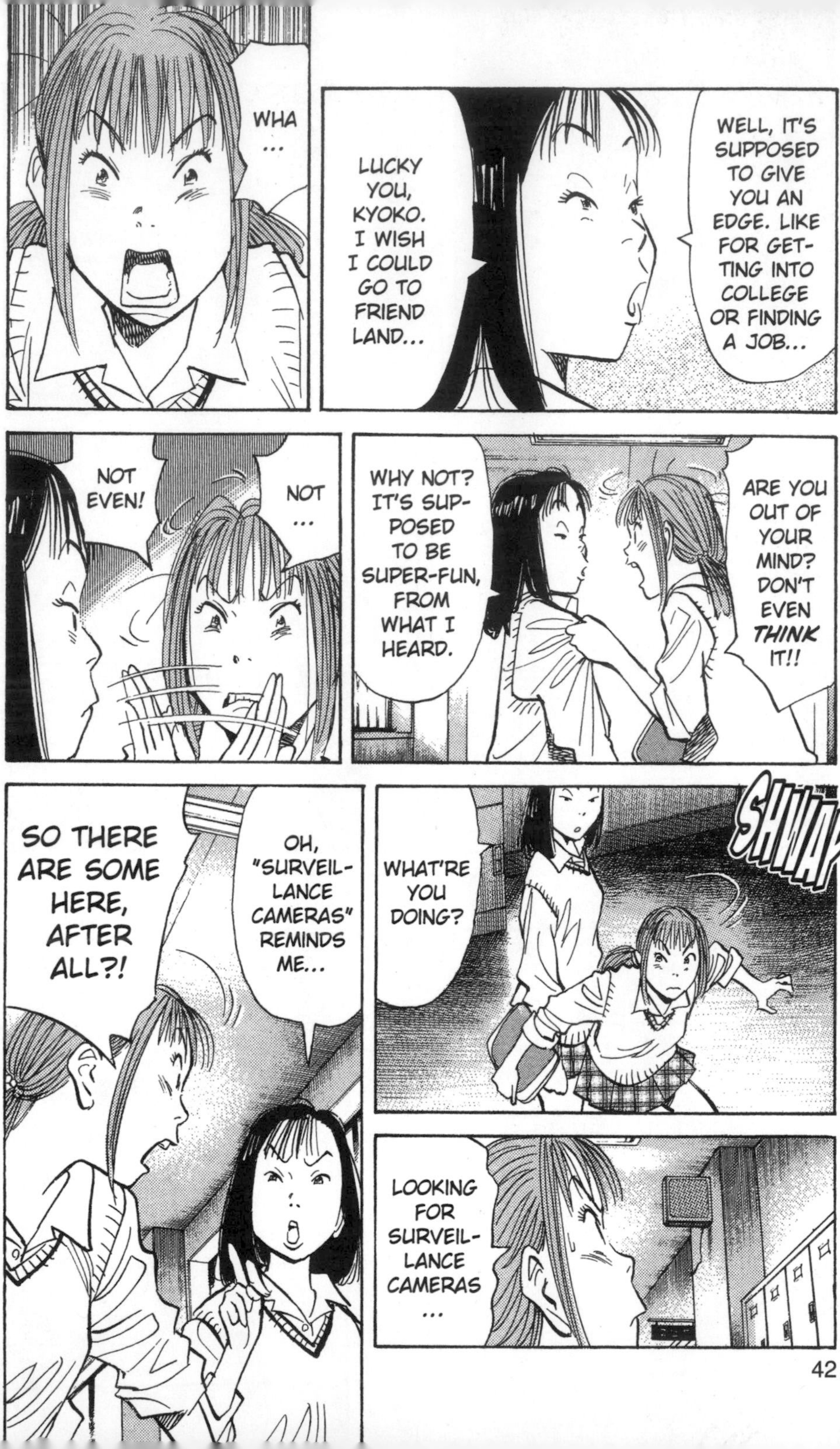
WELL, IT'S SUPPOSED TO GIVE YOU AN EDGE. LIKE FOR GET-TING INTO COLLEGE OR FINDING A JOB...
LUCKY YOU, KYOKO. I WISH I COULD GO TO FRIEND LAND...
WHA...
ARE YOU OUT OF YOUR MIND? DON'T EVEN *THINK* IT!!
WHY NOT? IT'S SUP-POSED TO BE SUPER-FUN, FROM WHAT I HEARD.
NOT...
NOT EVEN!
SHWAP
WHAT'RE YOU DOING?
LOOKING FOR SURVEIL-LANCE CAMERAS...
OH, "SURVEIL-LANCE CAMERAS" REMINDS ME...
SO THERE ARE SOME HERE, AFTER ALL?!

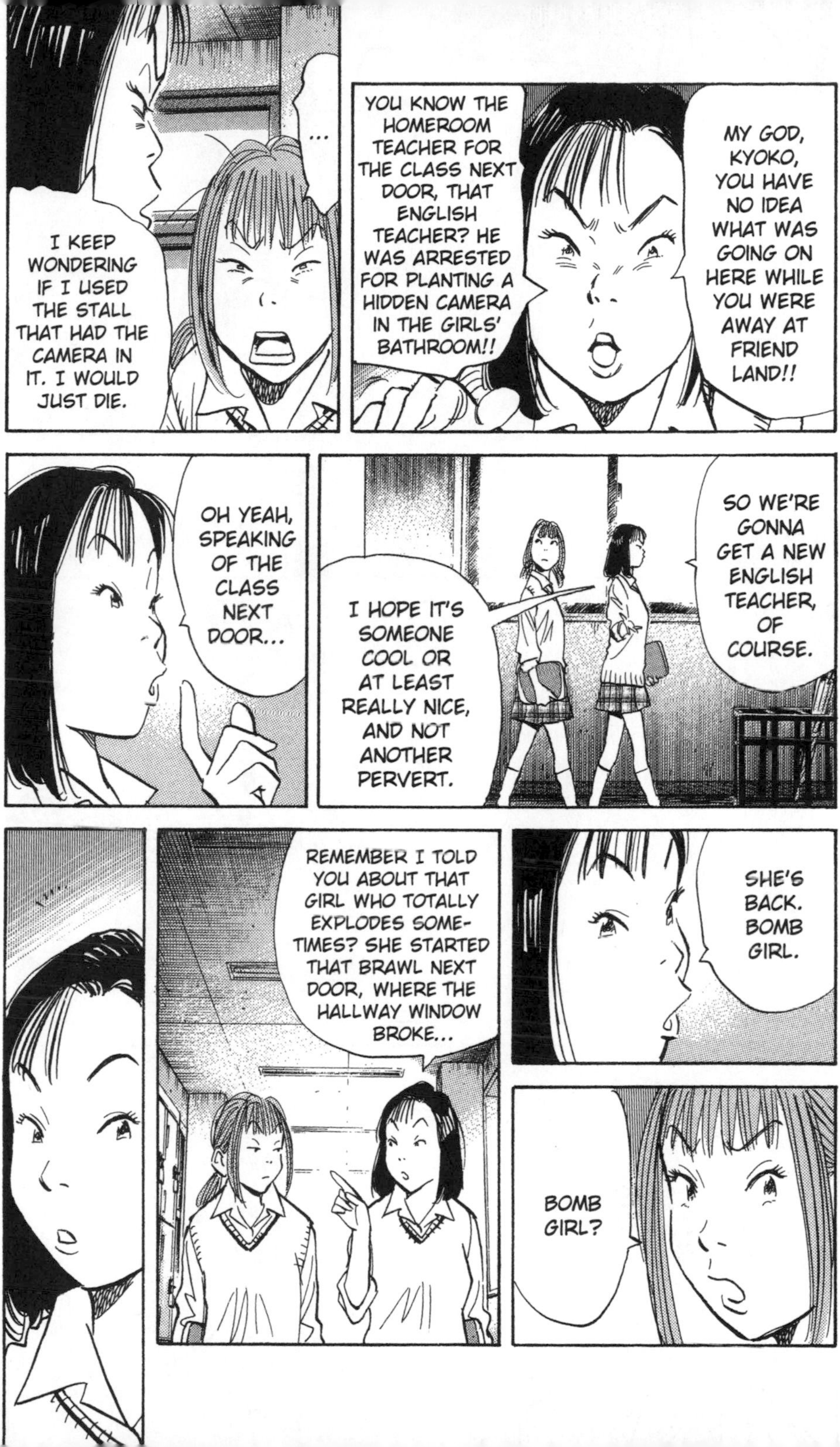
MY GOD, KYOKO, YOU HAVE NO IDEA WHAT WAS GOING ON HERE WHILE YOU WERE AWAY AT FRIEND LAND!!
YOU KNOW THE HOMEROOM TEACHER FOR THE CLASS NEXT DOOR, THAT ENGLISH TEACHER? HE WAS ARRESTED FOR PLANTING A HIDDEN CAMERA IN THE GIRLS' BATHROOM!!
...
I KEEP WONDERING IF I USED THE STALL THAT HAD THE CAMERA IN IT. I WOULD JUST DIE.
SO WE'RE GONNA GET A NEW ENGLISH TEACHER, OF COURSE.
I HOPE IT'S SOMEONE COOL OR AT LEAST REALLY NICE, AND NOT ANOTHER PERVERT.
OH YEAH, SPEAKING OF THE CLASS NEXT DOOR...
SHE'S BACK. BOMB GIRL.
BOMB GIRL?
REMEMBER I TOLD YOU ABOUT THAT GIRL WHO TOTALLY EXPLODES SOME-TIMES? SHE STARTED THAT BRAWL NEXT DOOR, WHERE THE HALLWAY WINDOW BROKE...

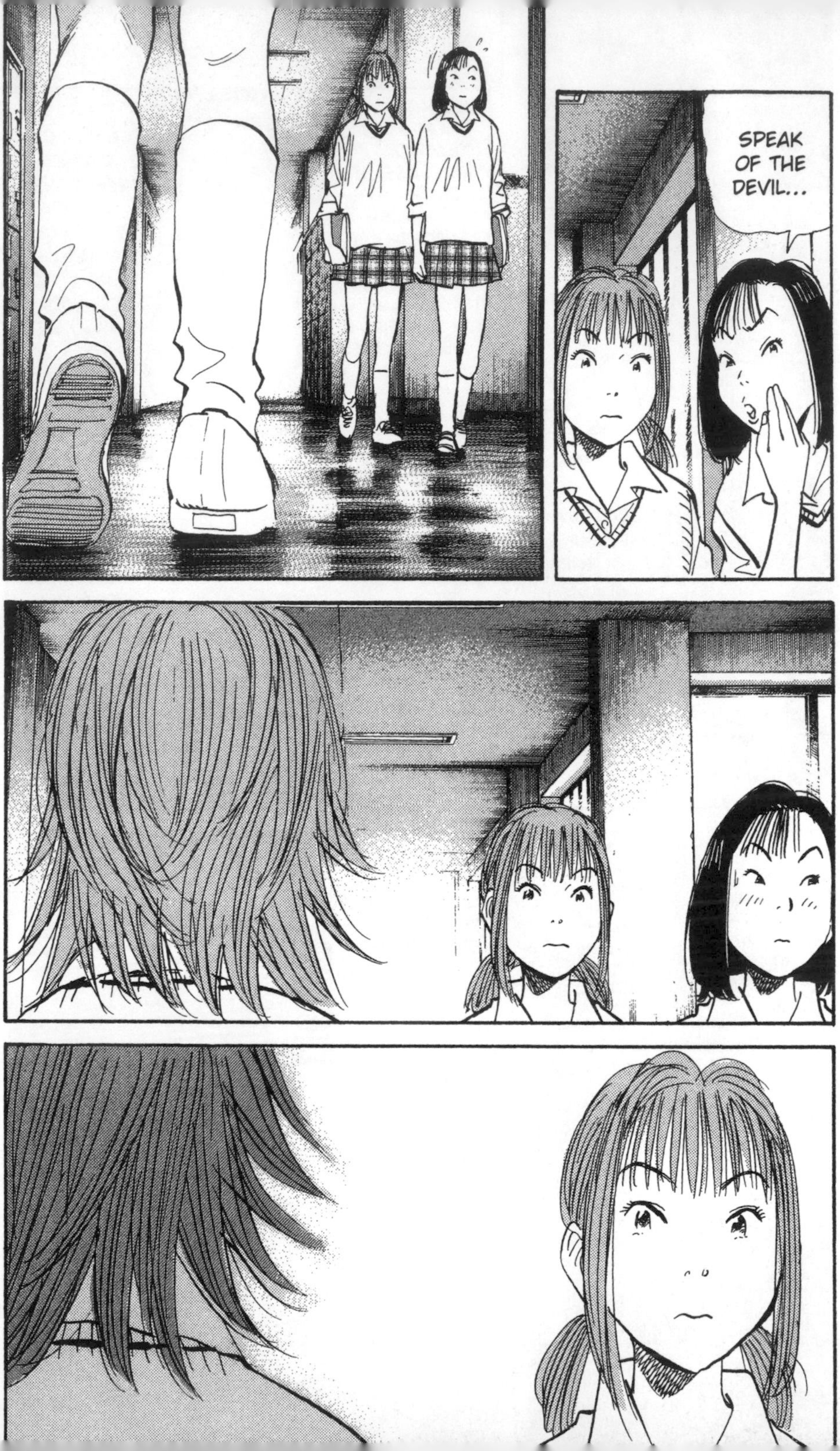
SPEAK OF THE DEVIL...

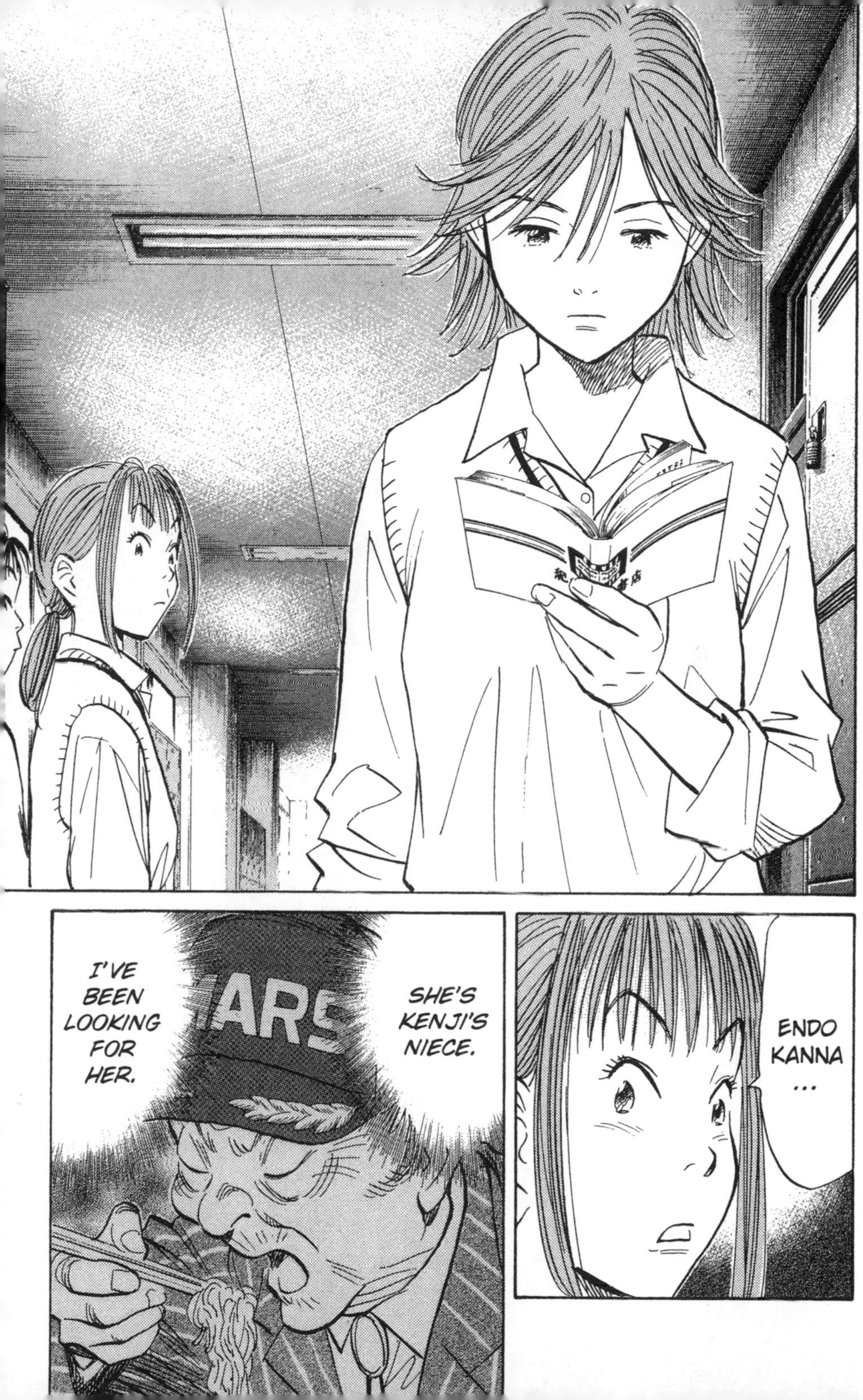
ENDO KANNA ...
SHE'S KENJI'S NIECE.
I'VE BEEN LOOKING FOR HER.

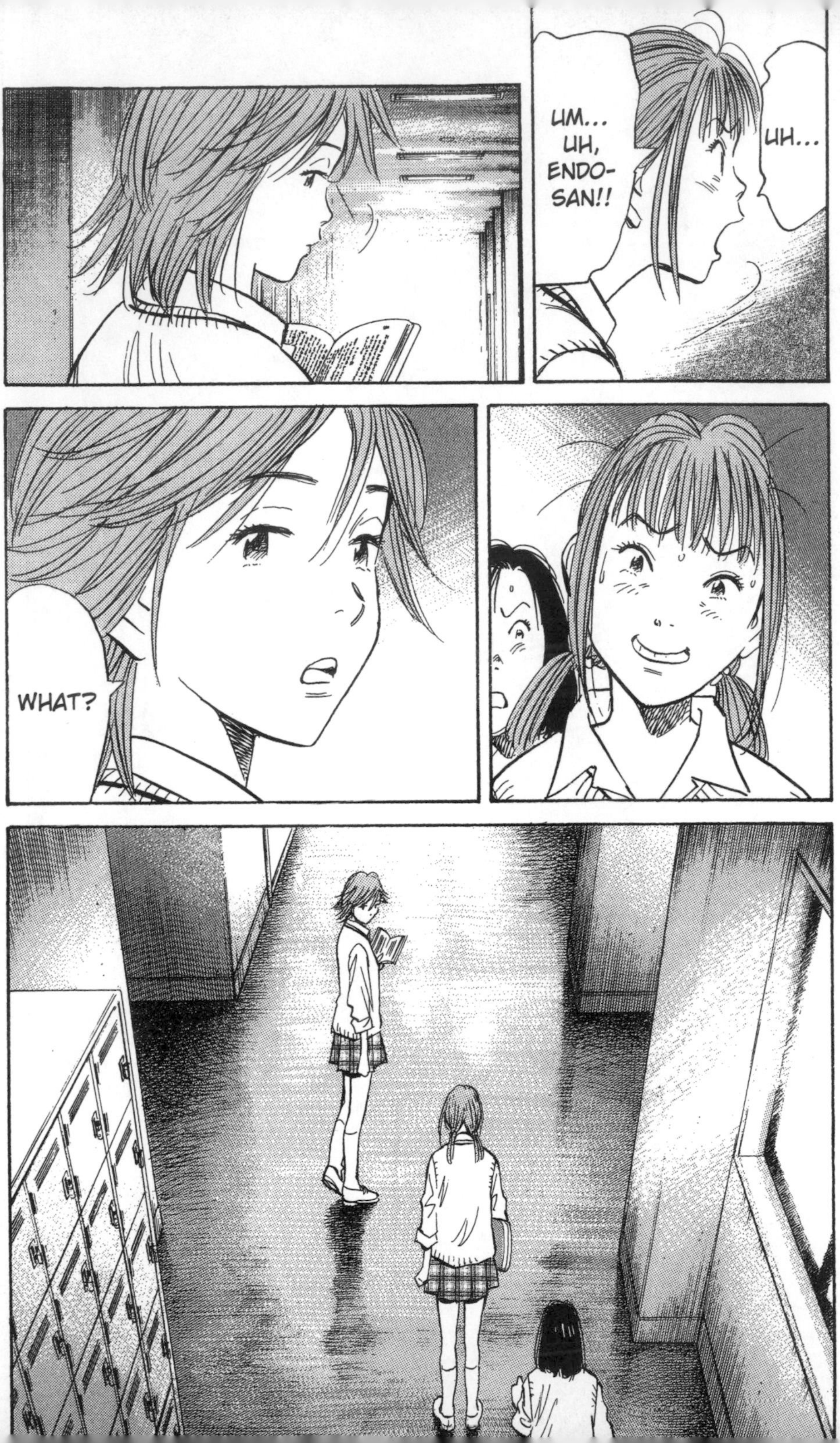
UH...
UM... UH, ENDO-SAN!!
WHAT?

Chapter 3 Surveillance

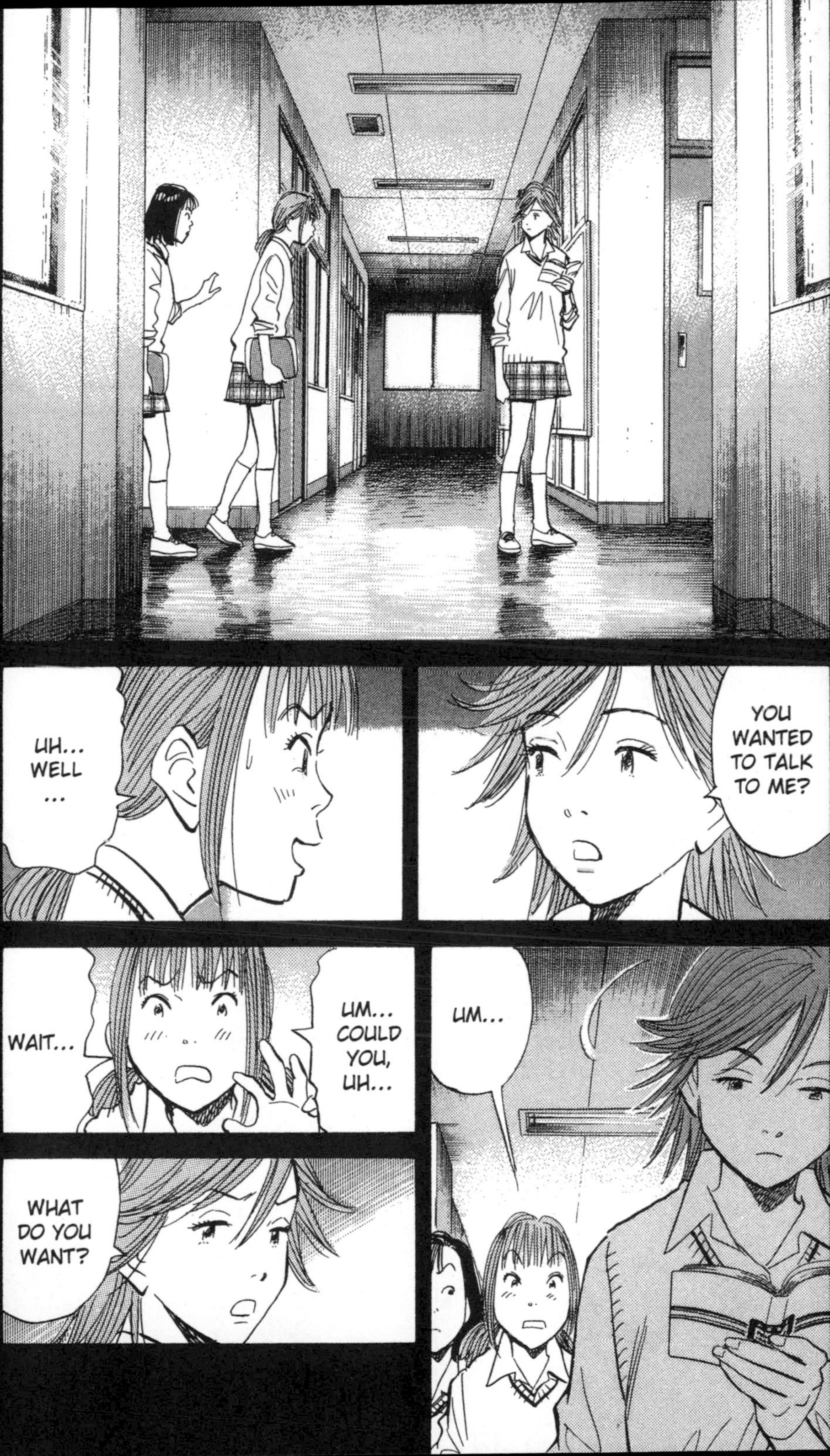

YOU WANTED TO TALK TO ME?
UH... WELL ...
UM...
UM... COULD YOU, UH...
WAIT...
WHAT DO YOU WANT?

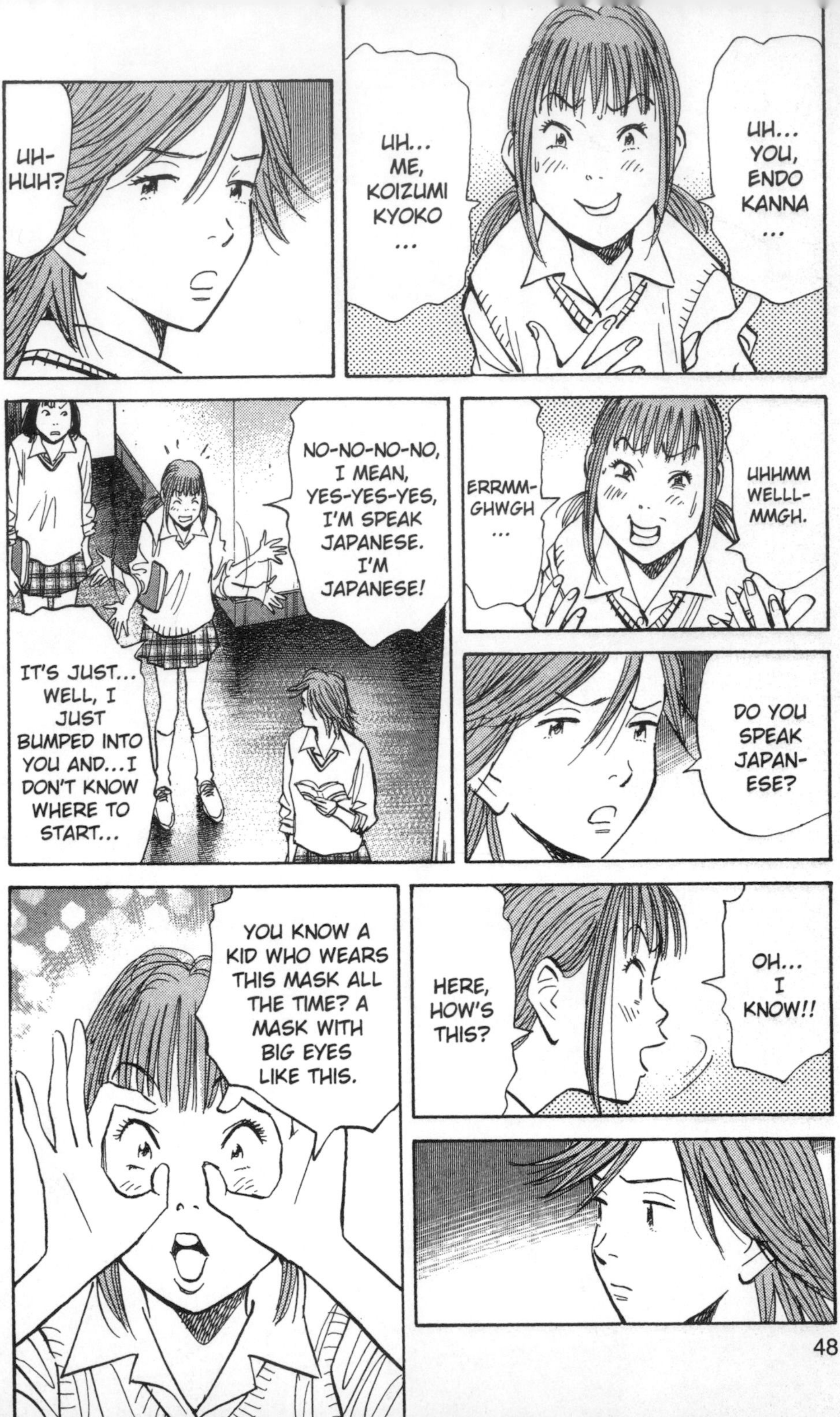

UH... YOU, ENDO KANNA ...
UH... ME, KOIZUMI KYOKO ...
UH-HUH?
UHHMM WELLL-MMGH.
ERRMM-GHWGH ...
DO YOU SPEAK JAPAN-ESE?
NO-NO-NO-NO, I MEAN, YES-YES-YES, I'M SPEAK JAPANESE. I'M JAPANESE!
IT'S JUST... WELL, I JUST BUMPED INTO YOU AND... I DON'T KNOW WHERE TO START...
OH... I KNOW!!
HERE, HOW'S THIS?
YOU KNOW A KID WHO WEARS THIS MASK ALL THE TIME? A MASK WITH BIG EYES LIKE THIS.

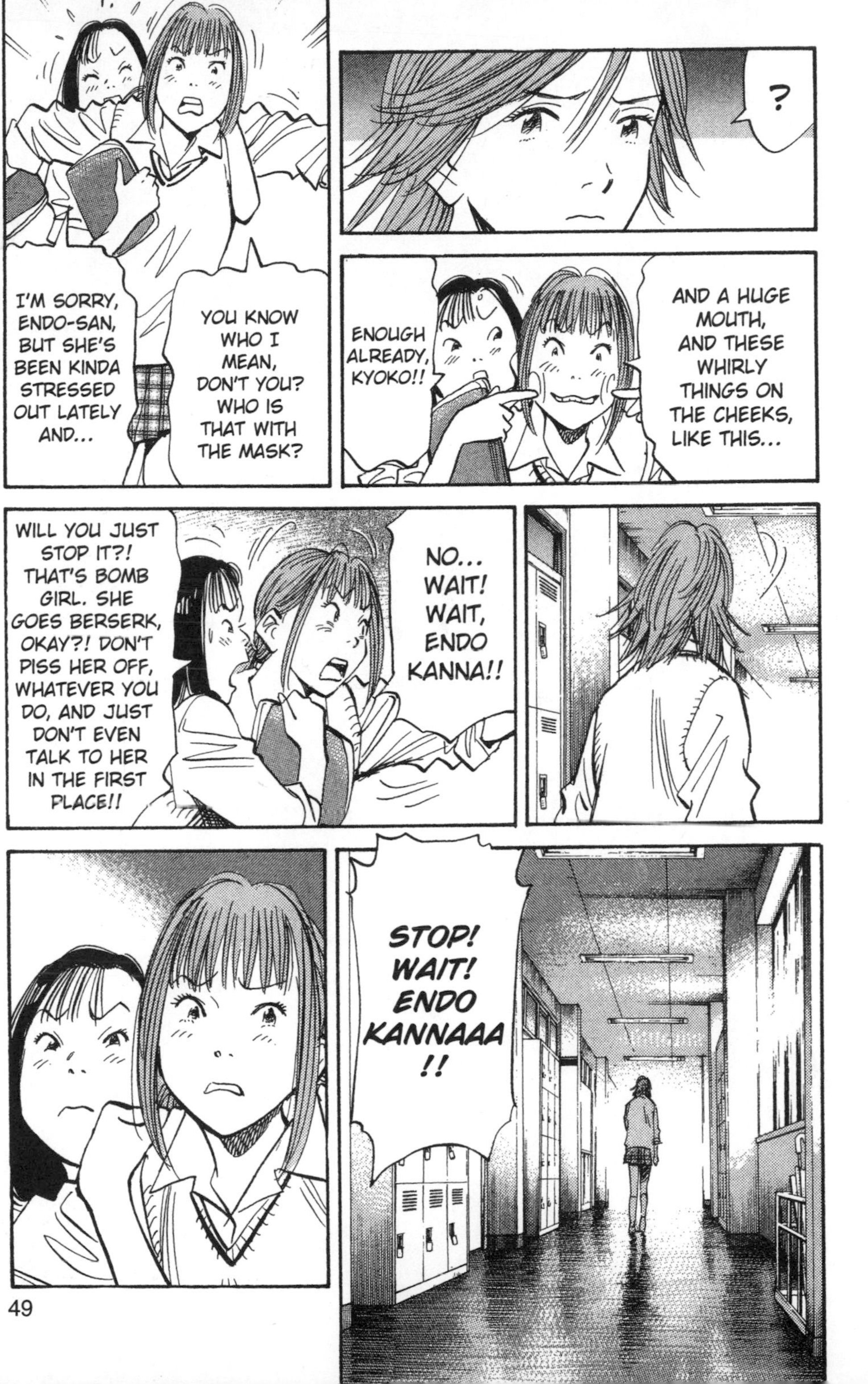
?
AND A HUGE MOUTH, AND THESE WHIRLY THINGS ON THE CHEEKS, LIKE THIS...
ENOUGH ALREADY, KYOKO!!
YOU KNOW WHO I MEAN, DON'T YOU? WHO IS THAT WITH THE MASK?
I'M SORRY, ENDO-SAN, BUT SHE'S BEEN KINDA STRESSED OUT LATELY AND...
NO... WAIT! WAIT, ENDO KANNA!!
WILL YOU JUST STOP IT?! THAT'S BOMB GIRL. SHE GOES BERSERK, OKAY?! DON'T PISS HER OFF, WHATEVER YOU DO, AND JUST DON'T EVEN TALK TO HER IN THE FIRST PLACE!!
STOP! WAIT! ENDO KANNAAA!!

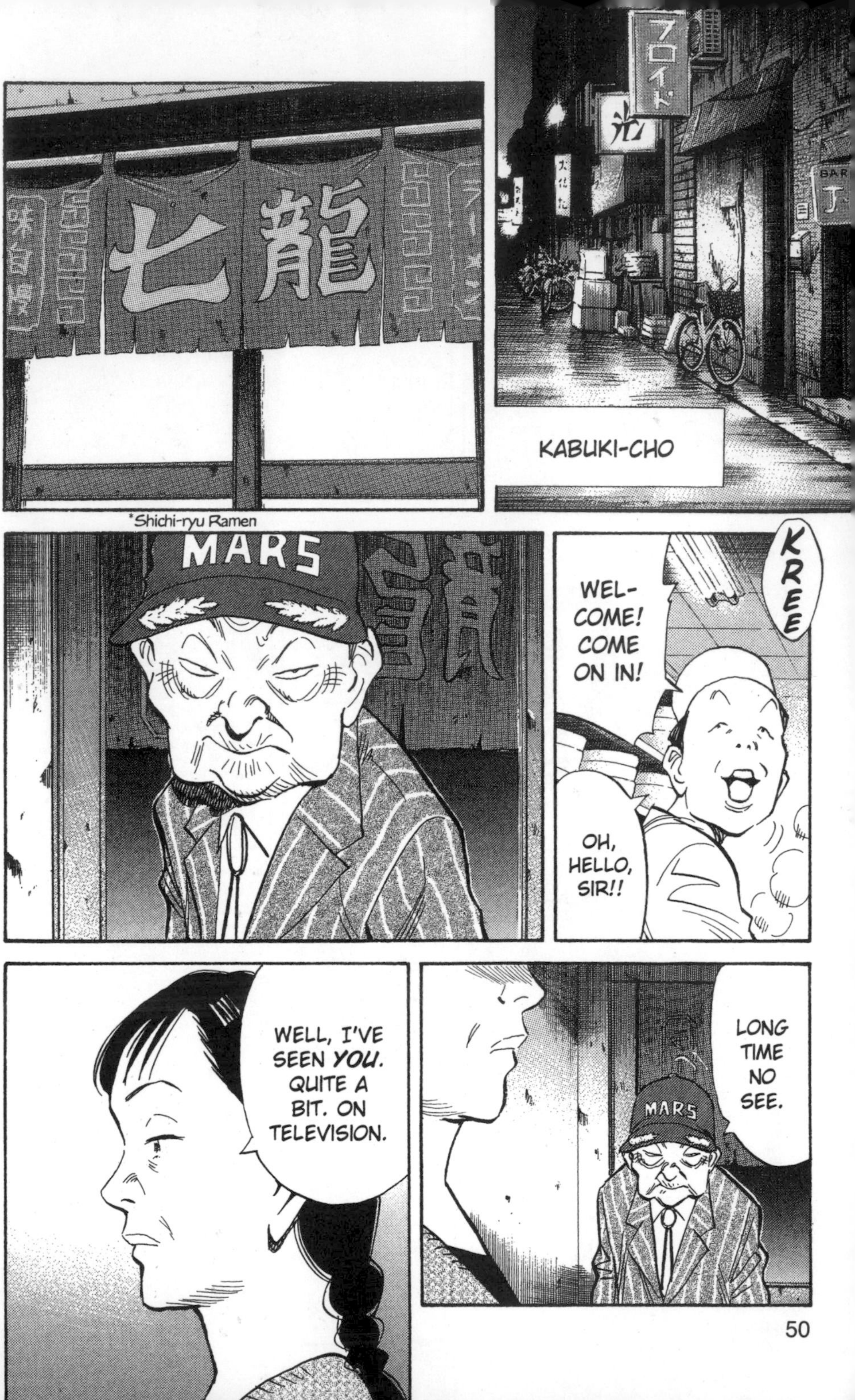
KABUKI-CHO
*Shichi-ryu Ramen
KREE
WEL-COME! COME ON IN!
OH, HELLO, SIR!!
LONG TIME NO SEE.
WELL, I'VE SEEN *YOU*. QUITE A BIT. ON TELEVISION.

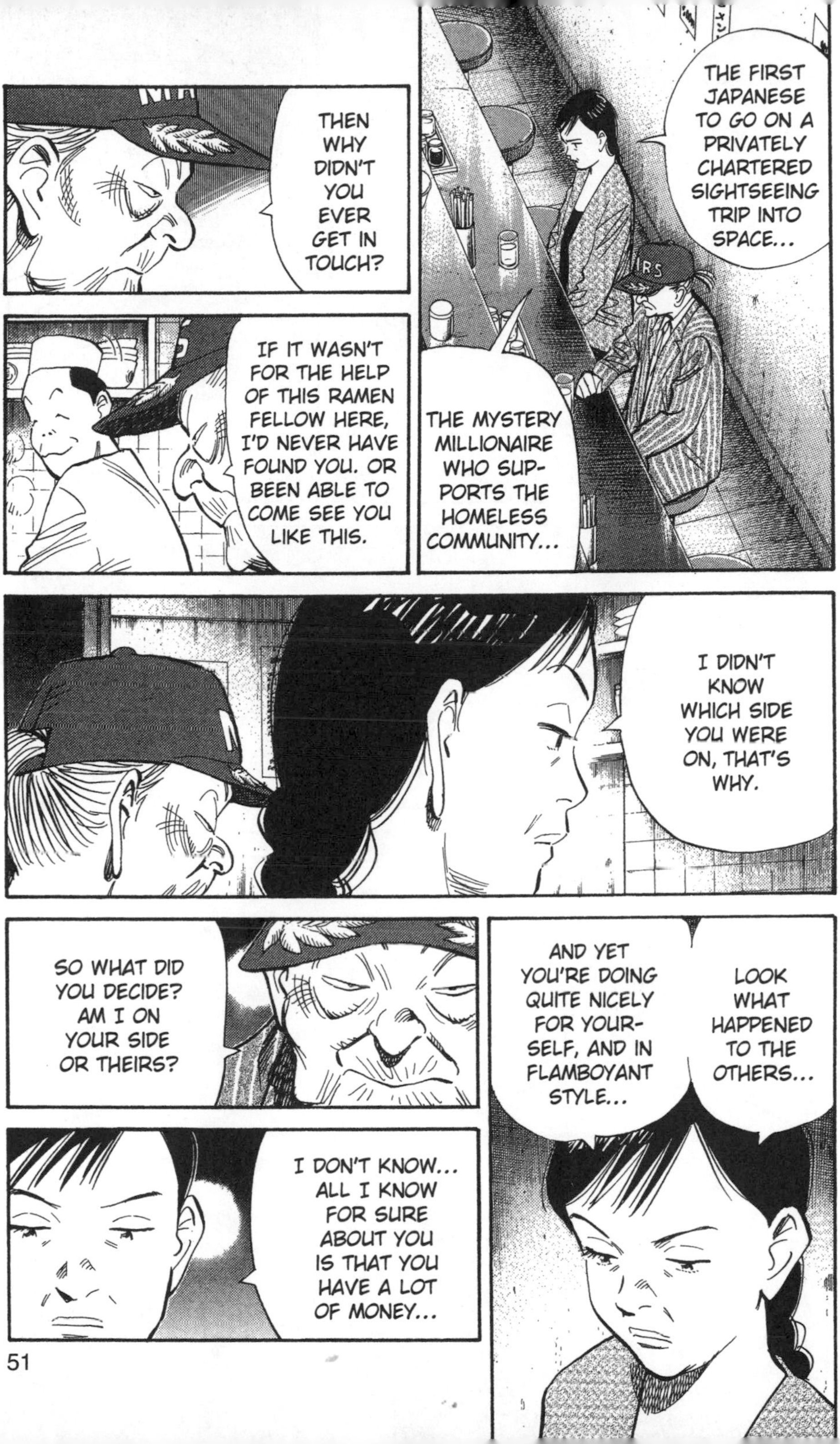
THE FIRST JAPANESE TO GO ON A PRIVATELY CHARTERED SIGHTSEEING TRIP INTO SPACE...
THE MYSTERY MILLIONAIRE WHO SUPPORTS THE HOMELESS COMMUNITY...
THEN WHY DIDN'T YOU EVER GET IN TOUCH?
IF IT WASN'T FOR THE HELP OF THIS RAMEN FELLOW HERE, I'D NEVER HAVE FOUND YOU. OR BEEN ABLE TO COME SEE YOU LIKE THIS.
I DIDN'T KNOW WHICH SIDE YOU WERE ON, THAT'S WHY.
LOOK WHAT HAPPENED TO THE OTHERS...
AND YET YOU'RE DOING QUITE NICELY FOR YOURSELF, AND IN FLAMBOYANT STYLE...
SO WHAT DID YOU DECIDE? AM I ON YOUR SIDE OR THEIRS?
I DON'T KNOW... ALL I KNOW FOR SURE ABOUT YOU IS THAT YOU HAVE A LOT OF MONEY...

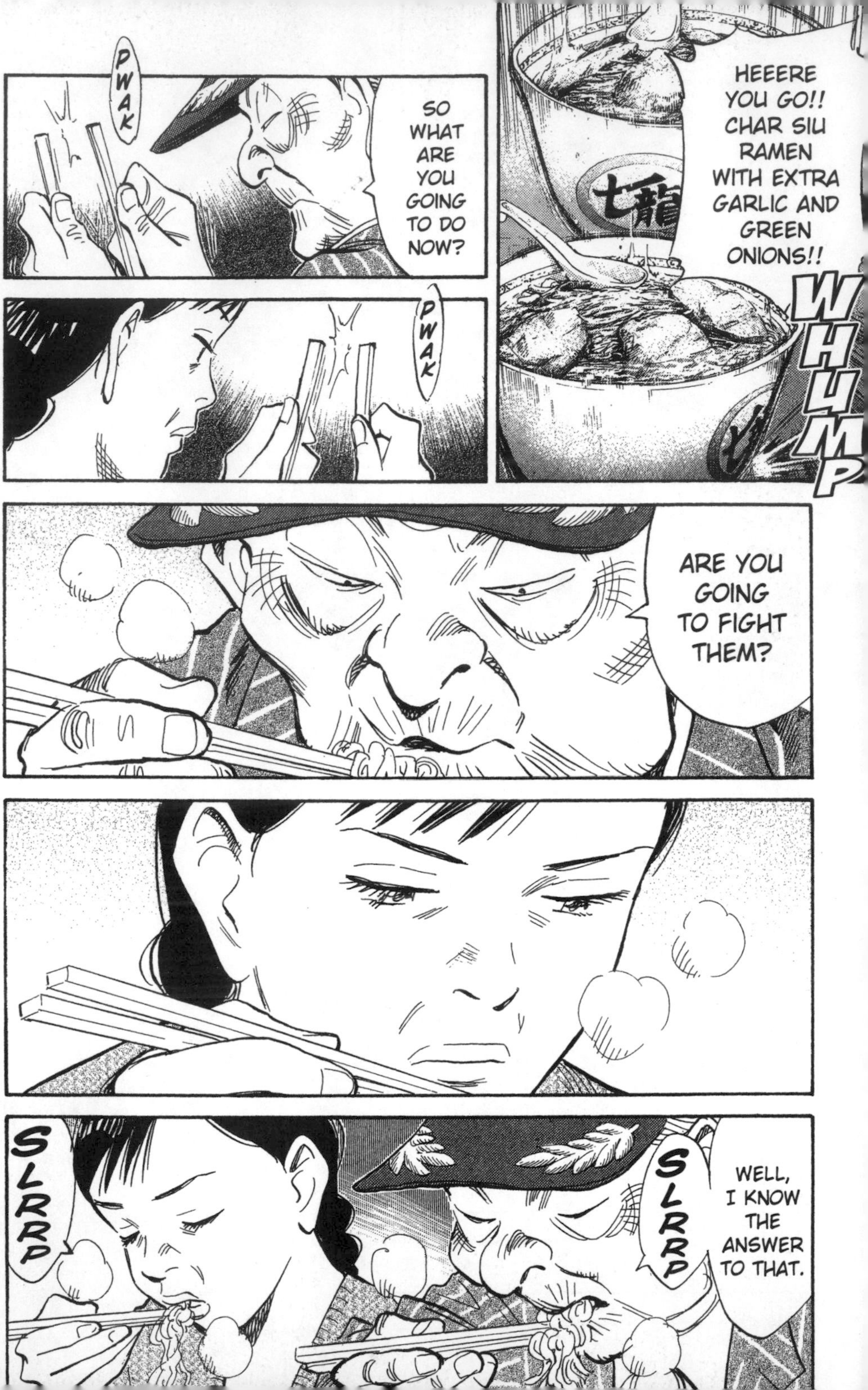
HEEERE YOU GO!! CHAR SIU RAMEN WITH EXTRA GARLIC AND GREEN ONIONS!!
WHUMP
PWAK
SO WHAT ARE YOU GOING TO DO NOW?
PWAK
ARE YOU GOING TO FIGHT THEM?
WELL, I KNOW THE ANSWER TO THAT.
SLRRP
SLRRP

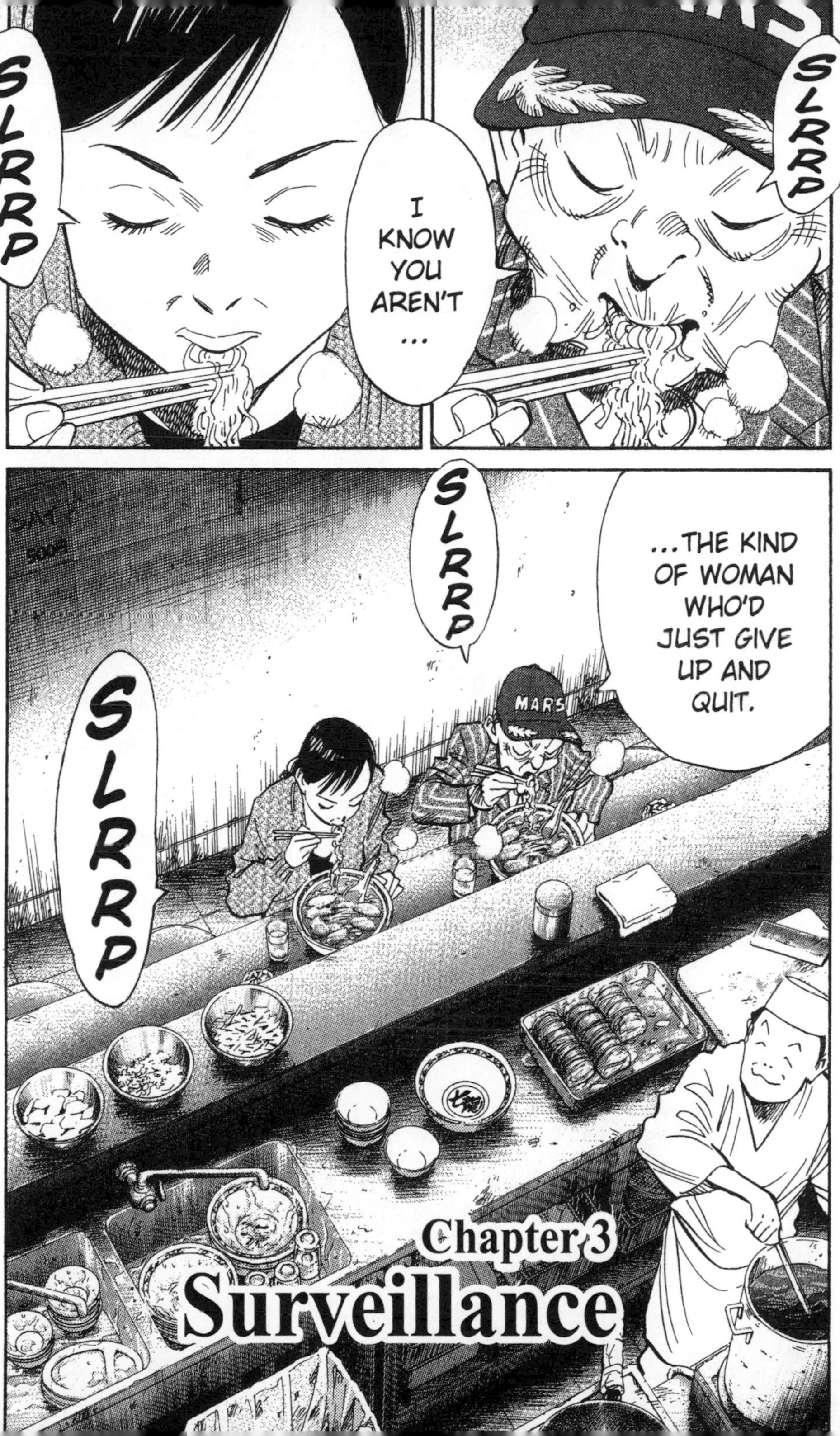
SLRRP
I KNOW YOU AREN'T ...
SLRRP
...THE KIND OF WOMAN WHO'D JUST GIVE UP AND QUIT.
SLRRP
SLRRP
MARS

Chapter 3
Surveillance

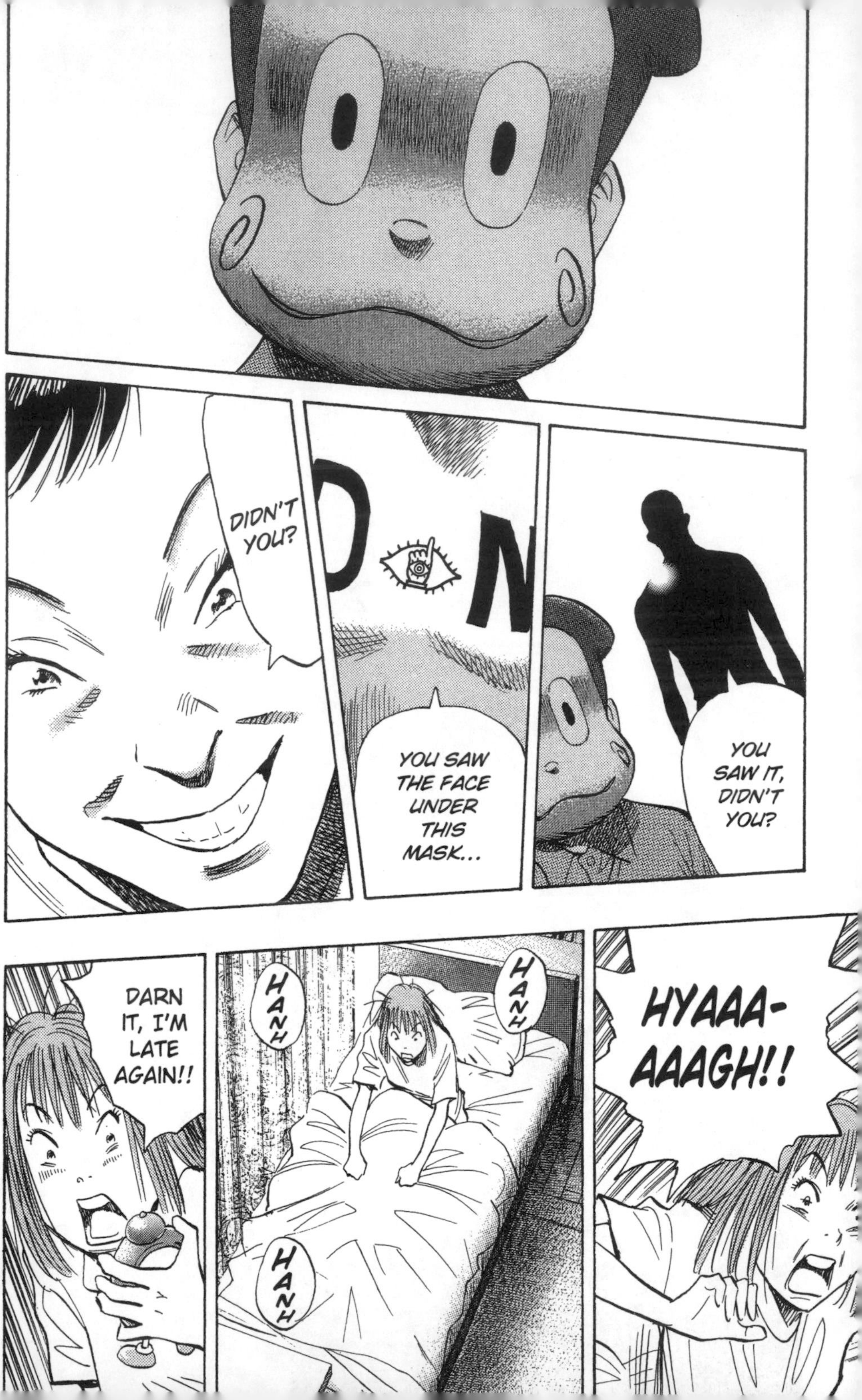
YOU SAW IT, DIDN'T YOU?
YOU SAW THE FACE UNDER THIS MASK...
DIDN'T YOU?
HYAAA-AAAGH!!
HANH
HANH
HANH
DARN IT, I'M LATE AGAIN!!

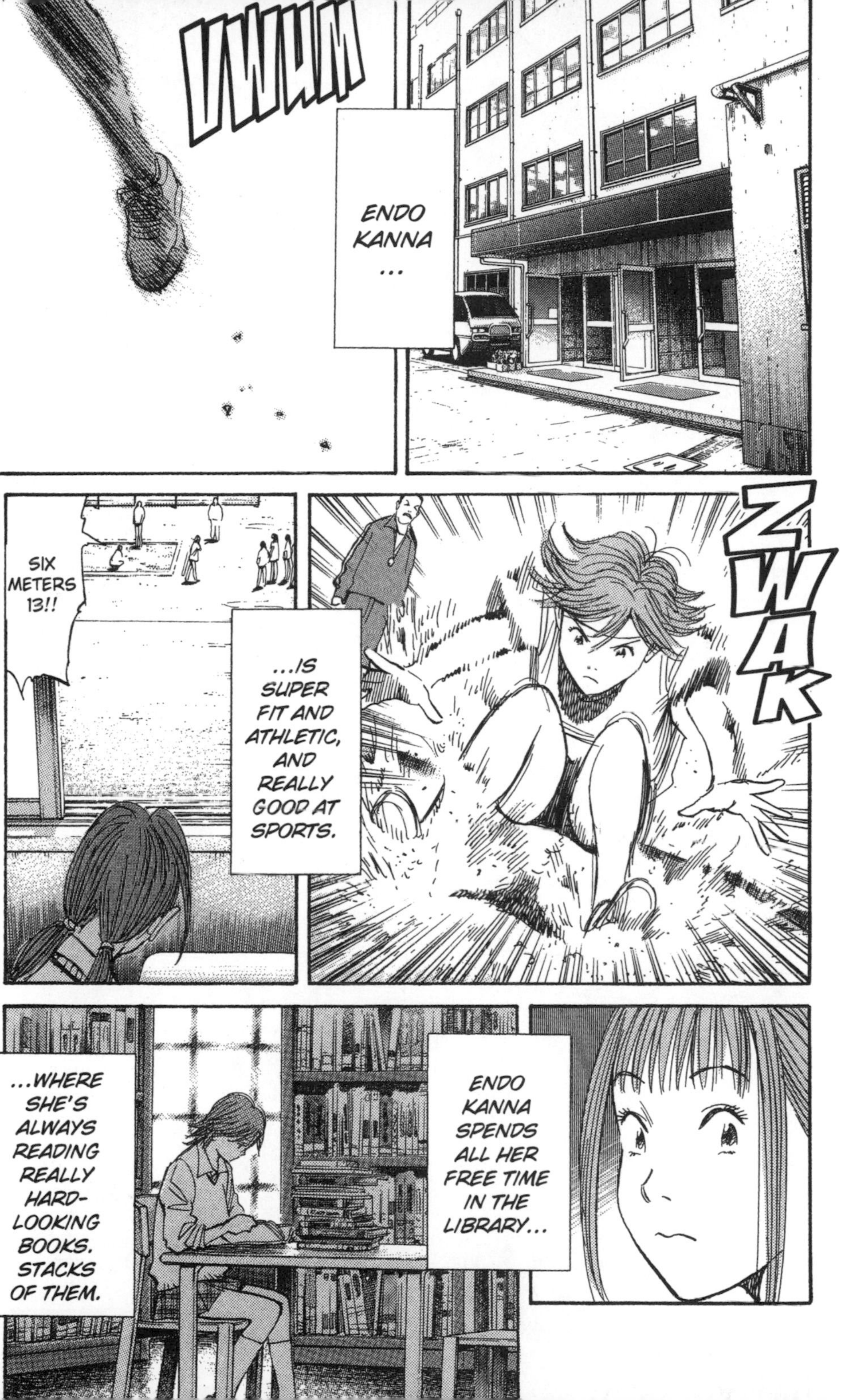
ENDO KANNA ...
VWUM
ZWAK
...IS SUPER FIT AND ATHLETIC, AND REALLY GOOD AT SPORTS.
SIX METERS 13!!
ENDO KANNA SPENDS ALL HER FREE TIME IN THE LIBRARY...
...WHERE SHE'S ALWAYS READING REALLY HARD-LOOKING BOOKS. STACKS OF THEM.

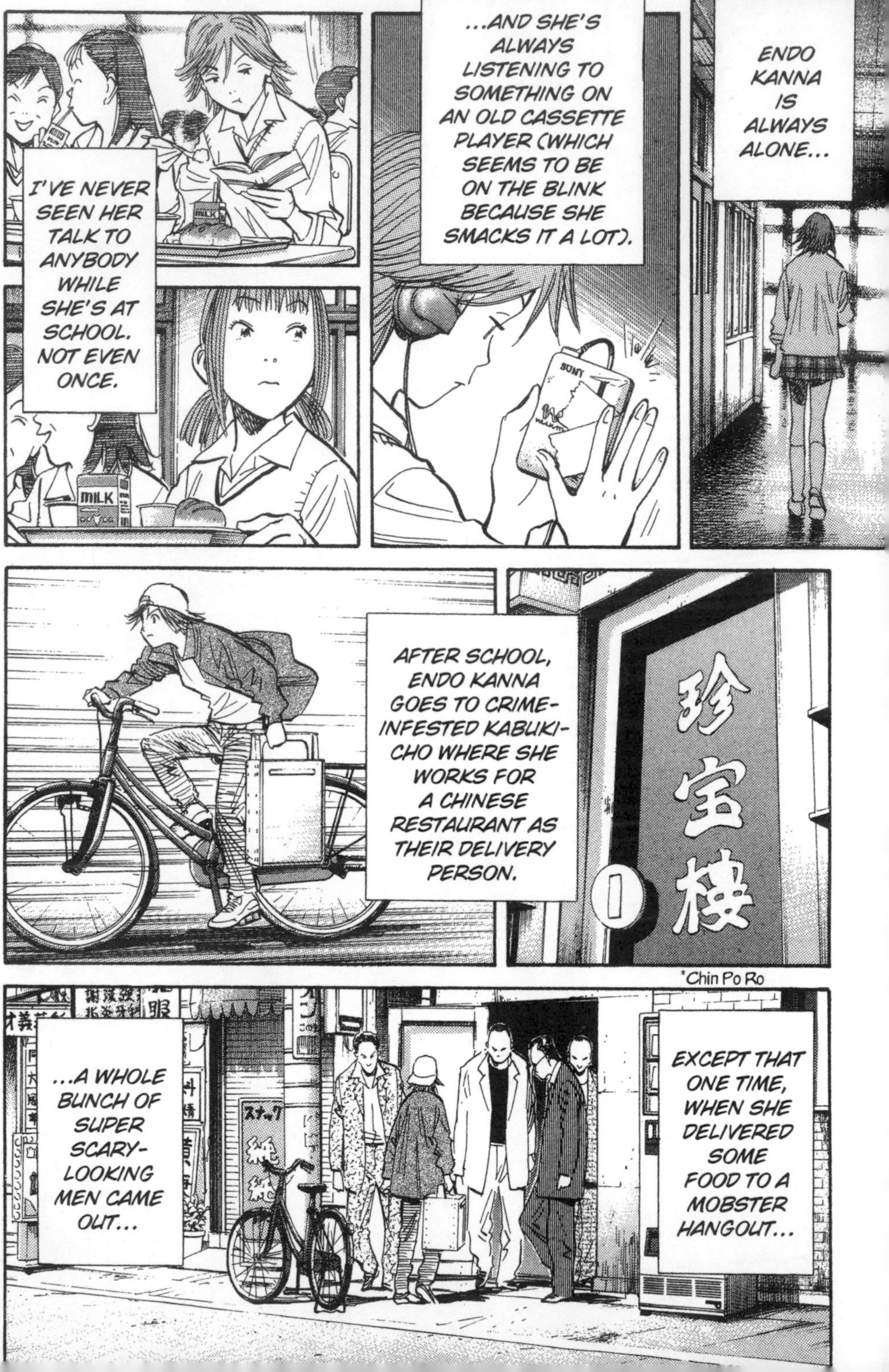
ENDO KANNA IS ALWAYS ALONE...
...AND SHE'S ALWAYS LISTENING TO SOMETHING ON AN OLD CASSETTE PLAYER (WHICH SEEMS TO BE ON THE BLINK BECAUSE SHE SMACKS IT A LOT).
I'VE NEVER SEEN HER TALK TO ANYBODY WHILE SHE'S AT SCHOOL. NOT EVEN ONCE.
珍宝楼
AFTER SCHOOL, ENDO KANNA GOES TO CRIME-INFESTED KABUKI-CHO WHERE SHE WORKS FOR A CHINESE RESTAURANT AS THEIR DELIVERY PERSON.
EXCEPT THAT ONE TIME, WHEN SHE DELIVERED SOME FOOD TO A MOBSTER HANGOUT...
...A WHOLE BUNCH OF SUPER SCARY-LOOKING MEN CAME OUT...
*Chin Po Ro

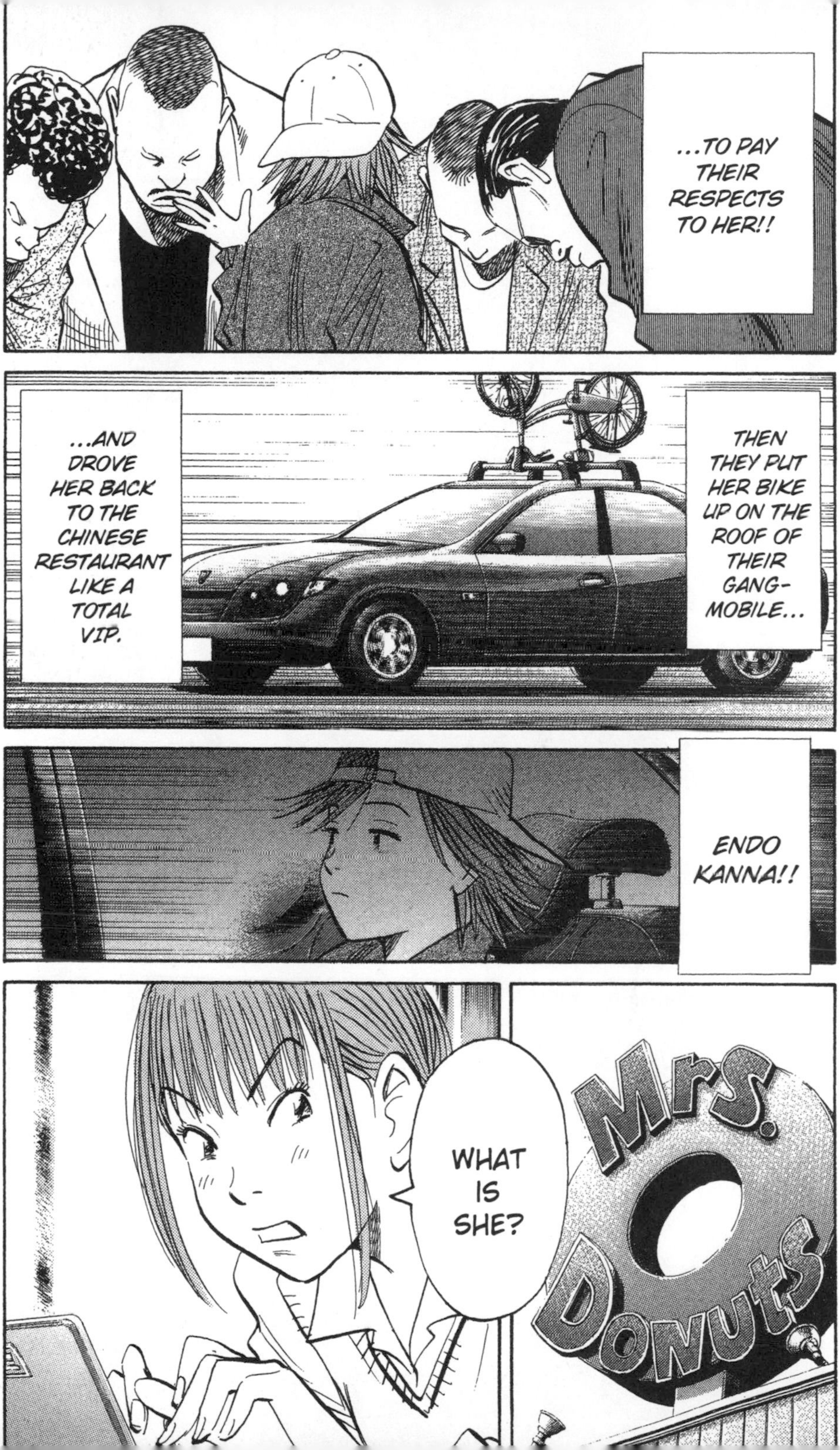
...TO PAY THEIR RESPECTS TO HER!!
THEN THEY PUT HER BIKE UP ON THE ROOF OF THEIR GANG-MOBILE...
...AND DROVE HER BACK TO THE CHINESE RESTAURANT LIKE A TOTAL VIP.
ENDO KANNA!!
Mrs. Donuts
WHAT IS SHE?

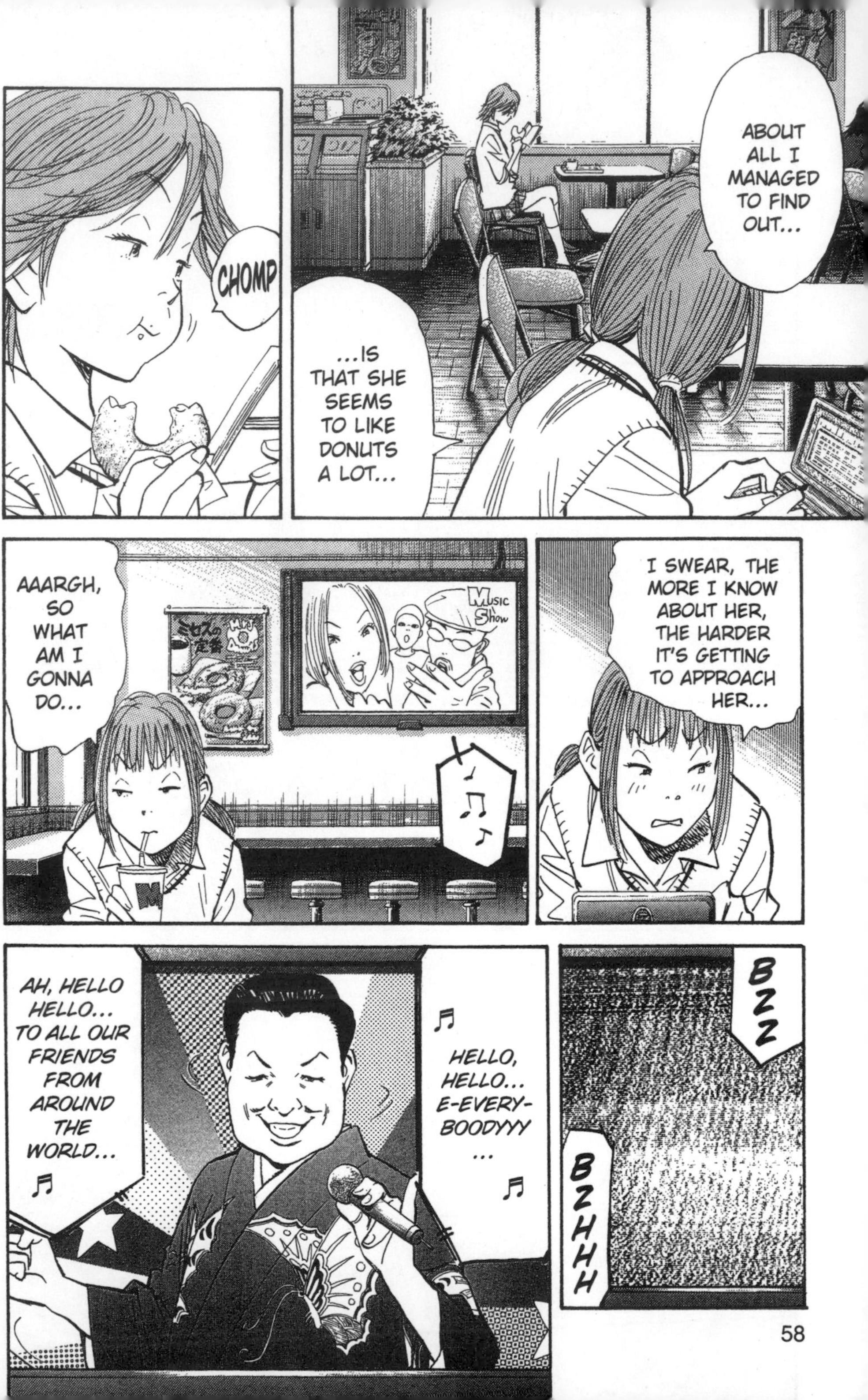
ABOUT ALL I MANAGED TO FIND OUT...
...IS THAT SHE SEEMS TO LIKE DONUTS A LOT...
CHOMP
I SWEAR, THE MORE I KNOW ABOUT HER, THE HARDER IT'S GETTING TO APPROACH HER...
AAARGH, SO WHAT AM I GONNA DO...
Music Show
BZZ
BZHHH
HELLO, HELLO... E-EVERY-BOODYYY ...
AH, HELLO HELLO... TO ALL OUR FRIENDS FROM AROUND THE WORLD...

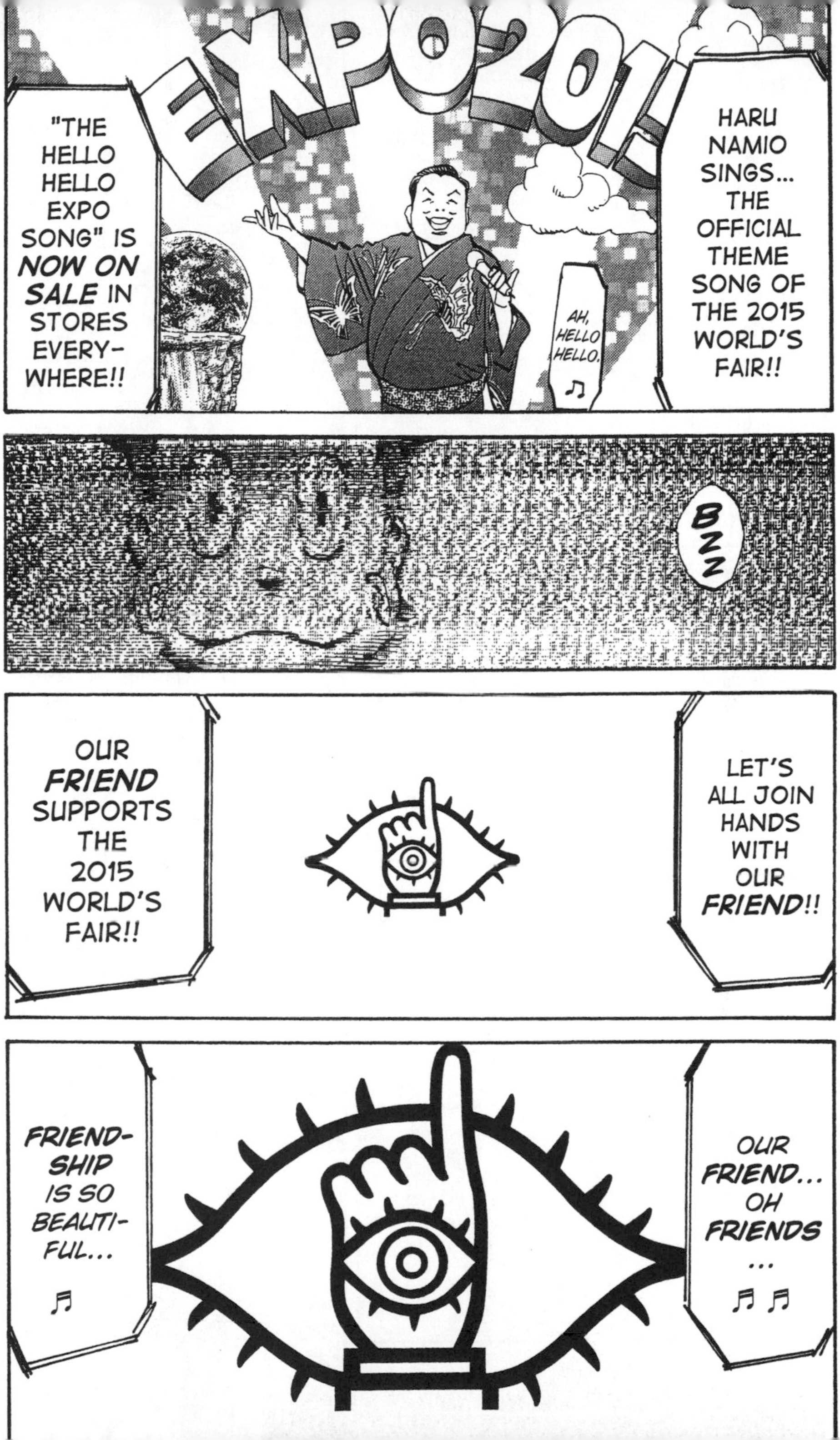
EXPO 2015
HARU NAMIO SINGS... THE OFFICIAL THEME SONG OF THE 2015 WORLD'S FAIR!!
AH, HELLO HELLO. ♫
"THE HELLO HELLO EXPO SONG" IS NOW ON SALE IN STORES EVERY-WHERE!!
BZZ
LET'S ALL JOIN HANDS WITH OUR FRIEND!!
OUR FRIEND SUPPORTS THE 2015 WORLD'S FAIR!!
OUR FRIEND... OH FRIENDS... ♬ ♬
FRIEND-SHIP IS SO BEAUTI-FUL... ♬

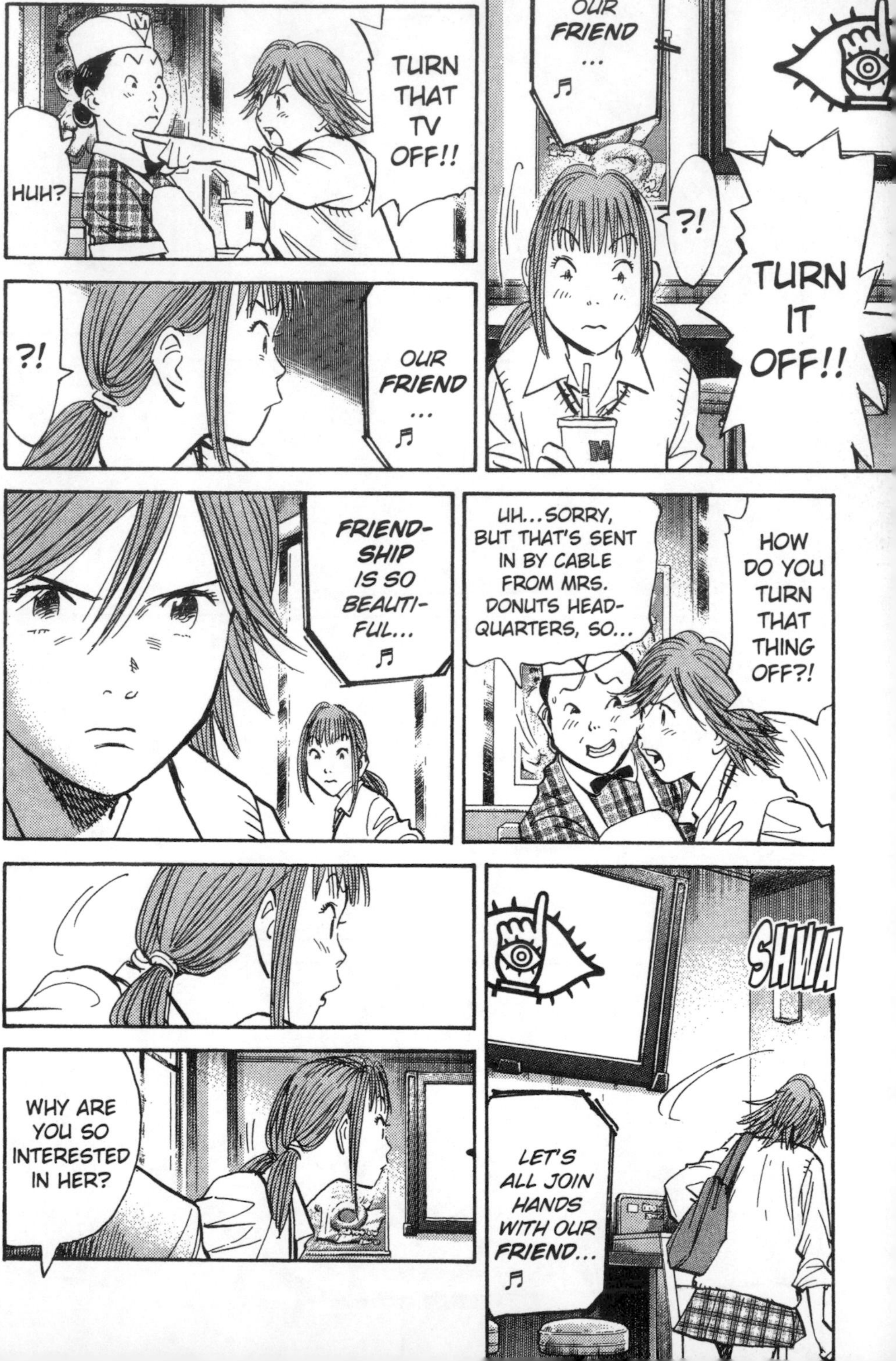
OUR FRIEND ... ♬
?!
TURN IT OFF!!
TURN THAT TV OFF!!
HUH?
?!
OUR FRIEND ... ♬
HOW DO YOU TURN THAT THING OFF?!
UH...SORRY, BUT THAT'S SENT IN BY CABLE FROM MRS. DONUTS HEAD-QUARTERS, SO...
FRIEND-SHIP IS SO BEAUTI-FUL... ♬
SHWA
LET'S ALL JOIN HANDS WITH OUR FRIEND... ♬
WHY ARE YOU SO INTERESTED IN HER?

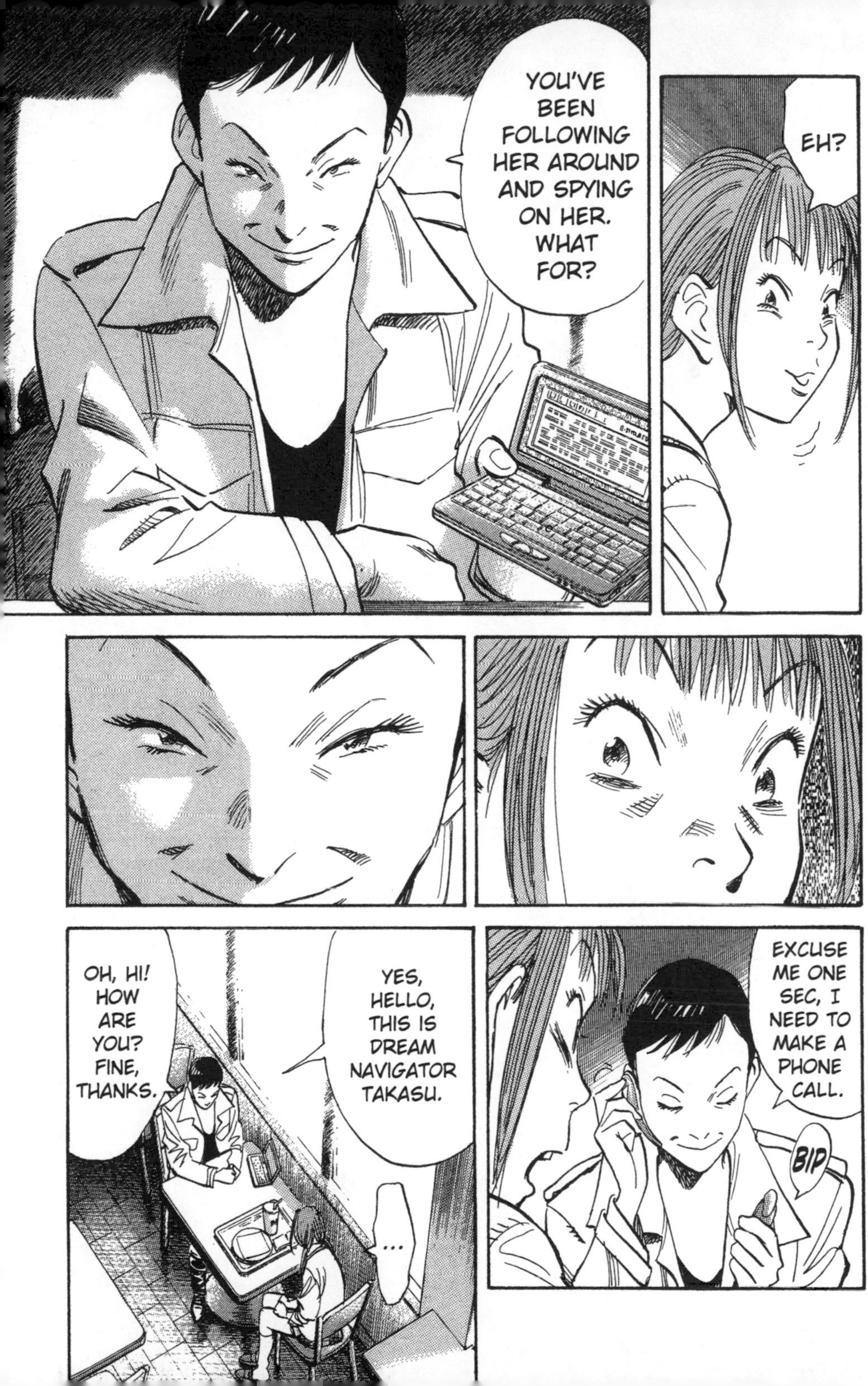
EH?
YOU'VE BEEN FOLLOWING HER AROUND AND SPYING ON HER. WHAT FOR?
EXCUSE ME ONE SEC, I NEED TO MAKE A PHONE CALL.
BIP
YES, HELLO, THIS IS DREAM NAVIGATOR TAKASU.
OH, HI! HOW ARE YOU? FINE, THANKS.
...

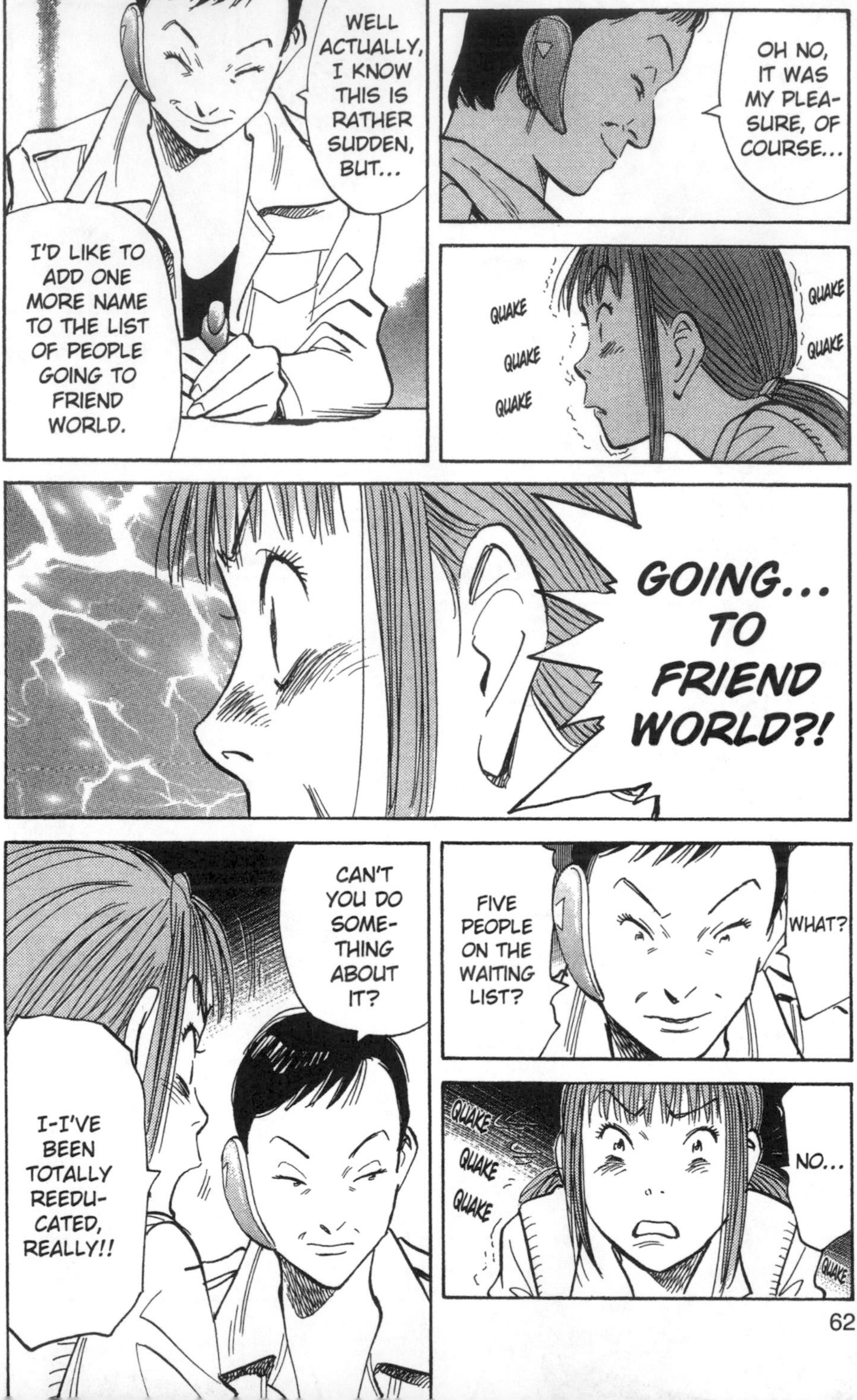
OH NO, IT WAS MY PLEASURE, OF COURSE...
QUAKE
QUAKE
QUAKE
QUAKE
QUAKE
WELL ACTUALLY, I KNOW THIS IS RATHER SUDDEN, BUT...
I'D LIKE TO ADD ONE MORE NAME TO THE LIST OF PEOPLE GOING TO FRIEND WORLD.
GOING... TO FRIEND WORLD?!
WHAT?
FIVE PEOPLE ON THE WAITING LIST?
NO...
QUAKE
QUAKE
QUAKE
QUAKE
CAN'T YOU DO SOMETHING ABOUT IT?
I-I'VE BEEN TOTALLY REEDUCATED, REALLY!!

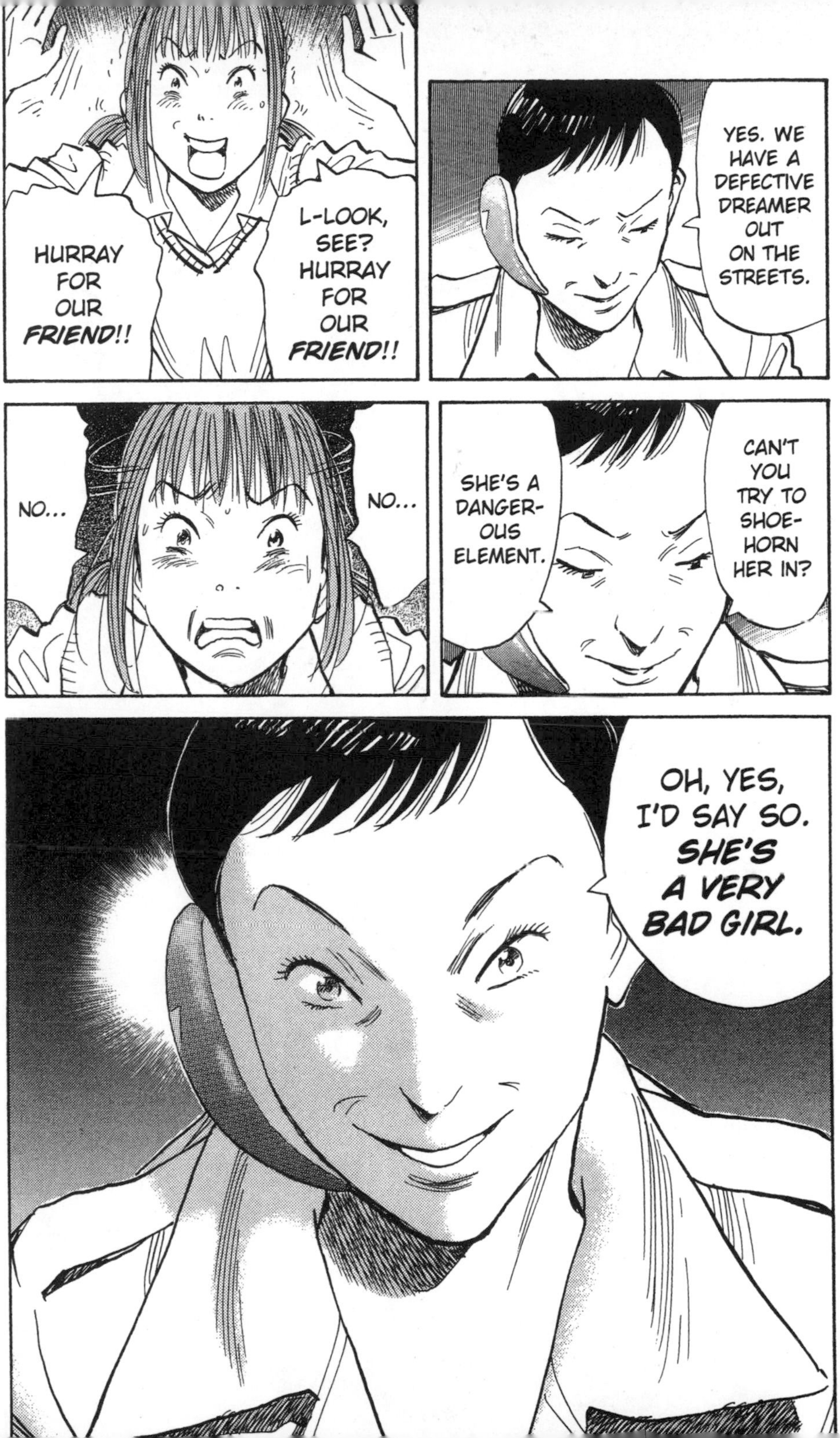

YES. WE HAVE A DEFECTIVE DREAMER OUT ON THE STREETS.
L-LOOK, SEE? HURRAY FOR OUR *FRIEND*!!
HURRAY FOR OUR *FRIEND*!!
CAN'T YOU TRY TO SHOEHORN HER IN?
SHE'S A DANGEROUS ELEMENT.
NO...
NO...
OH, YES, I'D SAY SO. ***SHE'S A VERY BAD GIRL.***

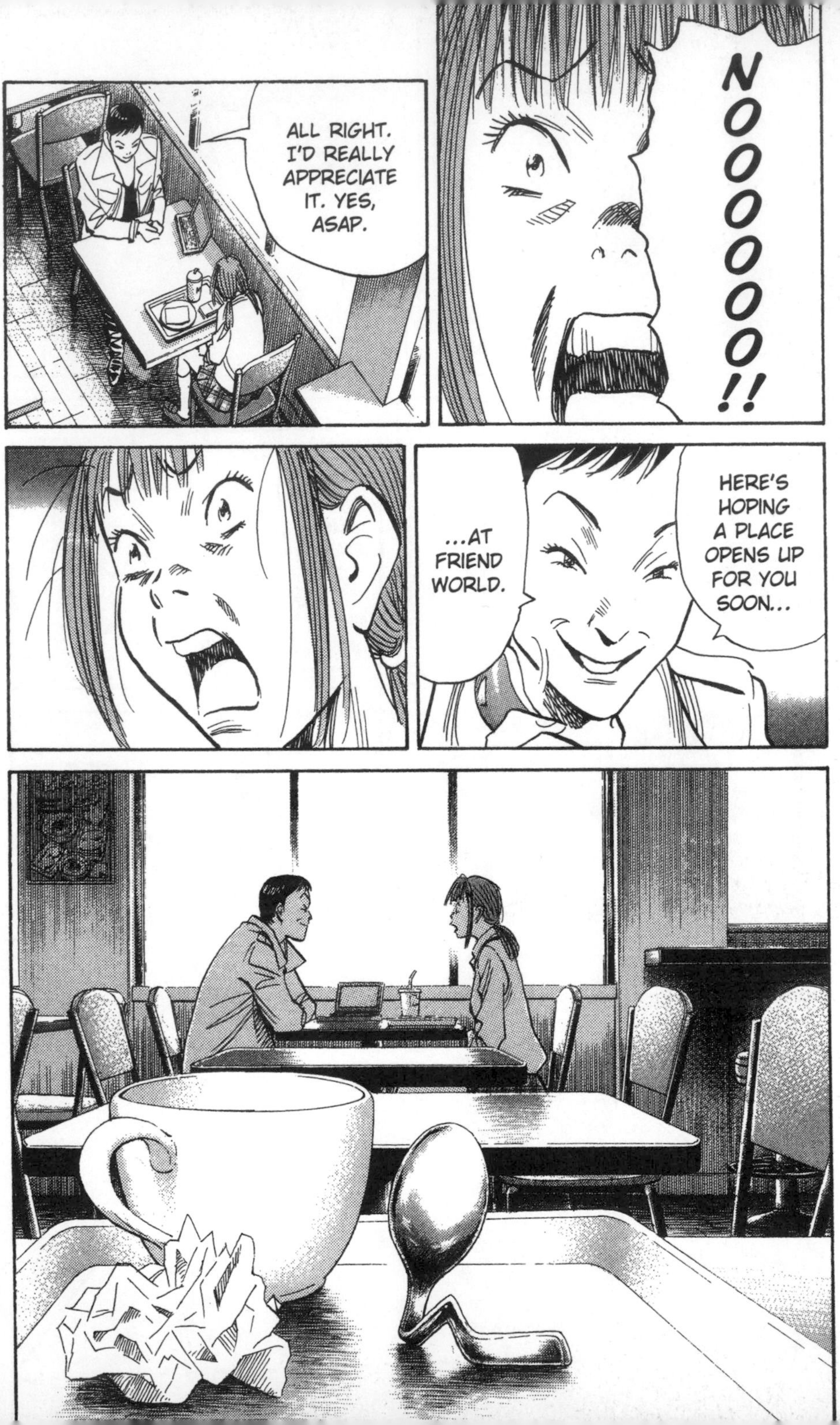
NOOOOOOO!!
ALL RIGHT. I'D REALLY APPRECIATE IT. YES, ASAP.
HERE'S HOPING A PLACE OPENS UP FOR YOU SOON...
...AT FRIEND WORLD.

Chapter 4 New Teacher

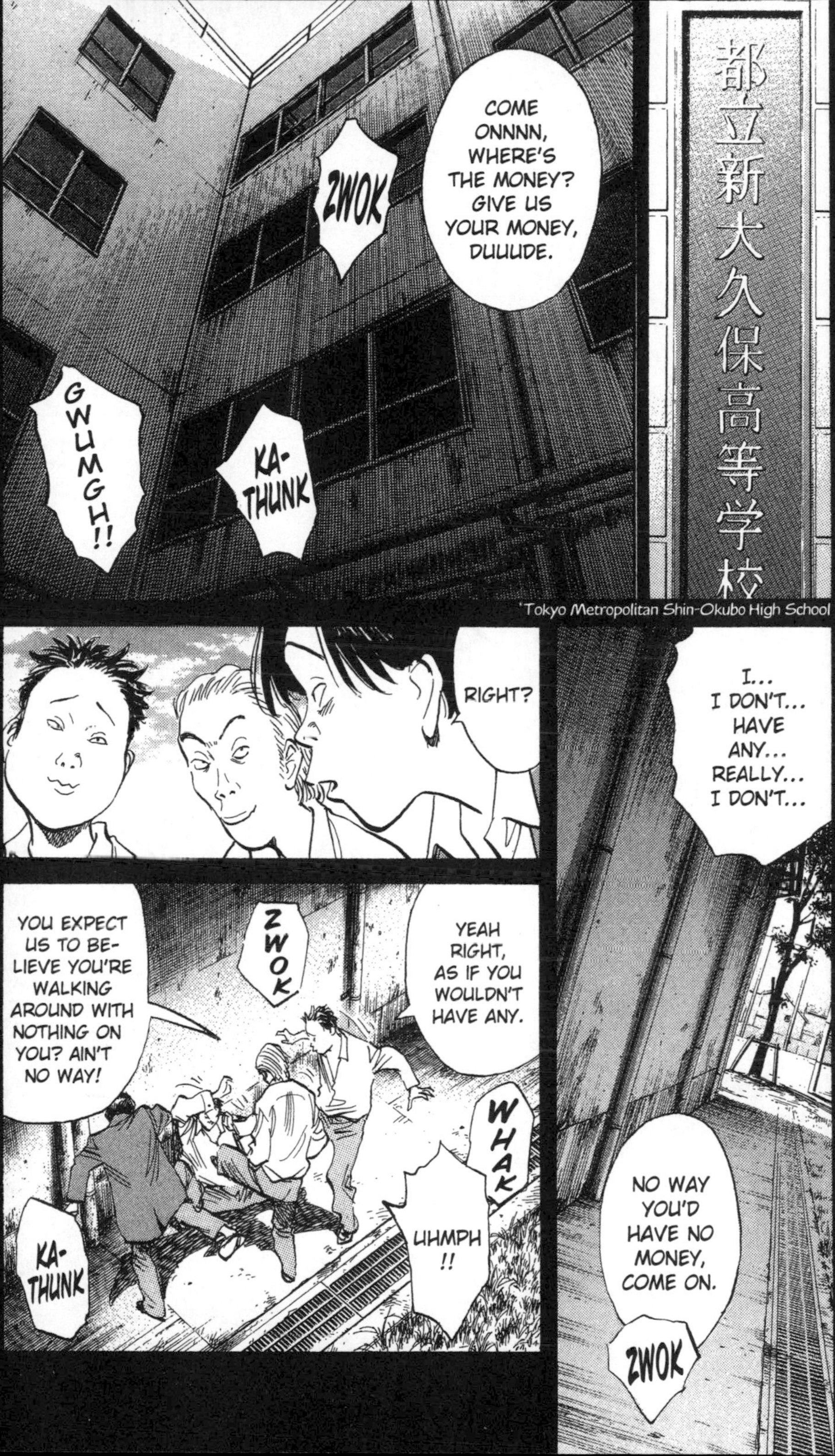
都立新大久保高等学校
*Tokyo Metropolitan Shin-Okubo High School
COME ONNNN, WHERE'S THE MONEY? GIVE US YOUR MONEY, DUUUDE.
ZWOK
KA-THUNK
GWUMGH!!
I... I DON'T... HAVE ANY... REALLY... I DON'T...
NO WAY YOU'D HAVE NO MONEY, COME ON.
ZWOK
RIGHT?
YEAH RIGHT, AS IF YOU WOULDN'T HAVE ANY.
ZWOK
YOU EXPECT US TO BE-LIEVE YOU'RE WALKING AROUND WITH NOTHING ON YOU? AIN'T NO WAY!
WHAK
UHMPH!!
KA-THUNK

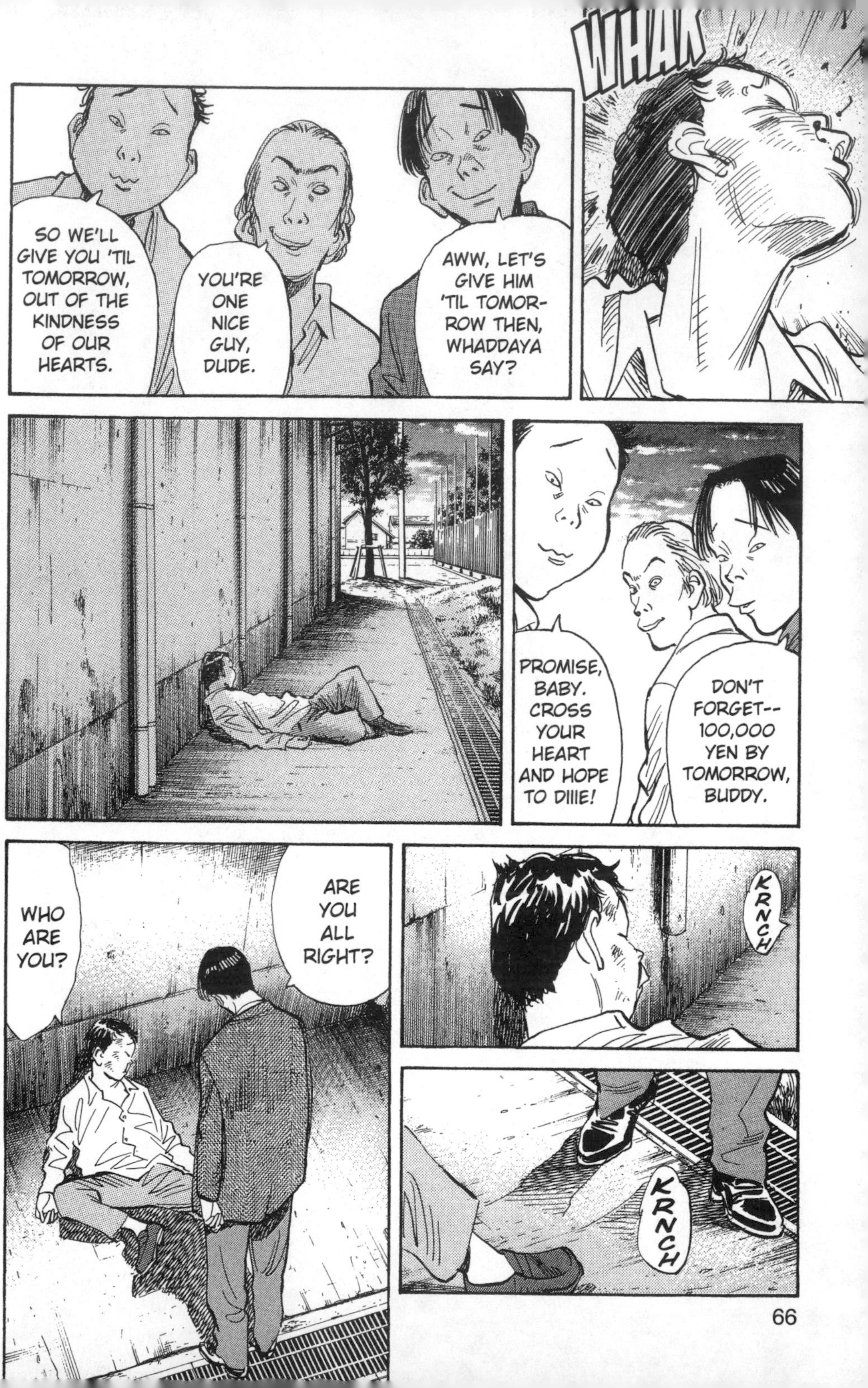
WHAK
AWW, LET'S GIVE HIM 'TIL TOMORROW THEN, WHADDAYA SAY?
YOU'RE ONE NICE GUY, DUDE.
SO WE'LL GIVE YOU 'TIL TOMORROW, OUT OF THE KINDNESS OF OUR HEARTS.
DON'T FORGET-- 100,000 YEN BY TOMORROW, BUDDY.
PROMISE, BABY. CROSS YOUR HEART AND HOPE TO DIIIE!
KRNCH
KRNCH
ARE YOU ALL RIGHT?
WHO ARE YOU?

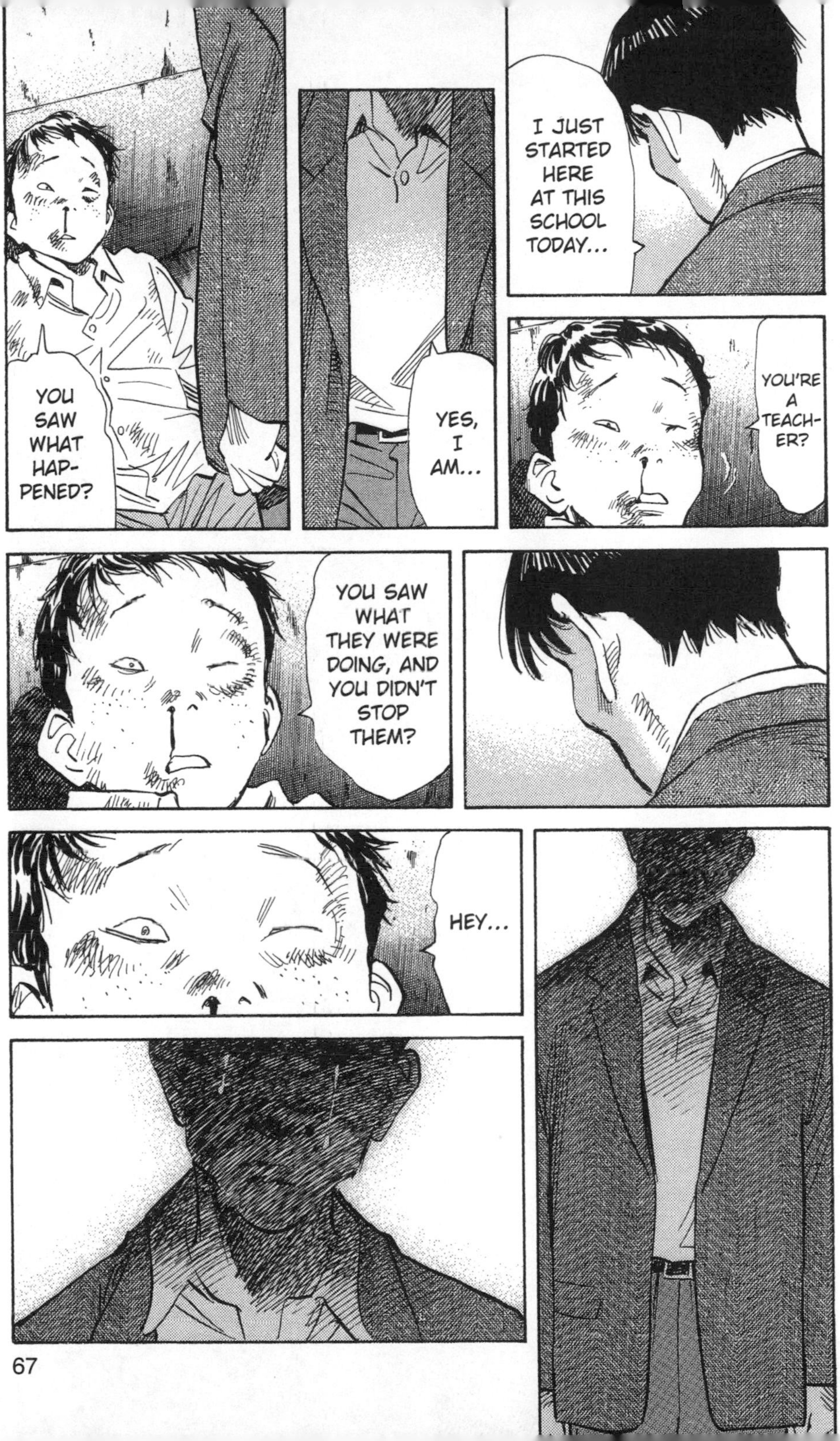
I JUST STARTED HERE AT THIS SCHOOL TODAY...
YOU'RE A TEACHER?
YES, I AM...
YOU SAW WHAT HAPPENED?
YOU SAW WHAT THEY WERE DOING, AND YOU DIDN'T STOP THEM?
HEY...

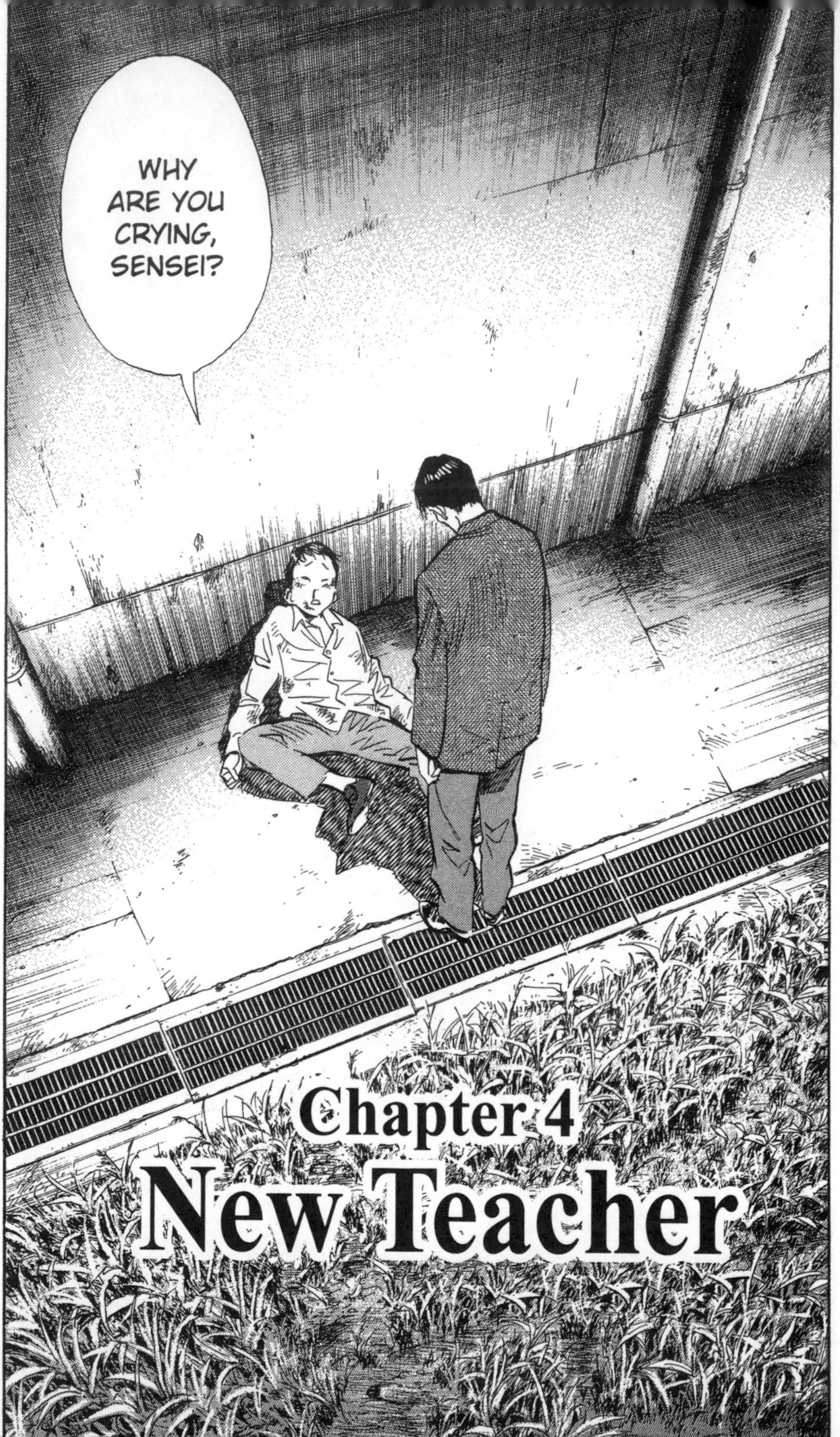
WHY ARE YOU CRYING, SENSEI?
Chapter 4
New Teacher

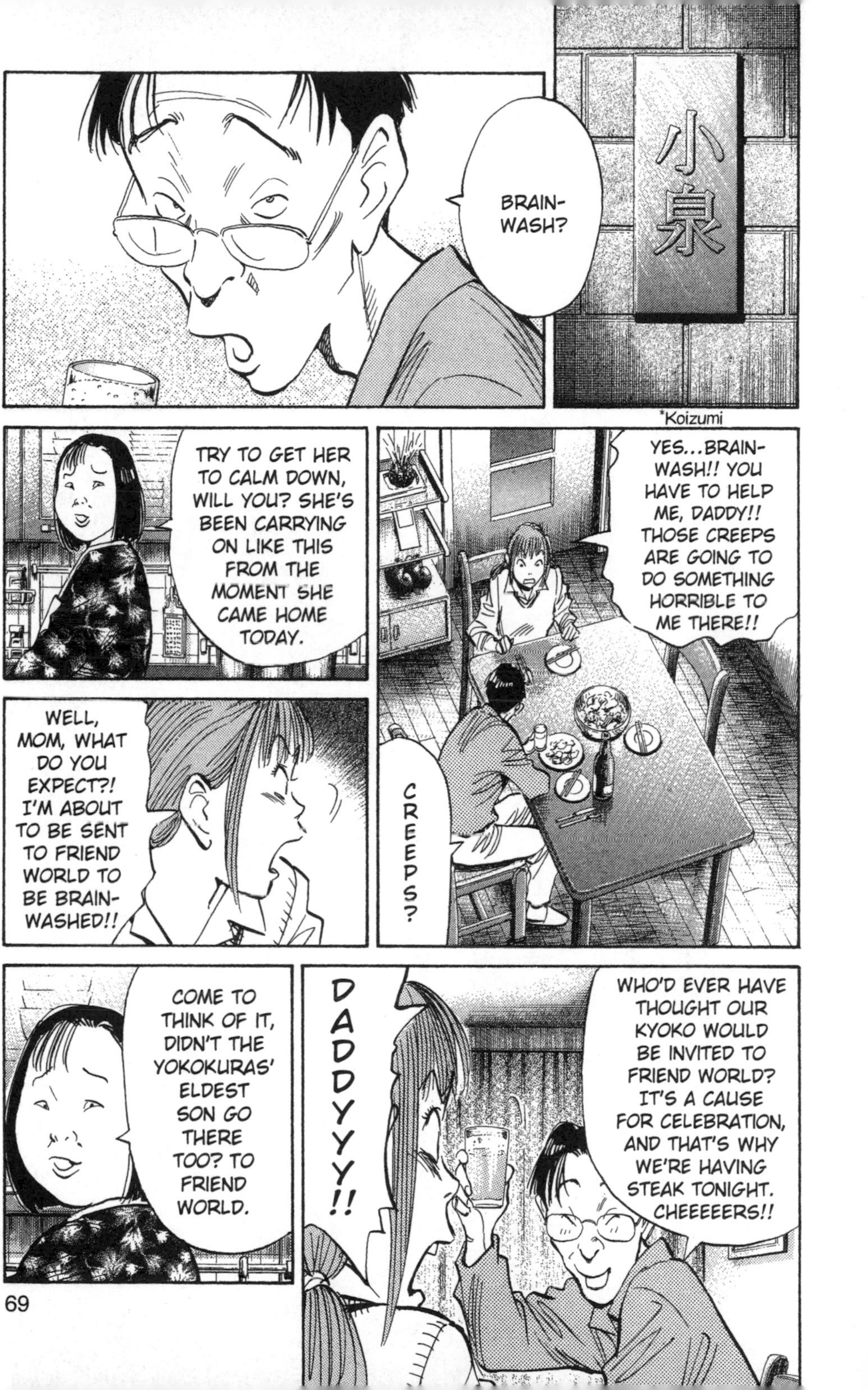
小泉
*Koizumi
BRAIN-WASH?
YES...BRAIN-WASH!! YOU HAVE TO HELP ME, DADDY!! THOSE CREEPS ARE GOING TO DO SOMETHING HORRIBLE TO ME THERE!!
CREEPS?
TRY TO GET HER TO CALM DOWN, WILL YOU? SHE'S BEEN CARRYING ON LIKE THIS FROM THE MOMENT SHE CAME HOME TODAY.
WELL, MOM, WHAT DO YOU EXPECT?! I'M ABOUT TO BE SENT TO FRIEND WORLD TO BE BRAIN-WASHED!!
WHO'D EVER HAVE THOUGHT OUR KYOKO WOULD BE INVITED TO FRIEND WORLD? IT'S A CAUSE FOR CELEBRATION, AND THAT'S WHY WE'RE HAVING STEAK TONIGHT. CHEEEEERS!!
DADDYYY!!
COME TO THINK OF IT, DIDN'T THE YOKOKURAS' ELDEST SON GO THERE TOO? TO FRIEND WORLD.

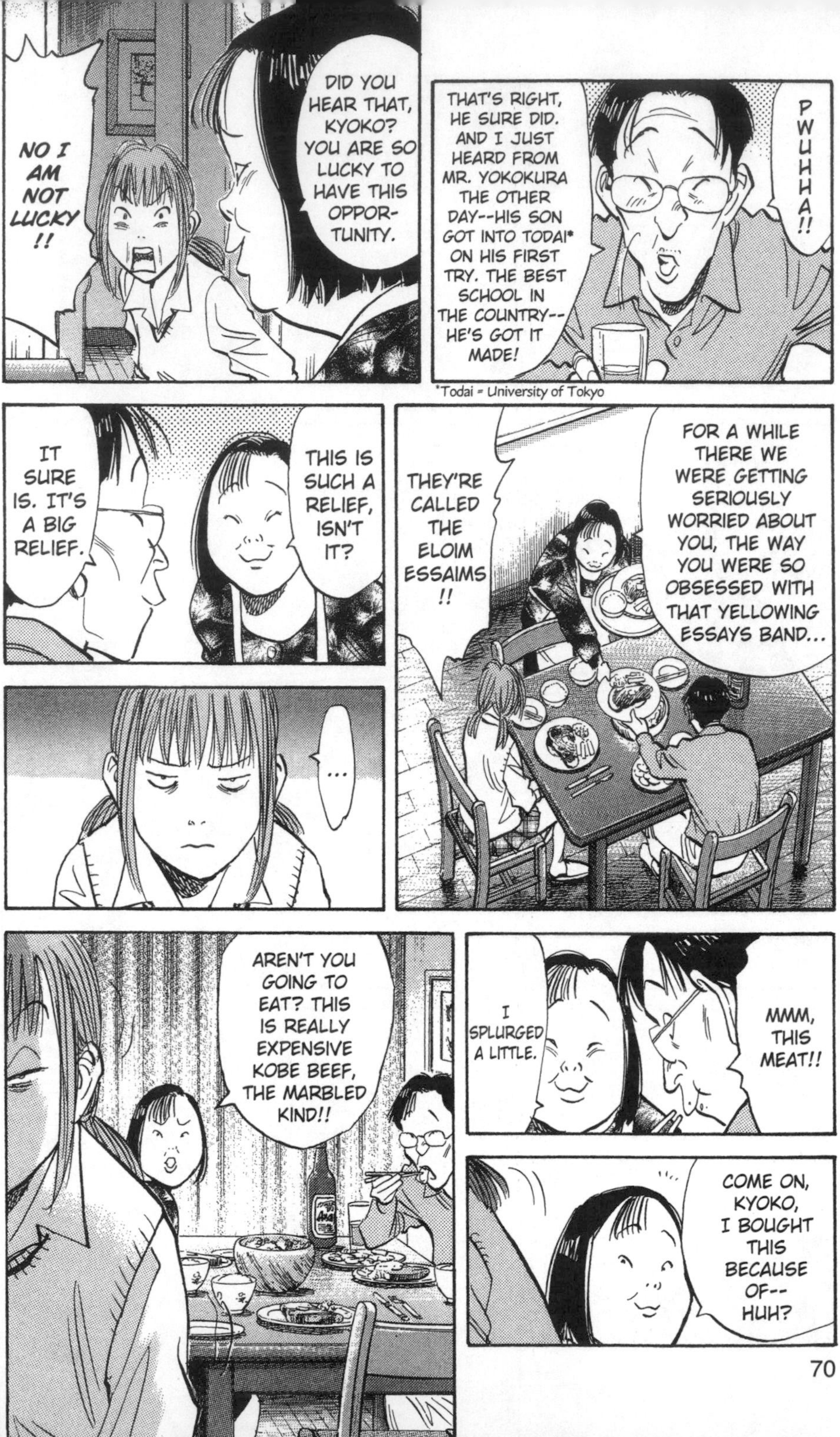
PWUHHA!!
THAT'S RIGHT, HE SURE DID. AND I JUST HEARD FROM MR. YOKOKURA THE OTHER DAY--HIS SON GOT INTO TODAI* ON HIS FIRST TRY. THE BEST SCHOOL IN THE COUNTRY-- HE'S GOT IT MADE!
DID YOU HEAR THAT, KYOKO? YOU ARE SO LUCKY TO HAVE THIS OPPOR-TUNITY.
NO I AM NOT LUCKY !!
FOR A WHILE THERE WE WERE GETTING SERIOUSLY WORRIED ABOUT YOU, THE WAY YOU WERE SO OBSESSED WITH THAT YELLOWING ESSAYS BAND...
THEY'RE CALLED THE ELOIM ESSAIMS !!
THIS IS SUCH A RELIEF, ISN'T IT?
IT SURE IS. IT'S A BIG RELIEF.
...
MMM, THIS MEAT!!
I SPLURGED A LITTLE.
COME ON, KYOKO, I BOUGHT THIS BECAUSE OF-- HUH?
AREN'T YOU GOING TO EAT? THIS IS REALLY EXPENSIVE KOBE BEEF, THE MARBLED KIND!!

*Todai = University of Tokyo

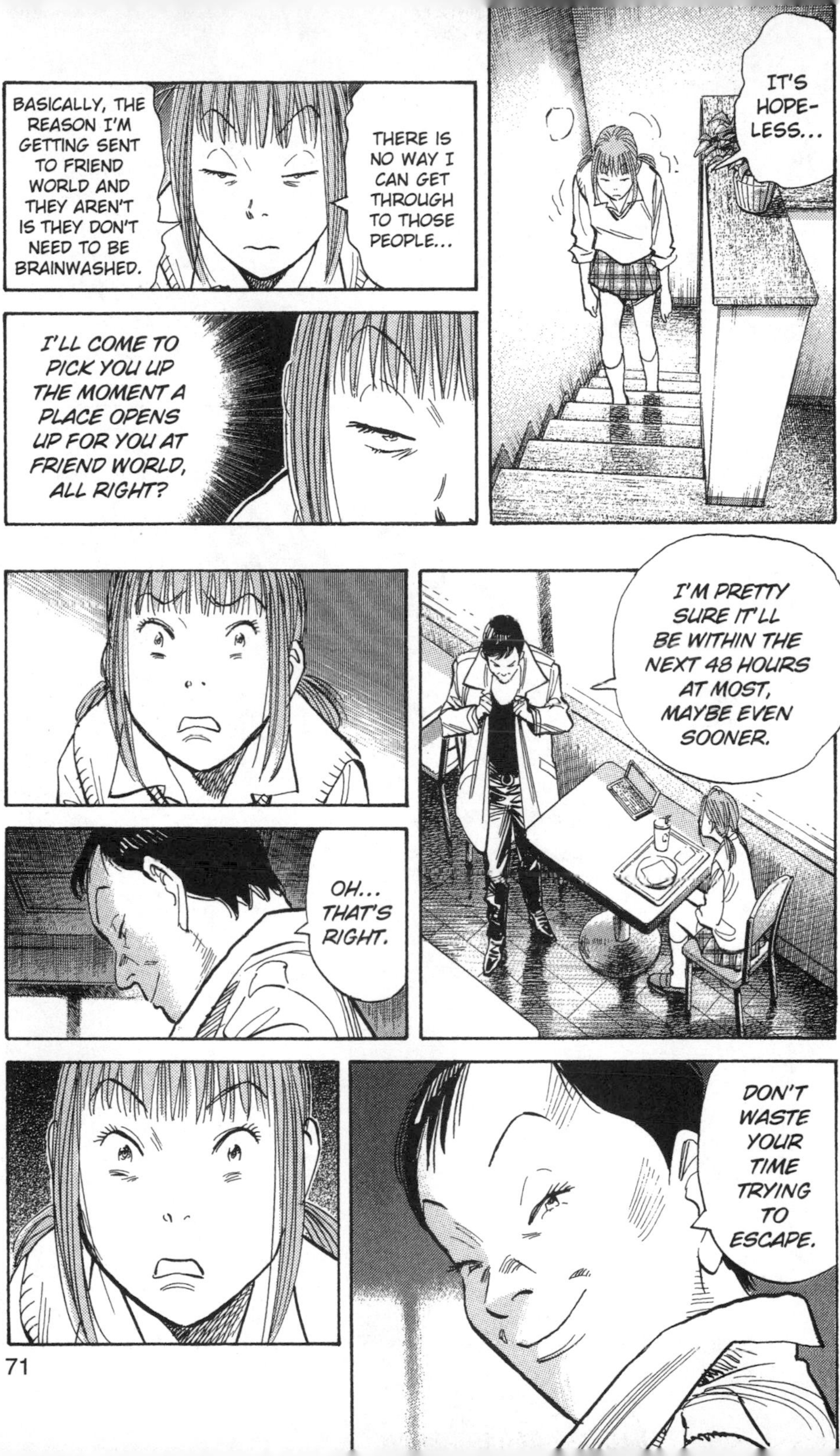
IT'S HOPE-LESS...
THERE IS NO WAY I CAN GET THROUGH TO THOSE PEOPLE...
BASICALLY, THE REASON I'M GETTING SENT TO FRIEND WORLD AND THEY AREN'T IS THEY DON'T NEED TO BE BRAINWASHED.
I'LL COME TO PICK YOU UP THE MOMENT A PLACE OPENS UP FOR YOU AT FRIEND WORLD, ALL RIGHT?
I'M PRETTY SURE IT'LL BE WITHIN THE NEXT 48 HOURS AT MOST, MAYBE EVEN SOONER.
OH... THAT'S RIGHT.
DON'T WASTE YOUR TIME TRYING TO ESCAPE.

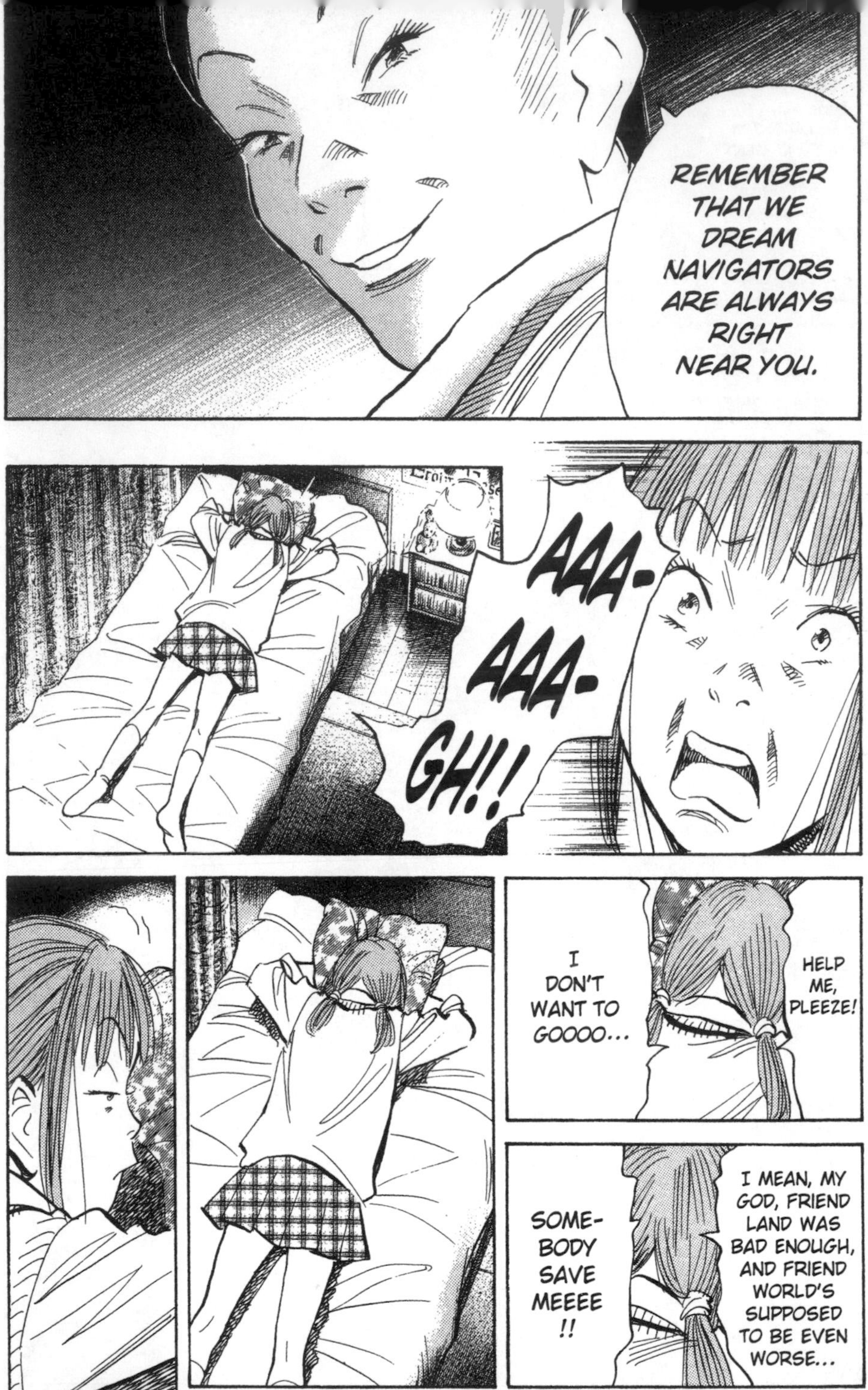
REMEMBER THAT WE DREAM NAVIGATORS ARE ALWAYS RIGHT NEAR YOU.
AAA-AAA-GH!!
HELP ME, PLEEZE!
I DON'T WANT TO GOOOO...
I MEAN, MY GOD, FRIEND LAND WAS BAD ENOUGH, AND FRIEND WORLD'S SUPPOSED TO BE EVEN WORSE...
SOME-BODY SAVE MEEEE !!

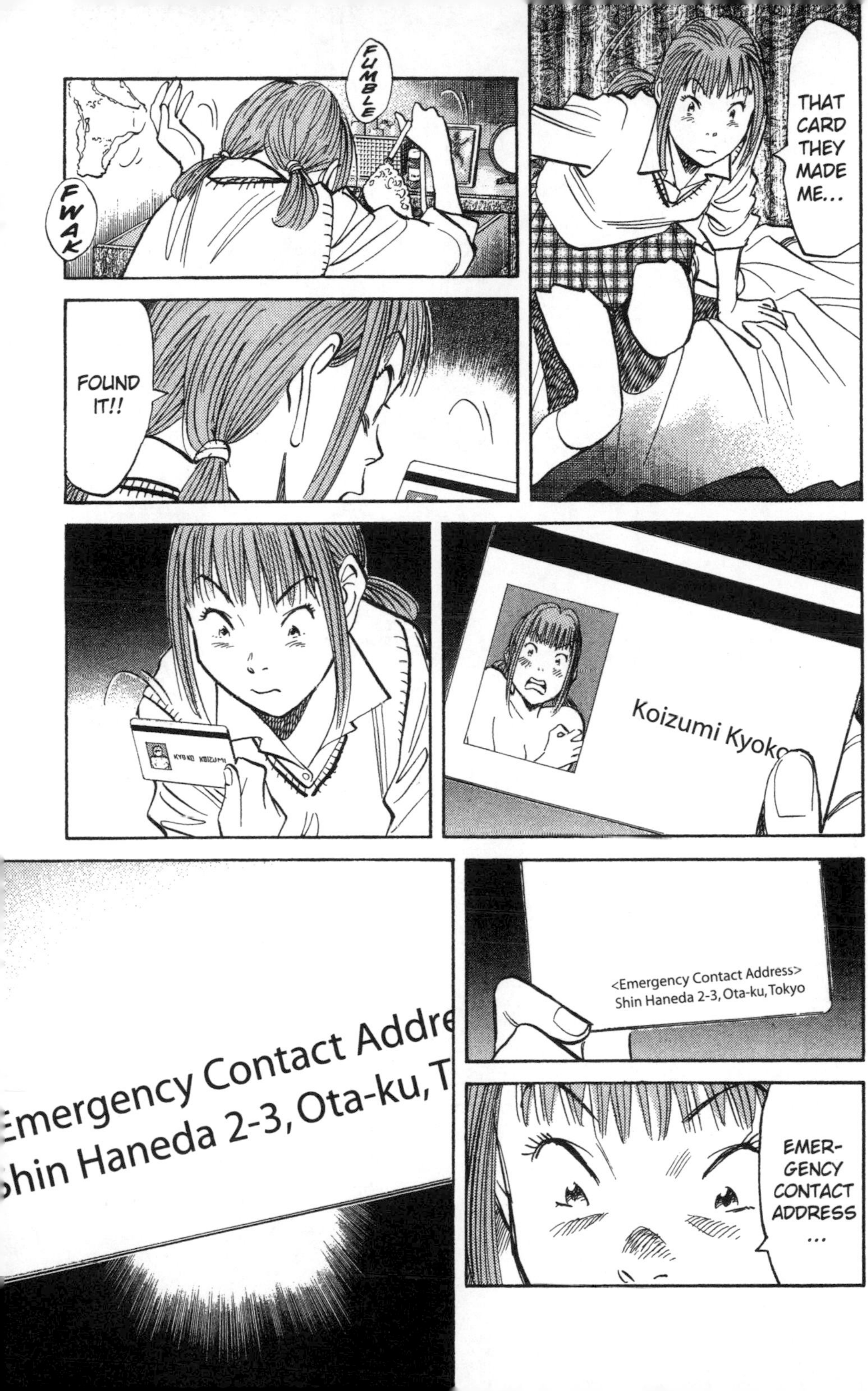
THAT CARD THEY MADE ME...
FUMBLE
FWAK
FOUND IT!!
Koizumi Kyoko
KYOKO KOIZUMI
<Emergency Contact Address>
Shin Haneda 2-3, Ota-ku, Tokyo
EMER-GENCY CONTACT ADDRESS...
Emergency Contact Addre
Shin Haneda 2-3, Ota-ku, T

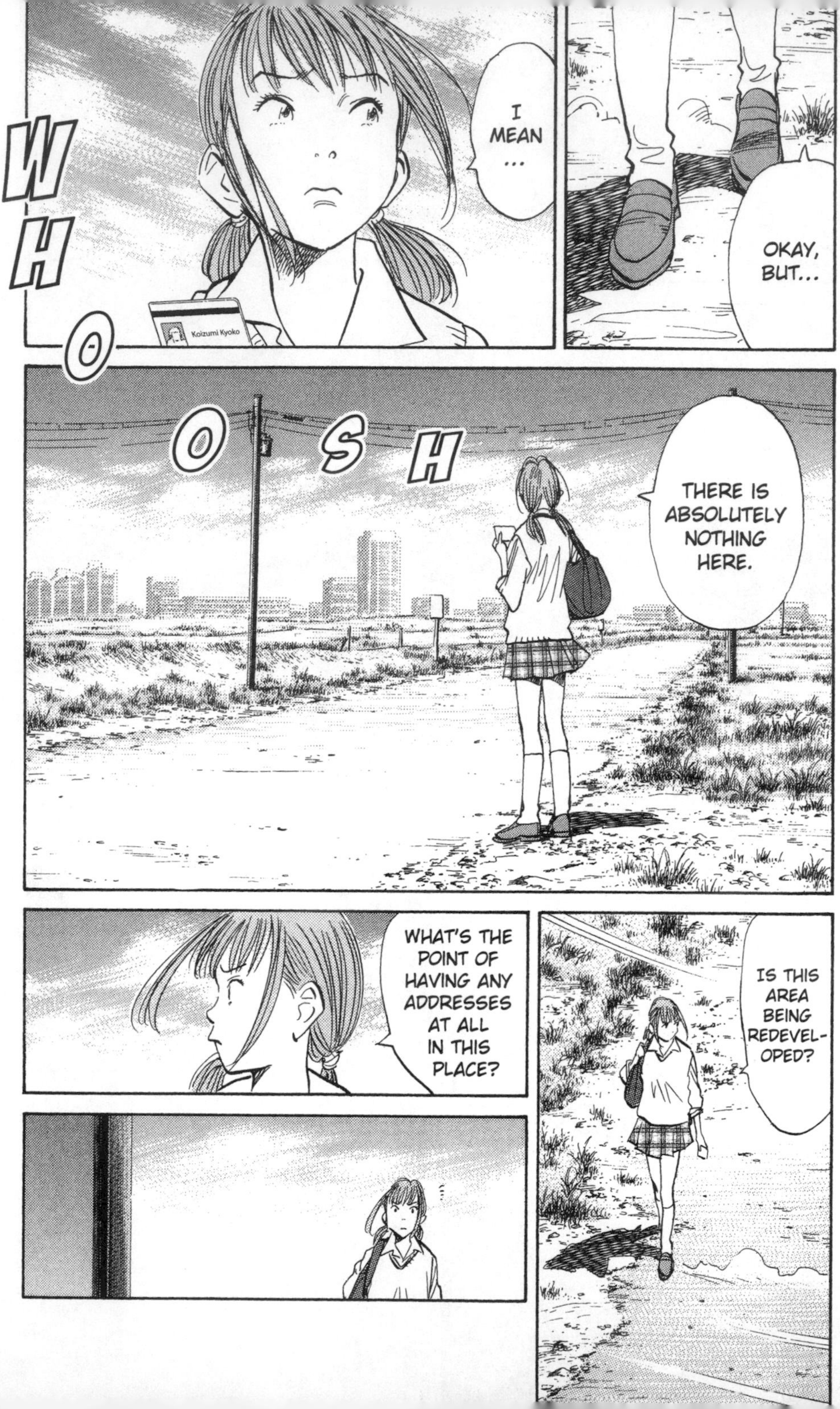

OKAY, BUT...
I MEAN ...
WHOOSH
Koizumi Kyoko
THERE IS ABSOLUTELY NOTHING HERE.
IS THIS AREA BEING REDEVEL-OPED?
WHAT'S THE POINT OF HAVING ANY ADDRESSES AT ALL IN THIS PLACE?

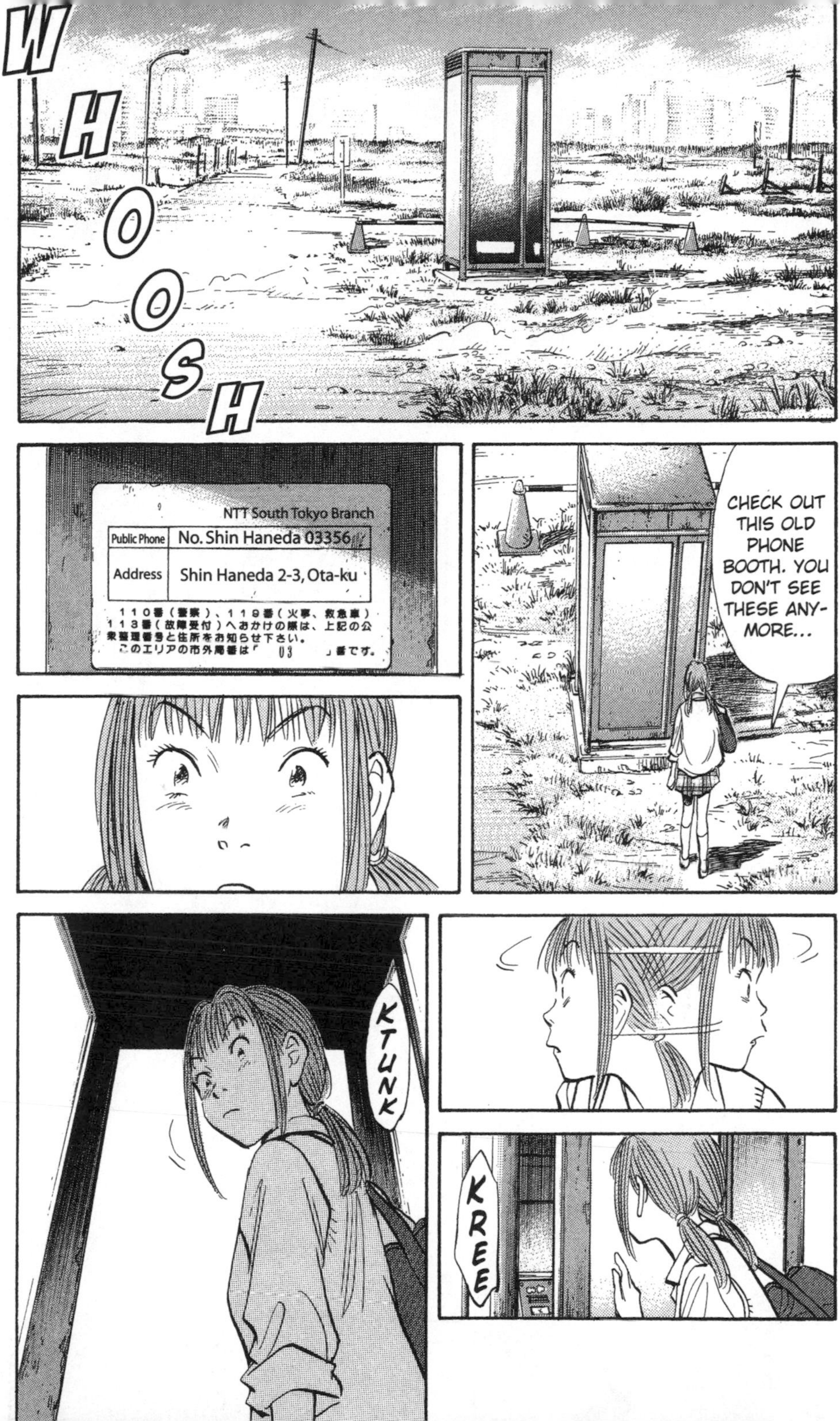
WHOOSH
CHECK OUT THIS OLD PHONE BOOTH. YOU DON'T SEE THESE ANYMORE...
NTT South Tokyo Branch
Public Phone
No. Shin Haneda 03356
Address
Shin Haneda 2-3, Ota-ku
110番（警察）、119番（火事、救急車）
113番（故障受付）へおかけの際は、上記の公衆電話番号と住所をお知らせ下さい。
このエリアの市外局番は「 03 」番です。
KREE
KTUNK

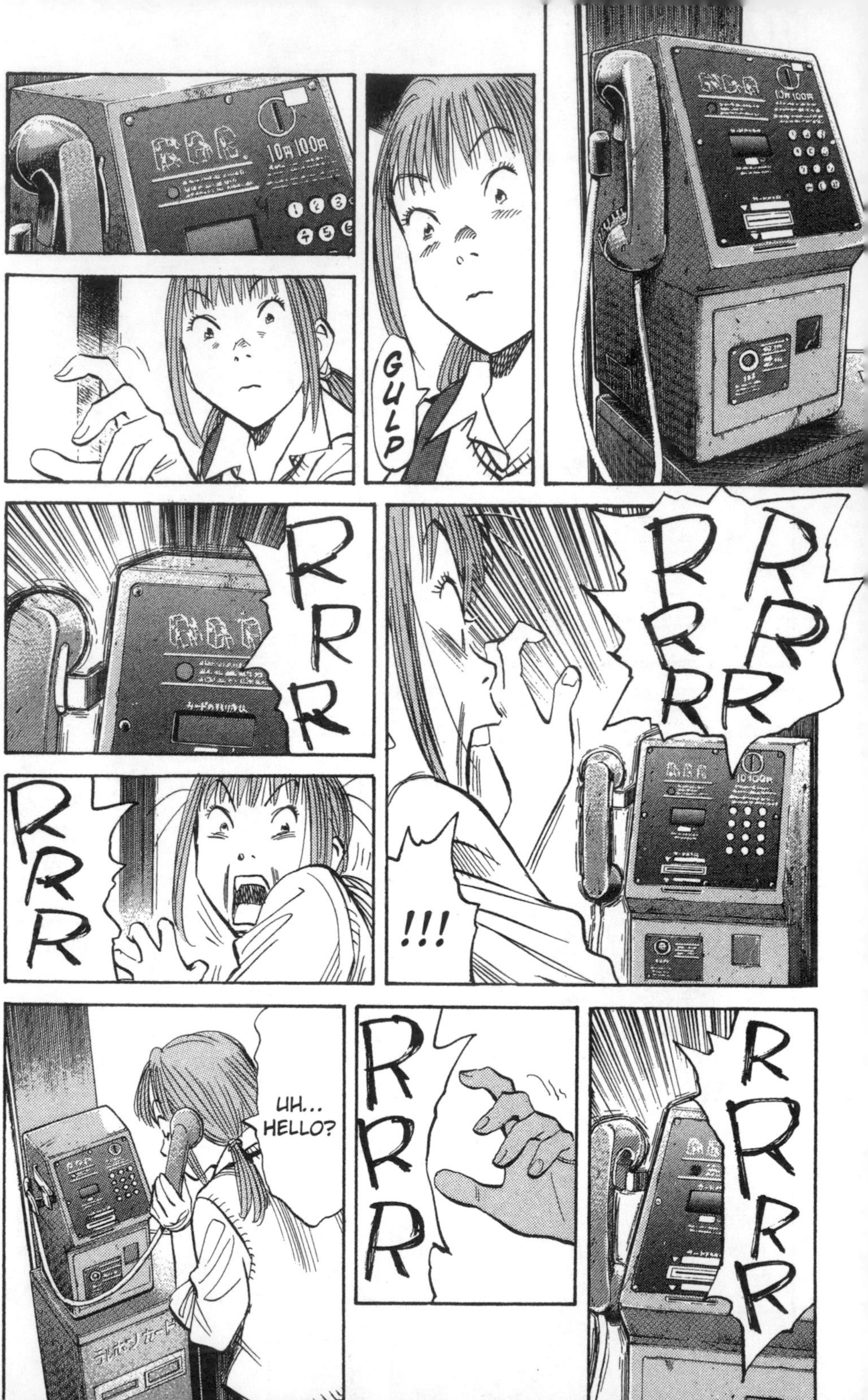
GULP
RRRRRRR
!!!
RRR
RRR
RRRRR
RRRR
UH... HELLO?

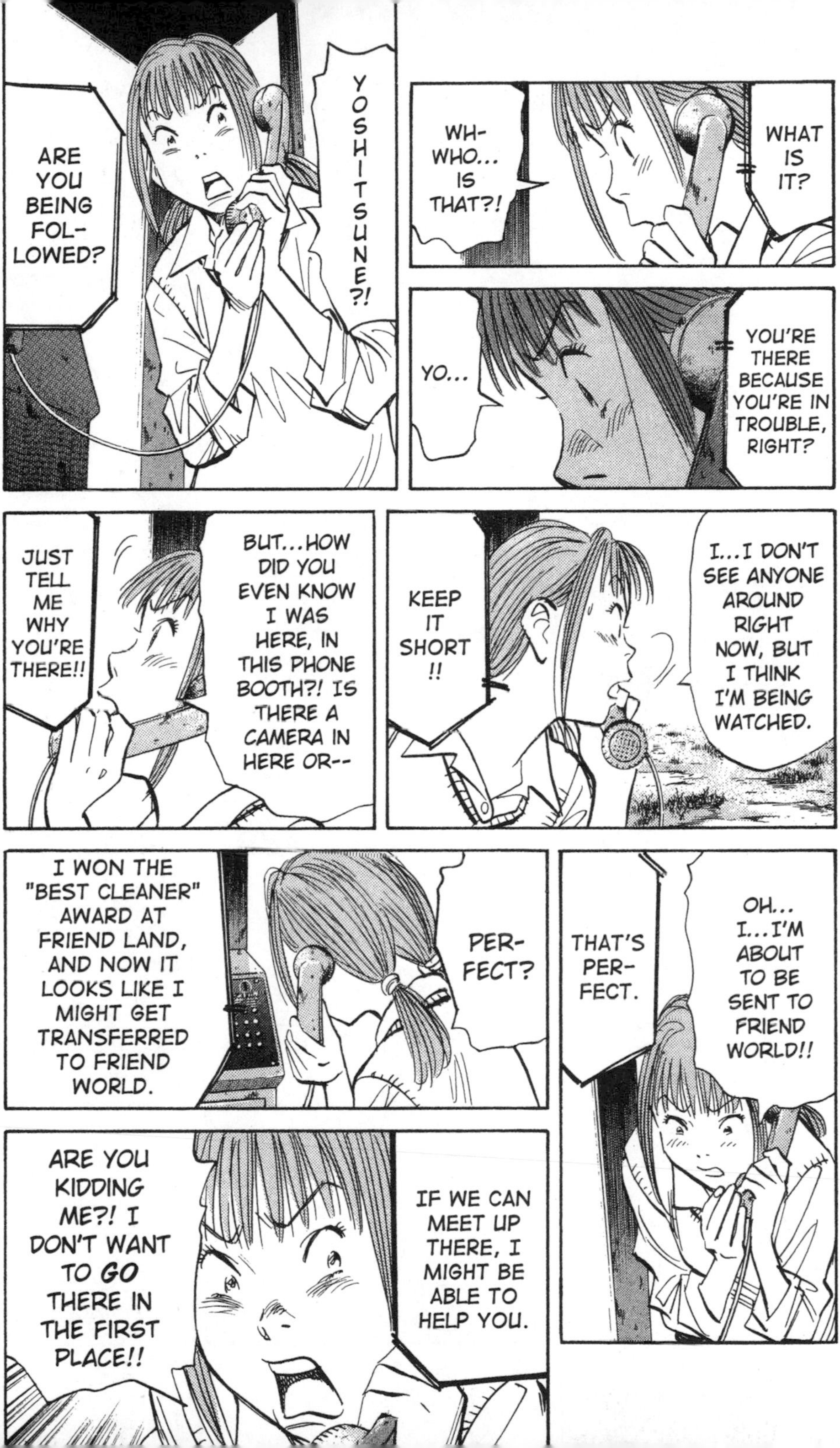
WHAT IS IT?
WH- WHO... IS THAT?!
YOU'RE THERE BECAUSE YOU'RE IN TROUBLE, RIGHT?
YO...
YOSHITSUNE?!
ARE YOU BEING FOL- LOWED?
I...I DON'T SEE ANYONE AROUND RIGHT NOW, BUT I THINK I'M BEING WATCHED.
KEEP IT SHORT !!
BUT...HOW DID YOU EVEN KNOW I WAS HERE, IN THIS PHONE BOOTH?! IS THERE A CAMERA IN HERE OR--
JUST TELL ME WHY YOU'RE THERE!!
OH... I...I'M ABOUT TO BE SENT TO FRIEND WORLD!!
THAT'S PER- FECT.
PER- FECT?
I WON THE "BEST CLEANER" AWARD AT FRIEND LAND, AND NOW IT LOOKS LIKE I MIGHT GET TRANSFERRED TO FRIEND WORLD.
IF WE CAN MEET UP THERE, I MIGHT BE ABLE TO HELP YOU.
ARE YOU KIDDING ME?! I DON'T WANT TO GO THERE IN THE FIRST PLACE!!

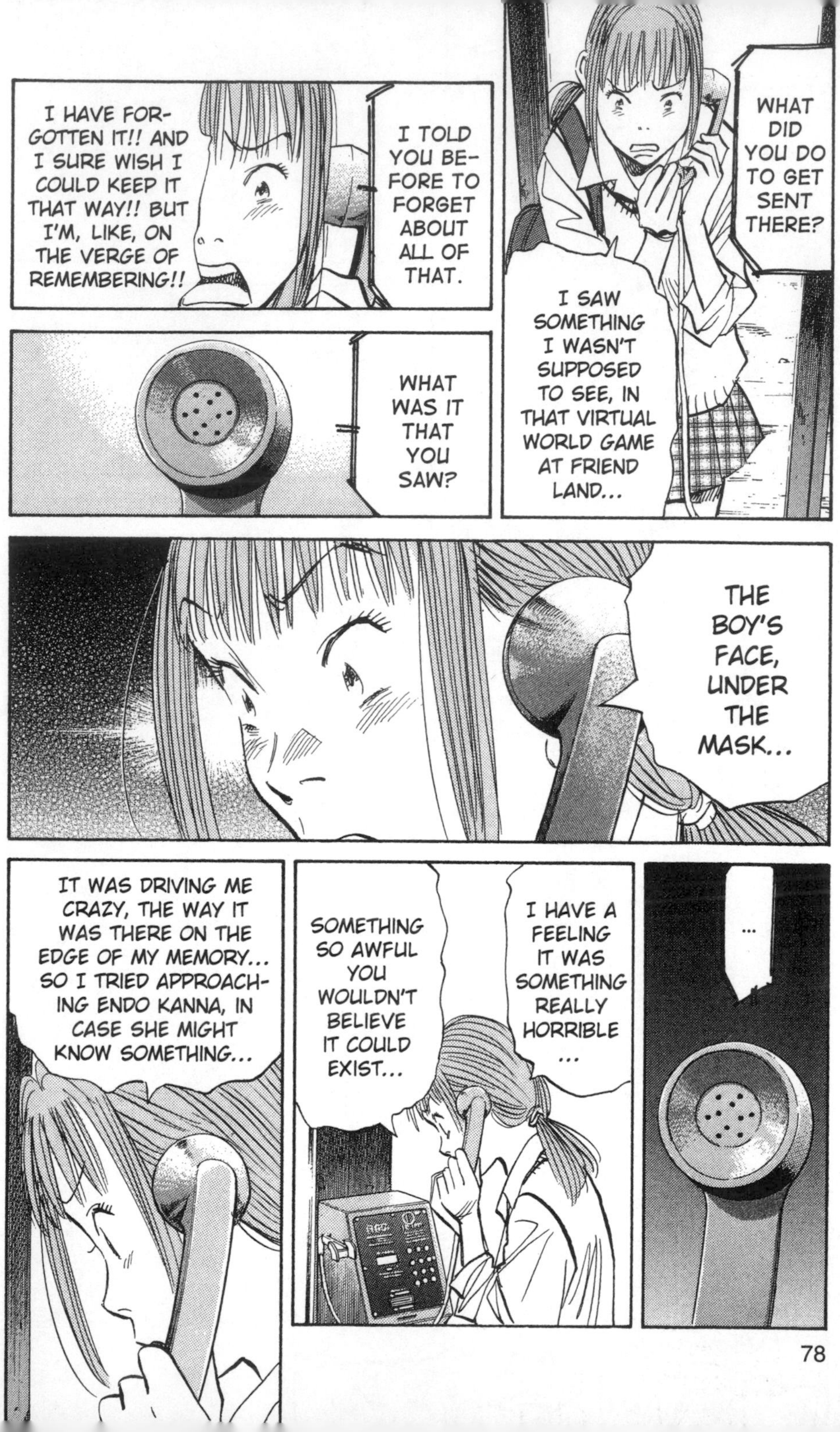
WHAT DID YOU DO TO GET SENT THERE?
I SAW SOMETHING I WASN'T SUPPOSED TO SEE, IN THAT VIRTUAL WORLD GAME AT FRIEND LAND...
I TOLD YOU BE-FORE TO FORGET ABOUT ALL OF THAT.
I HAVE FOR-GOTTEN IT!! AND I SURE WISH I COULD KEEP IT THAT WAY!! BUT I'M, LIKE, ON THE VERGE OF REMEMBERING!!
WHAT WAS IT THAT YOU SAW?
THE BOY'S FACE, UNDER THE MASK...
...
I HAVE A FEELING IT WAS SOMETHING REALLY HORRIBLE...
SOMETHING SO AWFUL YOU WOULDN'T BELIEVE IT COULD EXIST...
IT WAS DRIVING ME CRAZY, THE WAY IT WAS THERE ON THE EDGE OF MY MEMORY... SO I TRIED APPROACH-ING ENDO KANNA, IN CASE SHE MIGHT KNOW SOMETHING...

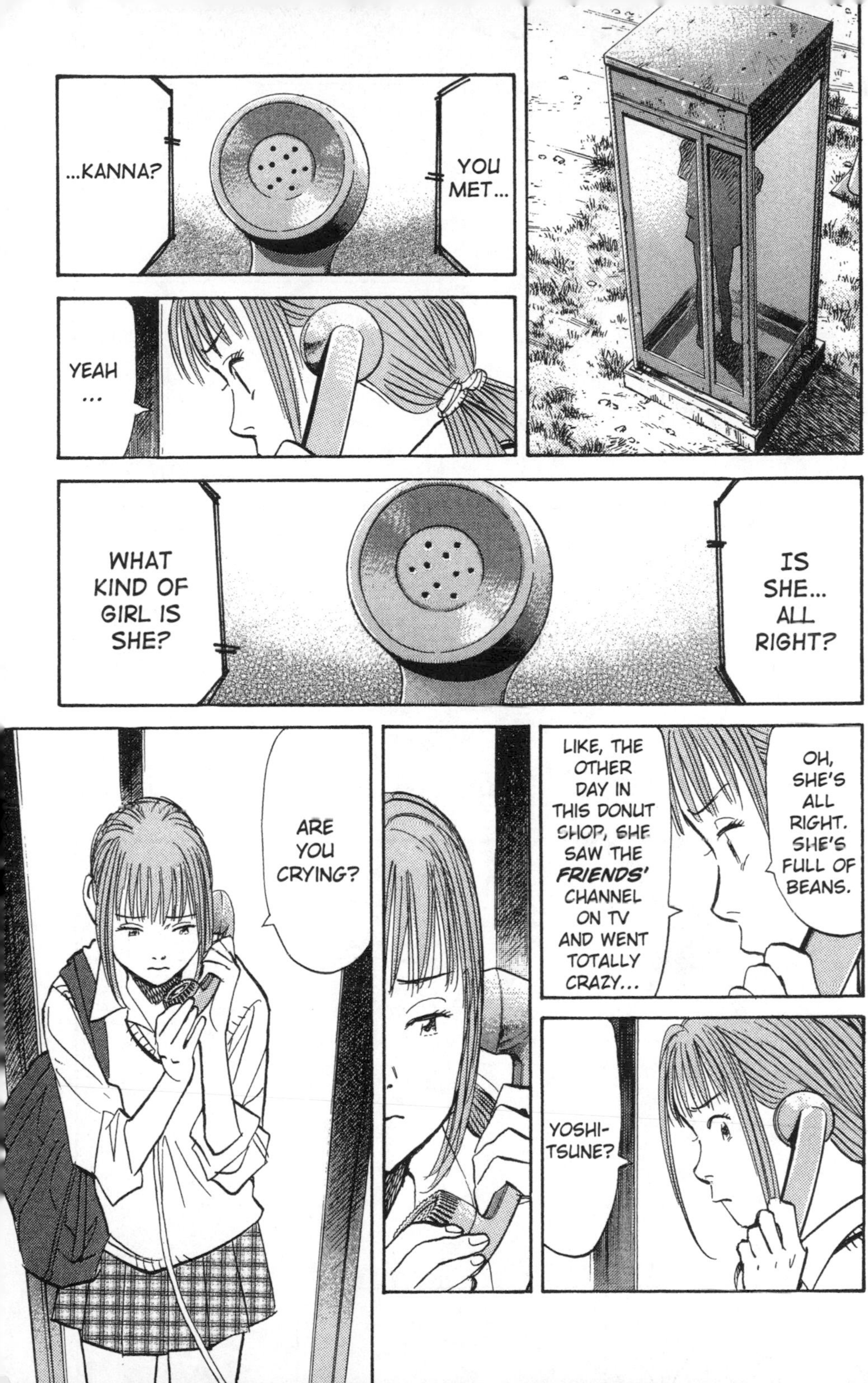
YOU MET...
...KANNA?
YEAH ...
IS SHE... ALL RIGHT?
WHAT KIND OF GIRL IS SHE?
OH, SHE'S ALL RIGHT. SHE'S FULL OF BEANS.
LIKE, THE OTHER DAY IN THIS DONUT SHOP, SHE SAW THE *FRIENDS'* CHANNEL ON TV AND WENT TOTALLY CRAZY...
YOSHI-TSUNE?
ARE YOU CRYING?

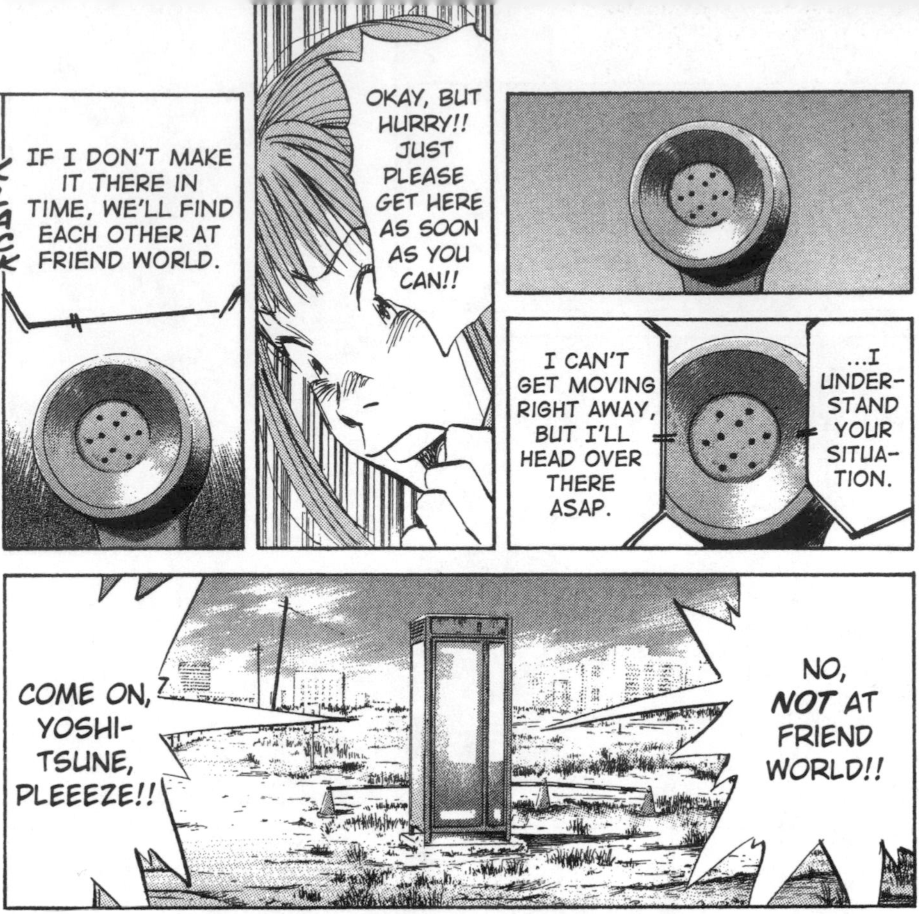
...I UNDERSTAND YOUR SITUATION.
I CAN'T GET MOVING RIGHT AWAY, BUT I'LL HEAD OVER THERE ASAP.
OKAY, BUT HURRY!! JUST PLEASE GET HERE AS SOON AS YOU CAN!!
IF I DON'T MAKE IT THERE IN TIME, WE'LL FIND EACH OTHER AT FRIEND WORLD.
KLACK
NO, ***NOT*** AT FRIEND WORLD!!
COME ON, YOSHI-TSUNE, PLEEEZE!!

*Tokyo Metropolitan Shin-Okubo High School

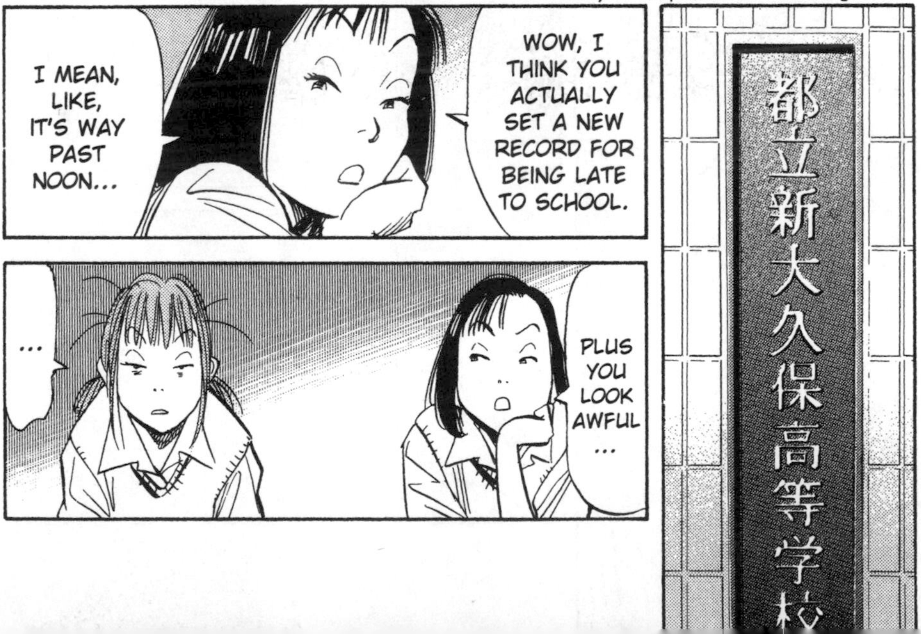
都立新大久保高等学校
WOW, I THINK YOU ACTUALLY SET A NEW RECORD FOR BEING LATE TO SCHOOL.
I MEAN, LIKE, IT'S WAY PAST NOON...
PLUS YOU LOOK AWFUL...
...

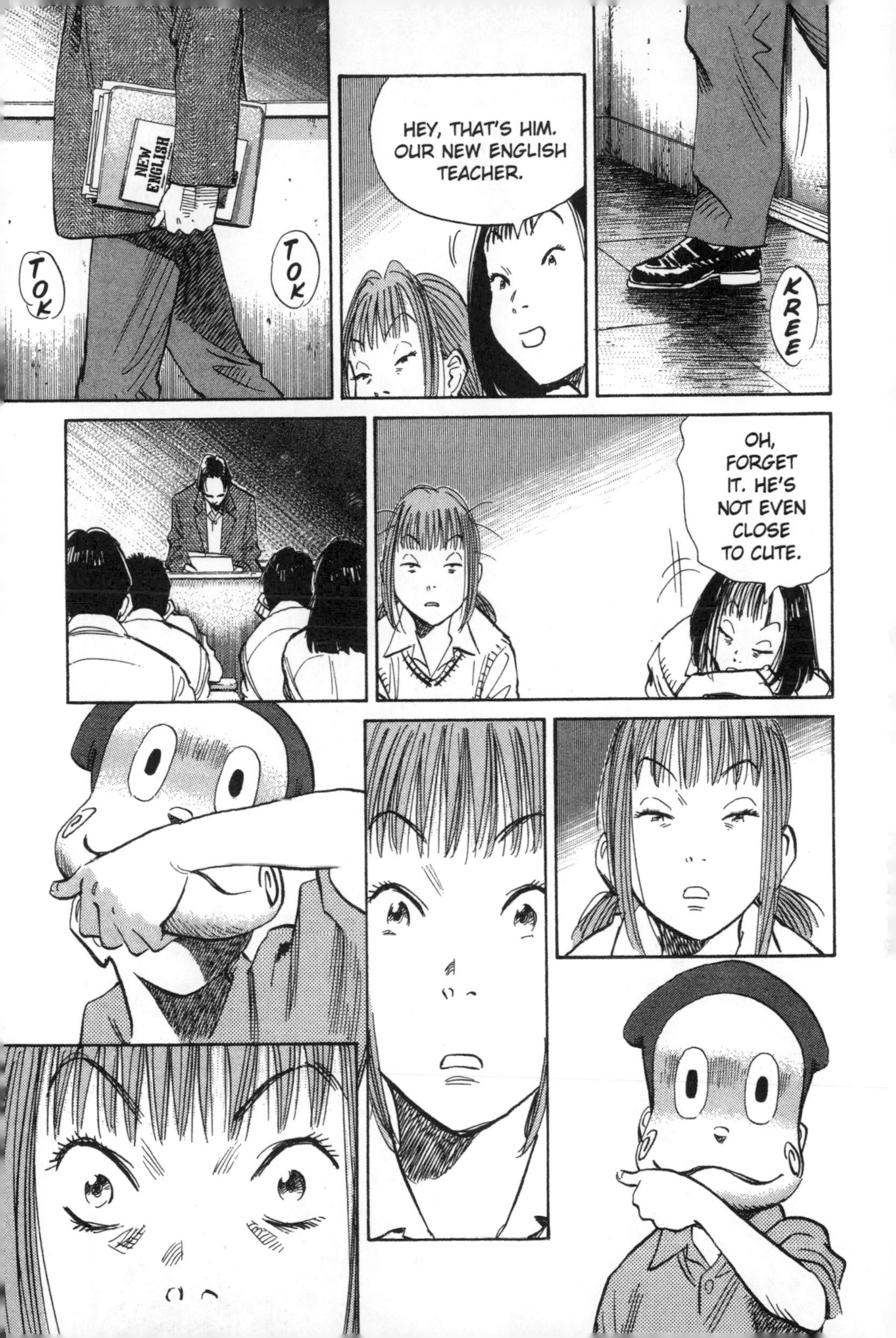
KREE
HEY, THAT'S HIM. OUR NEW ENGLISH TEACHER.
NEW ENGLISH
TOK
TOK
OH, FORGET IT. HE'S NOT EVEN CLOSE TO CUTE.

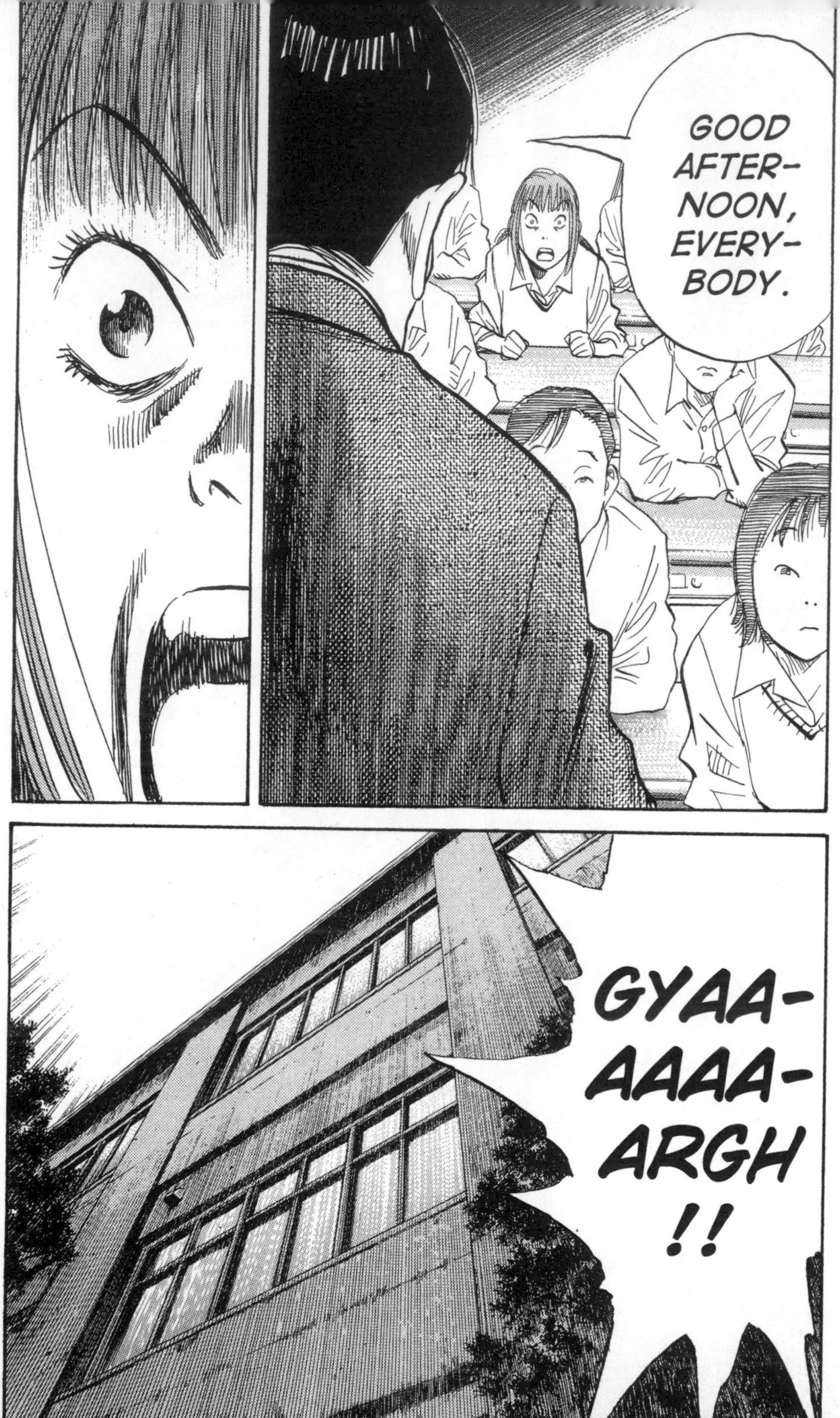
GOOD AFTER-NOON, EVERY-BODY.
GYAA-AAAA-ARGH!!

Chapter 5 Horror Explained

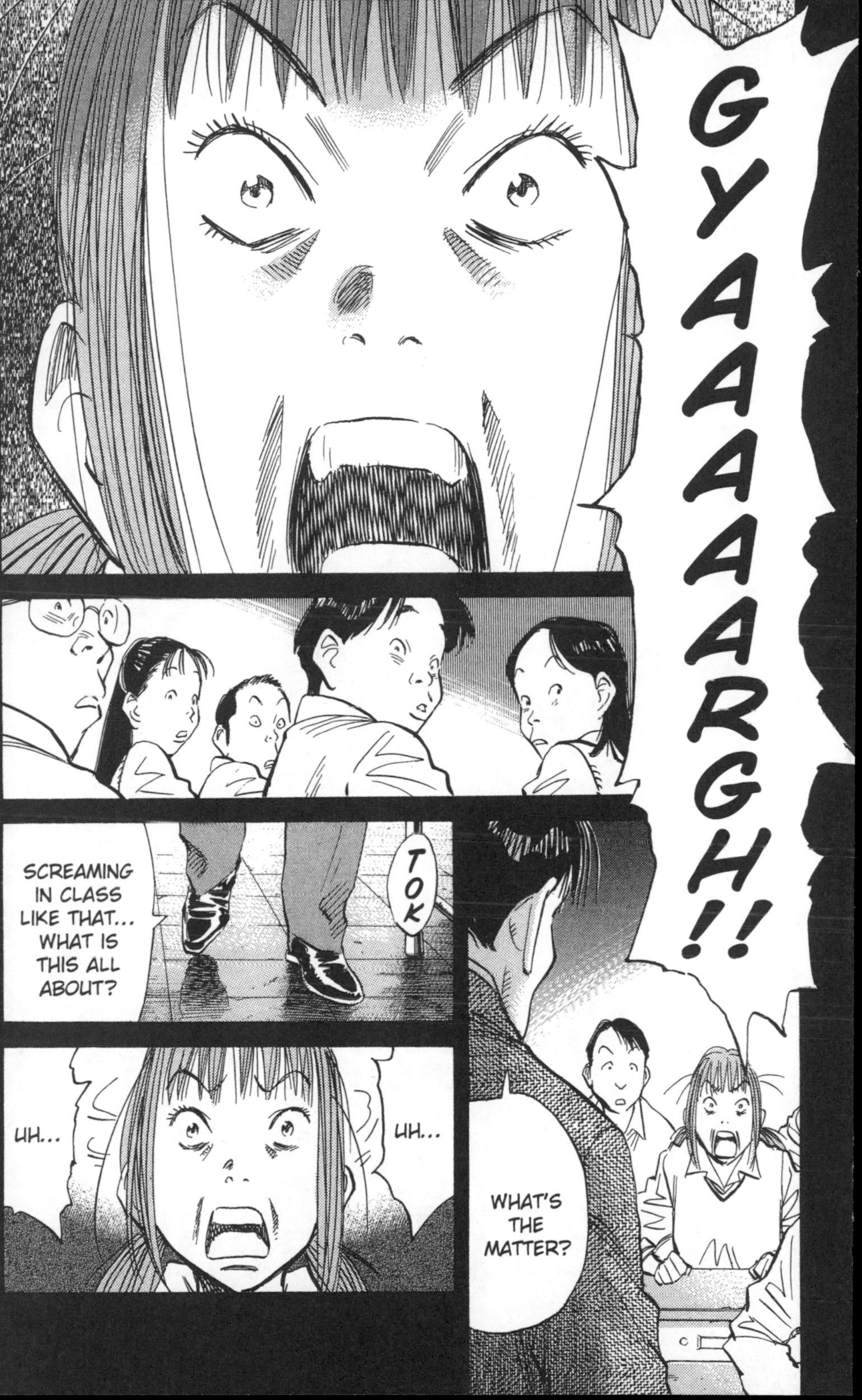
GYAAAAARGH!!
WHAT'S THE MATTER?
TOK
SCREAMING IN CLASS LIKE THAT... WHAT IS THIS ALL ABOUT?
UH...
UH...

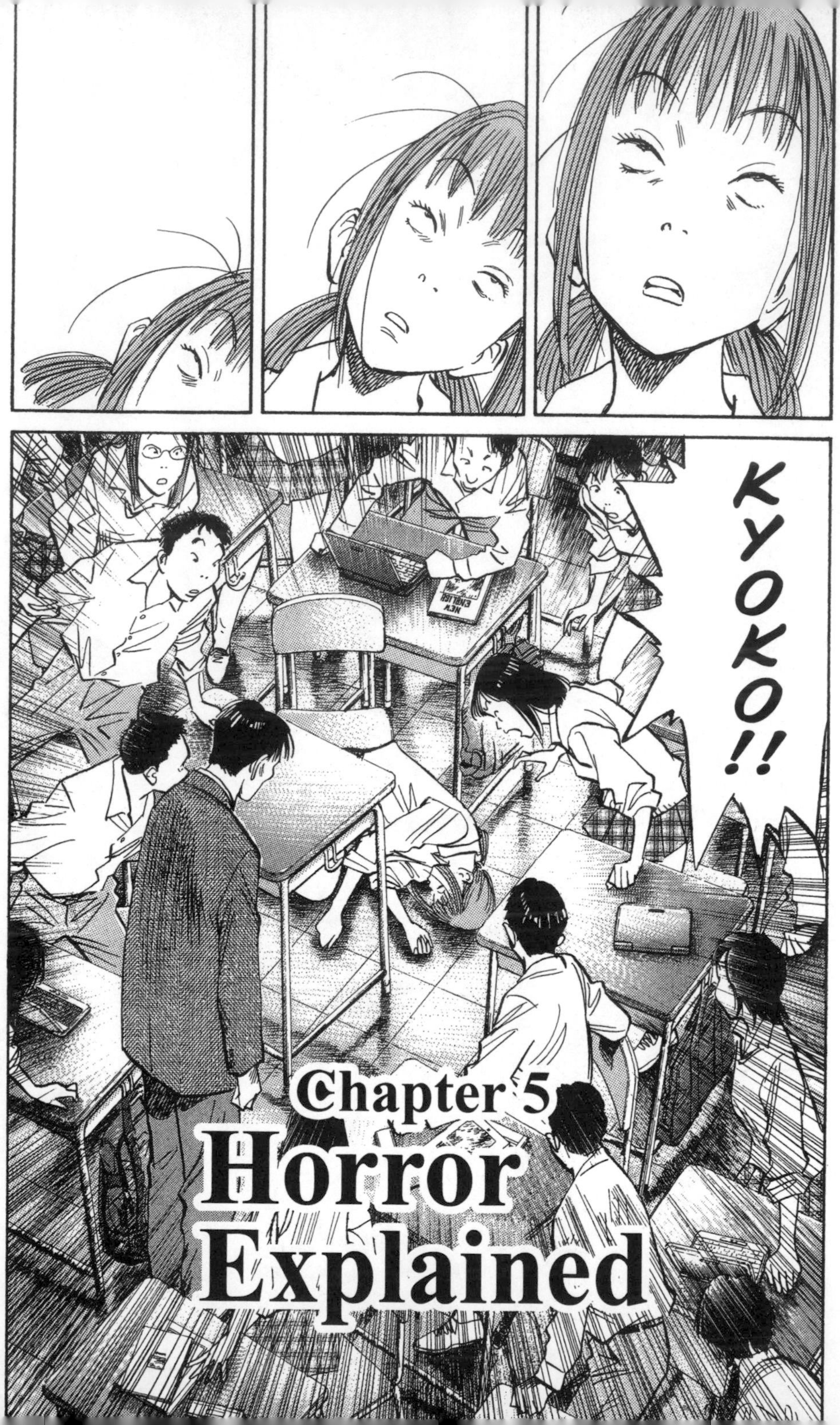
KYOKO!!

Chapter 5
Horror Explained

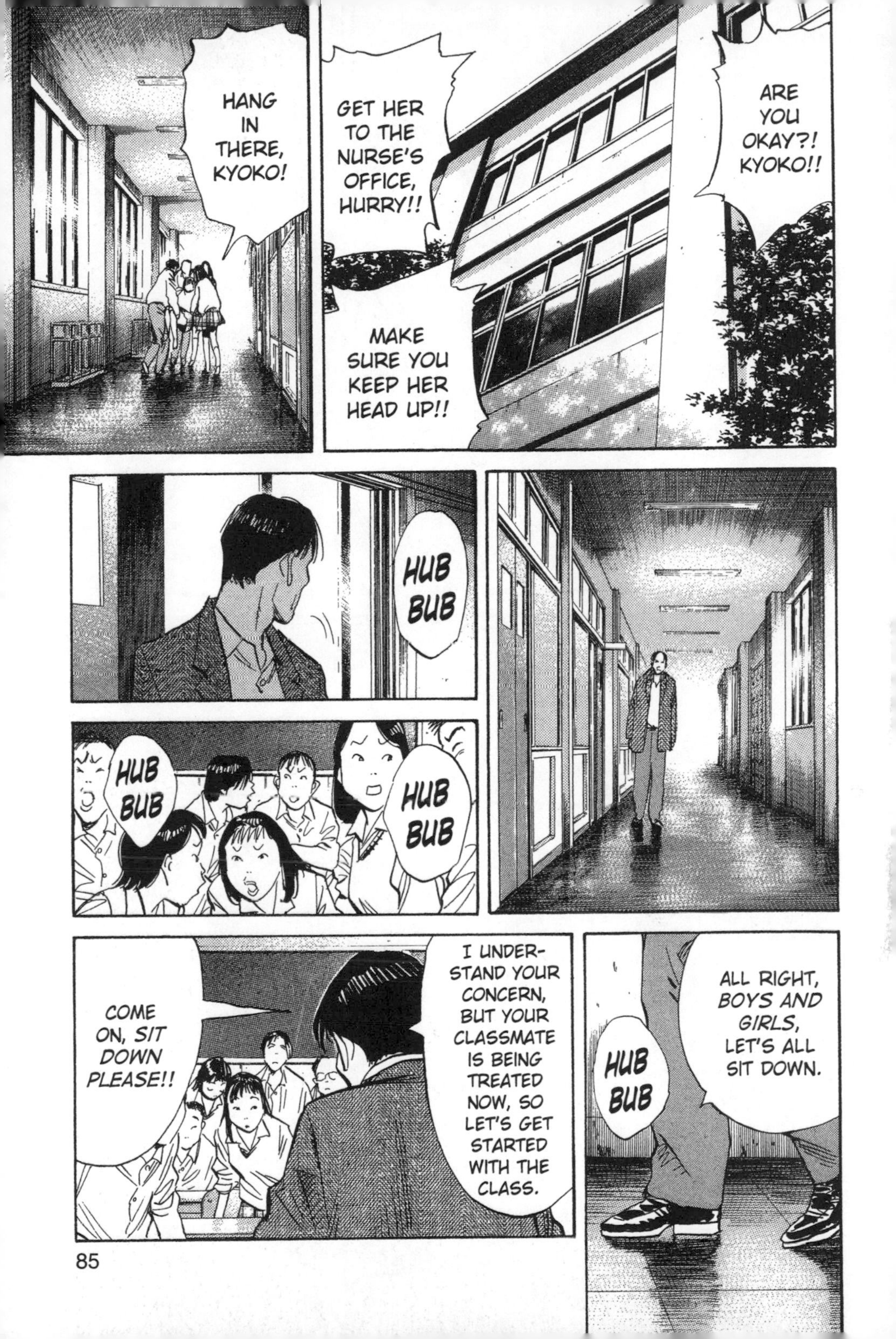

ARE YOU OKAY?! KYOKO!!
GET HER TO THE NURSE'S OFFICE, HURRY!!
MAKE SURE YOU KEEP HER HEAD UP!!
HANG IN THERE, KYOKO!
HUB BUB
HUB BUB
HUB BUB
ALL RIGHT, BOYS AND GIRLS, LET'S ALL SIT DOWN.
HUB BUB
I UNDER-STAND YOUR CONCERN, BUT YOUR CLASSMATE IS BEING TREATED NOW, SO LET'S GET STARTED WITH THE CLASS.
COME ON, SIT DOWN PLEASE!!

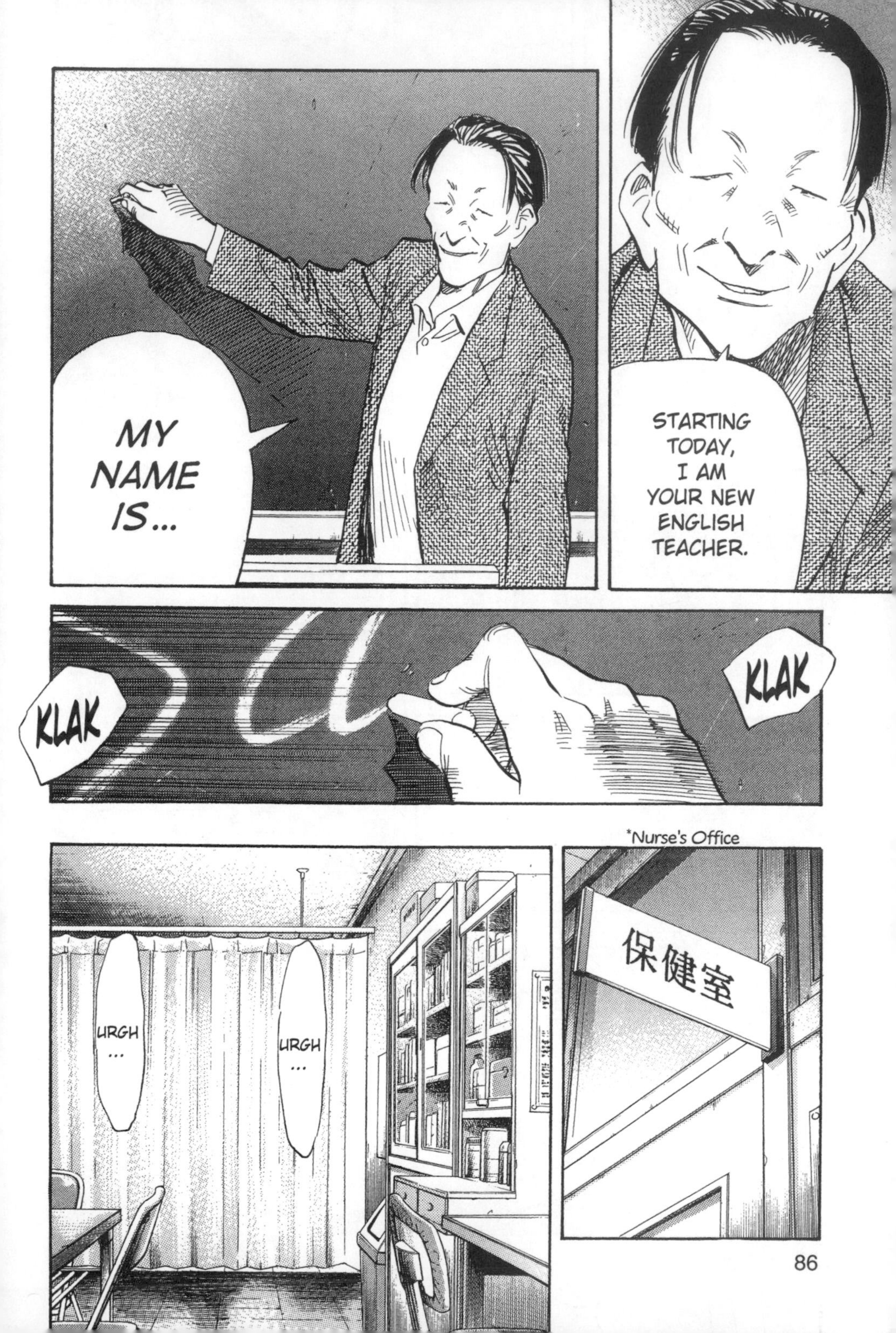
STARTING TODAY, I AM YOUR NEW ENGLISH TEACHER.
MY NAME IS...
KLAK
KLAK
*Nurse's Office
保健室
URGH ...
URGH ...

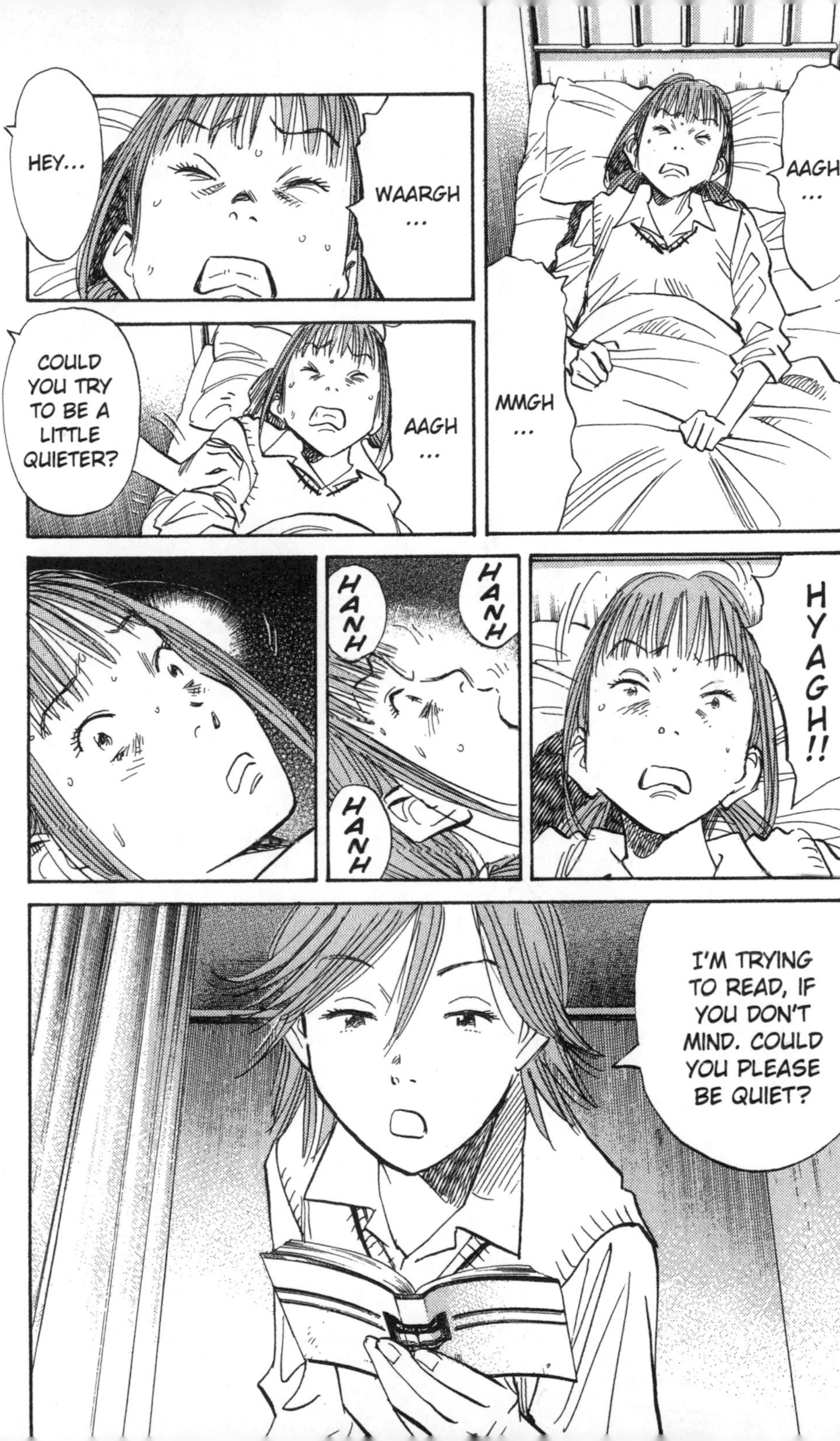
AAGH...
MMGH...
WAARGH...
HEY...
AAGH...
COULD YOU TRY TO BE A LITTLE QUIETER?
HYAGH!!
HANH
HANH
HANH
I'M TRYING TO READ, IF YOU DON'T MIND. COULD YOU PLEASE BE QUIET?

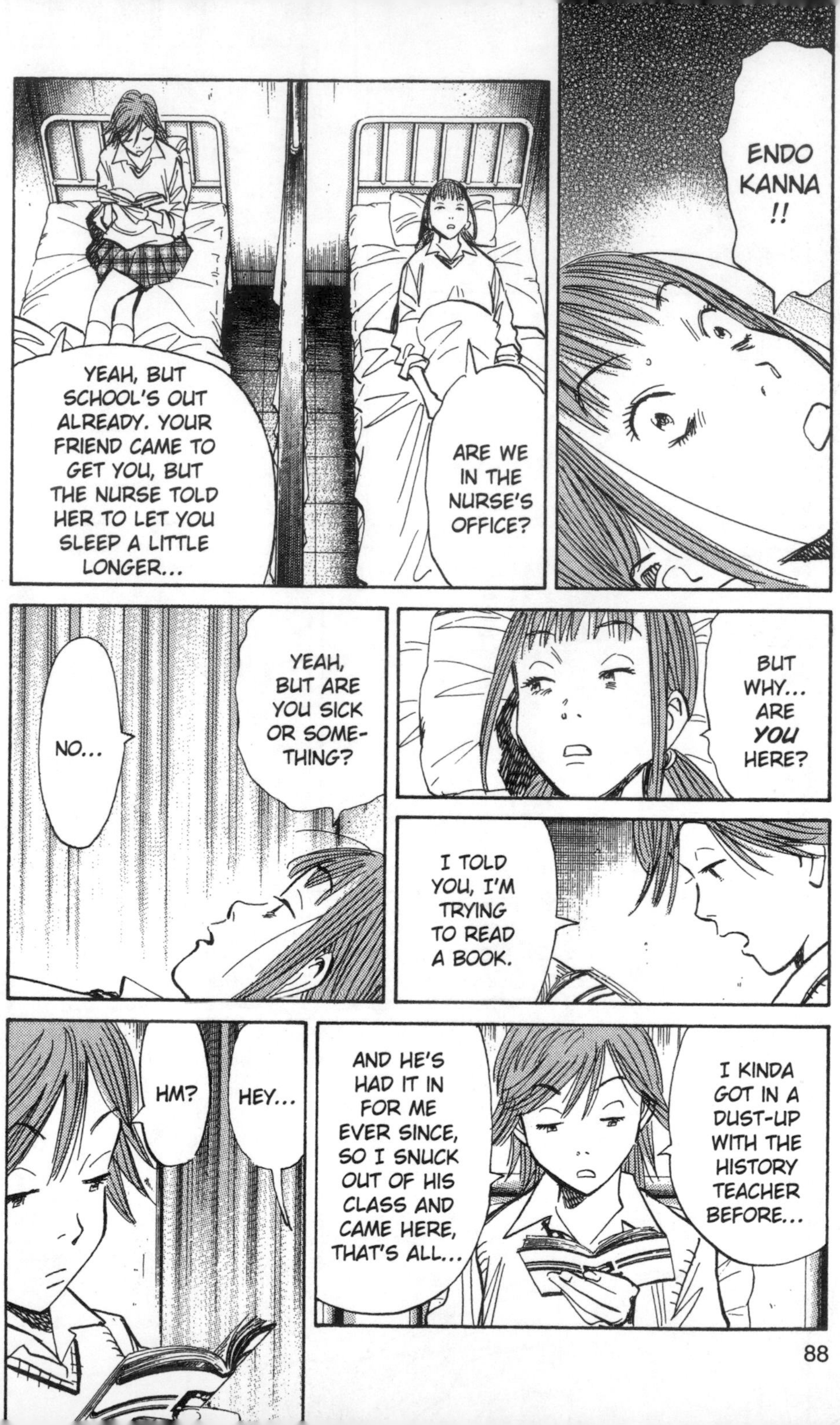
ENDO KANNA!!
ARE WE IN THE NURSE'S OFFICE?
YEAH, BUT SCHOOL'S OUT ALREADY. YOUR FRIEND CAME TO GET YOU, BUT THE NURSE TOLD HER TO LET YOU SLEEP A LITTLE LONGER...
BUT WHY... ARE *YOU* HERE?
I TOLD YOU, I'M TRYING TO READ A BOOK.
YEAH, BUT ARE YOU SICK OR SOME-THING?
NO...
I KINDA GOT IN A DUST-UP WITH THE HISTORY TEACHER BEFORE...
AND HE'S HAD IT IN FOR ME EVER SINCE, SO I SNUCK OUT OF HIS CLASS AND CAME HERE, THAT'S ALL...
HEY...
HM?

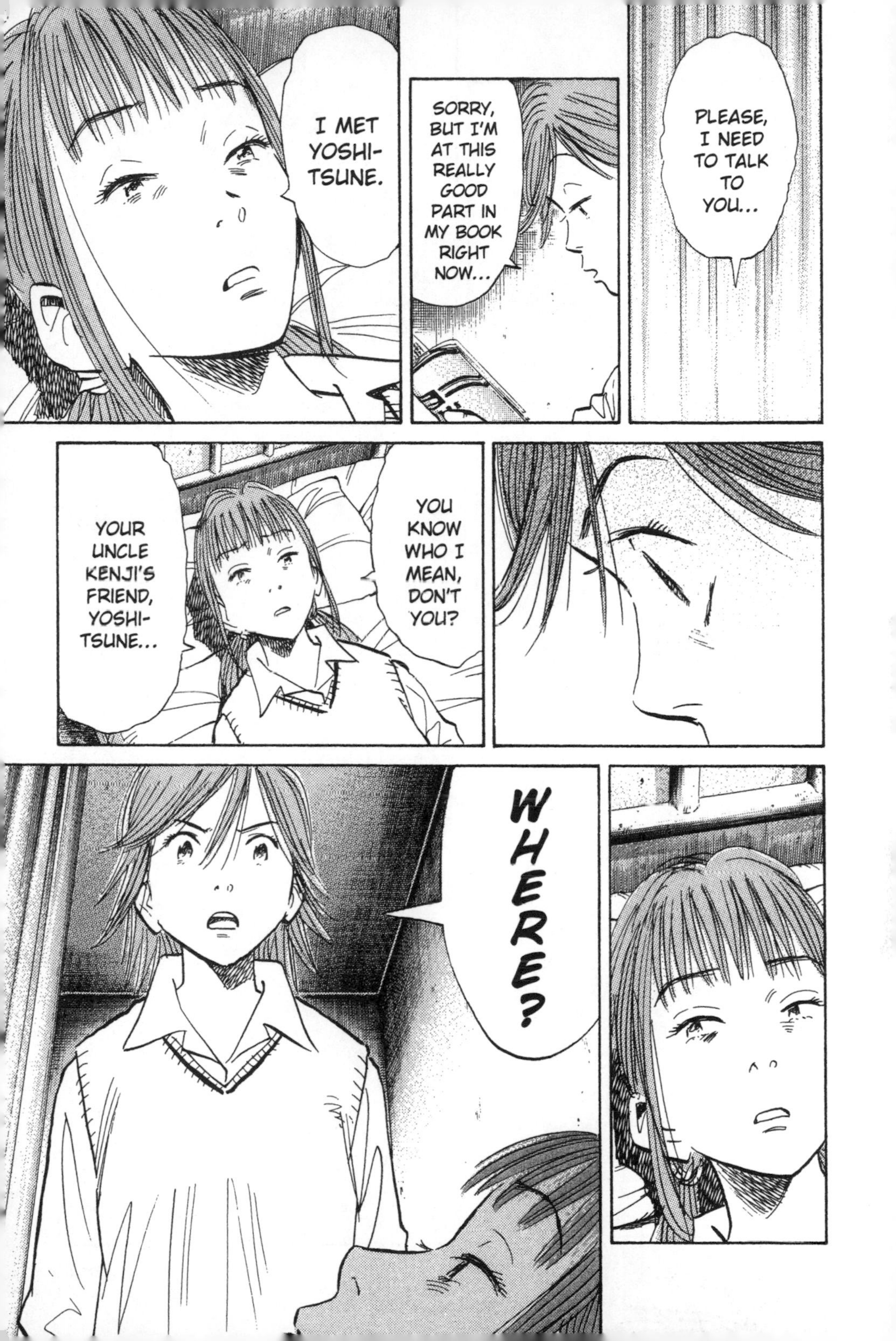
PLEASE, I NEED TO TALK TO YOU...
SORRY, BUT I'M AT THIS REALLY GOOD PART IN MY BOOK RIGHT NOW...
I MET YOSHI-TSUNE.
YOU KNOW WHO I MEAN, DON'T YOU?
YOUR UNCLE KENJI'S FRIEND, YOSHI-TSUNE...
WHERE?

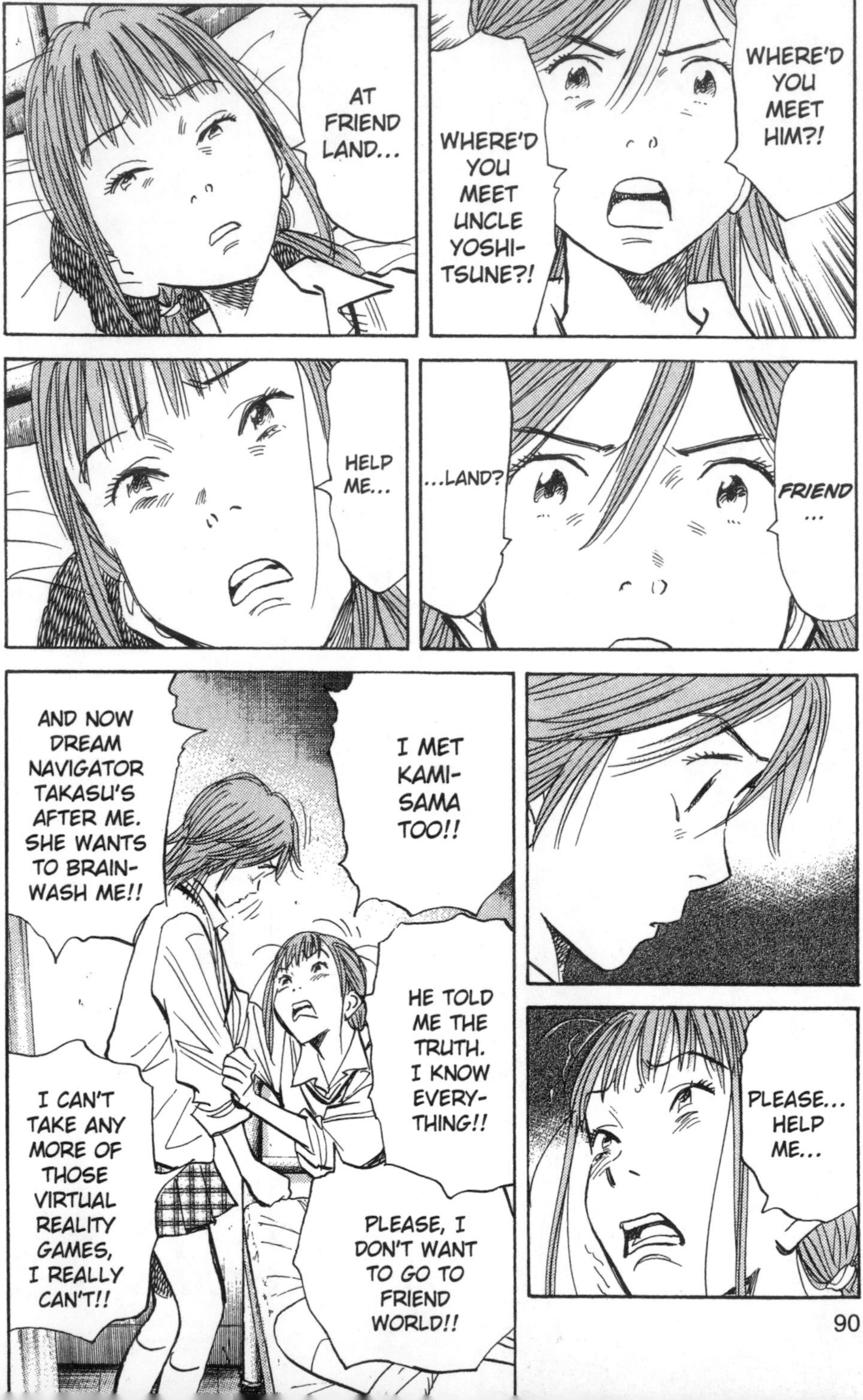
WHERE'D YOU MEET HIM?!
WHERE'D YOU MEET UNCLE YOSHI-TSUNE?!
AT FRIEND LAND...
FRIEND ...
...LAND?
HELP ME...
PLEASE... HELP ME...
I MET KAMI-SAMA TOO!!
AND NOW DREAM NAVIGATOR TAKASU'S AFTER ME. SHE WANTS TO BRAIN-WASH ME!!
HE TOLD ME THE TRUTH. I KNOW EVERY-THING!!
I CAN'T TAKE ANY MORE OF THOSE VIRTUAL REALITY GAMES, I REALLY CAN'T!!
PLEASE, I DON'T WANT TO GO TO FRIEND WORLD!!

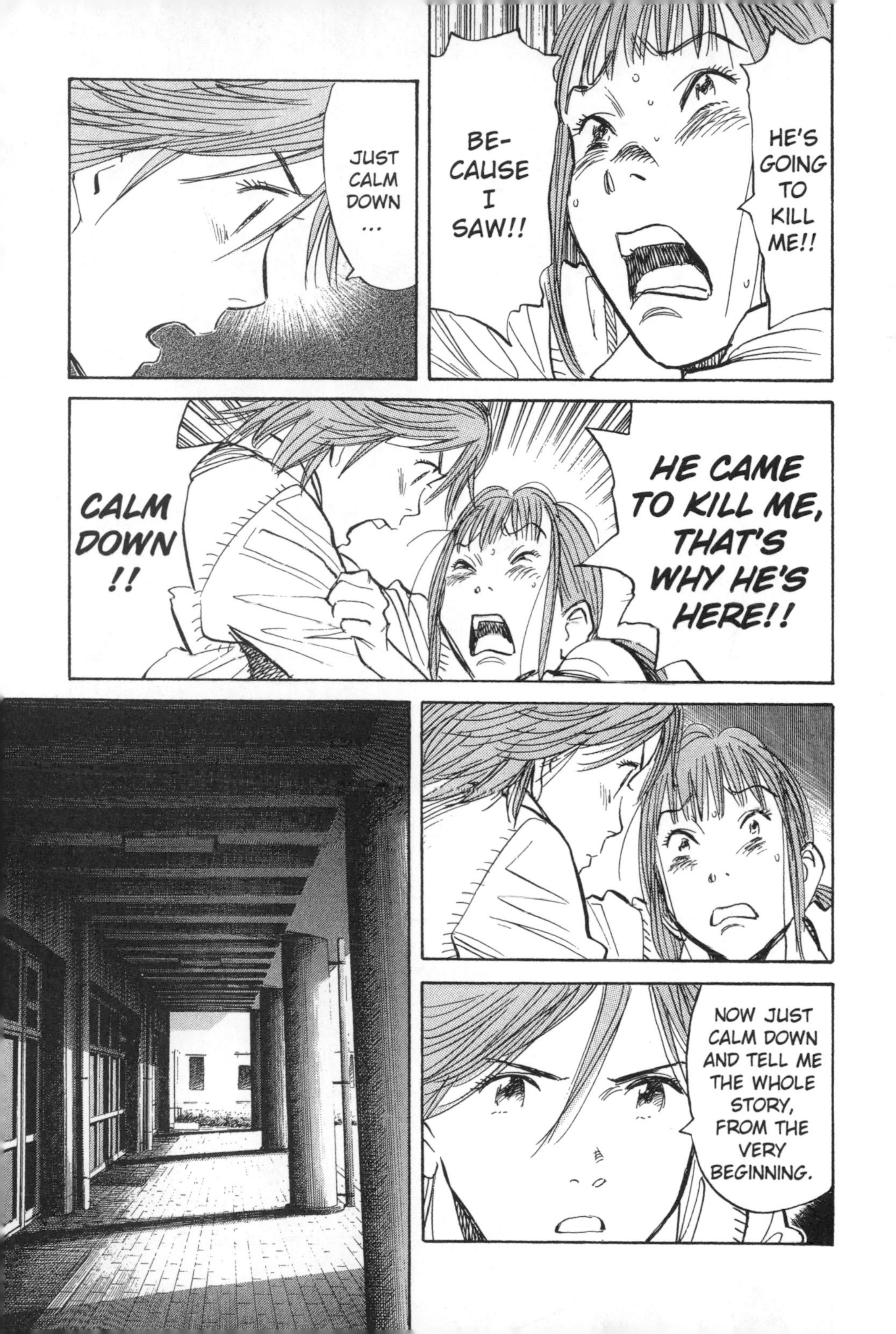
HE'S GOING TO KILL ME!!
BE-CAUSE I SAW!!
JUST CALM DOWN ...
HE CAME TO KILL ME, THAT'S WHY HE'S HERE!!
CALM DOWN !!
NOW JUST CALM DOWN AND TELL ME THE WHOLE STORY, FROM THE VERY BEGINNING.

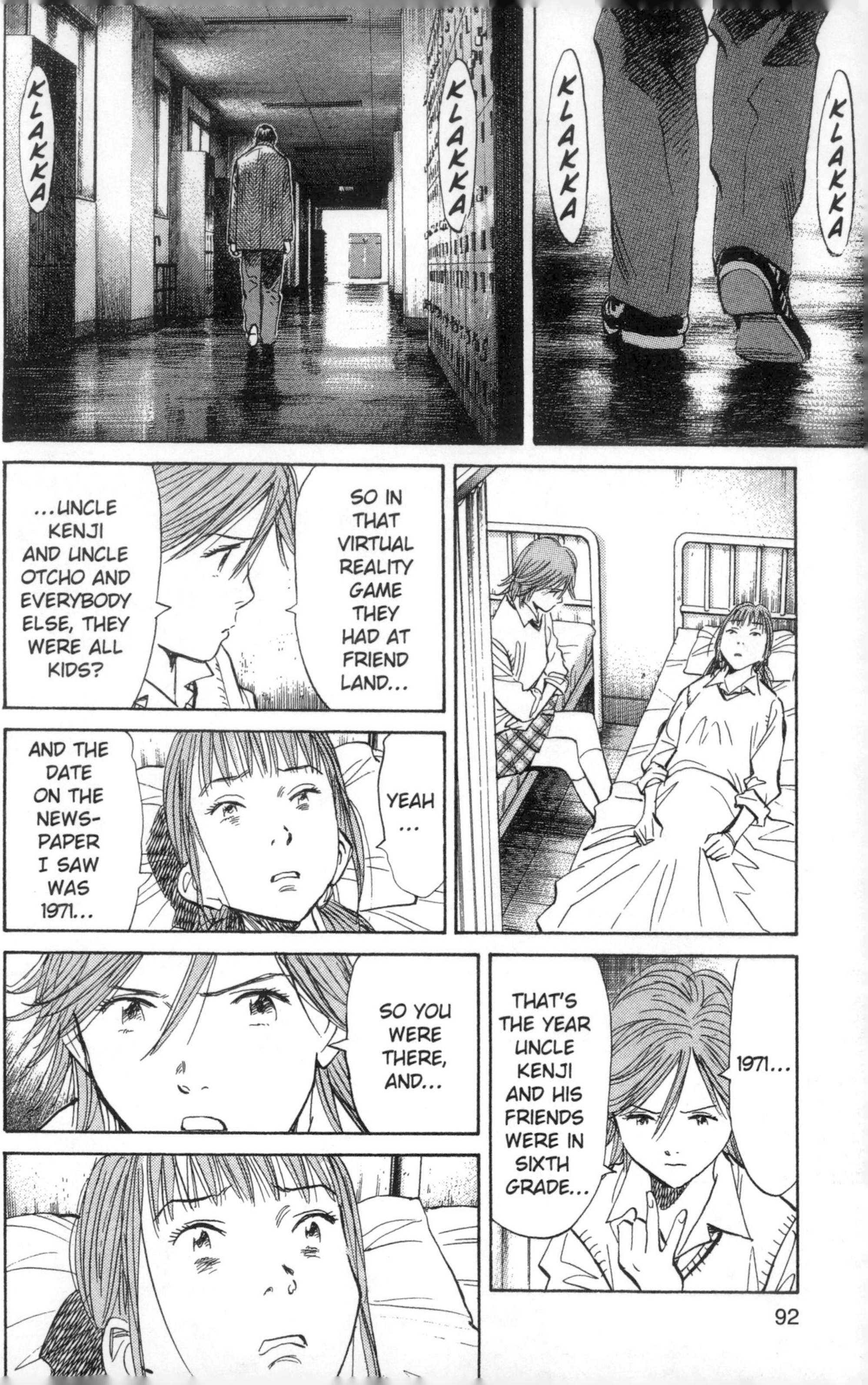
KLAKKA
KLAKKA
KLAKKA
KLAKKA
SO IN THAT VIRTUAL REALITY GAME THEY HAD AT FRIEND LAND...
...UNCLE KENJI AND UNCLE OTCHO AND EVERYBODY ELSE, THEY WERE ALL KIDS?
YEAH ...
AND THE DATE ON THE NEWS-PAPER I SAW WAS 1971...
1971...
THAT'S THE YEAR UNCLE KENJI AND HIS FRIENDS WERE IN SIXTH GRADE...
SO YOU WERE THERE, AND...

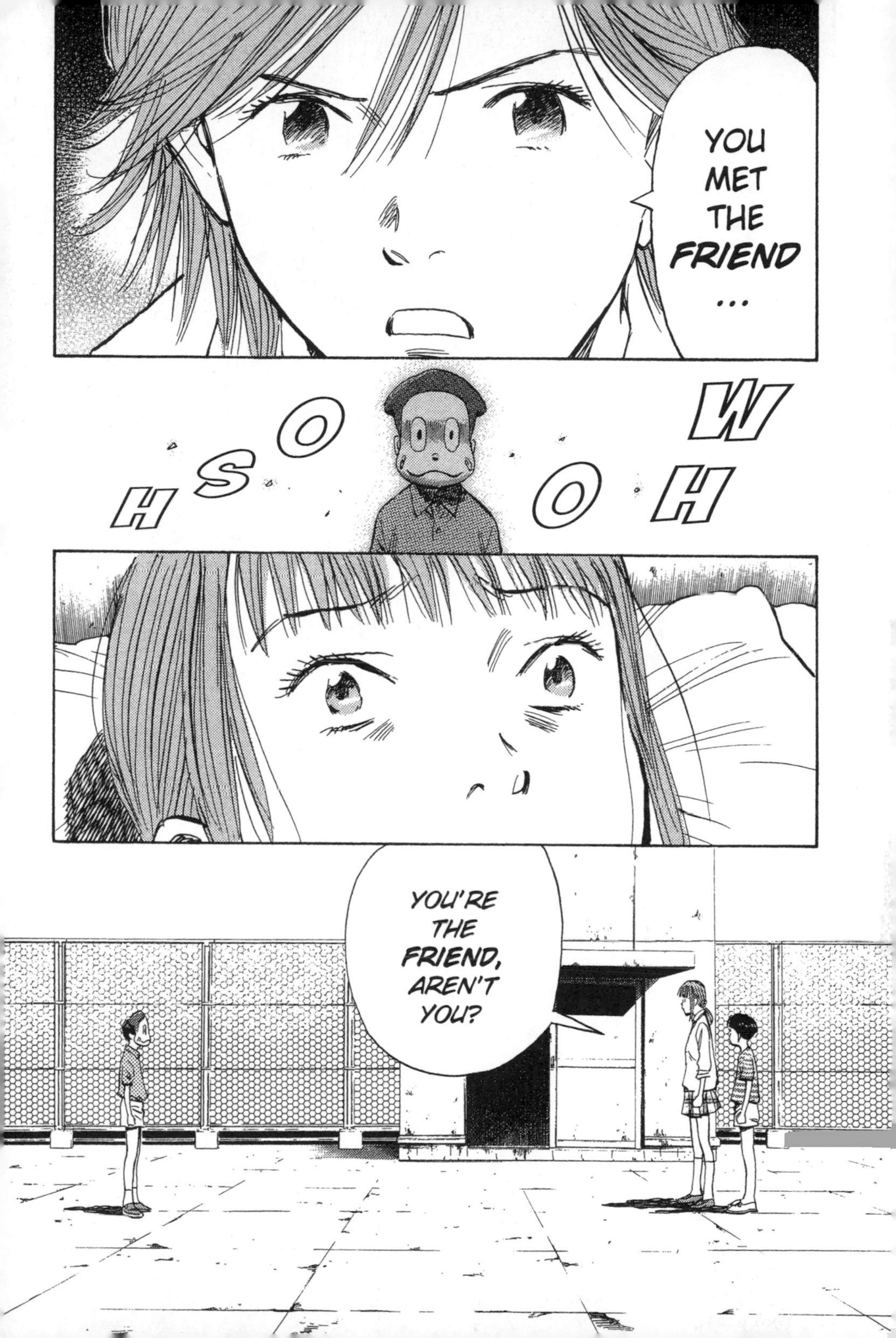
YOU MET THE FRIEND ...
WHOOSH
YOU'RE THE FRIEND, AREN'T YOU?

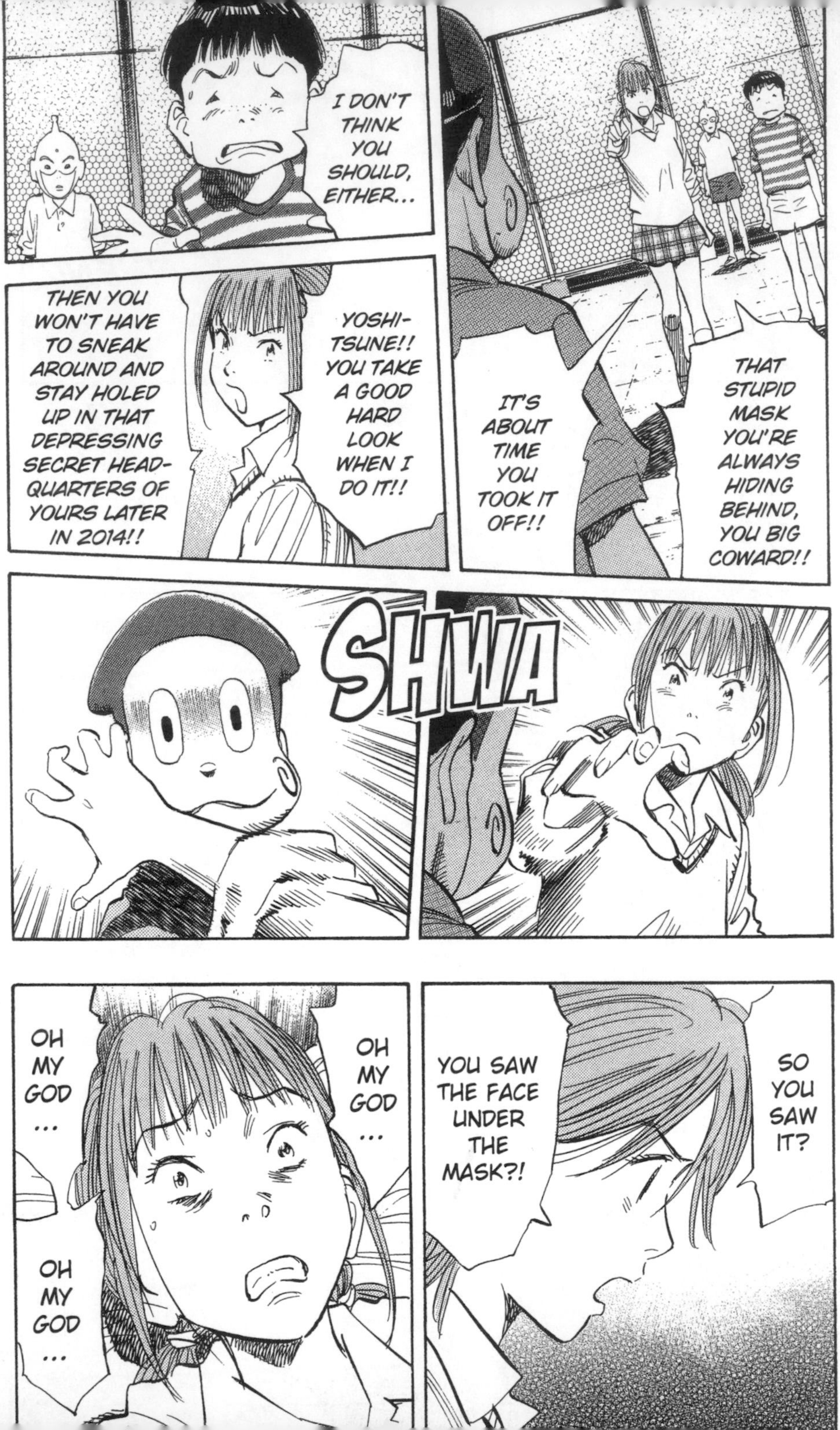
THAT STUPID MASK YOU'RE ALWAYS HIDING BEHIND, YOU BIG COWARD!!
IT'S ABOUT TIME YOU TOOK IT OFF!!
I DON'T THINK YOU SHOULD, EITHER...
YOSHI-TSUNE!! YOU TAKE A GOOD HARD LOOK WHEN I DO IT!!
THEN YOU WON'T HAVE TO SNEAK AROUND AND STAY HOLED UP IN THAT DEPRESSING SECRET HEAD-QUARTERS OF YOURS LATER IN 2014!!
SHWA
SO YOU SAW IT?
YOU SAW THE FACE UNDER THE MASK?!
OH MY GOD ...
OH MY GOD ...
OH MY GOD ...

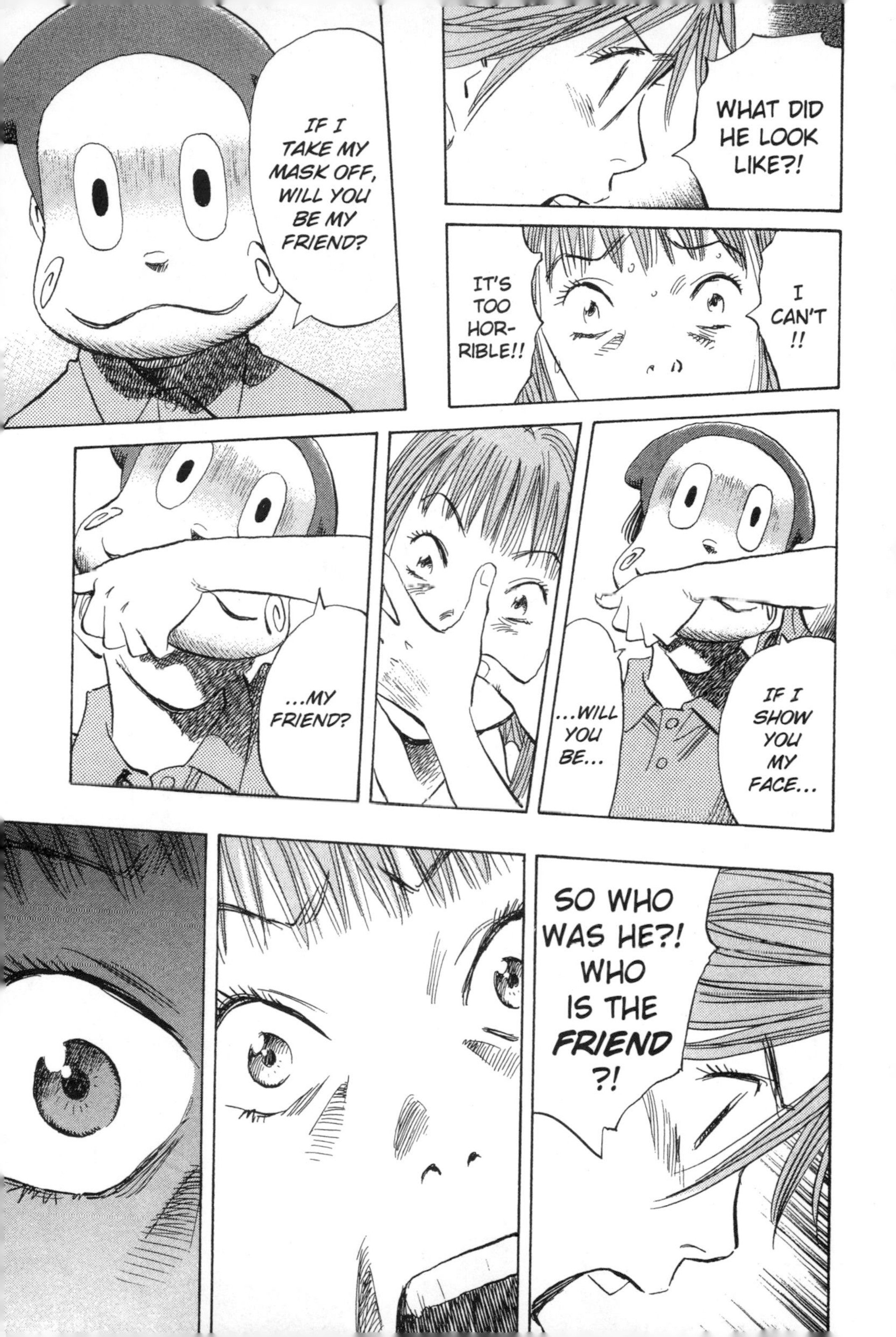
WHAT DID HE LOOK LIKE?!
I CAN'T !!
IT'S TOO HOR-RIBLE!!
IF I TAKE MY MASK OFF, WILL YOU BE MY FRIEND?
IF I SHOW YOU MY FACE...
...WILL YOU BE...
...MY FRIEND?
SO WHO WAS HE?! WHO IS THE FRIEND ?!

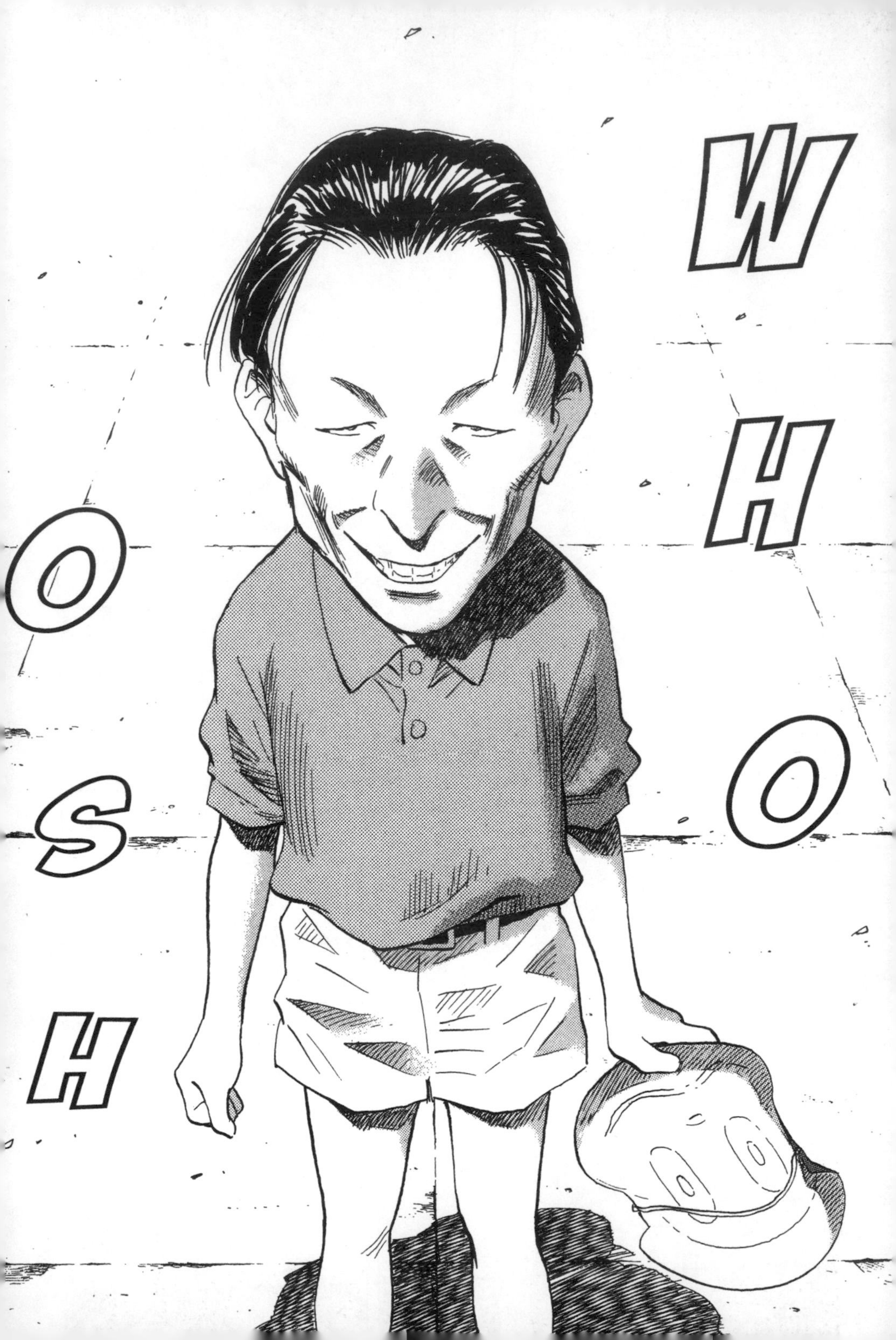
WHOOSH

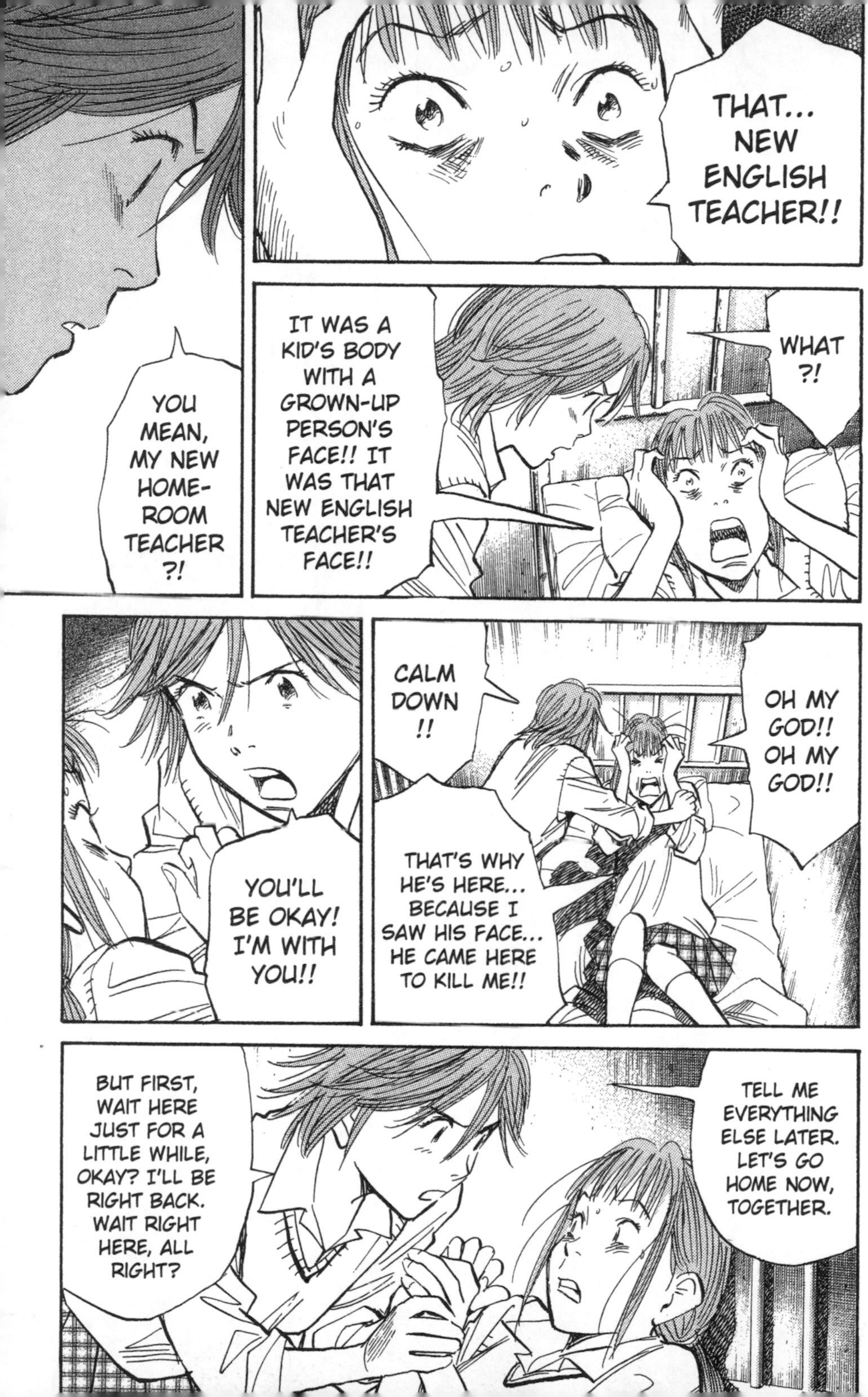
THAT... NEW ENGLISH TEACHER!!
WHAT?!
IT WAS A KID'S BODY WITH A GROWN-UP PERSON'S FACE!! IT WAS THAT NEW ENGLISH TEACHER'S FACE!!
YOU MEAN, MY NEW HOME-ROOM TEACHER?!
OH MY GOD!! OH MY GOD!!
CALM DOWN!!
THAT'S WHY HE'S HERE... BECAUSE I SAW HIS FACE... HE CAME HERE TO KILL ME!!
YOU'LL BE OKAY! I'M WITH YOU!!
TELL ME EVERYTHING ELSE LATER. LET'S GO HOME NOW, TOGETHER.
BUT FIRST, WAIT HERE JUST FOR A LITTLE WHILE, OKAY? I'LL BE RIGHT BACK. WAIT RIGHT HERE, ALL RIGHT?

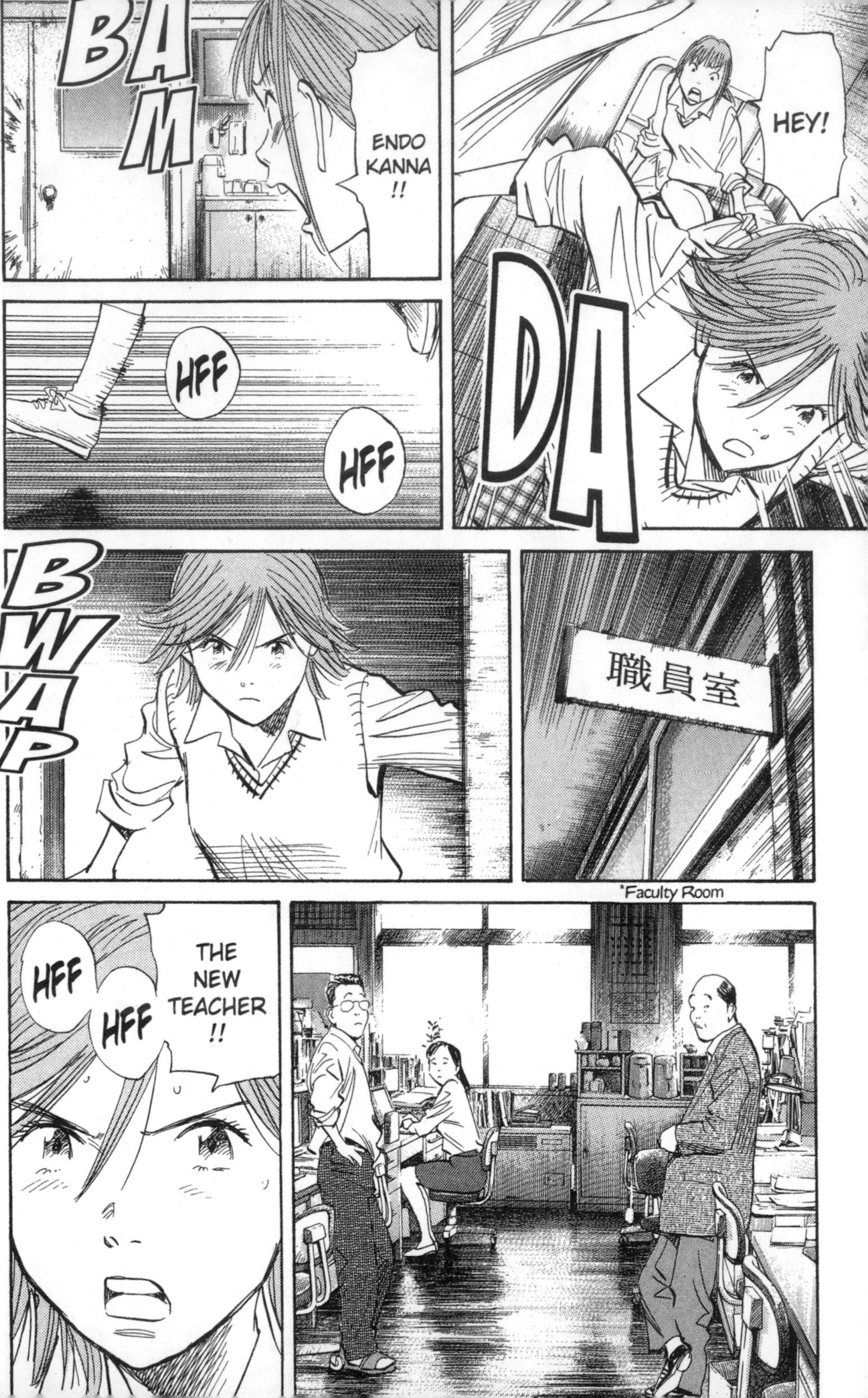
HEY!
DA
BAM
ENDO KANNA !!
HFF
HFF
職員室
*Faculty Room
BWAP
HFF
HFF
THE NEW TEACHER !!

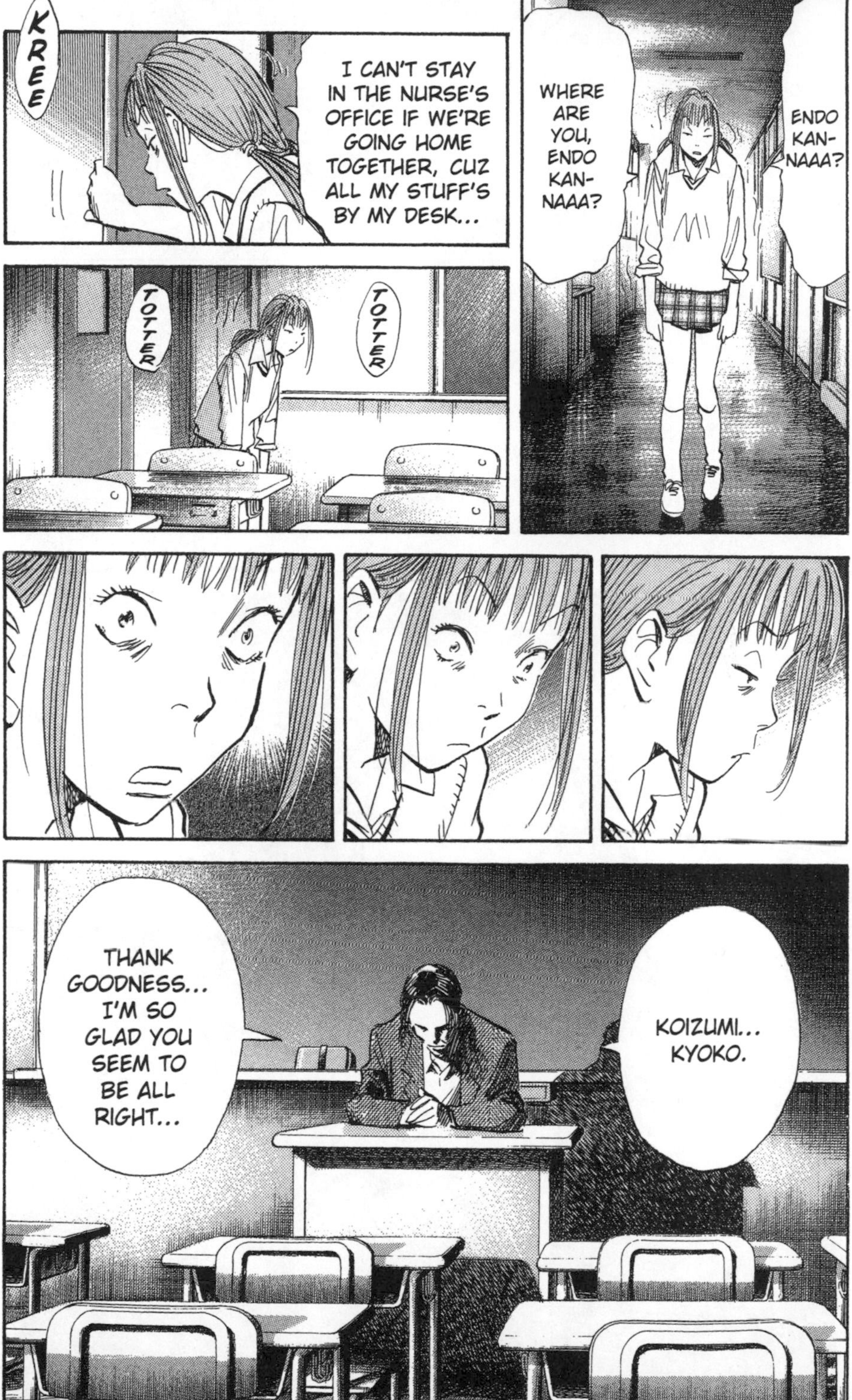
WHERE ARE YOU, ENDO KAN-NAAA?
ENDO KAN-NAAA?
KREE
I CAN'T STAY IN THE NURSE'S OFFICE IF WE'RE GOING HOME TOGETHER, CUZ ALL MY STUFF'S BY MY DESK...
TOTTER
TOTTER
KOIZUMI... KYOKO.
THANK GOODNESS... I'M SO GLAD YOU SEEM TO BE ALL RIGHT...

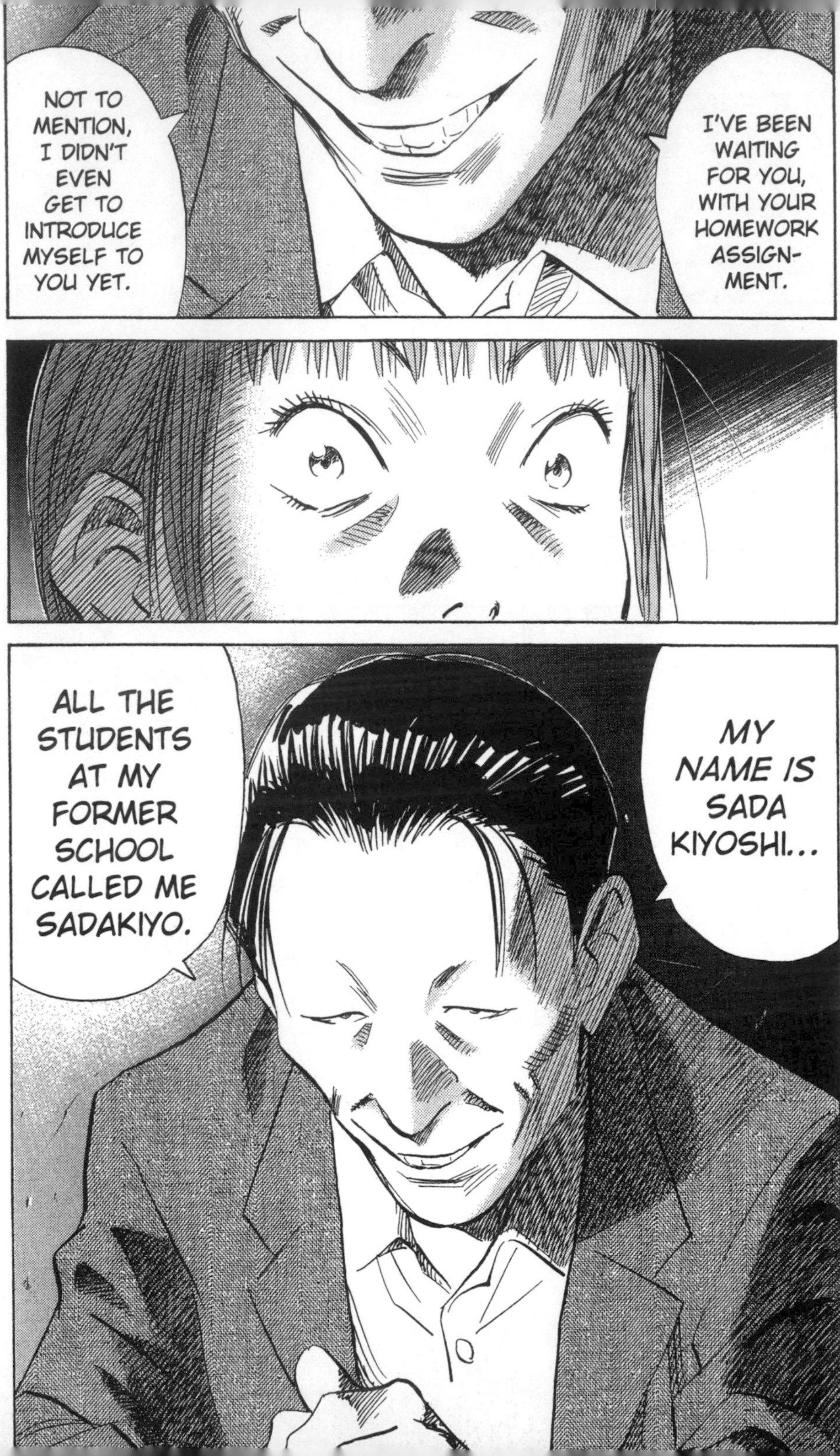
I'VE BEEN WAITING FOR YOU, WITH YOUR HOMEWORK ASSIGN-MENT.
NOT TO MENTION, I DIDN'T EVEN GET TO INTRODUCE MYSELF TO YOU YET.
MY NAME IS SADA KIYOSHI...
ALL THE STUDENTS AT MY FORMER SCHOOL CALLED ME SADAKIYO.

Chapter 6 Collector

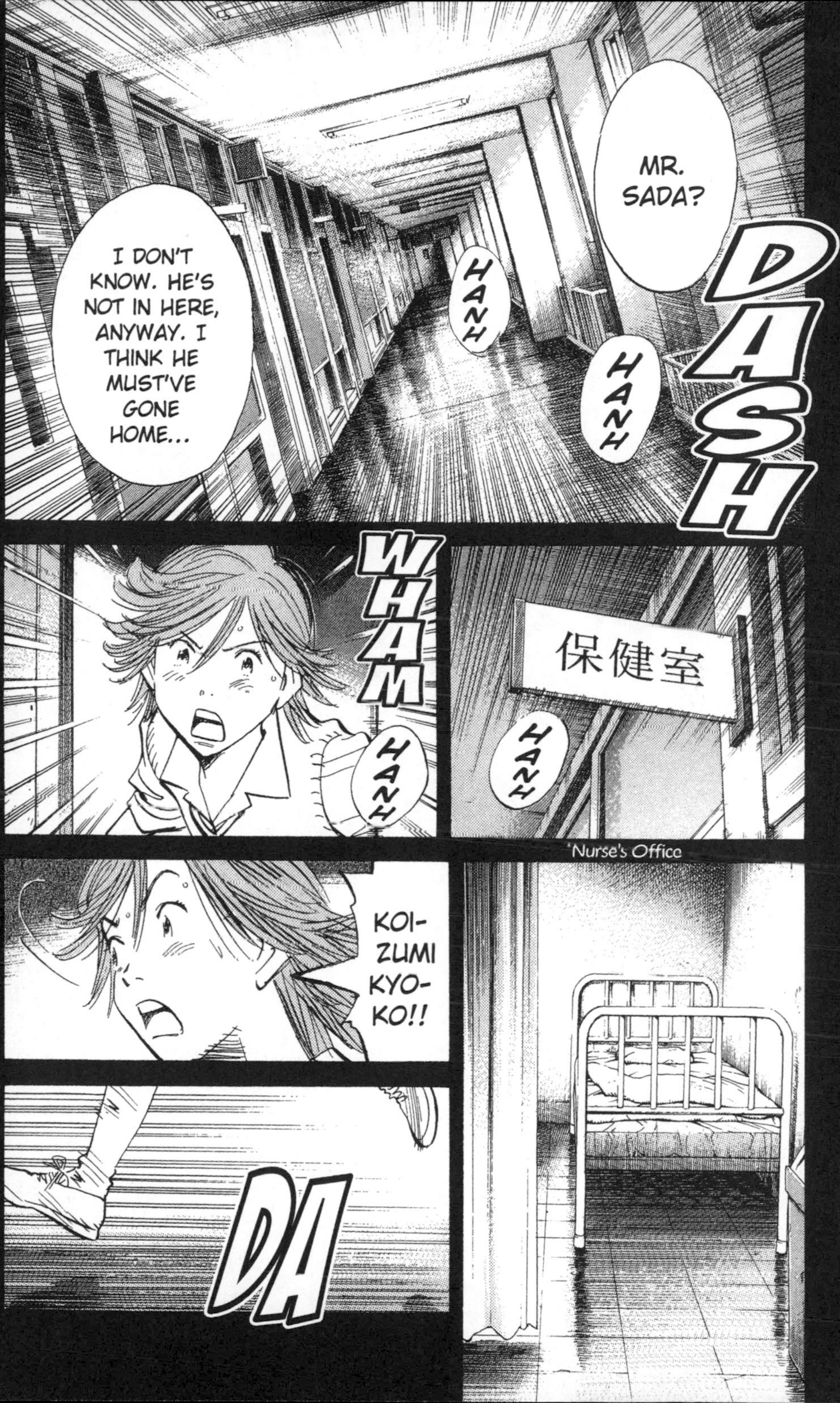
MR. SADA?
DASH
HANH HANH
HANH HANH
I DON'T KNOW. HE'S NOT IN HERE, ANYWAY. I THINK HE MUST'VE GONE HOME...
保健室
HANH HANH
WHAM
HANH HANH
*Nurse's Office
KOI-ZUMI KYO-KO!!
DA

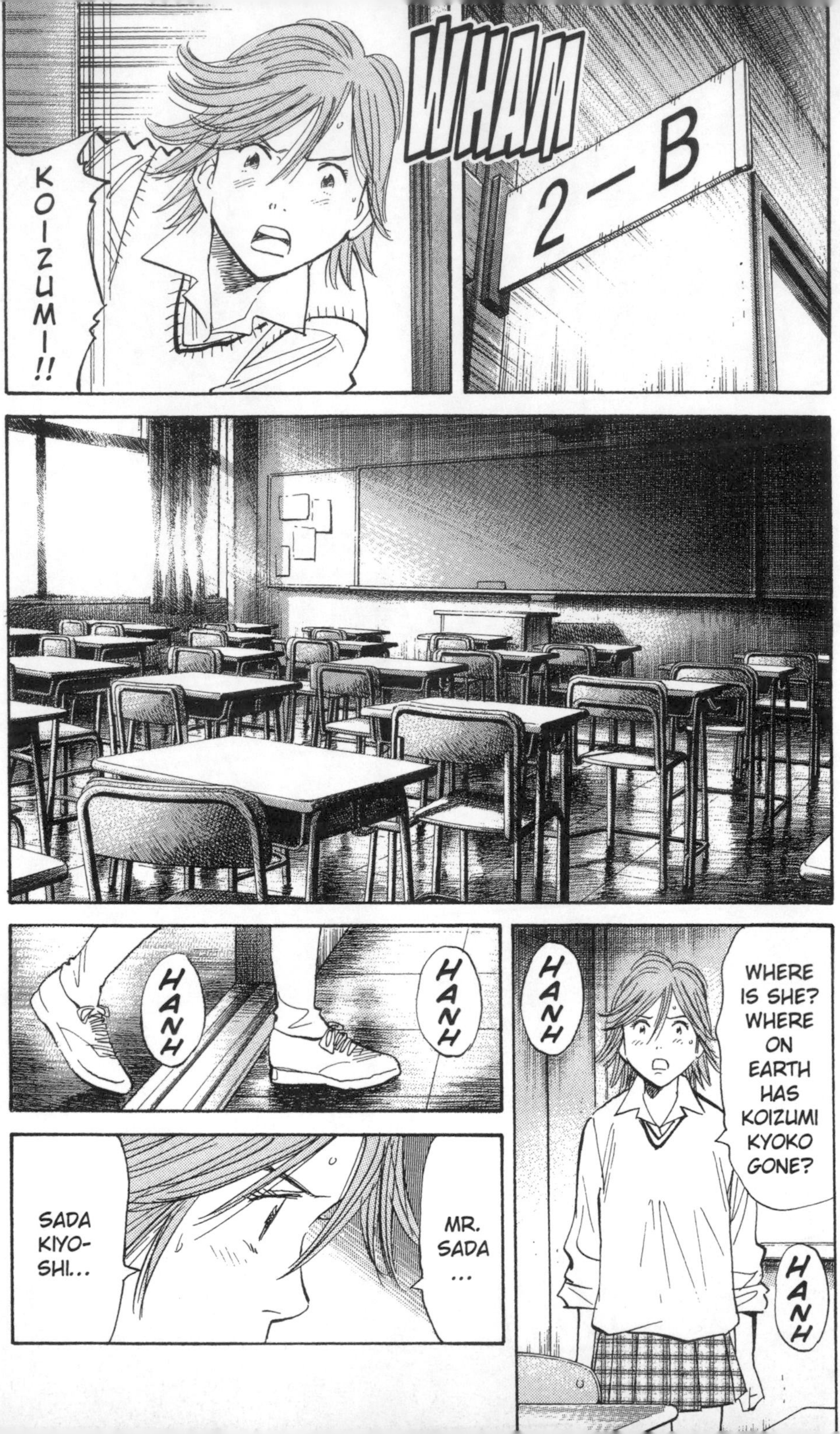
WHAM
2-B
KOIZUMI!!
HANH
WHERE IS SHE? WHERE ON EARTH HAS KOIZUMI KYOKO GONE?
HANH
HANH
HANH
MR. SADA ...
SADA KIYOSHI...

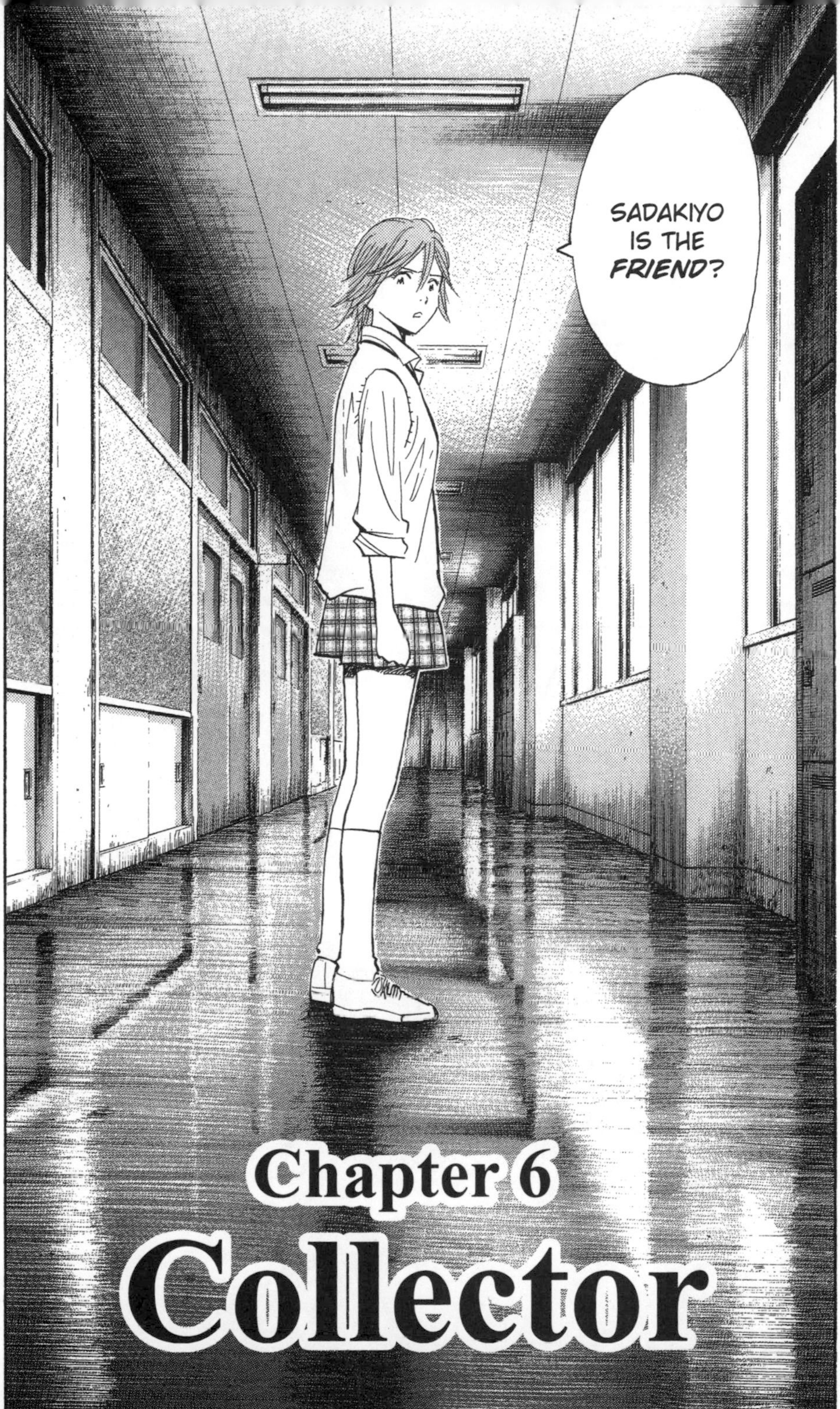
SADAKIYO IS THE *FRIEND*?

Chapter 6
Collector

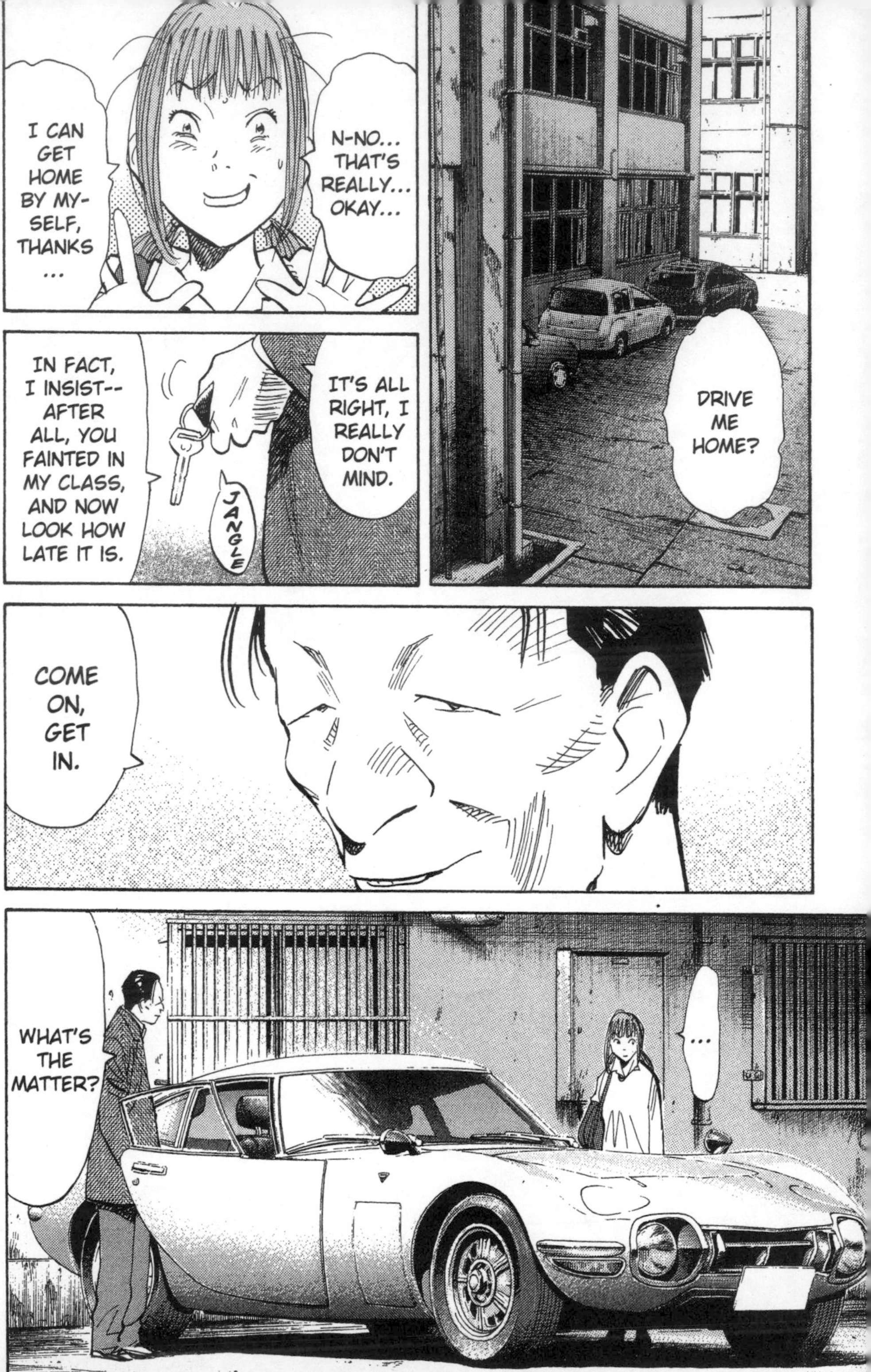
DRIVE ME HOME?
N-NO... THAT'S REALLY... OKAY...
I CAN GET HOME BY MY-SELF, THANKS ...
IT'S ALL RIGHT, I REALLY DON'T MIND.
JANGLE
IN FACT, I INSIST-- AFTER ALL, YOU FAINTED IN MY CLASS, AND NOW LOOK HOW LATE IT IS.
COME ON, GET IN.
...
WHAT'S THE MATTER?

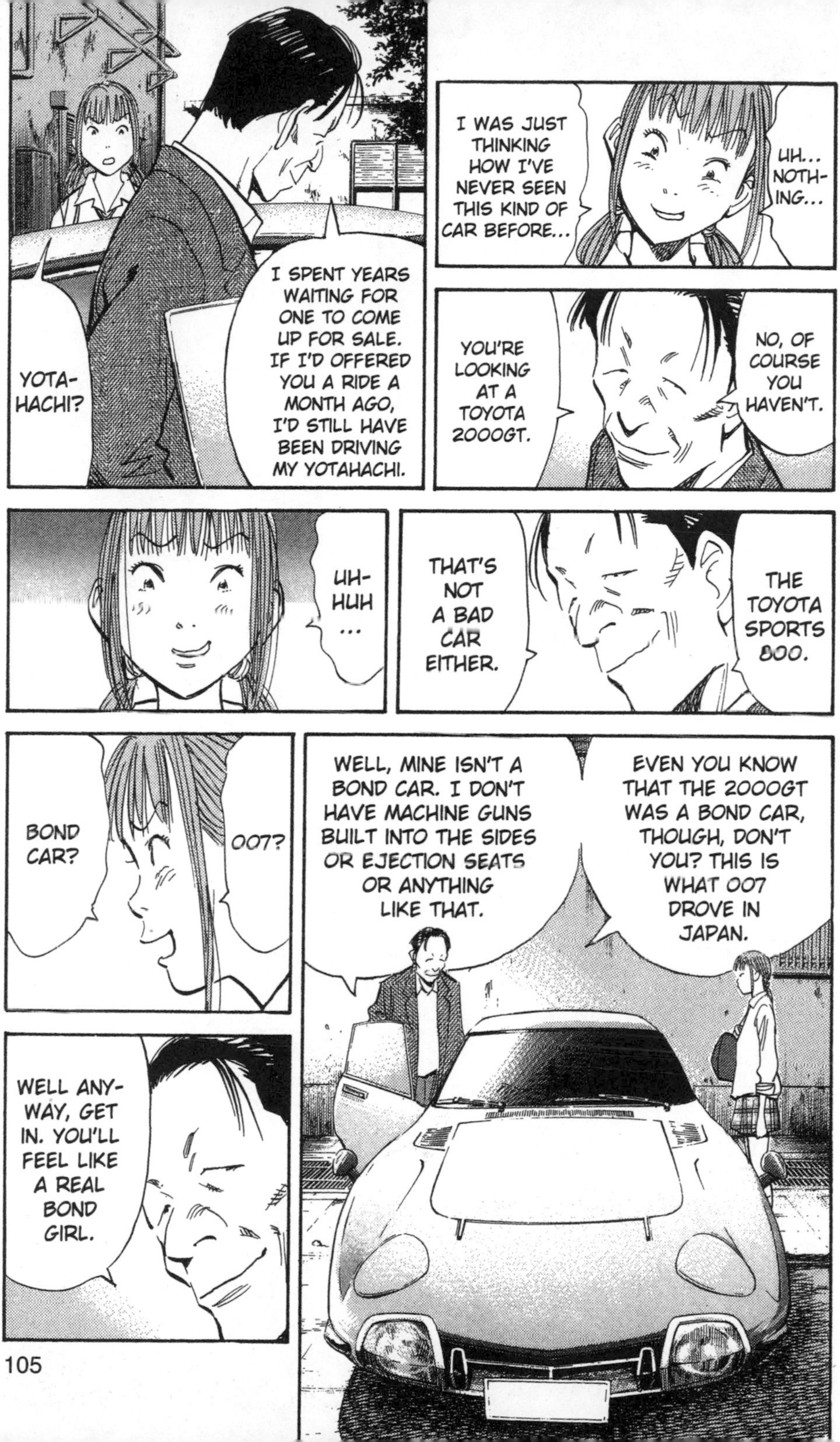
UH... NOTHING...
I WAS JUST THINKING HOW I'VE NEVER SEEN THIS KIND OF CAR BEFORE...
NO, OF COURSE YOU HAVEN'T.
YOU'RE LOOKING AT A TOYOTA 2000GT.
I SPENT YEARS WAITING FOR ONE TO COME UP FOR SALE. IF I'D OFFERED YOU A RIDE A MONTH AGO, I'D STILL HAVE BEEN DRIVING MY YOTAHACHI.
YOTA-HACHI?
THE TOYOTA SPORTS 800.
THAT'S NOT A BAD CAR EITHER.
UH-HUH...
EVEN YOU KNOW THAT THE 2000GT WAS A BOND CAR, THOUGH, DON'T YOU? THIS IS WHAT 007 DROVE IN JAPAN.
WELL, MINE ISN'T A BOND CAR. I DON'T HAVE MACHINE GUNS BUILT INTO THE SIDES OR EJECTION SEATS OR ANYTHING LIKE THAT.
007?
BOND CAR?
WELL ANYWAY, GET IN. YOU'LL FEEL LIKE A REAL BOND GIRL.

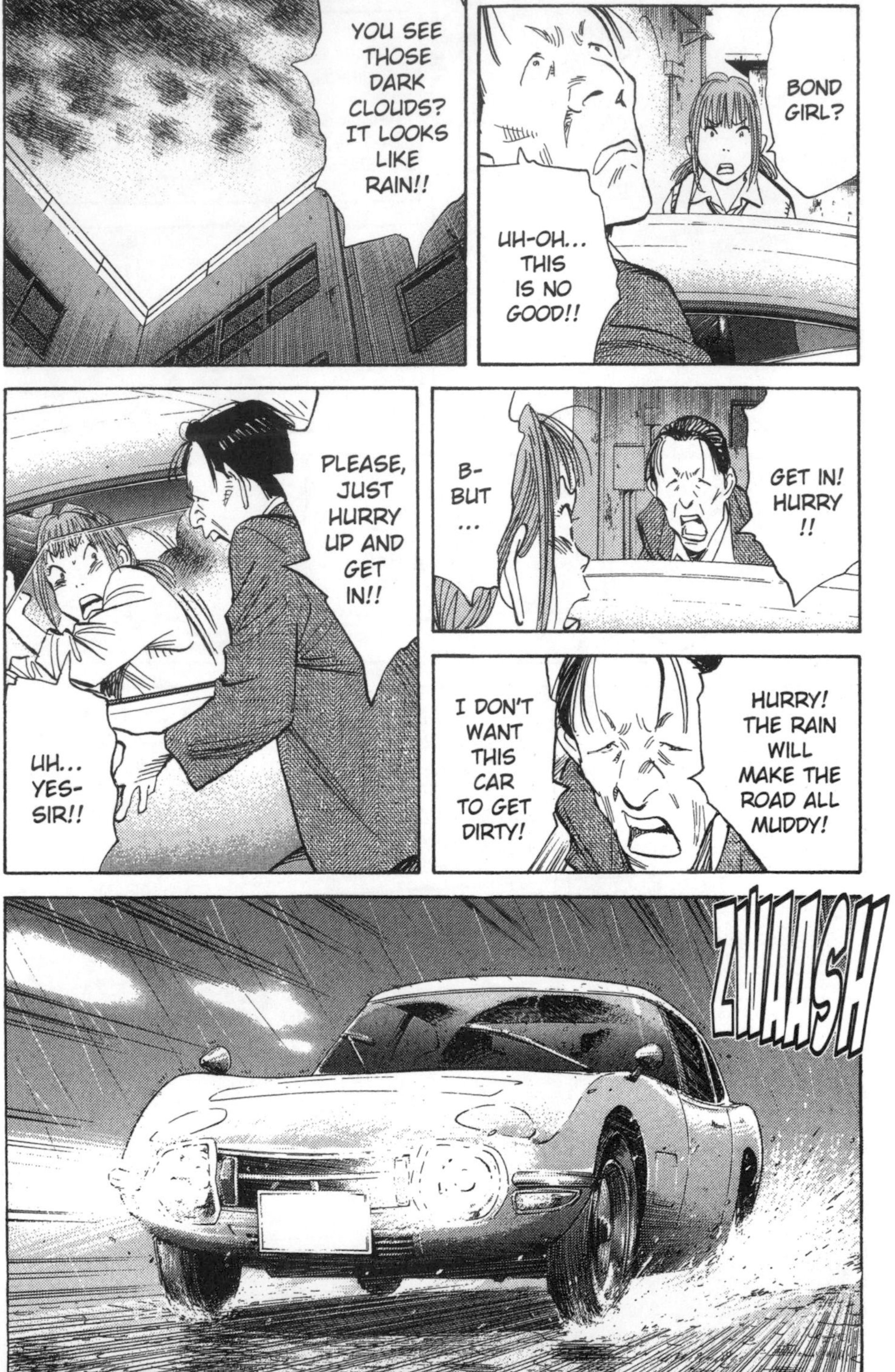
BOND GIRL?
UH-OH... THIS IS NO GOOD!!
YOU SEE THOSE DARK CLOUDS? IT LOOKS LIKE RAIN!!
GET IN! HURRY!!
B-BUT...
HURRY! THE RAIN WILL MAKE THE ROAD ALL MUDDY!
I DON'T WANT THIS CAR TO GET DIRTY!
PLEASE, JUST HURRY UP AND GET IN!!
UH... YES-SIR!!
ZWAASH

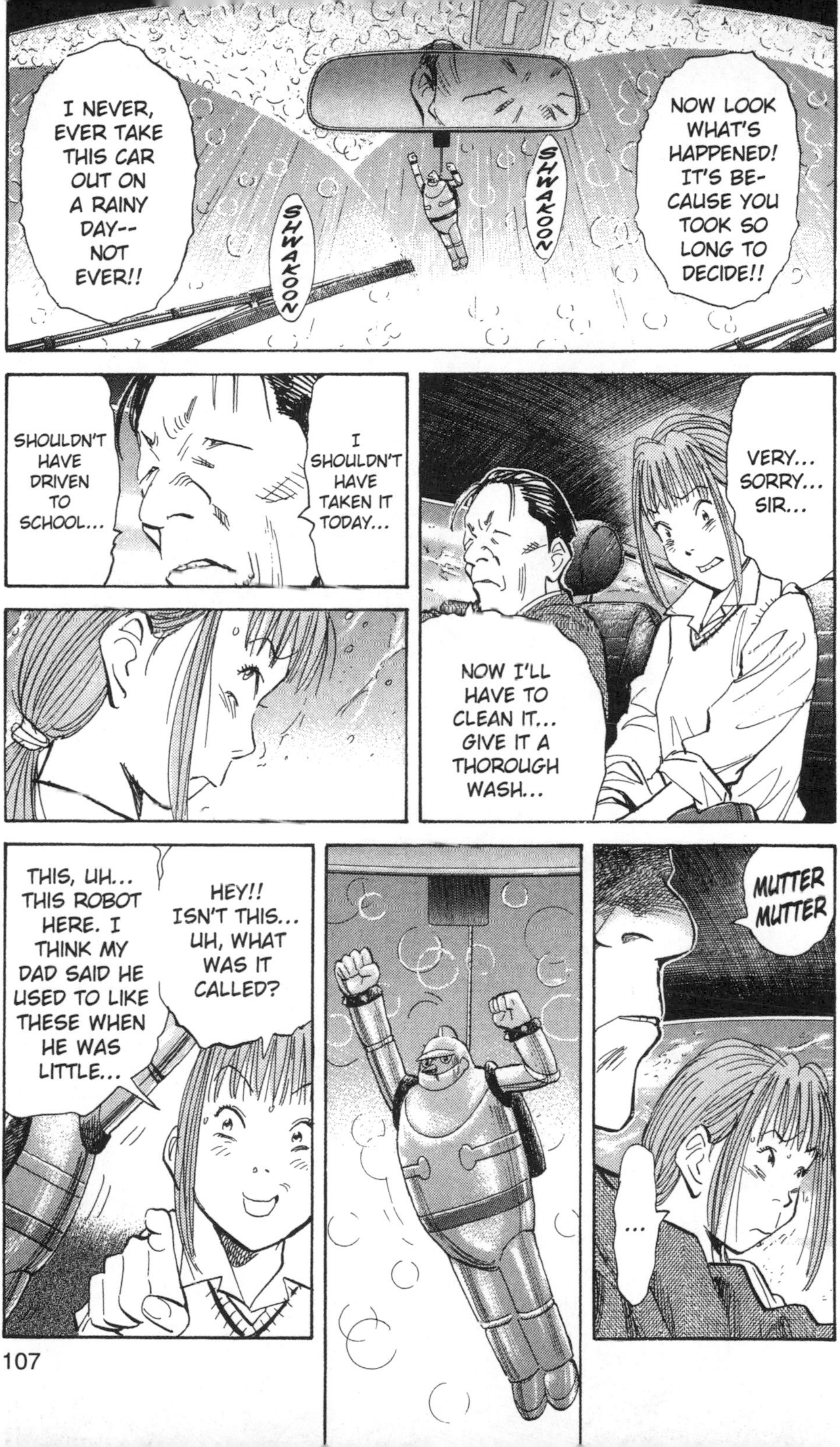
NOW LOOK WHAT'S HAPPENED! IT'S BE-CAUSE YOU TOOK SO LONG TO DECIDE!!
SHWAKOON
SHWAKOON
I NEVER, EVER TAKE THIS CAR OUT ON A RAINY DAY-- NOT EVER!!
VERY... SORRY... SIR...
NOW I'LL HAVE TO CLEAN IT... GIVE IT A THOROUGH WASH...
I SHOULDN'T HAVE TAKEN IT TODAY...
SHOULDN'T HAVE DRIVEN TO SCHOOL...
MUTTER MUTTER
...
HEY!! ISN'T THIS... UH, WHAT WAS IT CALLED?
THIS, UH... THIS ROBOT HERE. I THINK MY DAD SAID HE USED TO LIKE THESE WHEN HE WAS LITTLE...

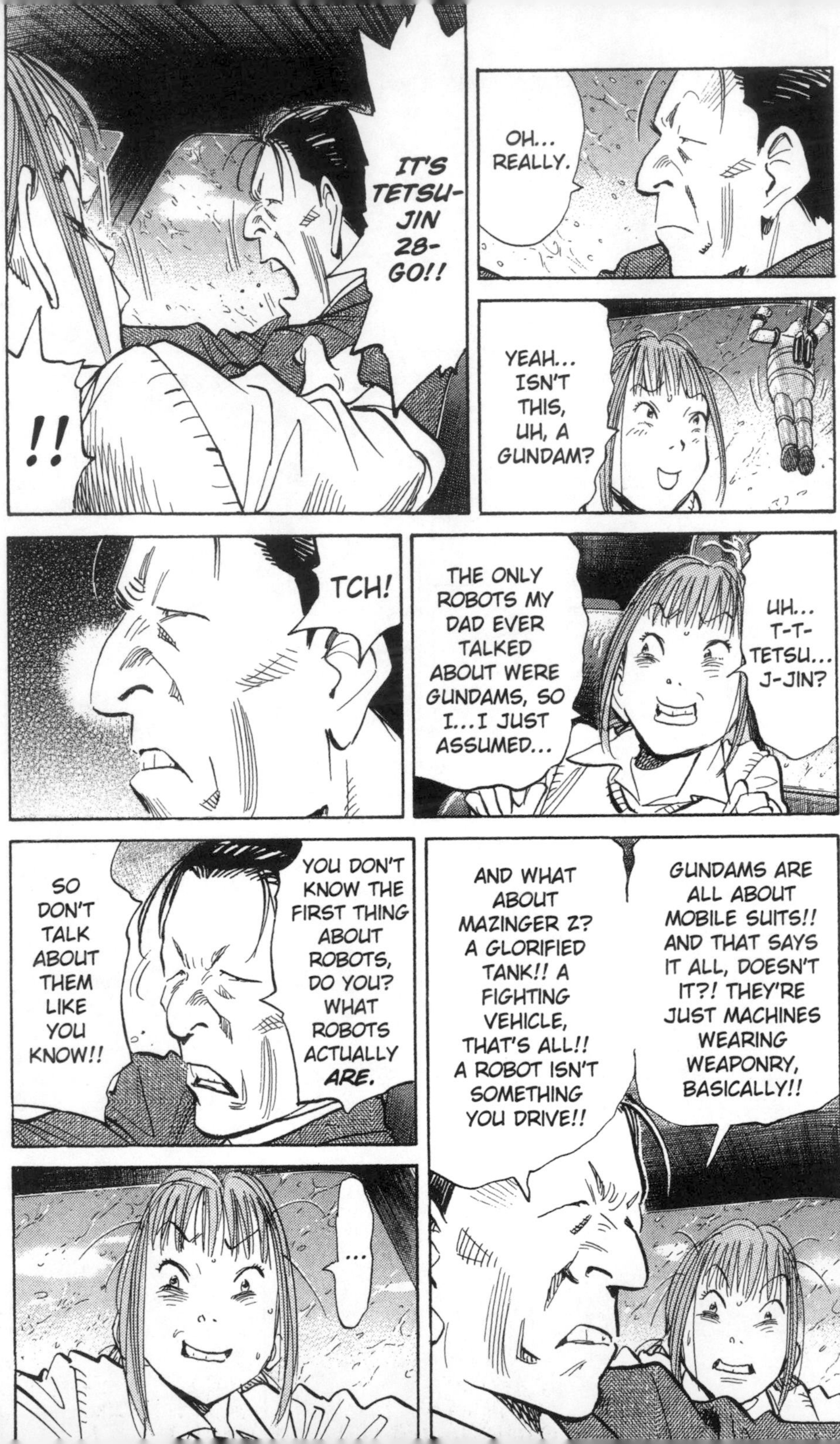
OH... REALLY.
YEAH... ISN'T THIS, UH, A GUNDAM?
IT'S TETSU-JIN 28-GO!!
!!
UH... T-T-TETSU... J-JIN?
THE ONLY ROBOTS MY DAD EVER TALKED ABOUT WERE GUNDAMS, SO I...I JUST ASSUMED...
TCH!
GUNDAMS ARE ALL ABOUT MOBILE SUITS!! AND THAT SAYS IT ALL, DOESN'T IT?! THEY'RE JUST MACHINES WEARING WEAPONRY, BASICALLY!!
AND WHAT ABOUT MAZINGER Z? A GLORIFIED TANK!! A FIGHTING VEHICLE, THAT'S ALL!! A ROBOT ISN'T SOMETHING YOU DRIVE!!
YOU DON'T KNOW THE FIRST THING ABOUT ROBOTS, DO YOU? WHAT ROBOTS ACTUALLY ARE.
SO DON'T TALK ABOUT THEM LIKE YOU KNOW!!
...

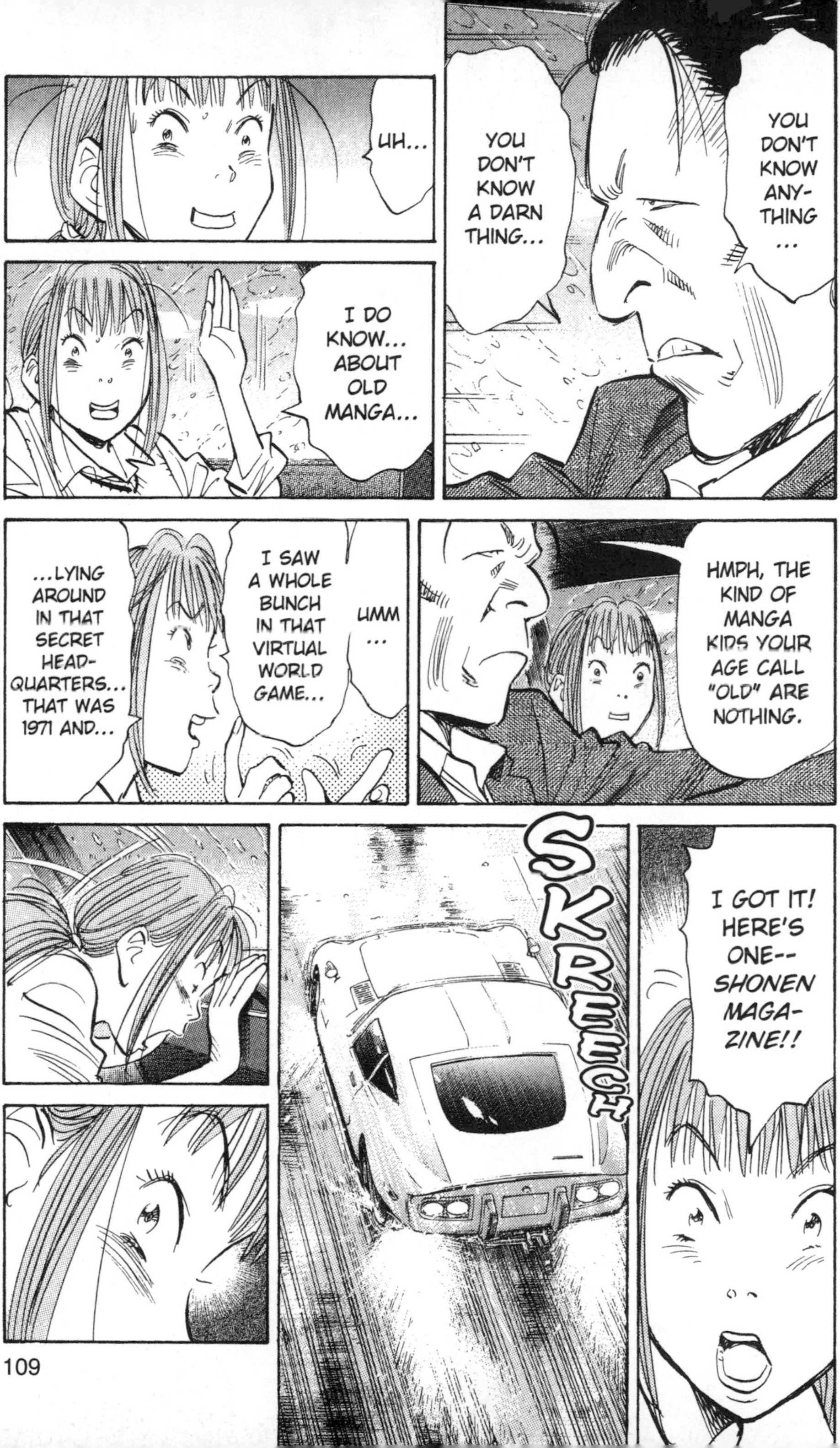
YOU DON'T KNOW ANYTHING...
YOU DON'T KNOW A DARN THING...
UH...
I DO KNOW... ABOUT OLD MANGA...
HMPH, THE KIND OF MANGA KIDS YOUR AGE CALL "OLD" ARE NOTHING.
UMM...
I SAW A WHOLE BUNCH IN THAT VIRTUAL WORLD GAME...
...LYING AROUND IN THAT SECRET HEADQUARTERS... THAT WAS 1971 AND...
I GOT IT! HERE'S ONE--SHONEN MAGAZINE!!
SKREECH

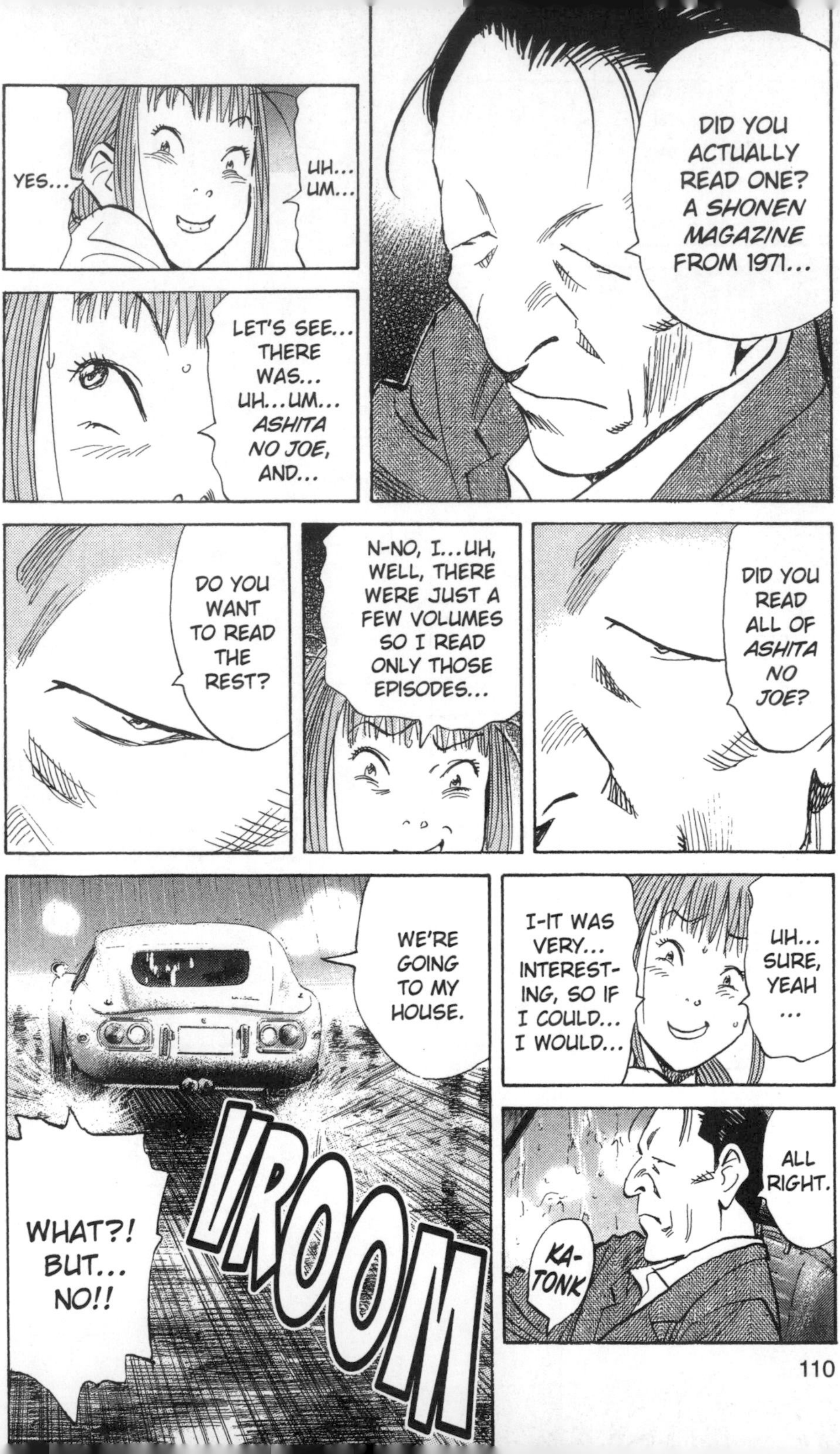

DID YOU ACTUALLY READ ONE? A *SHONEN MAGAZINE* FROM 1971...
UH... UM...
YES...
LET'S SEE... THERE WAS... UH...UM... *ASHITA NO JOE*, AND...
DID YOU READ ALL OF *ASHITA NO JOE*?
N-NO, I...UH, WELL, THERE WERE JUST A FEW VOLUMES SO I READ ONLY THOSE EPISODES...
DO YOU WANT TO READ THE REST?
UH... SURE, YEAH ...
I-IT WAS VERY... INTEREST-ING, SO IF I COULD... I WOULD...
ALL RIGHT.
KA-TONK
WE'RE GOING TO MY HOUSE.
VROOM
WHAT?! BUT... NO!!

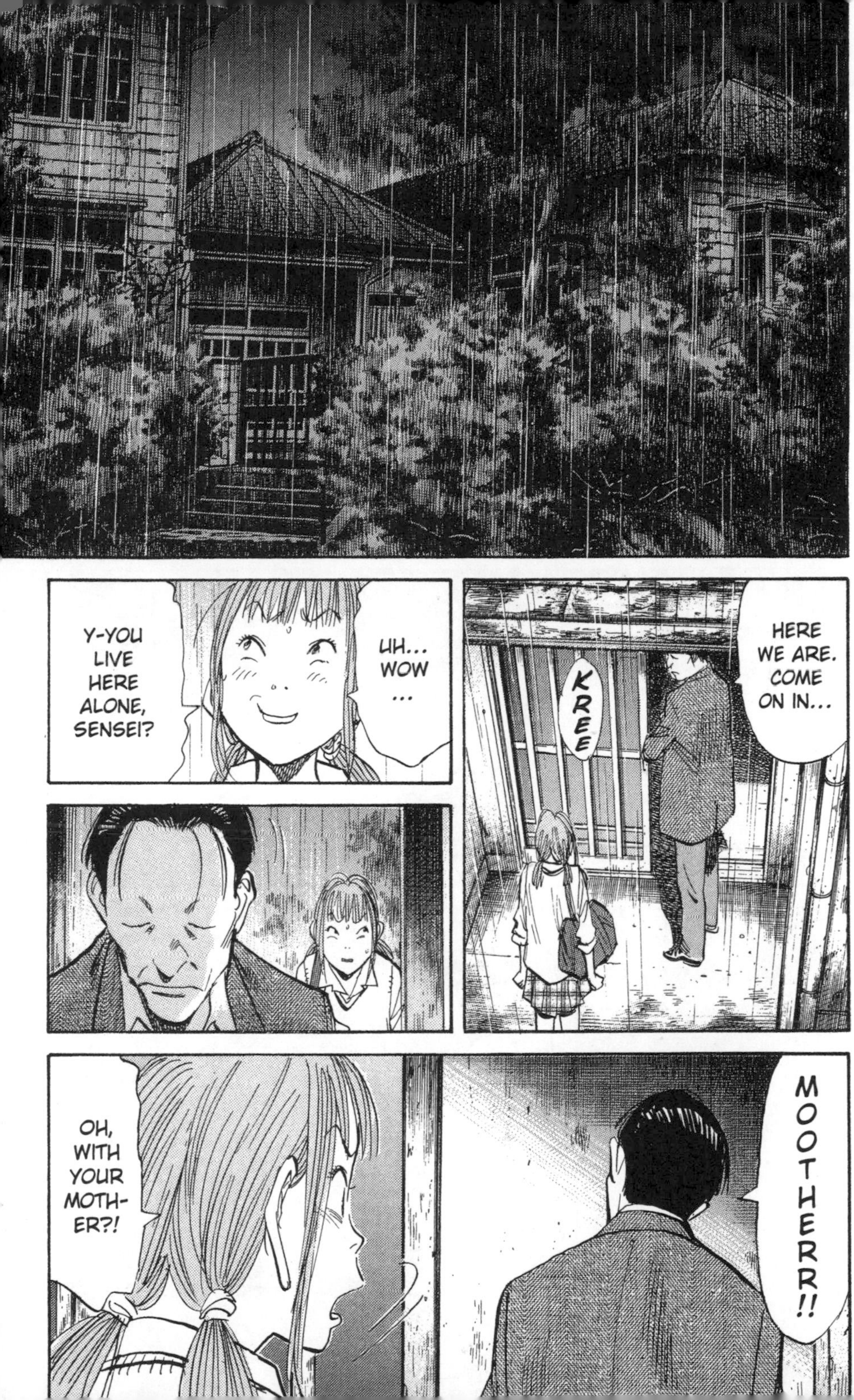
HERE WE ARE. COME ON IN...
KREE
UH... WOW ...
Y-YOU LIVE HERE ALONE, SENSEI?
MOOTHERR!!
OH, WITH YOUR MOTH-ER?!

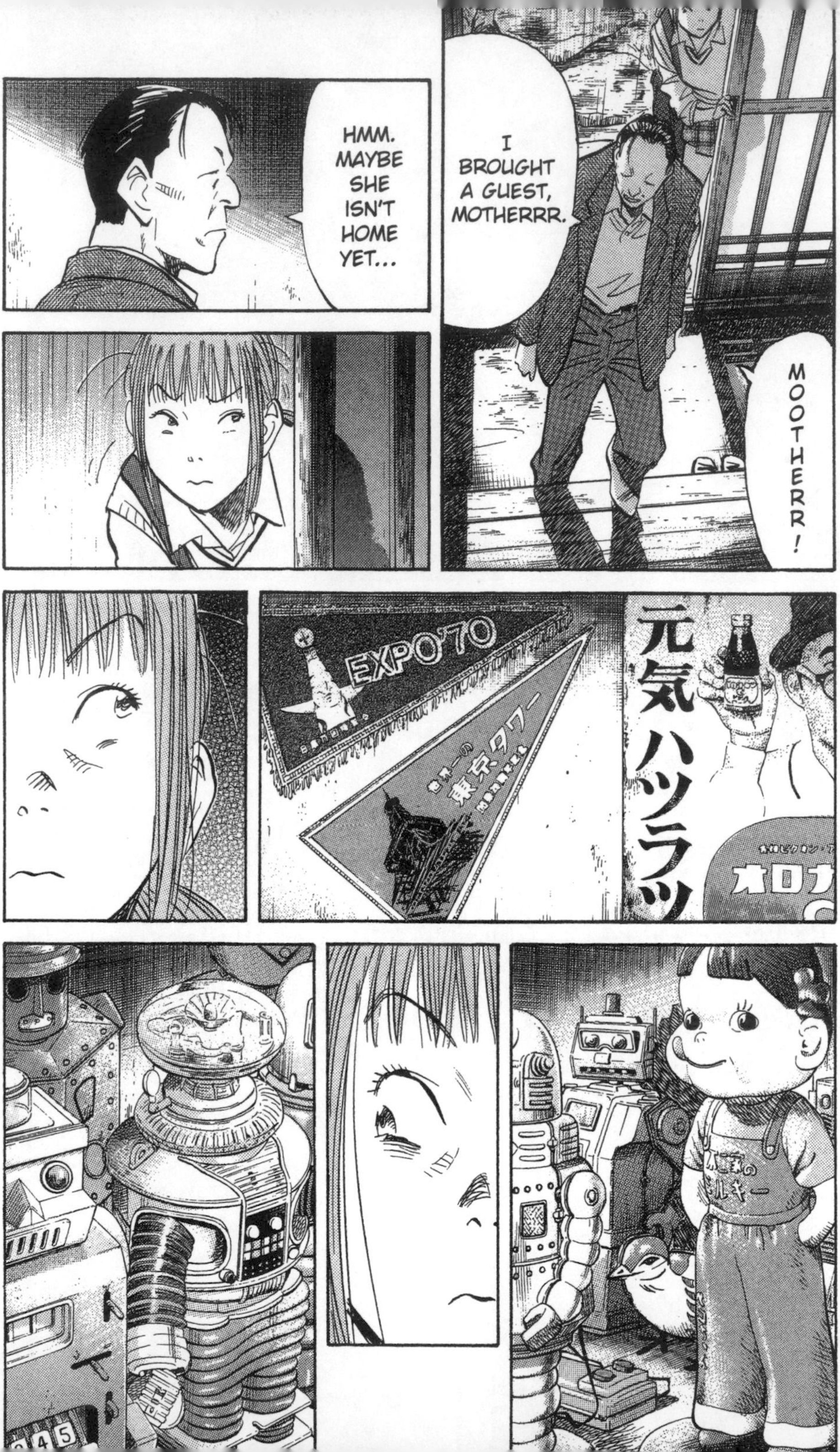
I BROUGHT A GUEST, MOTHERRR.
MOOTHERR!
HMM. MAYBE SHE ISN'T HOME YET...
元気ハツラツ
オロナ
EXPO'70
東京タワー

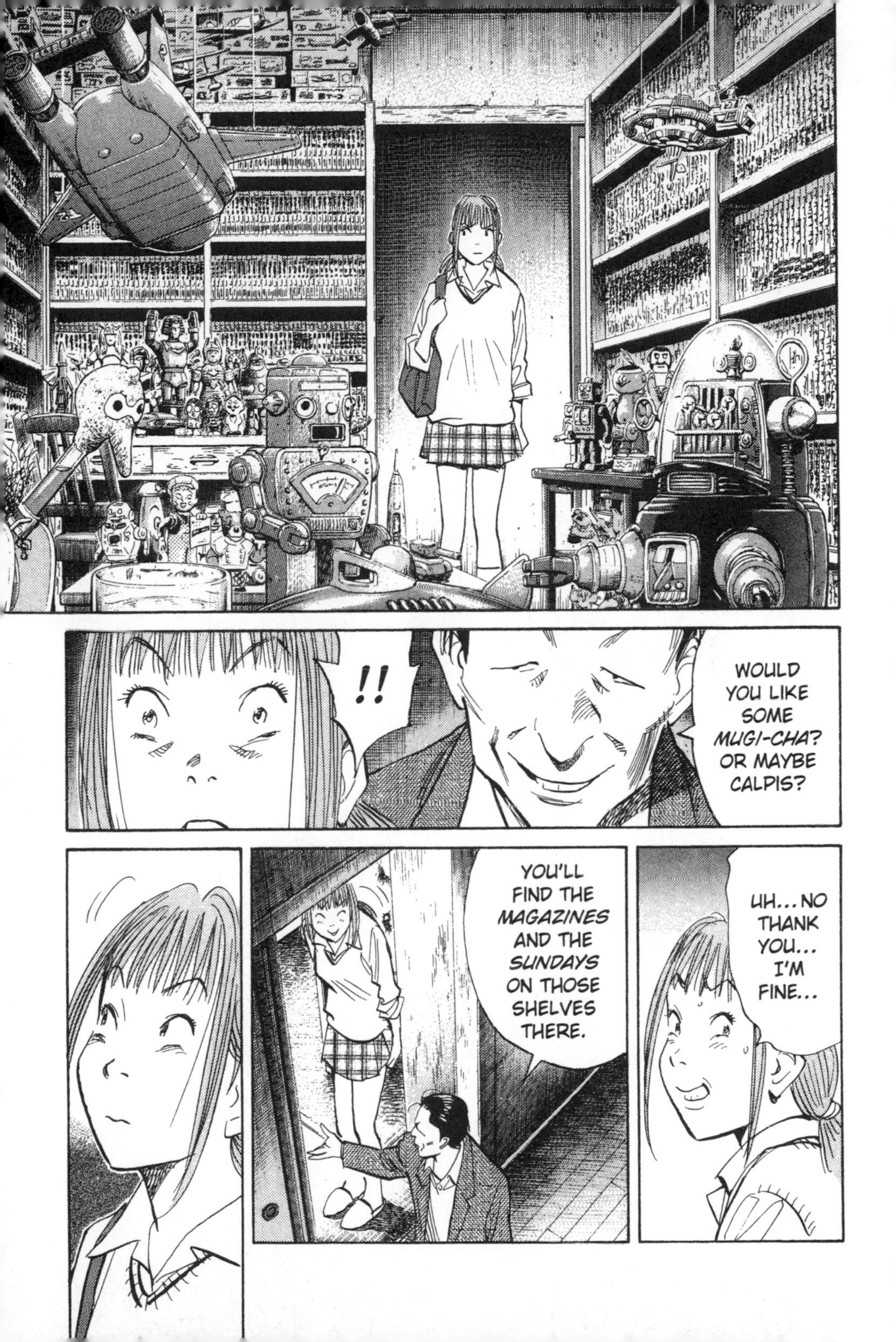

WOULD YOU LIKE SOME *MUGI-CHA*? OR MAYBE CALPIS?
!!
UH... NO THANK YOU... I'M FINE...
YOU'LL FIND THE *MAGAZINES* AND THE *SUNDAYS* ON THOSE SHELVES THERE.

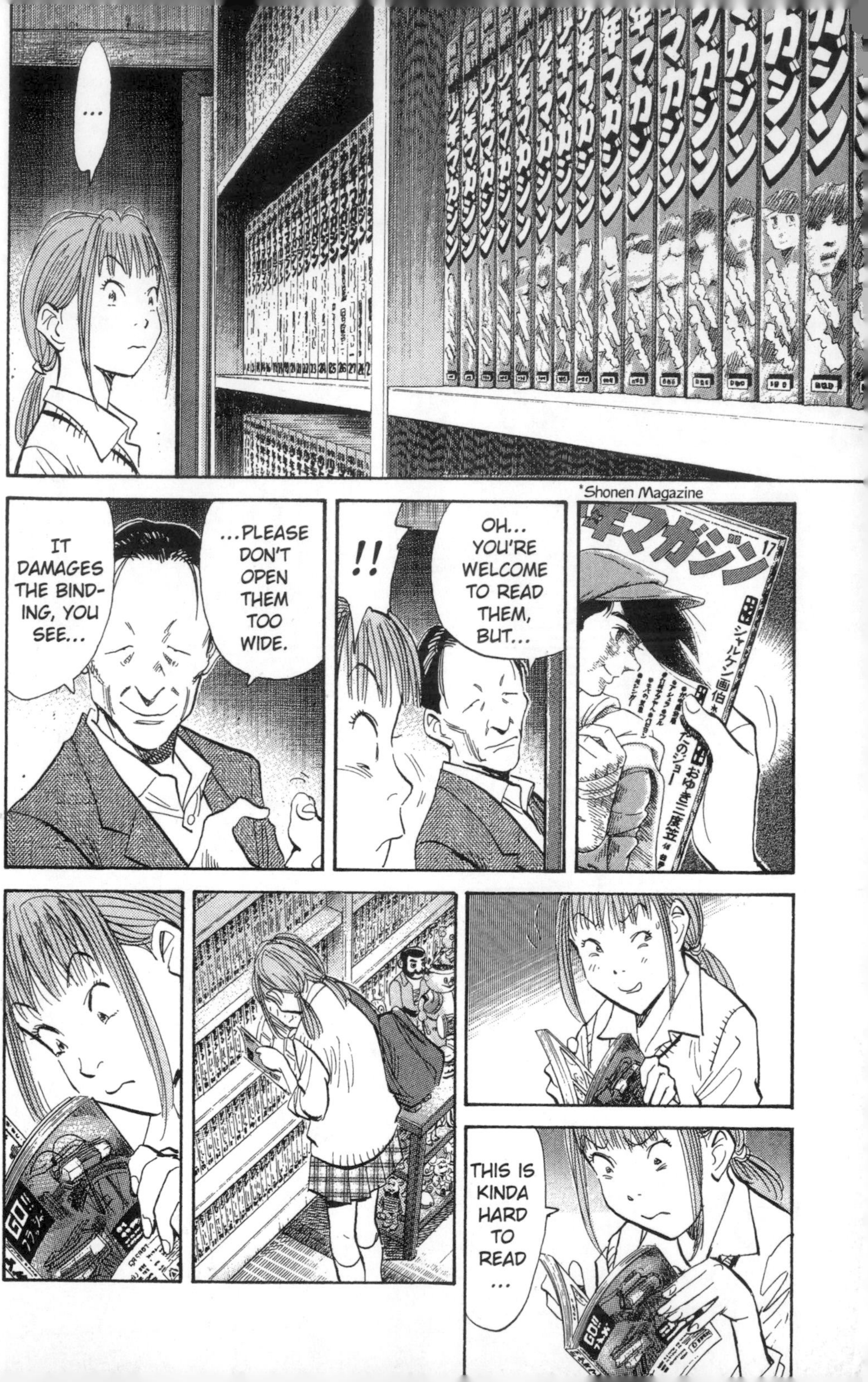
…
ガジン
*Shonen Magazine
年マガジン
17
シャルケン画伯
おゆき三度笠
たのジョー
OH… YOU'RE WELCOME TO READ THEM, BUT…
!!
…PLEASE DON'T OPEN THEM TOO WIDE.
IT DAMAGES THE BIND-ING, YOU SEE…
THIS IS KINDA HARD TO READ …
GO!!

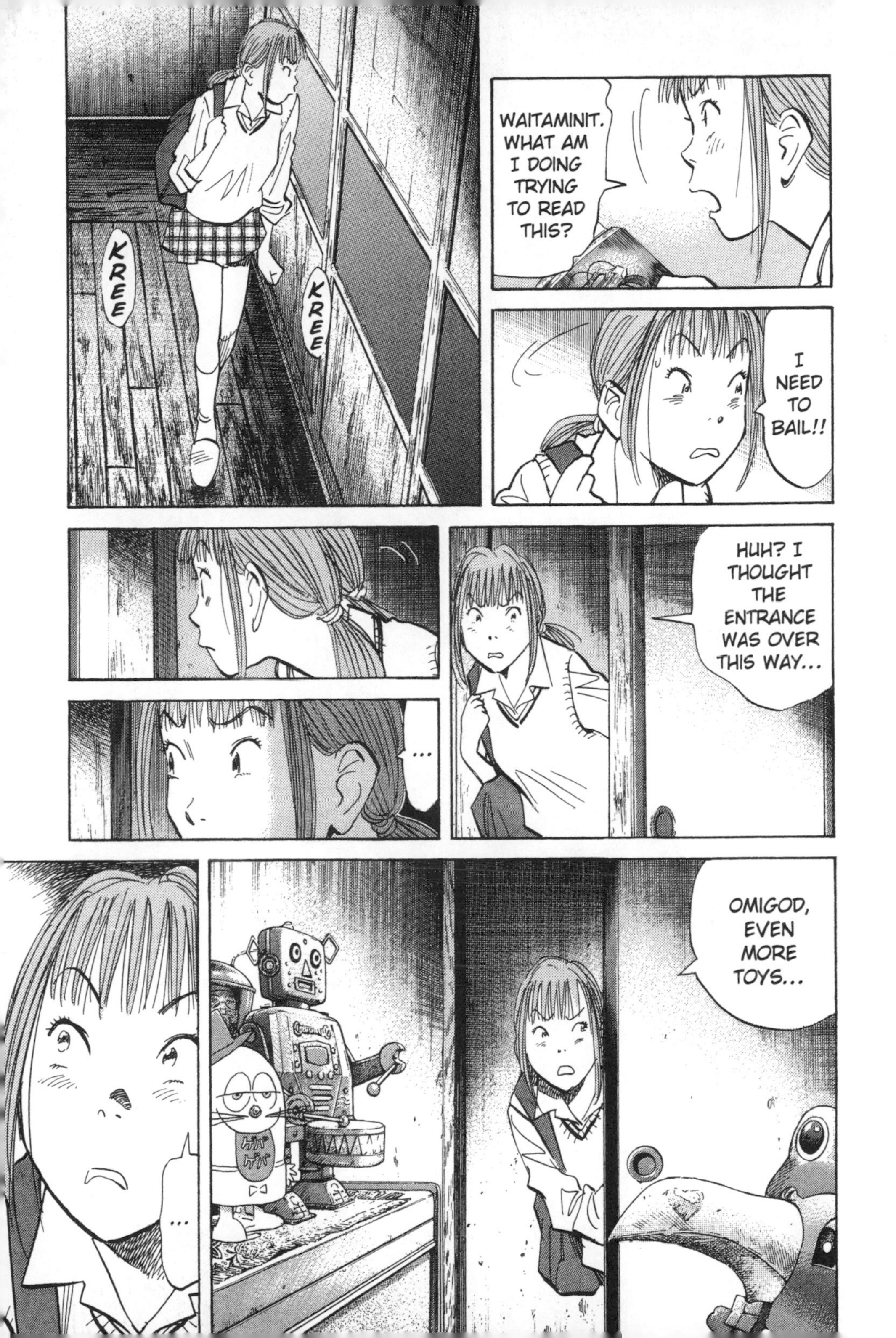
WAITAMINIT. WHAT AM I DOING TRYING TO READ THIS?
I NEED TO BAIL!!
KREE
KREE
HUH? I THOUGHT THE ENTRANCE WAS OVER THIS WAY...
...
OMIGOD, EVEN MORE TOYS...
...

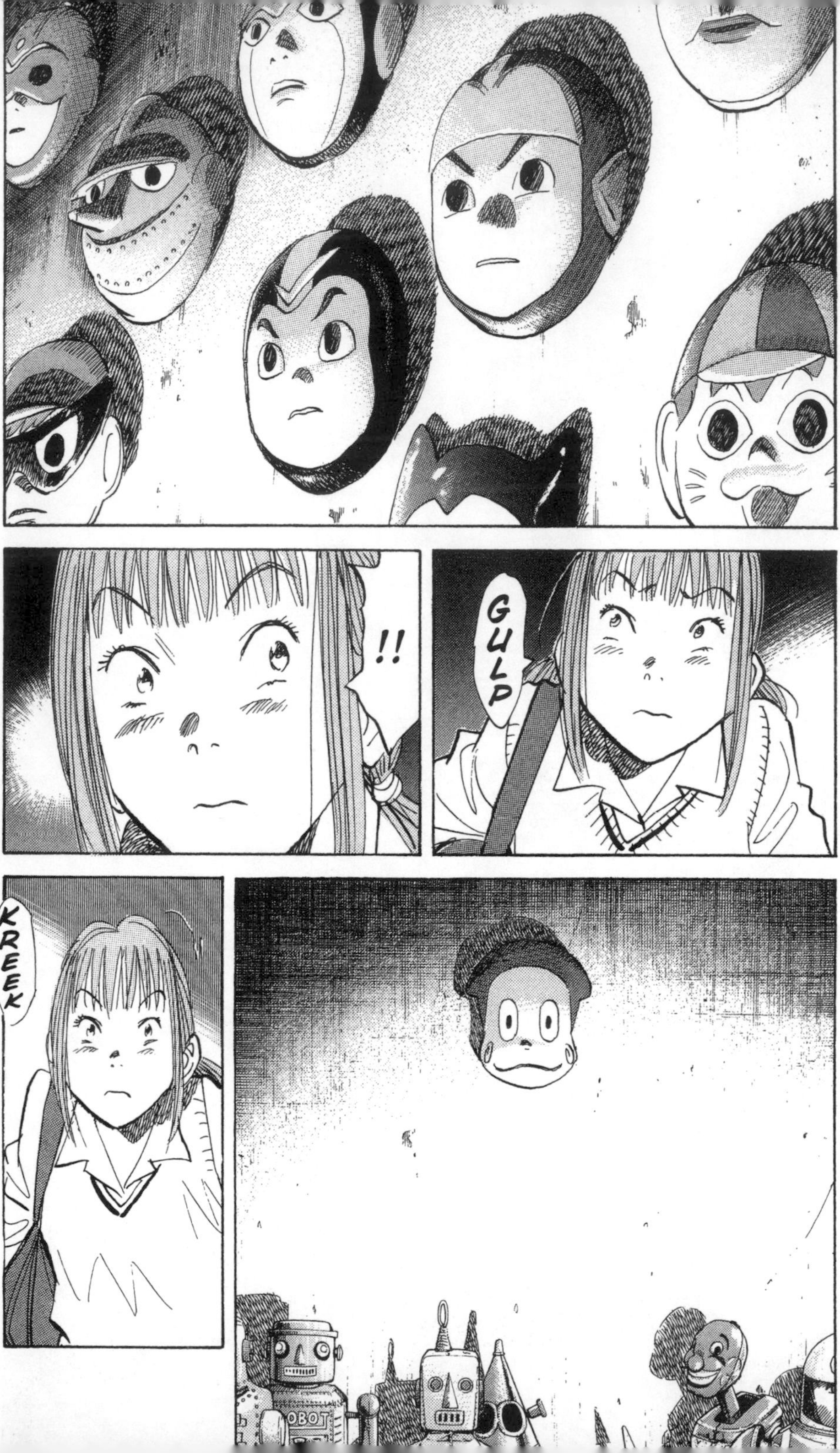
!!
GULP
KREEK

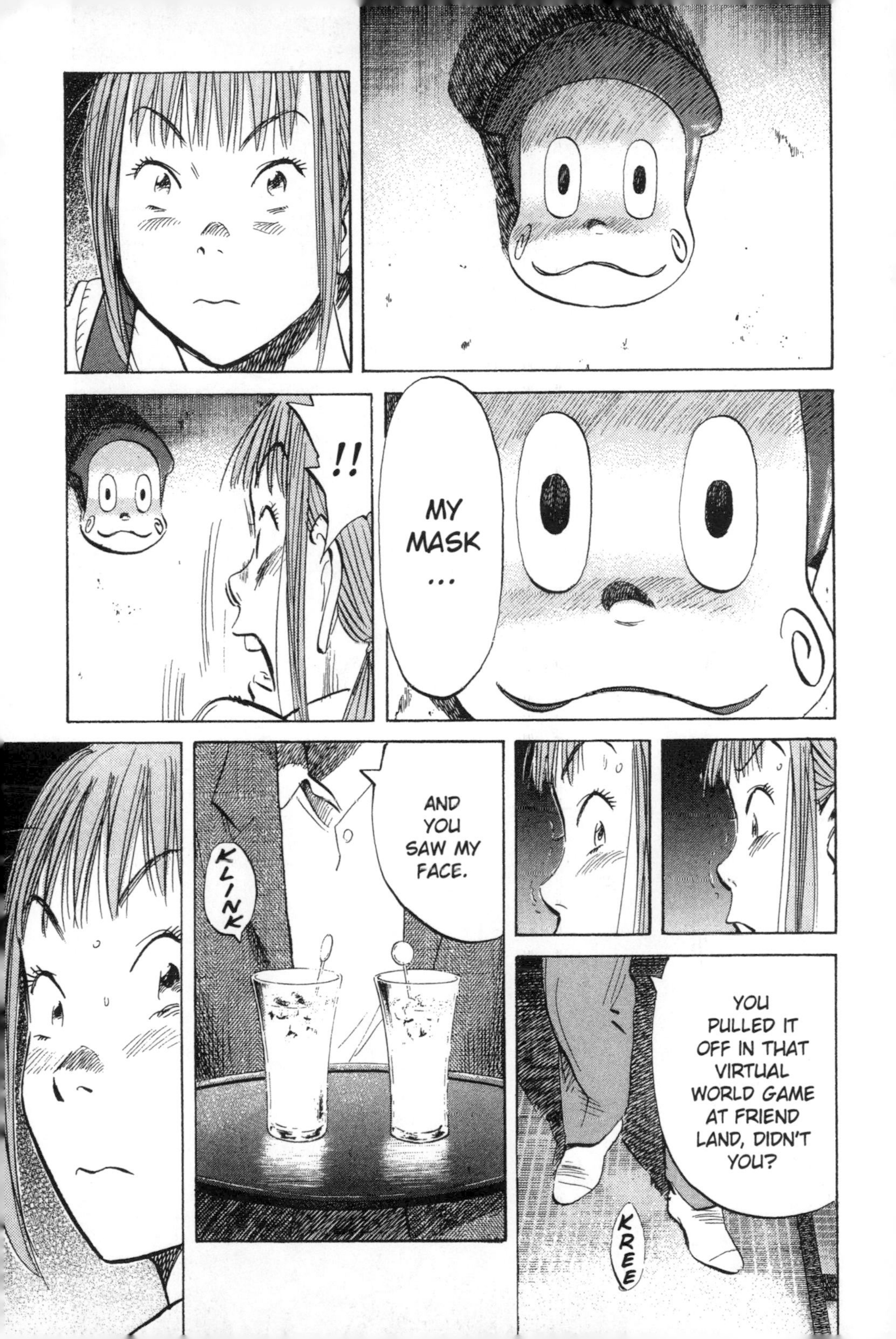
MY MASK ...
!!
YOU PULLED IT OFF IN THAT VIRTUAL WORLD GAME AT FRIEND LAND, DIDN'T YOU?
KREE
AND YOU SAW MY FACE.
KLINK

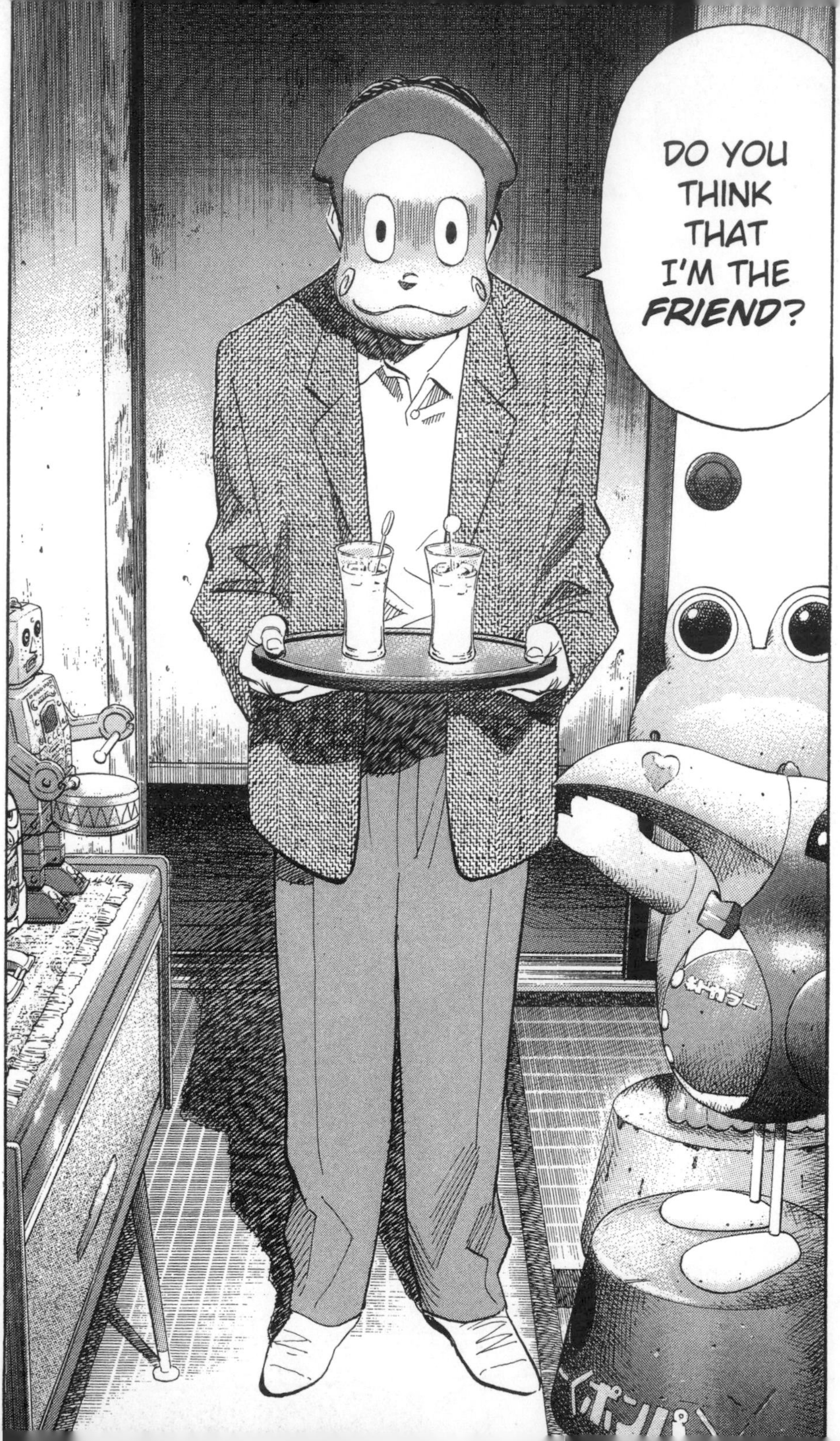
DO YOU THINK THAT I'M THE *FRIEND*?

Chapter 7 Hearing Voices

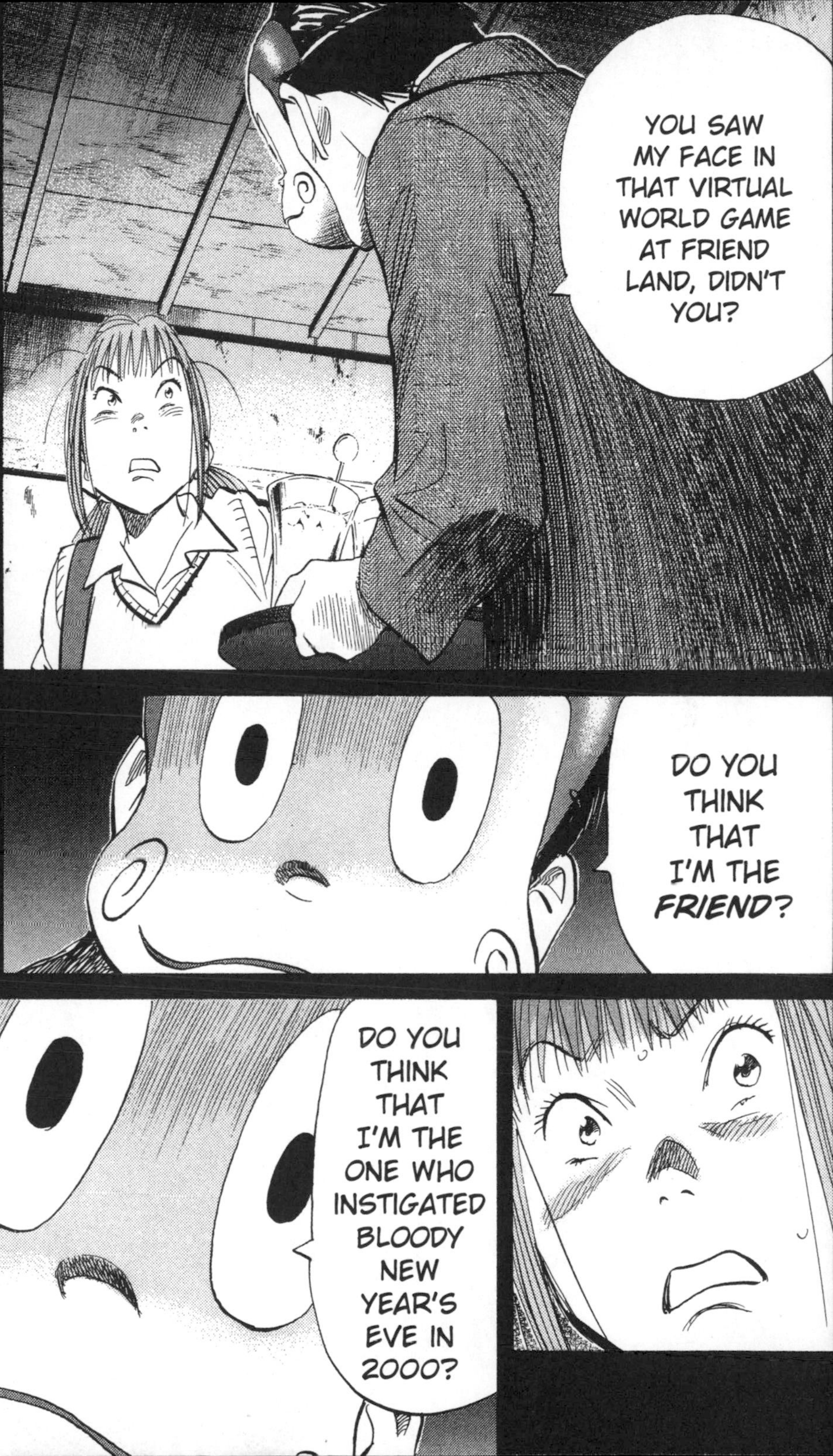
YOU SAW MY FACE IN THAT VIRTUAL WORLD GAME AT FRIEND LAND, DIDN'T YOU?
DO YOU THINK THAT I'M THE *FRIEND*?
DO YOU THINK THAT I'M THE ONE WHO INSTIGATED BLOODY NEW YEAR'S EVE IN 2000?

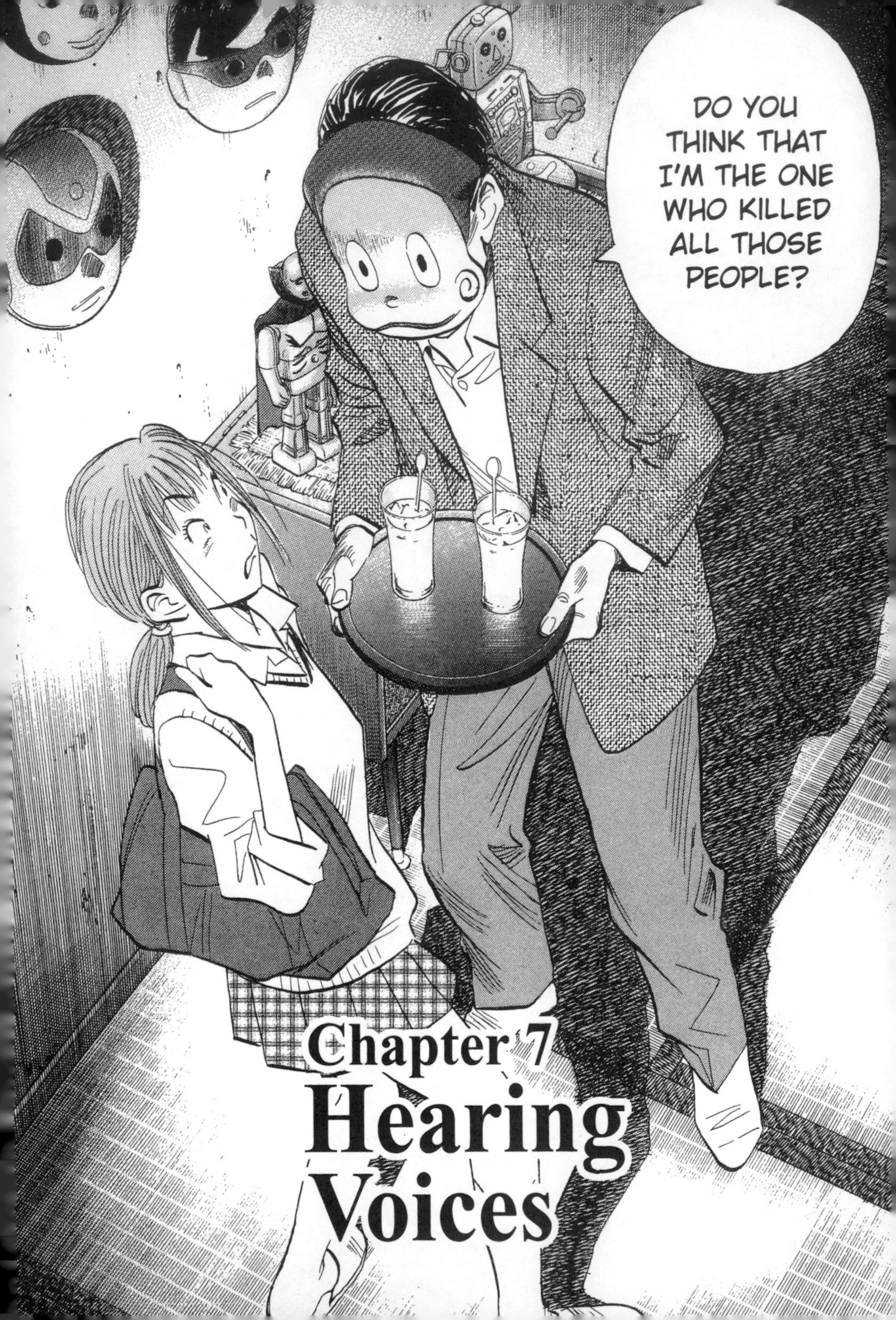
DO YOU THINK THAT I'M THE ONE WHO KILLED ALL THOSE PEOPLE?
Chapter 7
Hearing Voices

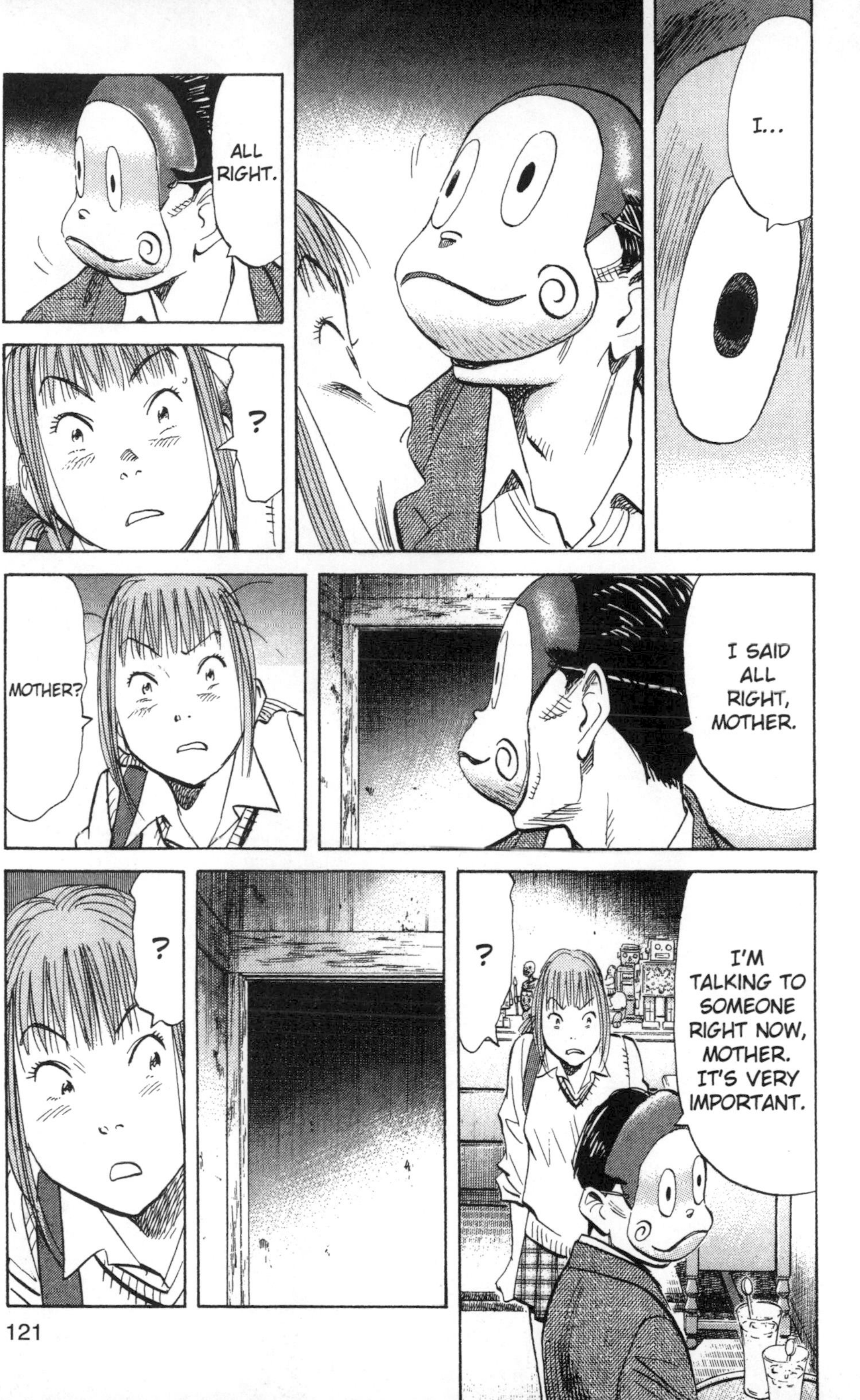
I...
ALL RIGHT.
?
I SAID ALL RIGHT, MOTHER.
MOTHER?
I'M TALKING TO SOMEONE RIGHT NOW, MOTHER. IT'S VERY IMPORTANT.
?
?

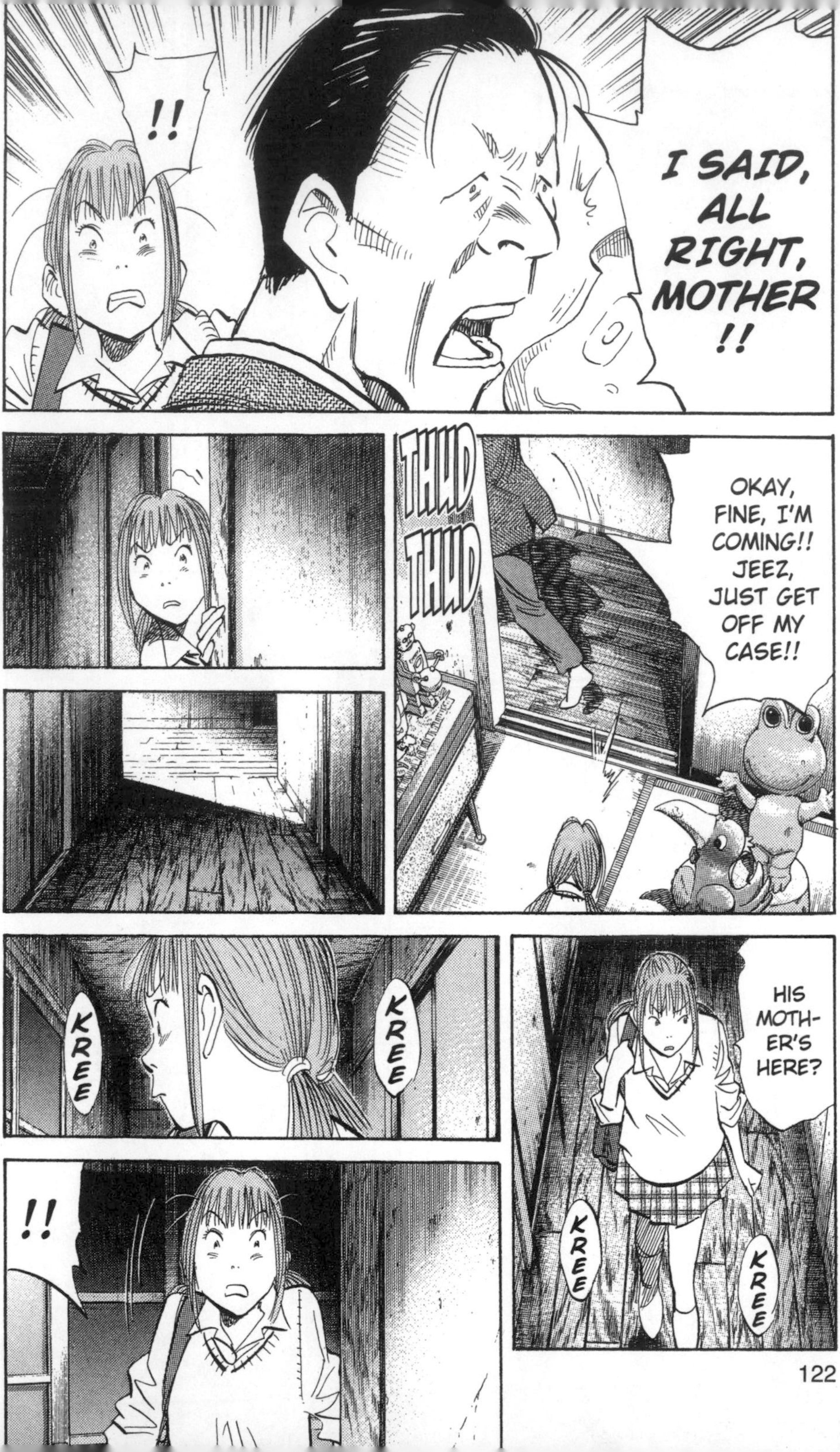
I SAID, ALL RIGHT, MOTHER!!
!!
THUD THUD
OKAY, FINE, I'M COMING!! JEEZ, JUST GET OFF MY CASE!!
HIS MOTHER'S HERE?
KREE
KREE
KREE
KREE
!!

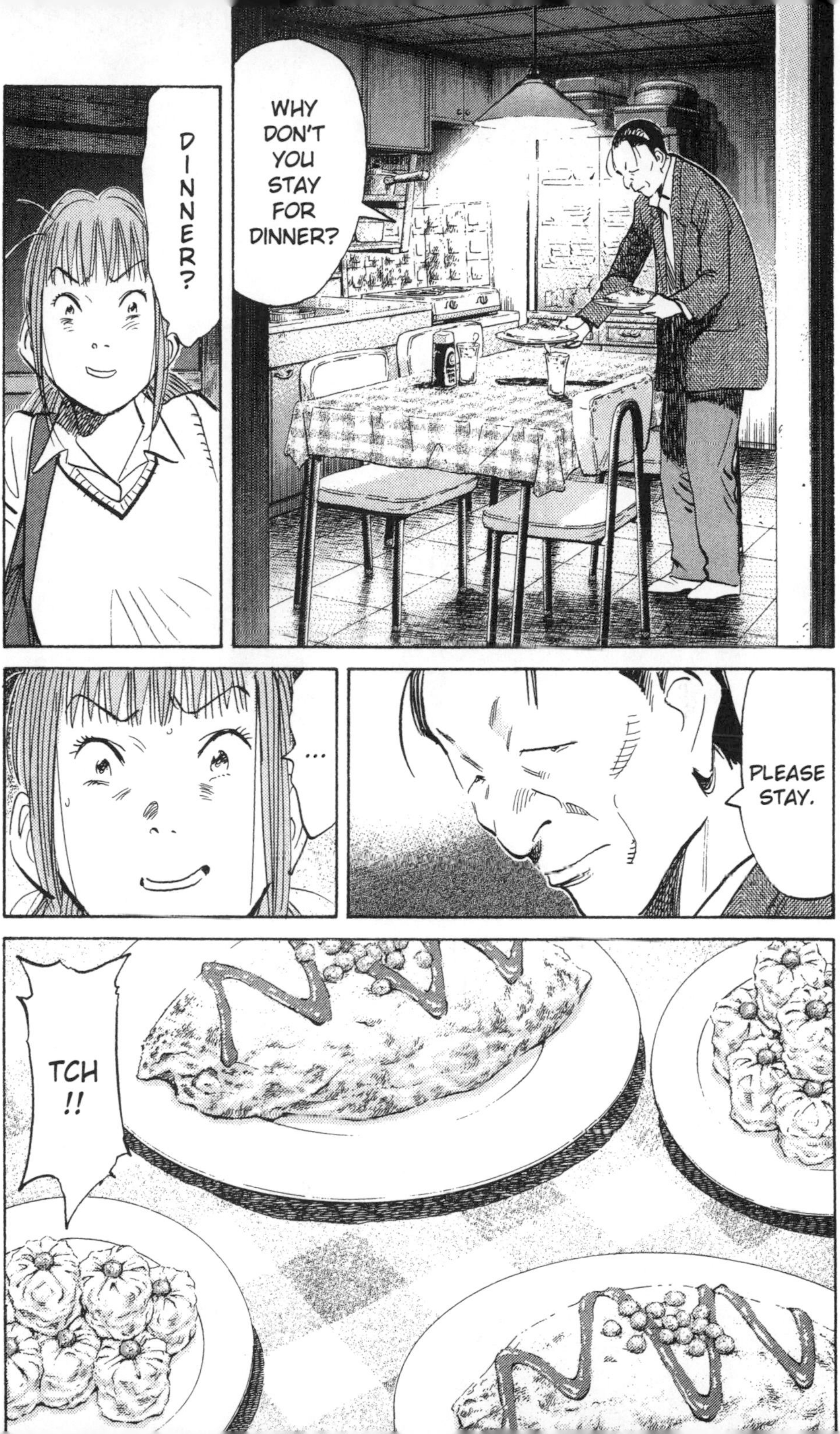

WHY DON'T YOU STAY FOR DINNER?
DINNER?
PLEASE STAY.
...
TCH !!

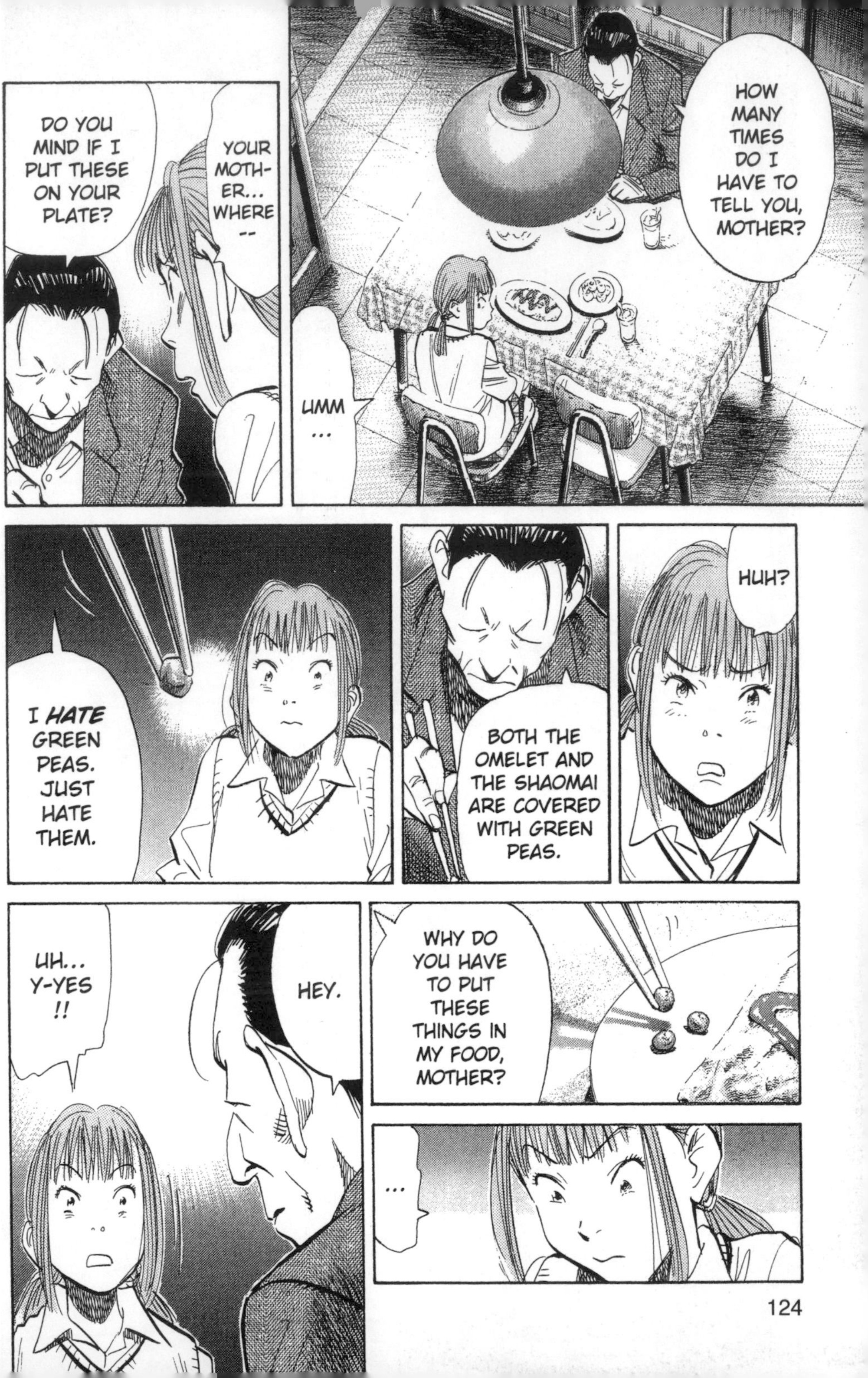
DO YOU MIND IF I PUT THESE ON YOUR PLATE?
YOUR MOTH-ER... WHERE --
UMM ...
HOW MANY TIMES DO I HAVE TO TELL YOU, MOTHER?
I *HATE* GREEN PEAS. JUST HATE THEM.
BOTH THE OMELET AND THE SHAOMAI ARE COVERED WITH GREEN PEAS.
HUH?
UH... Y-YES !!
HEY.
WHY DO YOU HAVE TO PUT THESE THINGS IN MY FOOD, MOTHER?
...

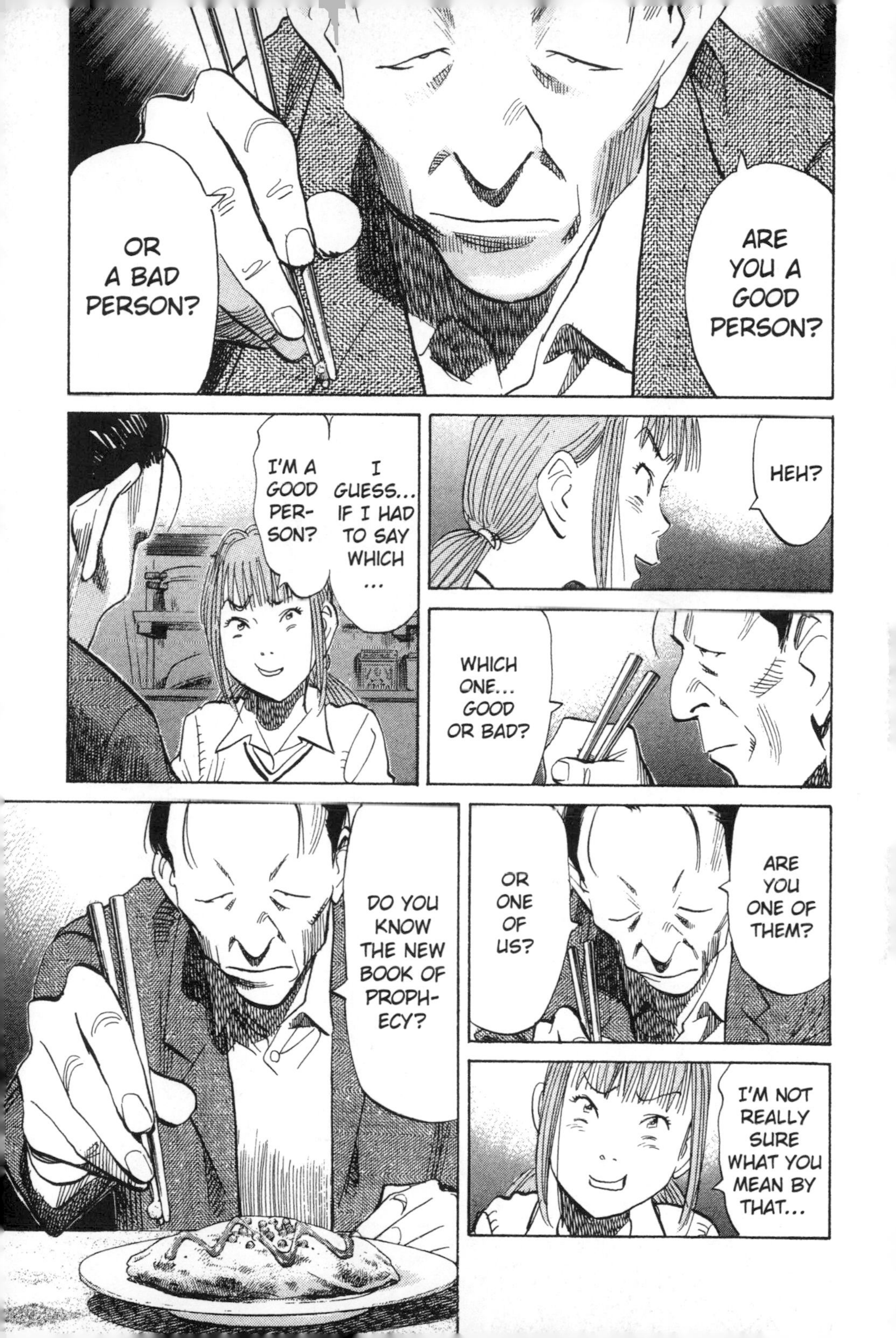
ARE YOU A GOOD PERSON?
OR A BAD PERSON?
HEH?
WHICH ONE... GOOD OR BAD?
I GUESS... IF I HAD TO SAY WHICH ...
I'M A GOOD PERSON?
ARE YOU ONE OF THEM?
OR ONE OF US?
I'M NOT REALLY SURE WHAT YOU MEAN BY THAT...
DO YOU KNOW THE NEW BOOK OF PROPHECY?

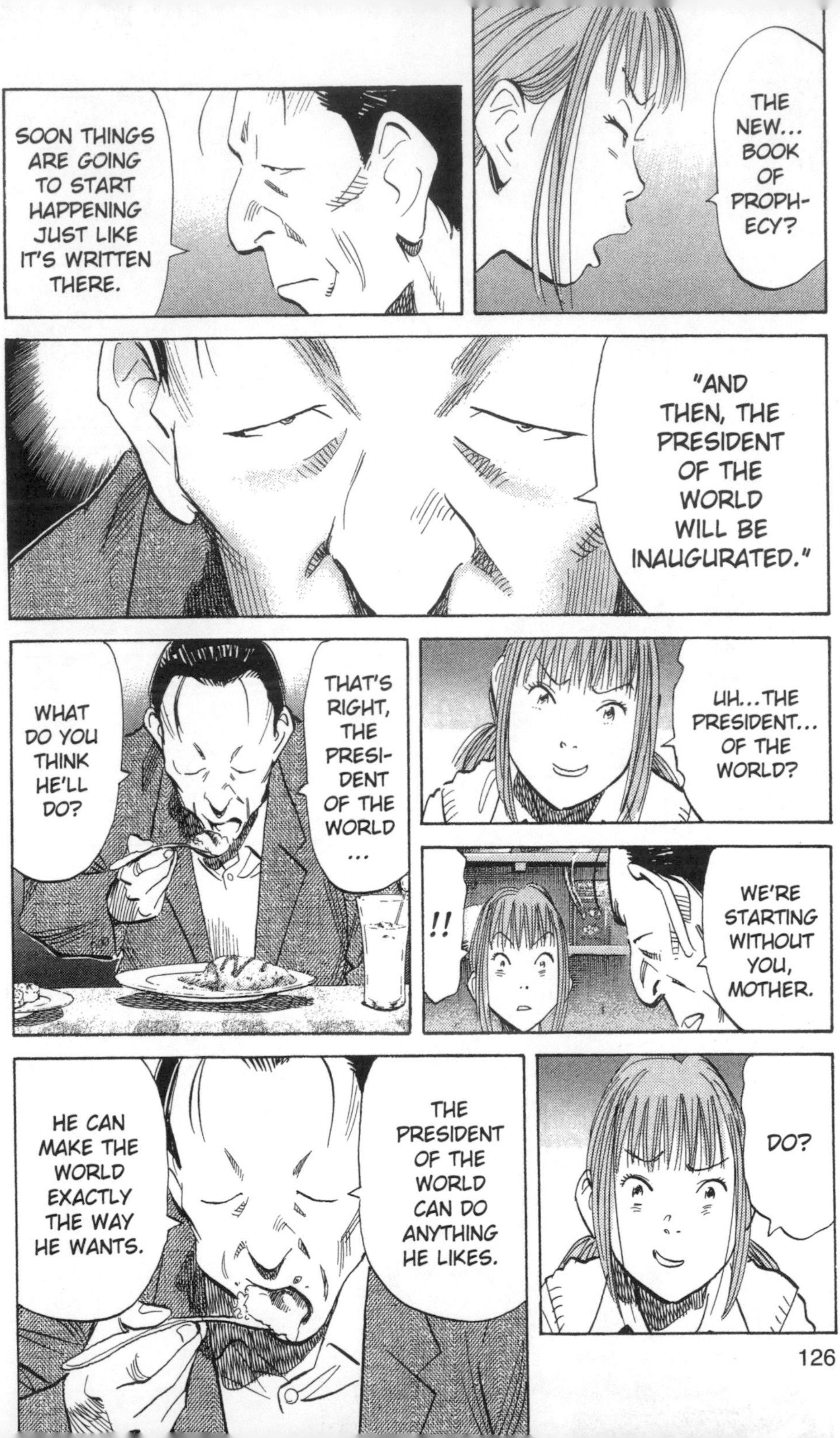

THE NEW... BOOK OF PROPHECY?
SOON THINGS ARE GOING TO START HAPPENING JUST LIKE IT'S WRITTEN THERE.
"AND THEN, THE PRESIDENT OF THE WORLD WILL BE INAUGURATED."
UH...THE PRESIDENT... OF THE WORLD?
WE'RE STARTING WITHOUT YOU, MOTHER.
!!
THAT'S RIGHT, THE PRESIDENT OF THE WORLD ...
WHAT DO YOU THINK HE'LL DO?
DO?
THE PRESIDENT OF THE WORLD CAN DO ANYTHING HE LIKES.
HE CAN MAKE THE WORLD EXACTLY THE WAY HE WANTS.

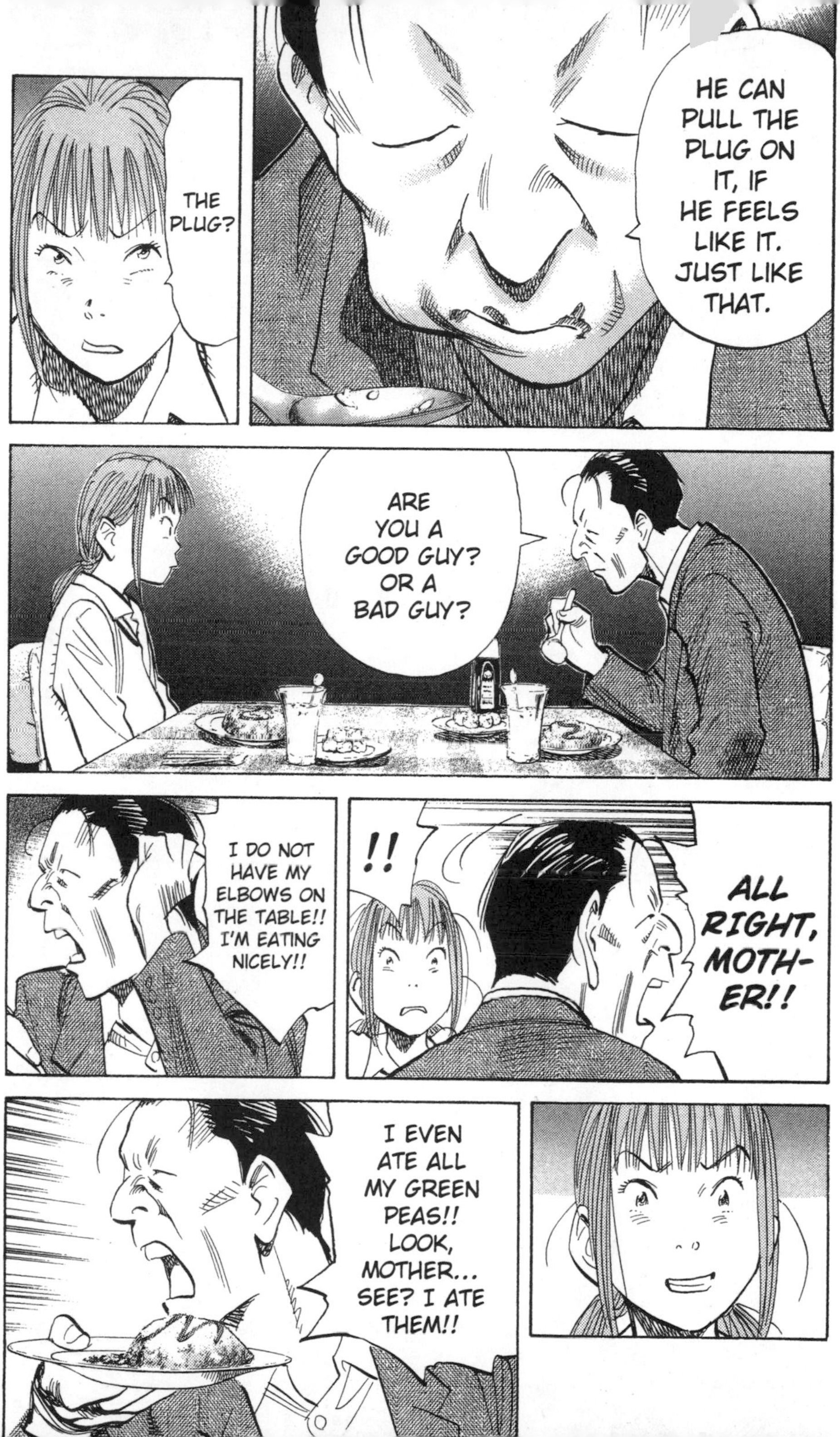
HE CAN PULL THE PLUG ON IT, IF HE FEELS LIKE IT. JUST LIKE THAT.
THE PLUG?
ARE YOU A GOOD GUY? OR A BAD GUY?
ALL RIGHT, MOTH-ER!!
!!
I DO NOT HAVE MY ELBOWS ON THE TABLE!! I'M EATING NICELY!!
I EVEN ATE ALL MY GREEN PEAS!! LOOK, MOTHER... SEE? I ATE THEM!!

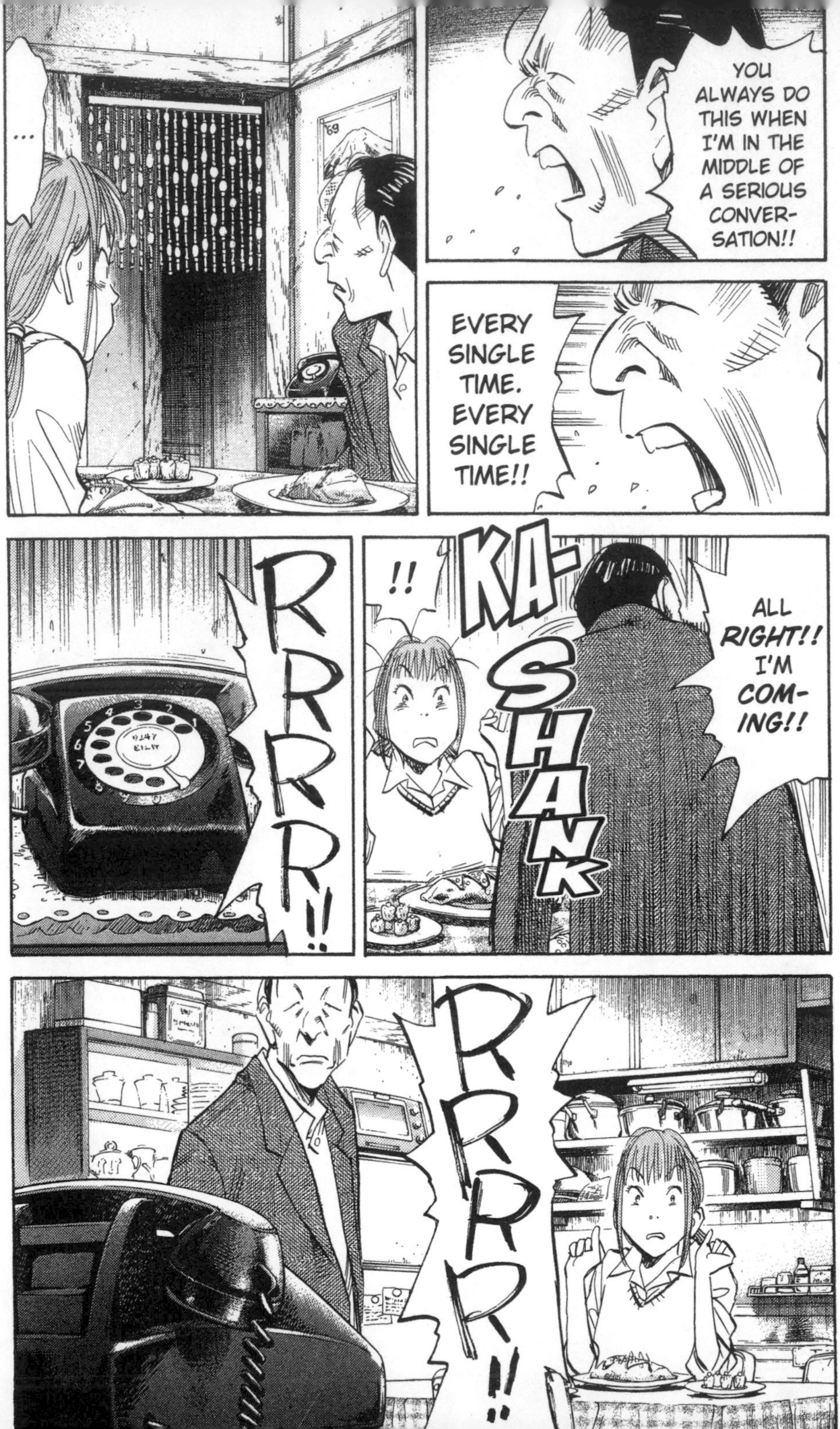
YOU ALWAYS DO THIS WHEN I'M IN THE MIDDLE OF A SERIOUS CONVER-SATION!!
EVERY SINGLE TIME. EVERY SINGLE TIME!!
...
KA-SHANK
!!
ALL RIGHT!! I'M COM-ING!!
RRRRR!!
RRRRR!!

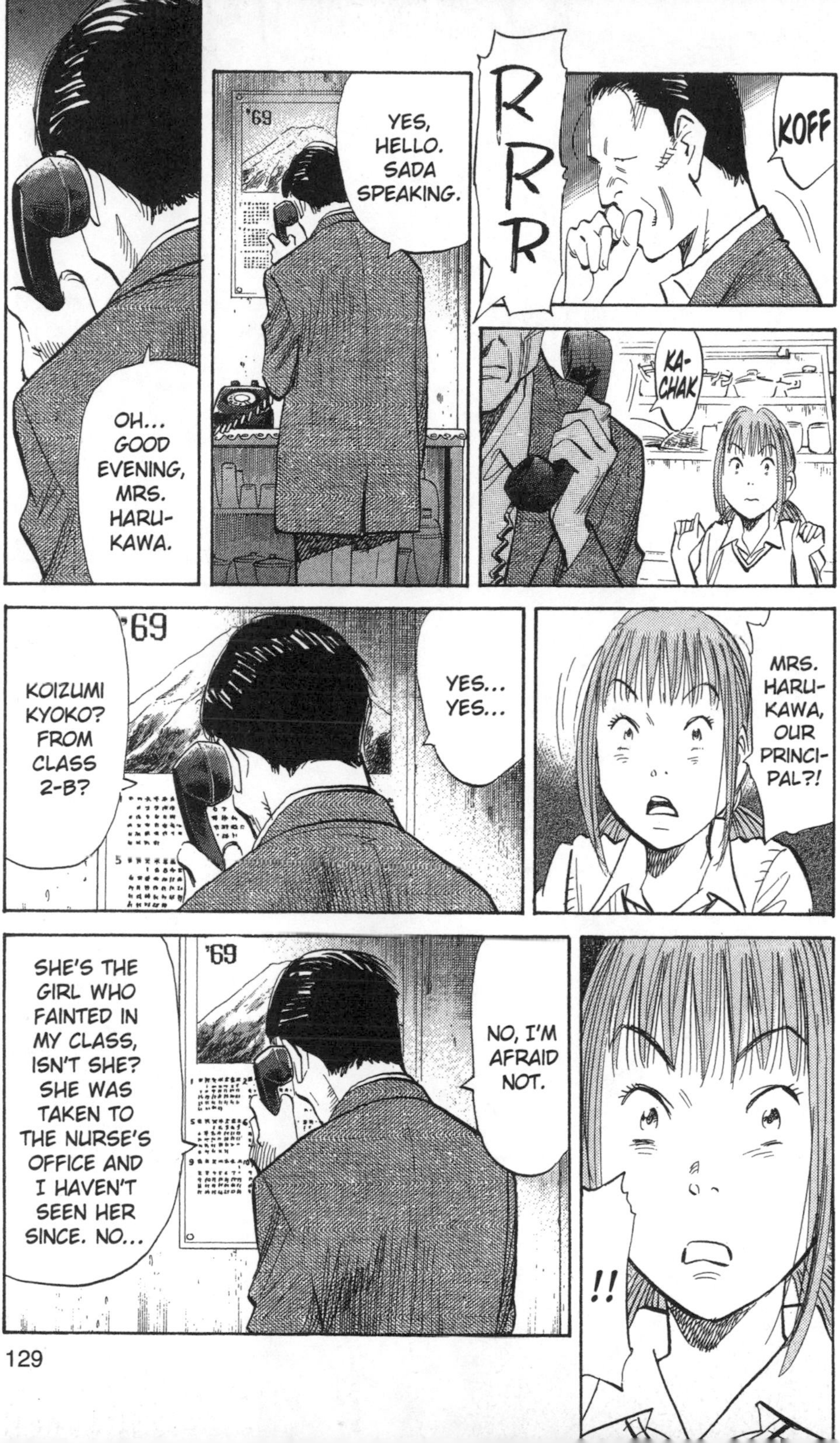
RRR
KOFF
KA-CHAK
YES, HELLO. SADA SPEAKING.
OH... GOOD EVENING, MRS. HARUKAWA.
MRS. HARUKAWA, OUR PRINCIPAL?!
YES... YES...
KOIZUMI KYOKO? FROM CLASS 2-B?
!!
NO, I'M AFRAID NOT.
SHE'S THE GIRL WHO FAINTED IN MY CLASS, ISN'T SHE? SHE WAS TAKEN TO THE NURSE'S OFFICE AND I HAVEN'T SEEN HER SINCE. NO...

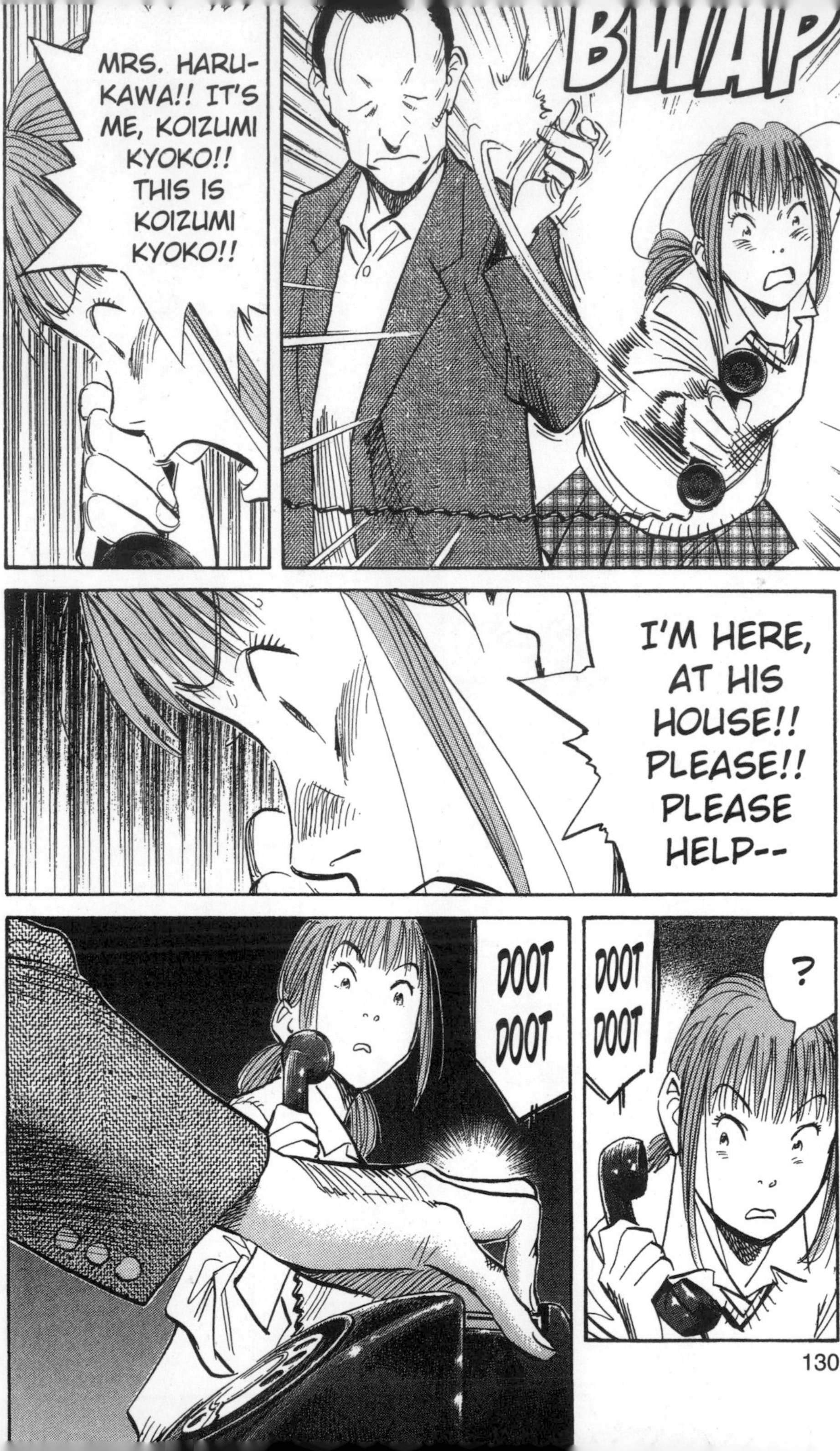
BWAP
MRS. HARUKAWA!! IT'S ME, KOIZUMI KYOKO!! THIS IS KOIZUMI KYOKO!!
I'M HERE, AT HIS HOUSE!! PLEASE!! PLEASE HELP--
DOOT DOOT
?
DOOT DOOT

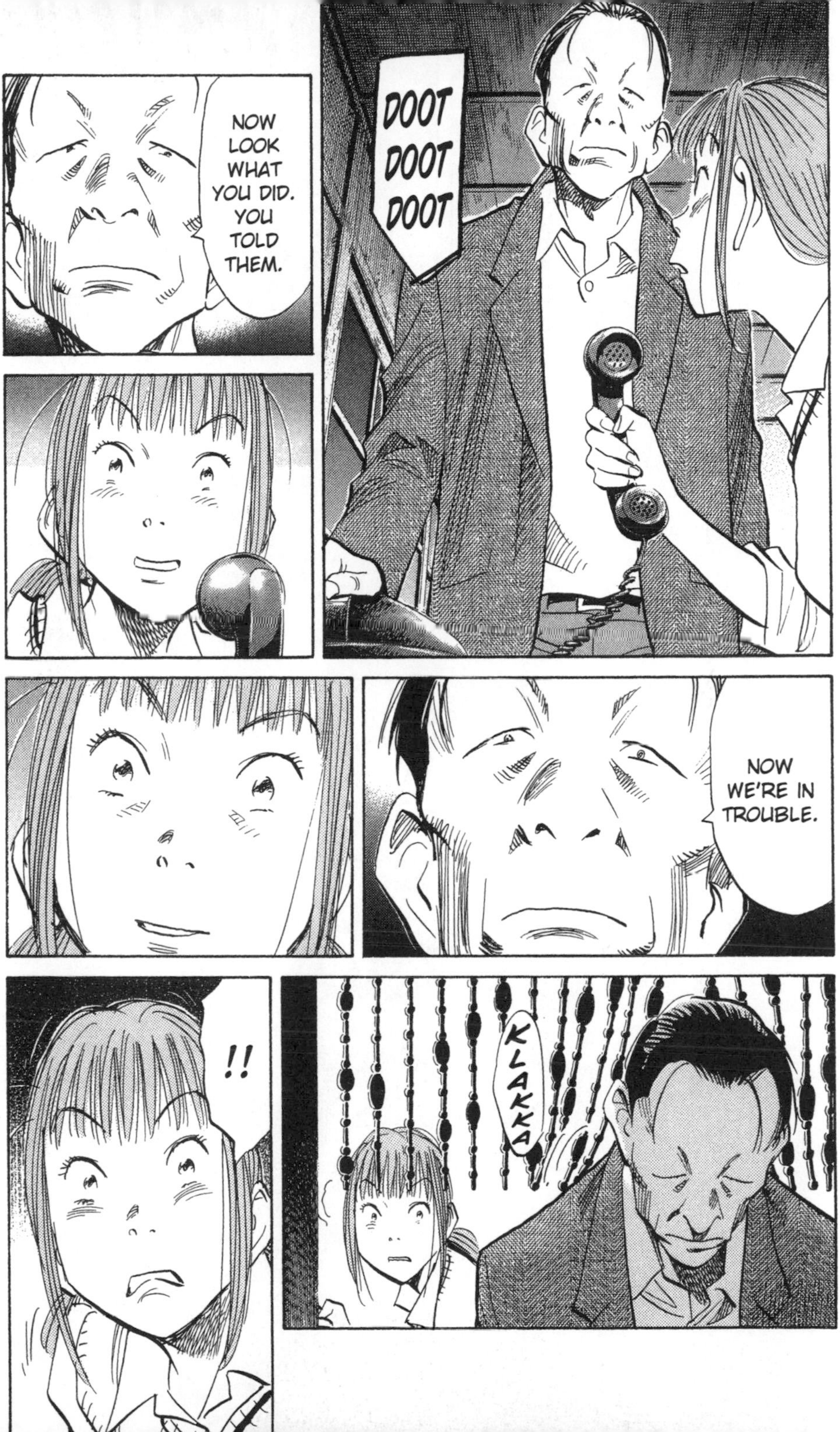
DOOT DOOT DOOT
NOW LOOK WHAT YOU DID. YOU TOLD THEM.
NOW WE'RE IN TROUBLE.
KLAKKA
!!

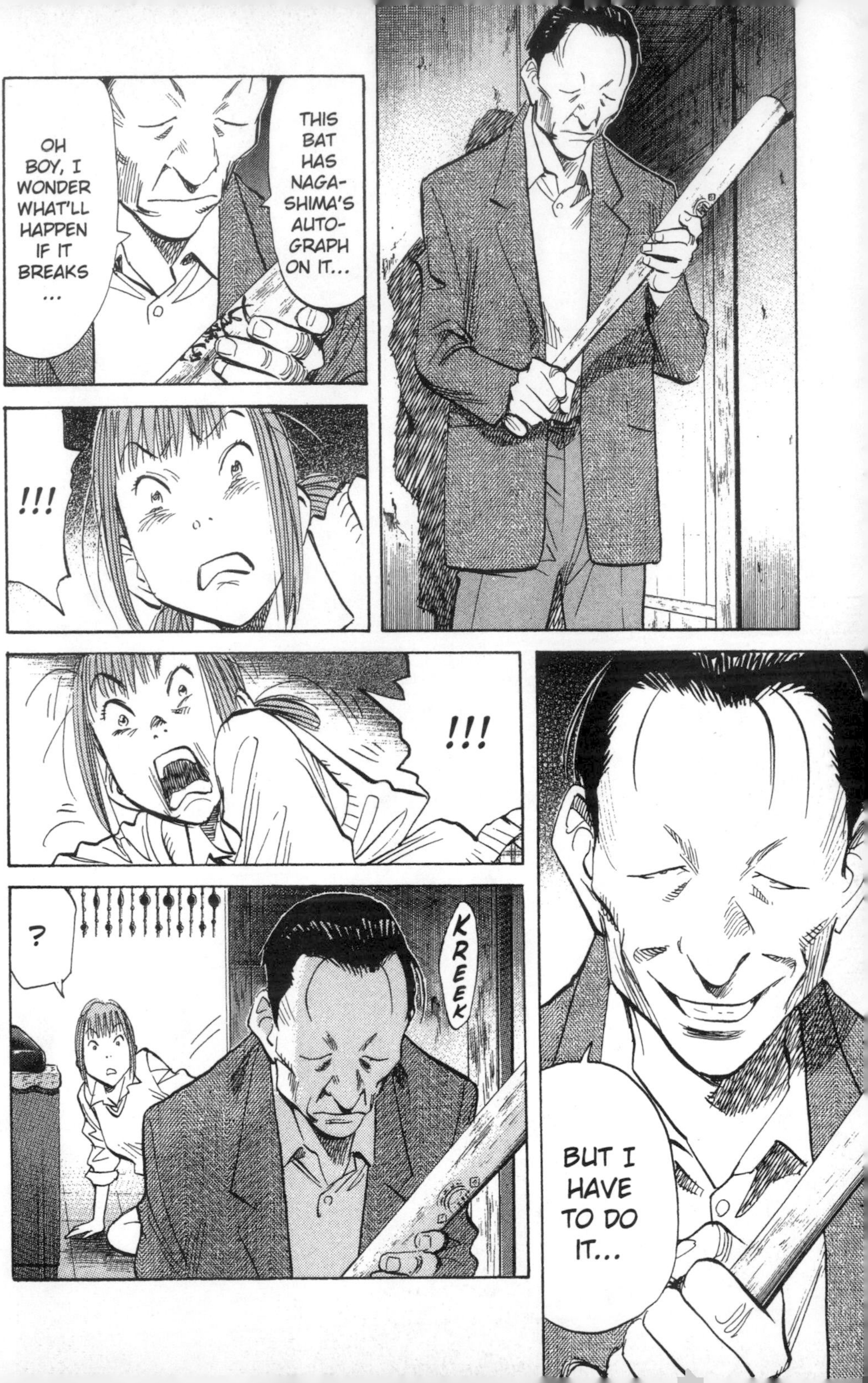
THIS BAT HAS NAGA-SHIMA'S AUTO-GRAPH ON IT...
OH BOY, I WONDER WHAT'LL HAPPEN IF IT BREAKS ...
!!!
BUT I HAVE TO DO IT...
!!!
KREEK
?

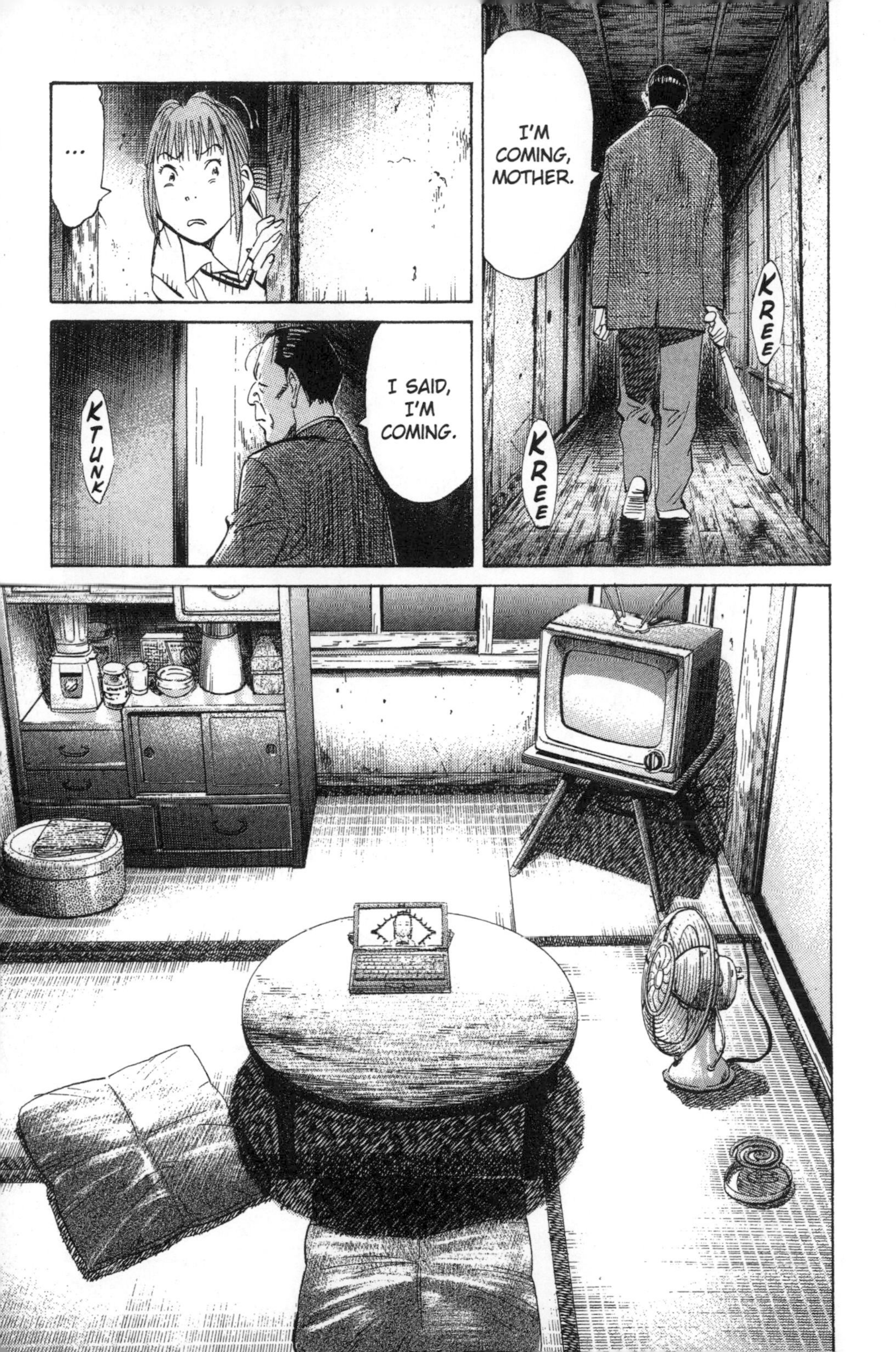
I'M COMING, MOTHER.
KREE
KREE
...
I SAID, I'M COMING.
KTUNK

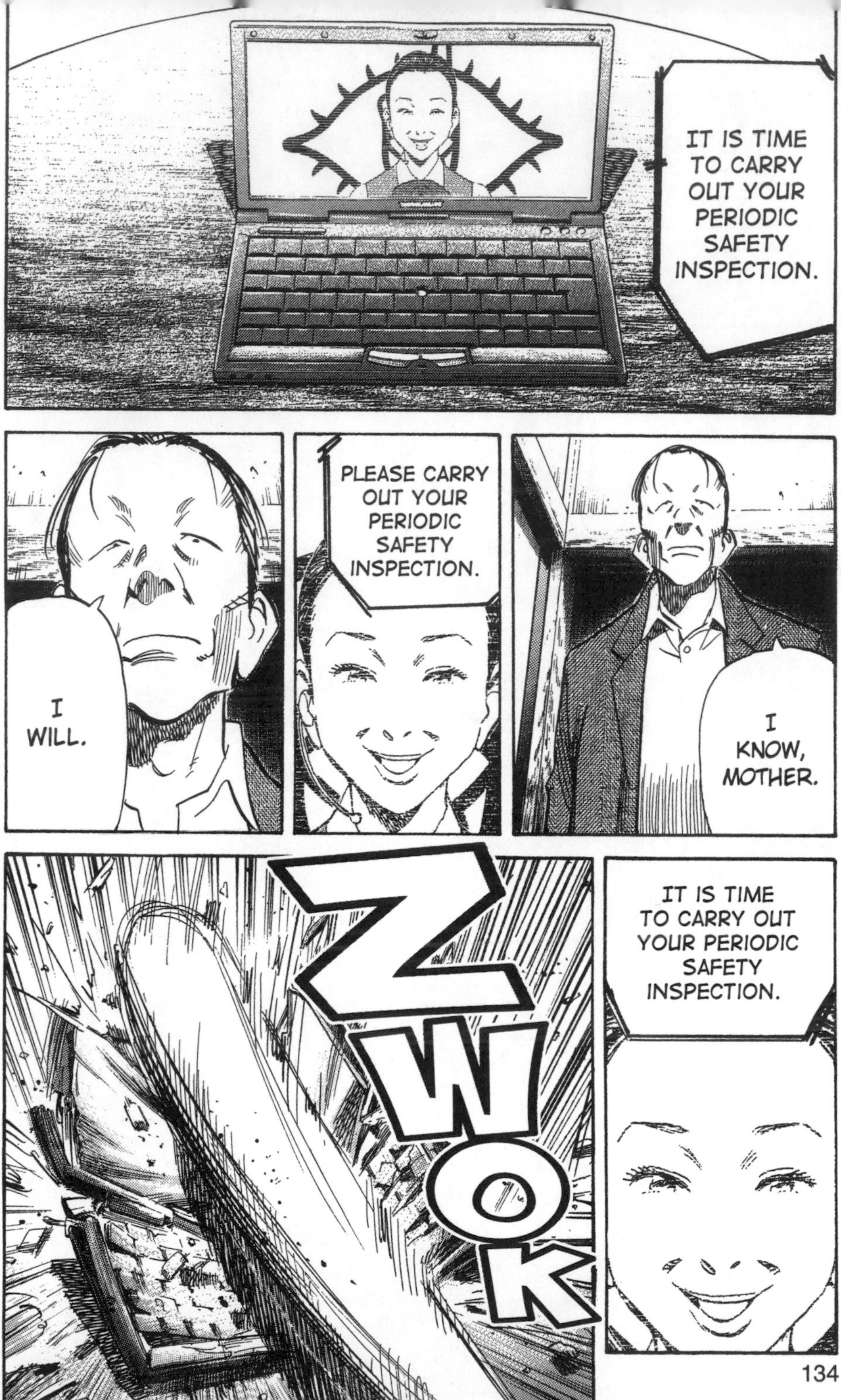
IT IS TIME TO CARRY OUT YOUR PERIODIC SAFETY INSPECTION.
I KNOW, MOTHER.
PLEASE CARRY OUT YOUR PERIODIC SAFETY INSPECTION.
I WILL.
IT IS TIME TO CARRY OUT YOUR PERIODIC SAFETY INSPECTION.
ZWOK

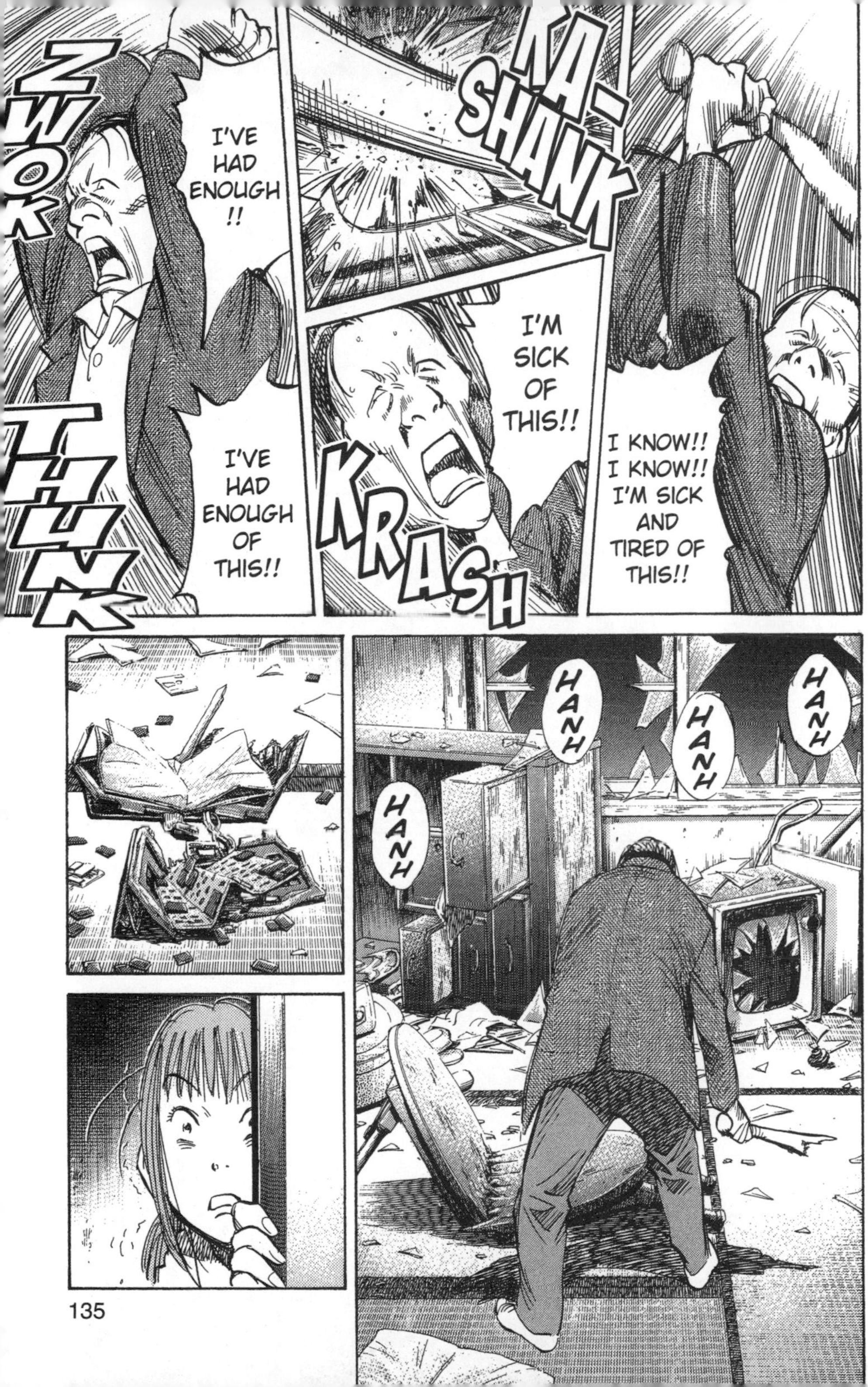
I KNOW!! I KNOW!! I'M SICK AND TIRED OF THIS!!
KA-SHANK
I'M SICK OF THIS!!
KRASH
ZWOK
I'VE HAD ENOUGH!!
I'VE HAD ENOUGH OF THIS!!
THUNK
HANH
HANH
HANH
HANH

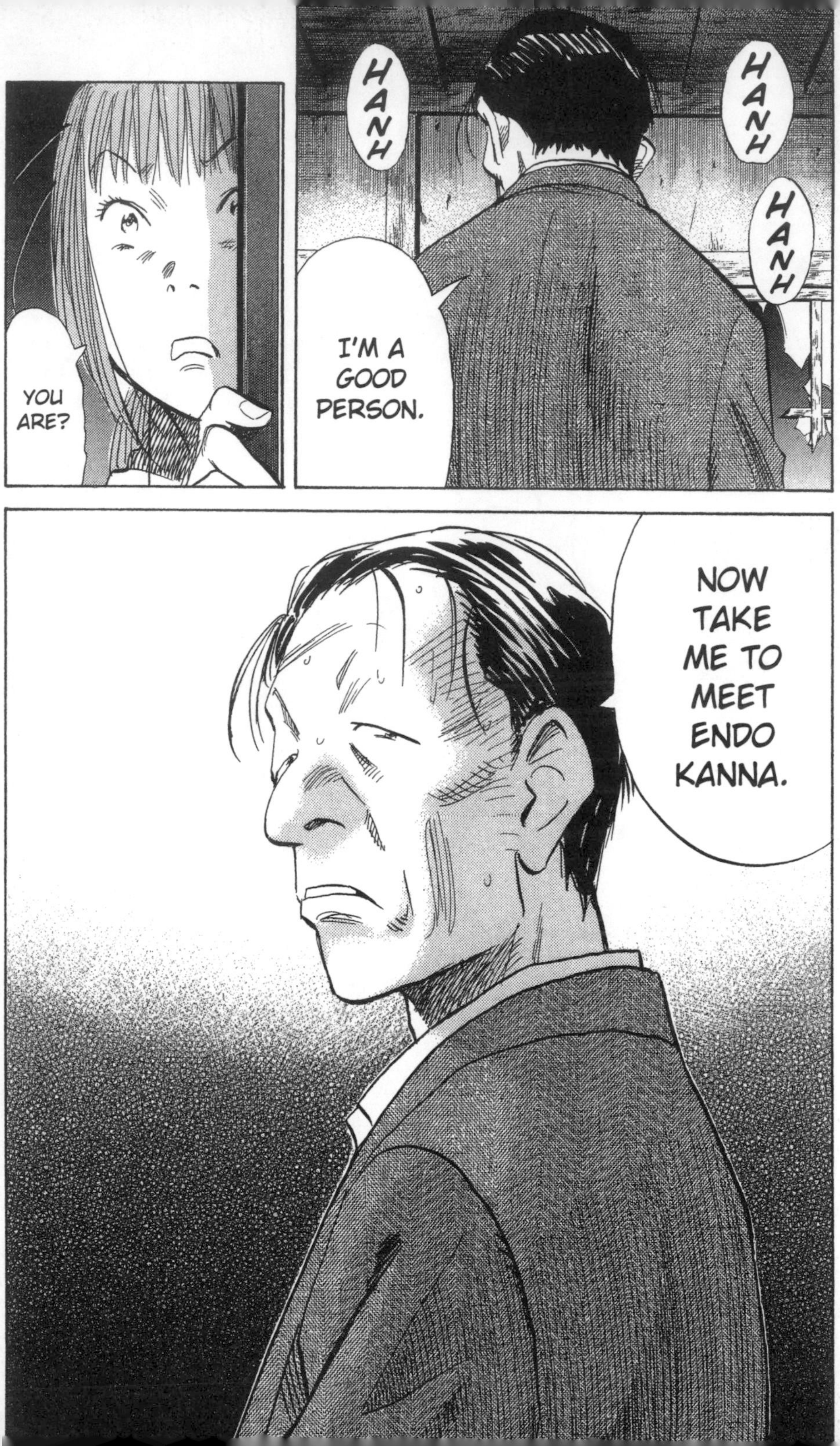
HANH
HANH
HANH
I'M A GOOD PERSON.
YOU ARE?
NOW TAKE ME TO MEET ENDO KANNA.

Chapter 8 Friend's Room

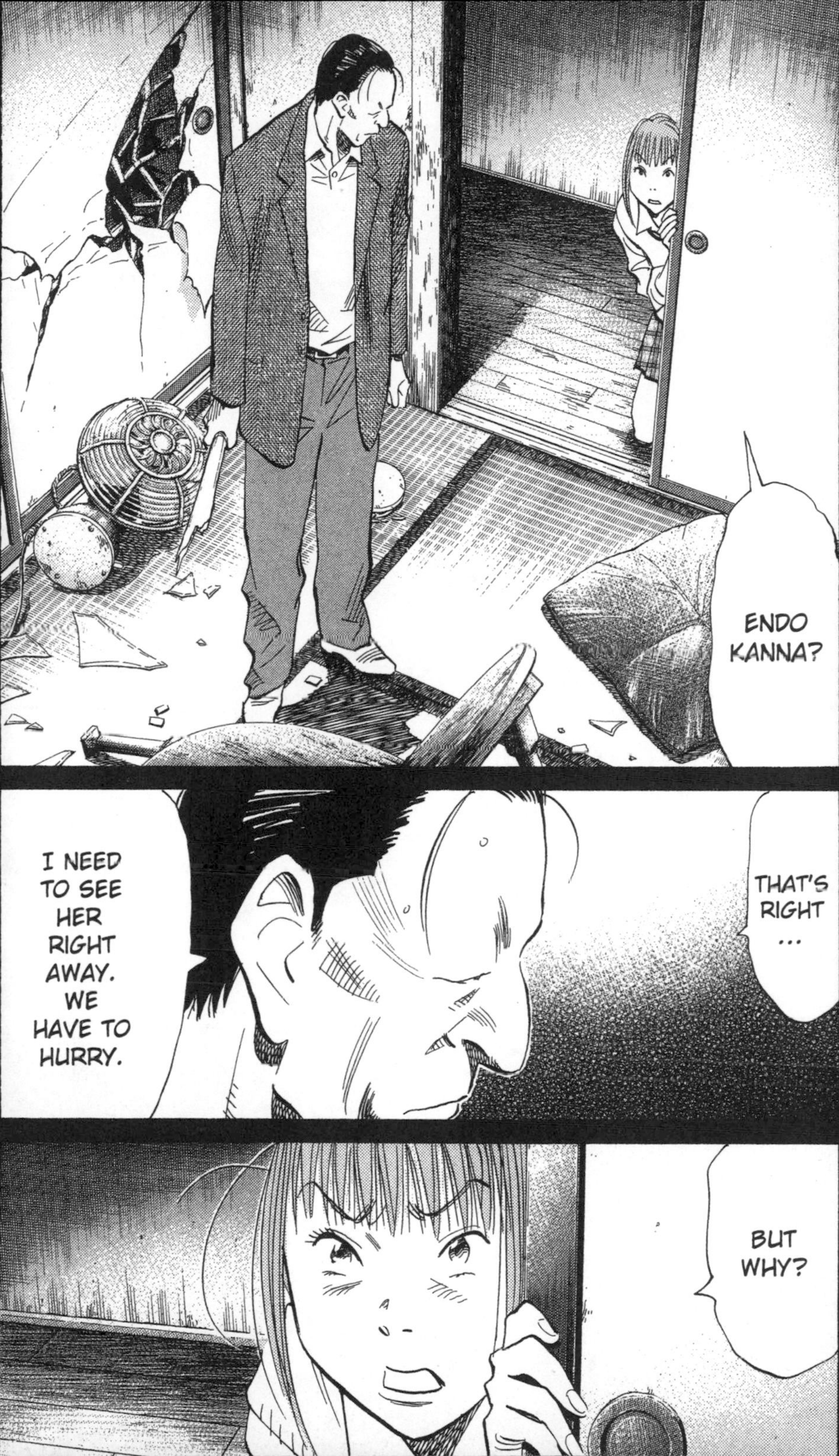
ENDO KANNA?
THAT'S RIGHT ...
I NEED TO SEE HER RIGHT AWAY. WE HAVE TO HURRY.
BUT WHY?

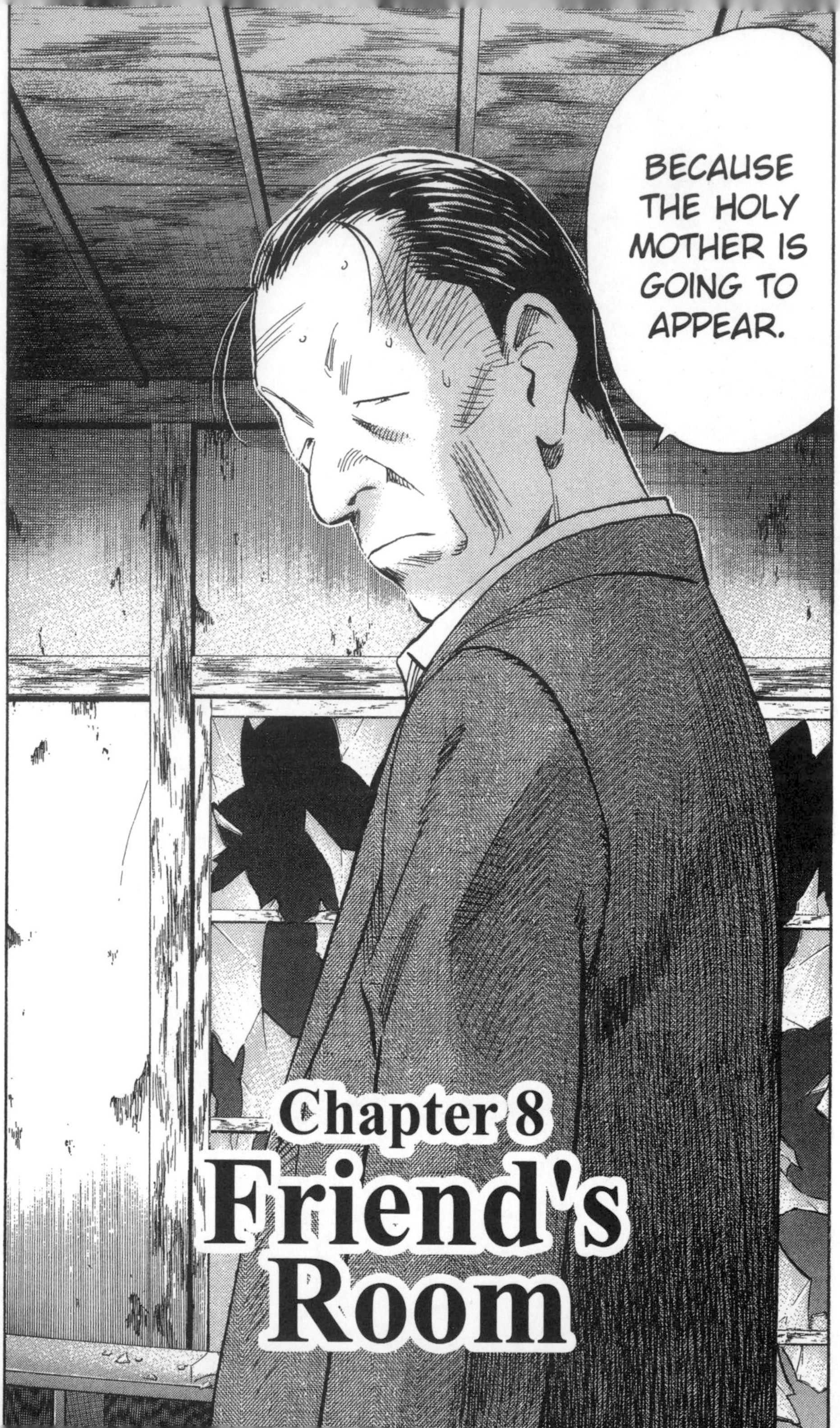
BECAUSE THE HOLY MOTHER IS GOING TO APPEAR.
Chapter 8
Friend's Room

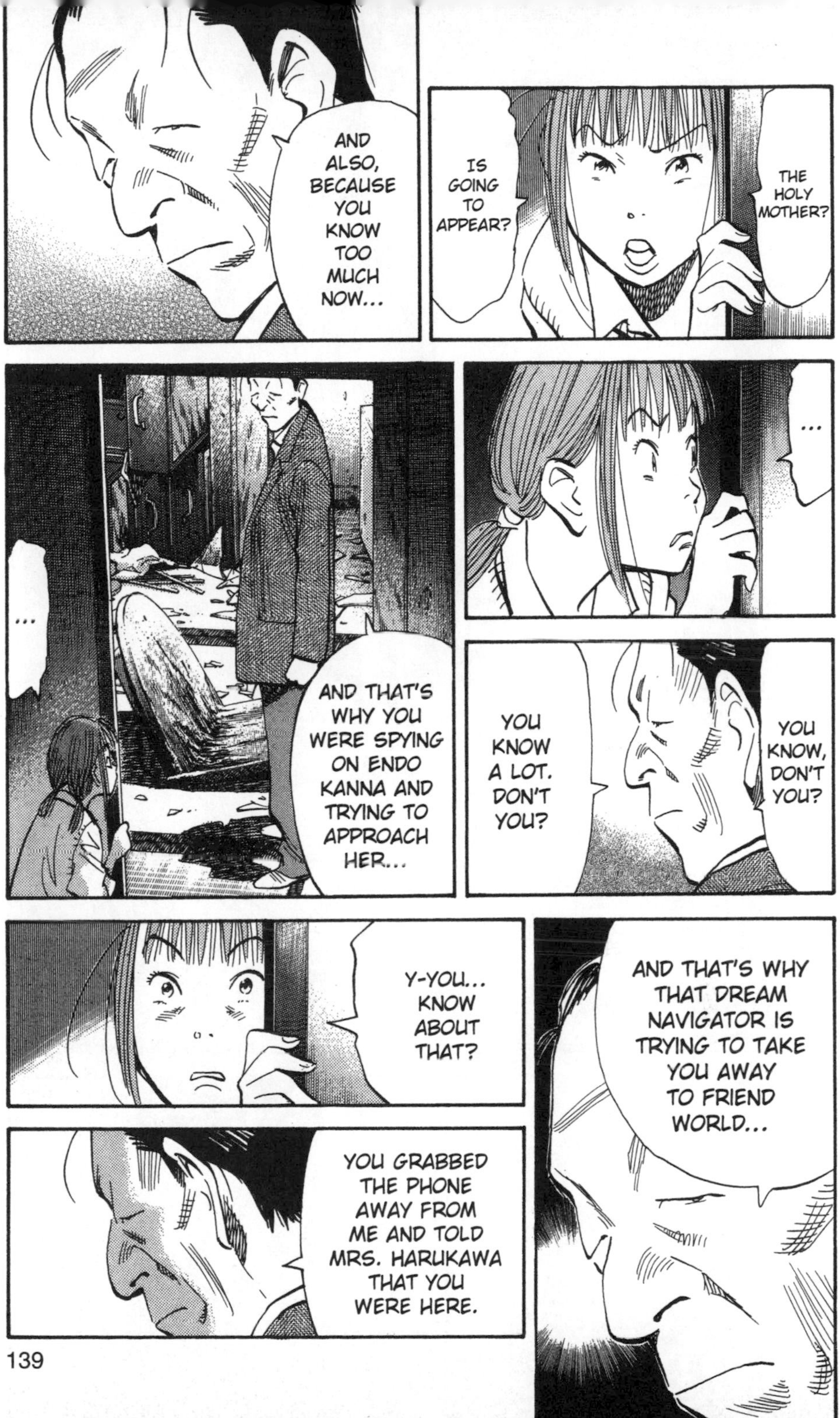
THE HOLY MOTHER?
IS GOING TO APPEAR?
AND ALSO, BECAUSE YOU KNOW TOO MUCH NOW...
...
YOU KNOW, DON'T YOU?
YOU KNOW A LOT. DON'T YOU?
AND THAT'S WHY YOU WERE SPYING ON ENDO KANNA AND TRYING TO APPROACH HER...
...
AND THAT'S WHY THAT DREAM NAVIGATOR IS TRYING TO TAKE YOU AWAY TO FRIEND WORLD...
Y-YOU... KNOW ABOUT THAT?
YOU GRABBED THE PHONE AWAY FROM ME AND TOLD MRS. HARUKAWA THAT YOU WERE HERE.

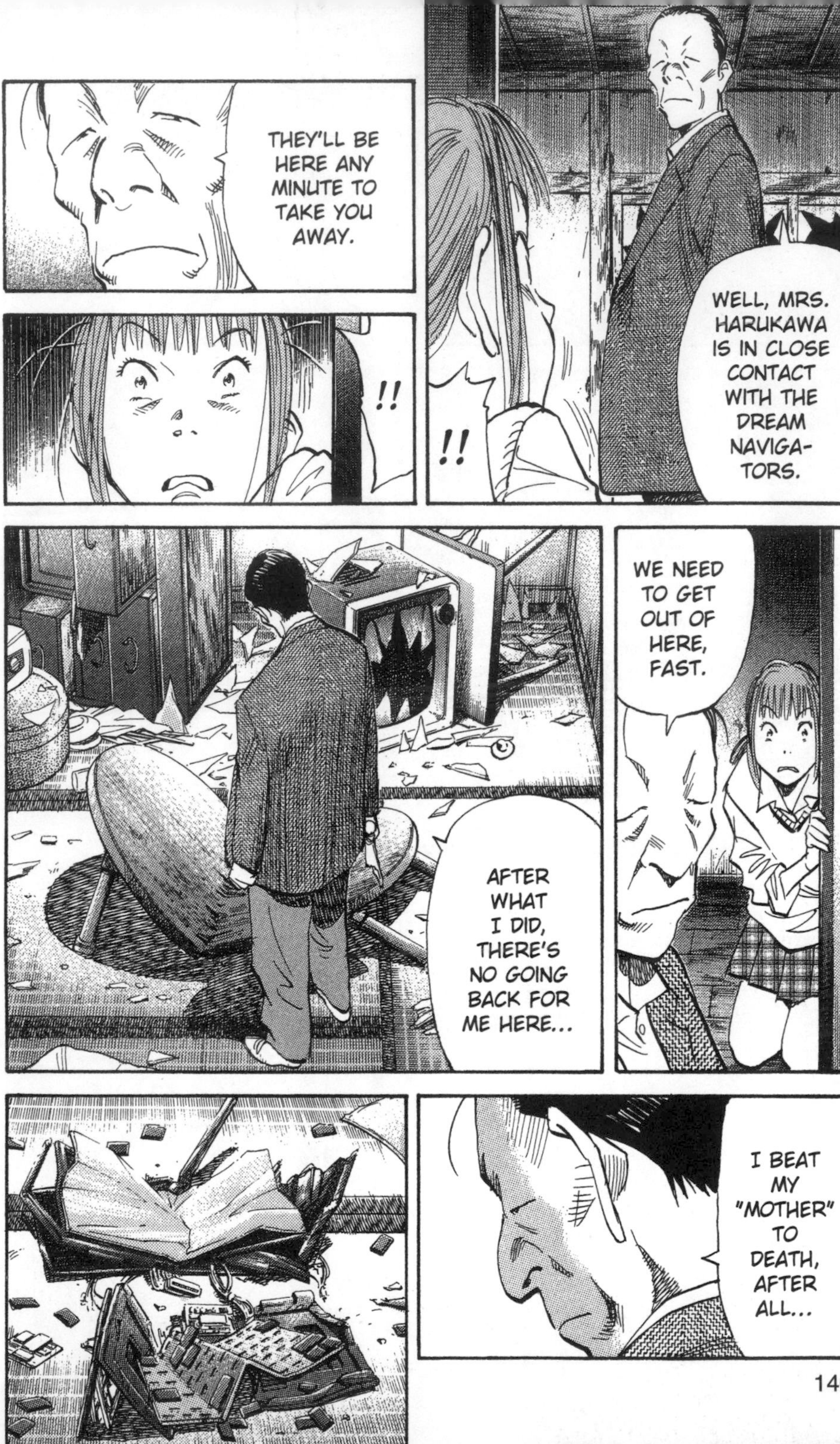
WELL, MRS. HARUKAWA IS IN CLOSE CONTACT WITH THE DREAM NAVIGA-TORS.
!!
THEY'LL BE HERE ANY MINUTE TO TAKE YOU AWAY.
!!
WE NEED TO GET OUT OF HERE, FAST.
AFTER WHAT I DID, THERE'S NO GOING BACK FOR ME HERE...
I BEAT MY "MOTHER" TO DEATH, AFTER ALL...

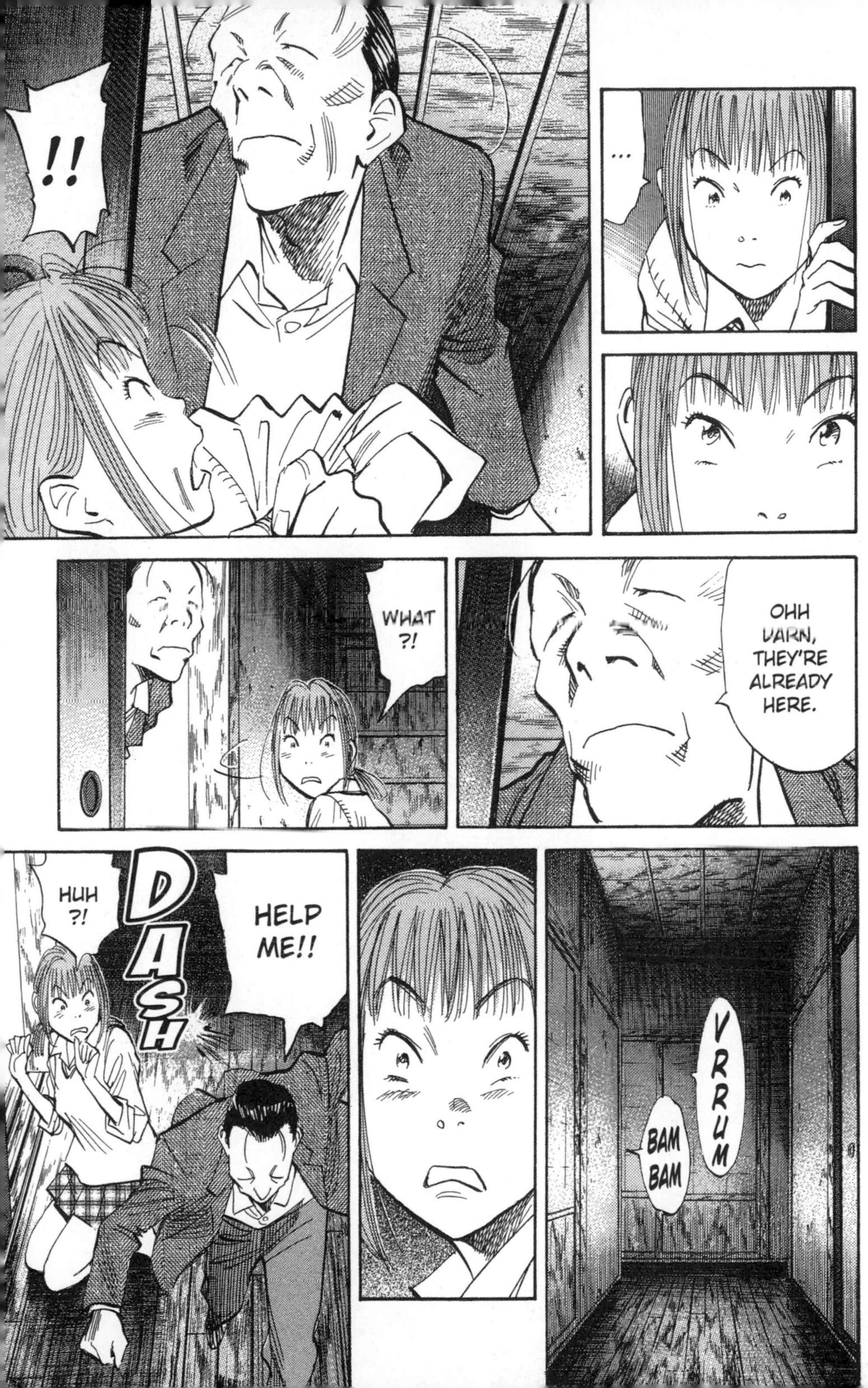
...
!!
OHH DARN, THEY'RE ALREADY HERE.
WHAT ?!
VRRUM
BAM BAM
HELP ME!!
DASH
HUH ?!

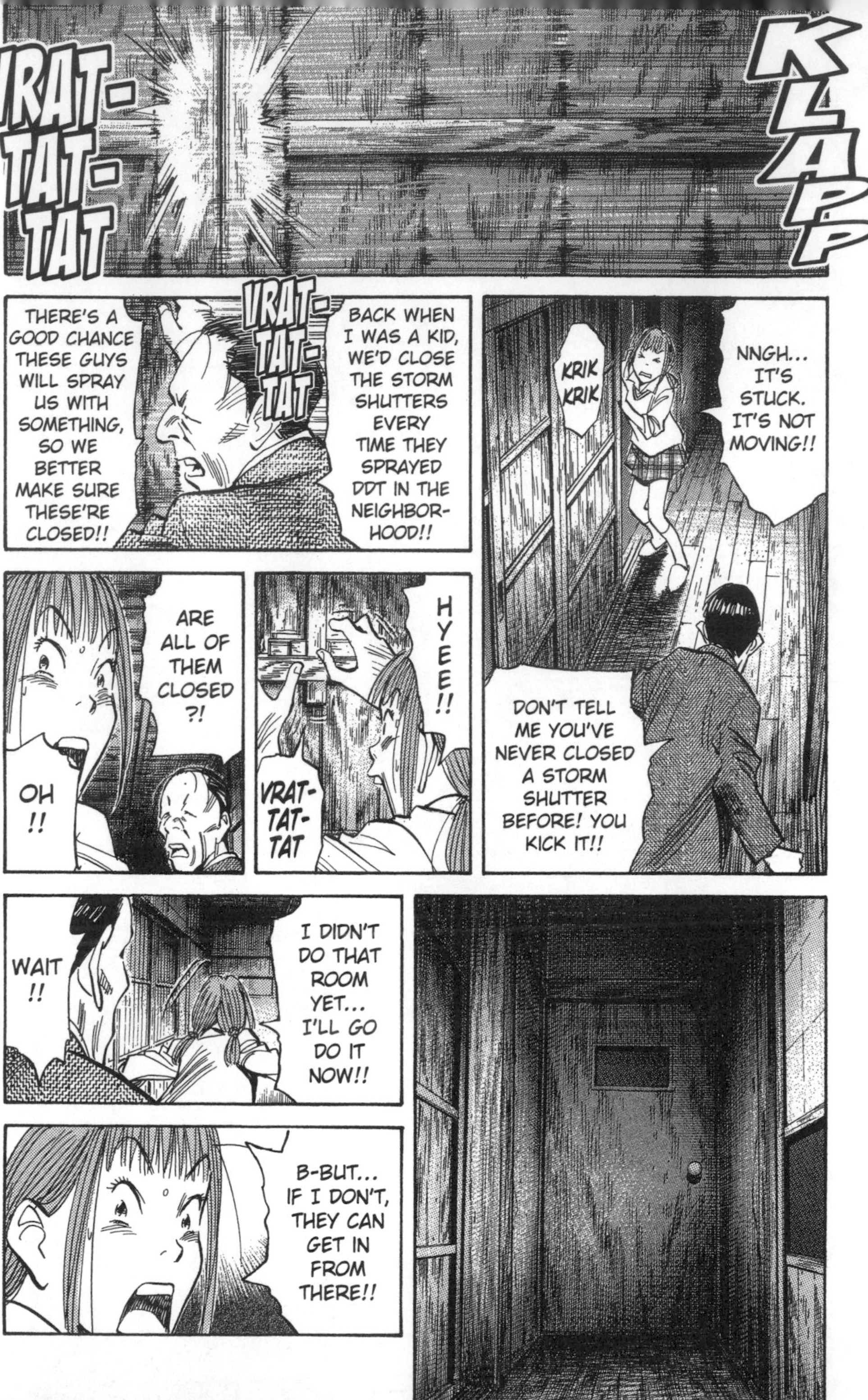
KLAPP
VRAT-TAT-TAT
NNGH... IT'S STUCK. IT'S NOT MOVING!!
KRIK KRIK
DON'T TELL ME YOU'VE NEVER CLOSED A STORM SHUTTER BEFORE! YOU KICK IT!!
BACK WHEN I WAS A KID, WE'D CLOSE THE STORM SHUTTERS EVERY TIME THEY SPRAYED DDT IN THE NEIGHBOR-HOOD!!
VRAT-TAT-TAT
THERE'S A GOOD CHANCE THESE GUYS WILL SPRAY US WITH SOMETHING, SO WE BETTER MAKE SURE THESE'RE CLOSED!!
HYEEE!!
VRAT-TAT-TAT
ARE ALL OF THEM CLOSED?!
OH!!
I DIDN'T DO THAT ROOM YET... I'LL GO DO IT NOW!!
WAIT!!
B-BUT... IF I DON'T, THEY CAN GET IN FROM THERE!!

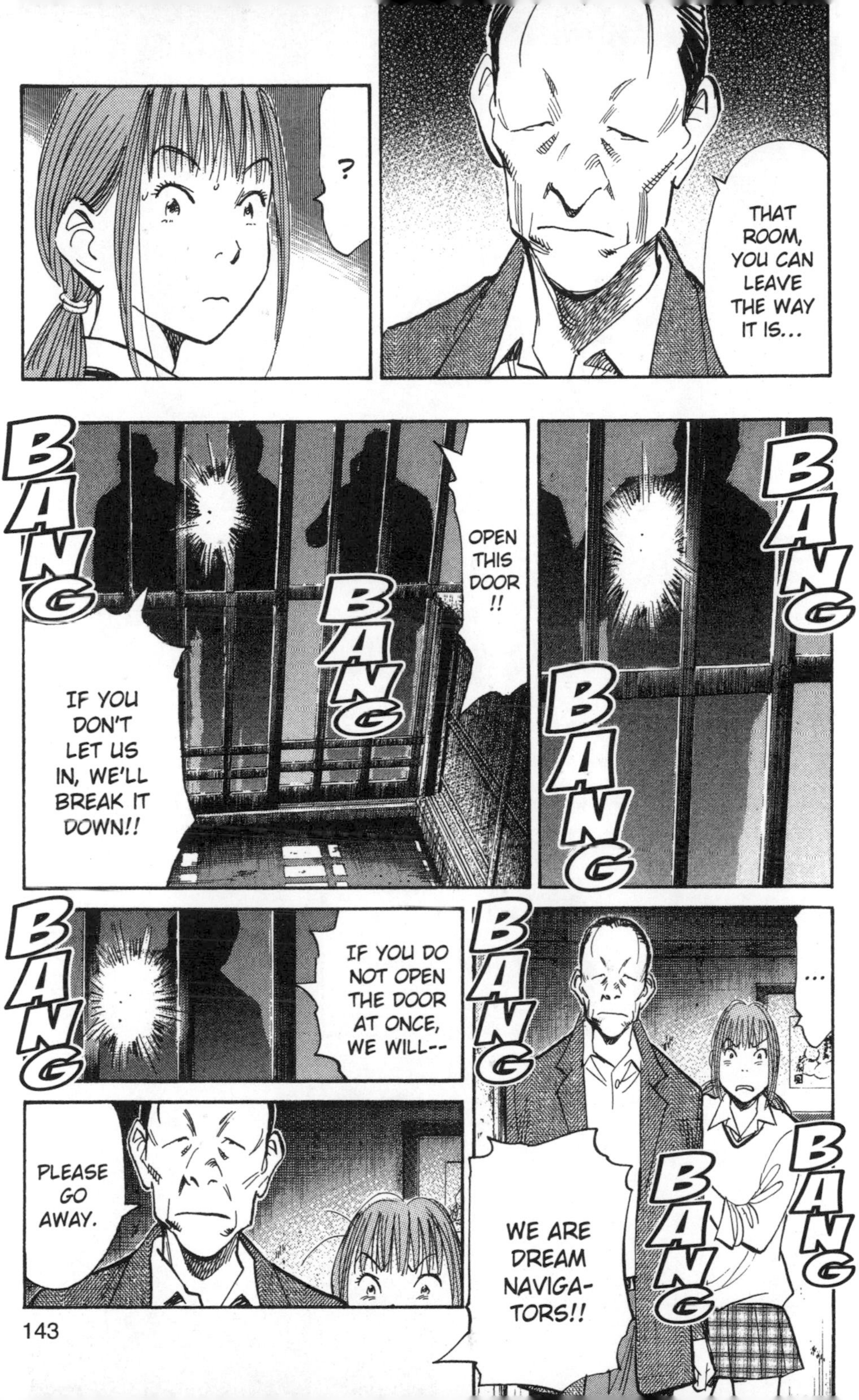
THAT ROOM, YOU CAN LEAVE THE WAY IT IS...
?
BANG
BANG
OPEN THIS DOOR!!
BANG
BANG
IF YOU DON'T LET US IN, WE'LL BREAK IT DOWN!!
...
BANG
BANG
BANG
WE ARE DREAM NAVIGATORS!!
IF YOU DO NOT OPEN THE DOOR AT ONCE, WE WILL--
BANG
PLEASE GO AWAY.

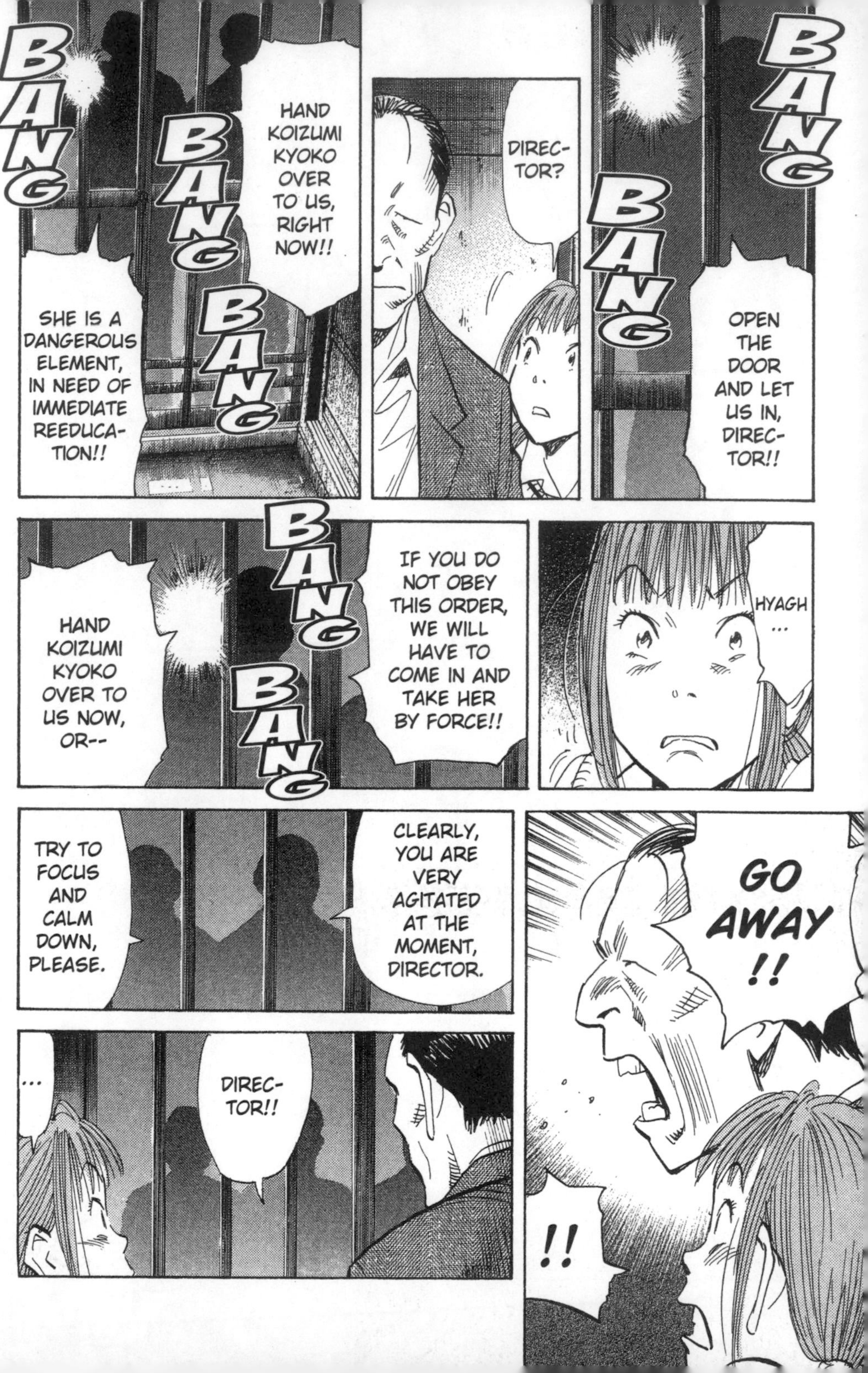
BANG
BANG
OPEN THE DOOR AND LET US IN, DIRECTOR!!
DIREC-TOR?
BANG
HAND KOIZUMI KYOKO OVER TO US, RIGHT NOW!!
BANG
BANG
SHE IS A DANGEROUS ELEMENT, IN NEED OF IMMEDIATE REEDUCA-TION!!
HYAGH ...
BANG
IF YOU DO NOT OBEY THIS ORDER, WE WILL HAVE TO COME IN AND TAKE HER BY FORCE!!
BANG
HAND KOIZUMI KYOKO OVER TO US NOW, OR--
GO AWAY!!
!!
CLEARLY, YOU ARE VERY AGITATED AT THE MOMENT, DIRECTOR.
TRY TO FOCUS AND CALM DOWN, PLEASE.
DIREC-TOR!!
...

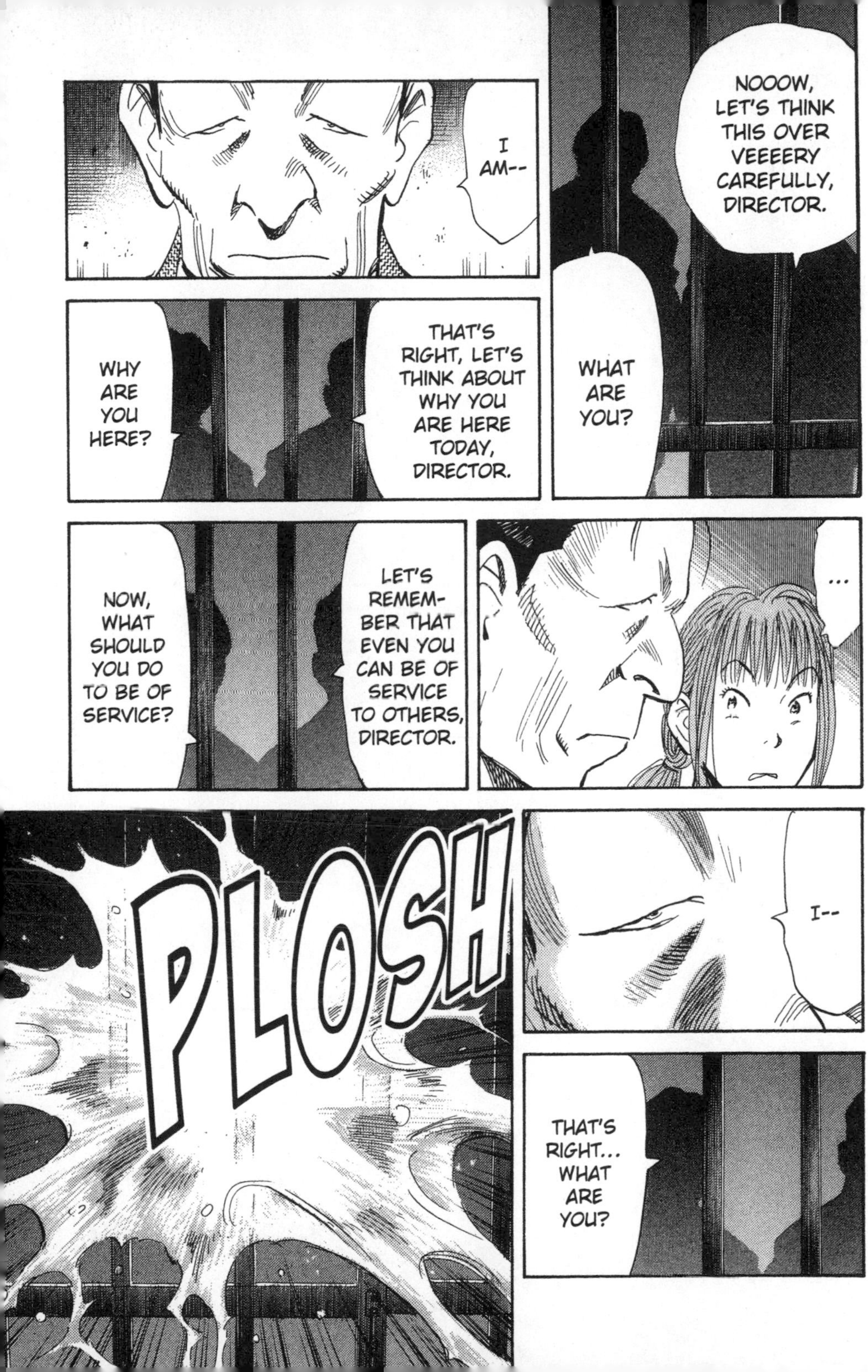
NOOOW, LET'S THINK THIS OVER VEEEERY CAREFULLY, DIRECTOR.
WHAT ARE YOU?
I AM--
THAT'S RIGHT, LET'S THINK ABOUT WHY YOU ARE HERE TODAY, DIRECTOR.
WHY ARE YOU HERE?
...
LET'S REMEMBER THAT EVEN YOU CAN BE OF SERVICE TO OTHERS, DIRECTOR.
NOW, WHAT SHOULD YOU DO TO BE OF SERVICE?
I--
THAT'S RIGHT... WHAT ARE YOU?
PLOSH

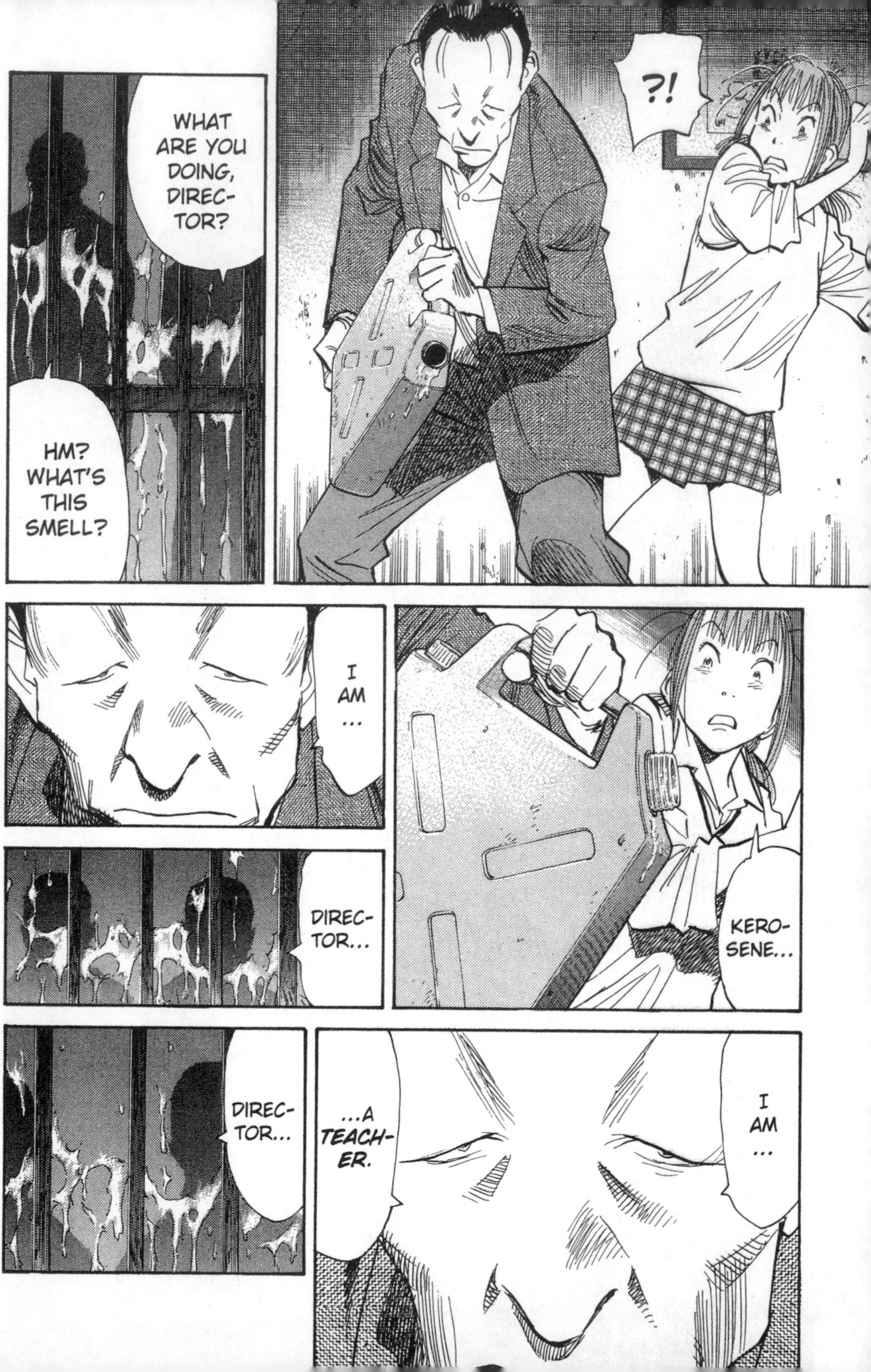
?!
WHAT ARE YOU DOING, DIRECTOR?
HM? WHAT'S THIS SMELL?
KEROSENE...
I AM...
DIRECTOR...
I AM...
...A *TEACHER*.
DIRECTOR...

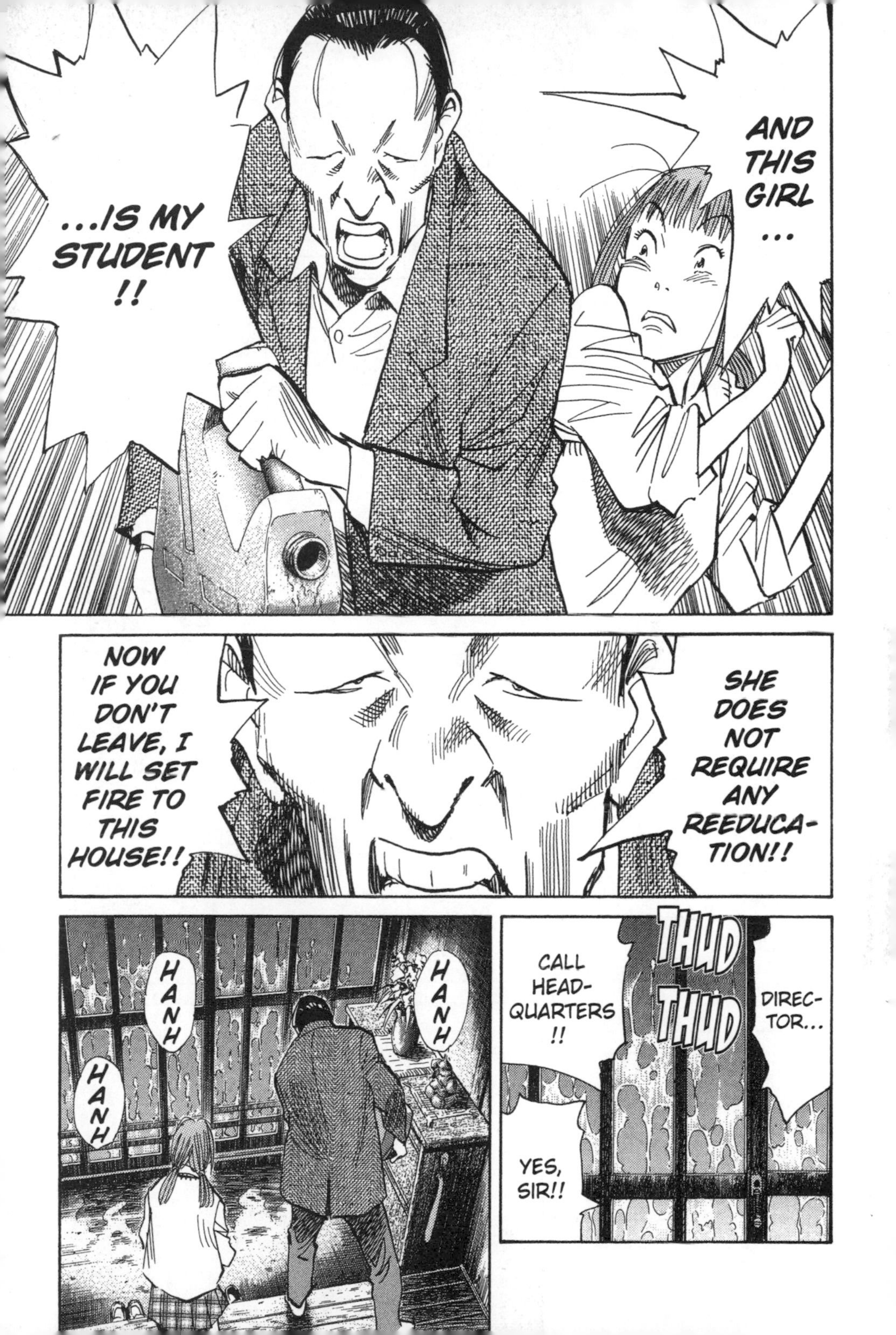
AND THIS GIRL...
...IS MY STUDENT!!
SHE DOES NOT REQUIRE ANY REEDUCATION!!
NOW IF YOU DON'T LEAVE, I WILL SET FIRE TO THIS HOUSE!!
THUD THUD
DIREC-TOR...
CALL HEAD-QUARTERS!!
YES, SIR!!
HANH HANH
HANH HANH

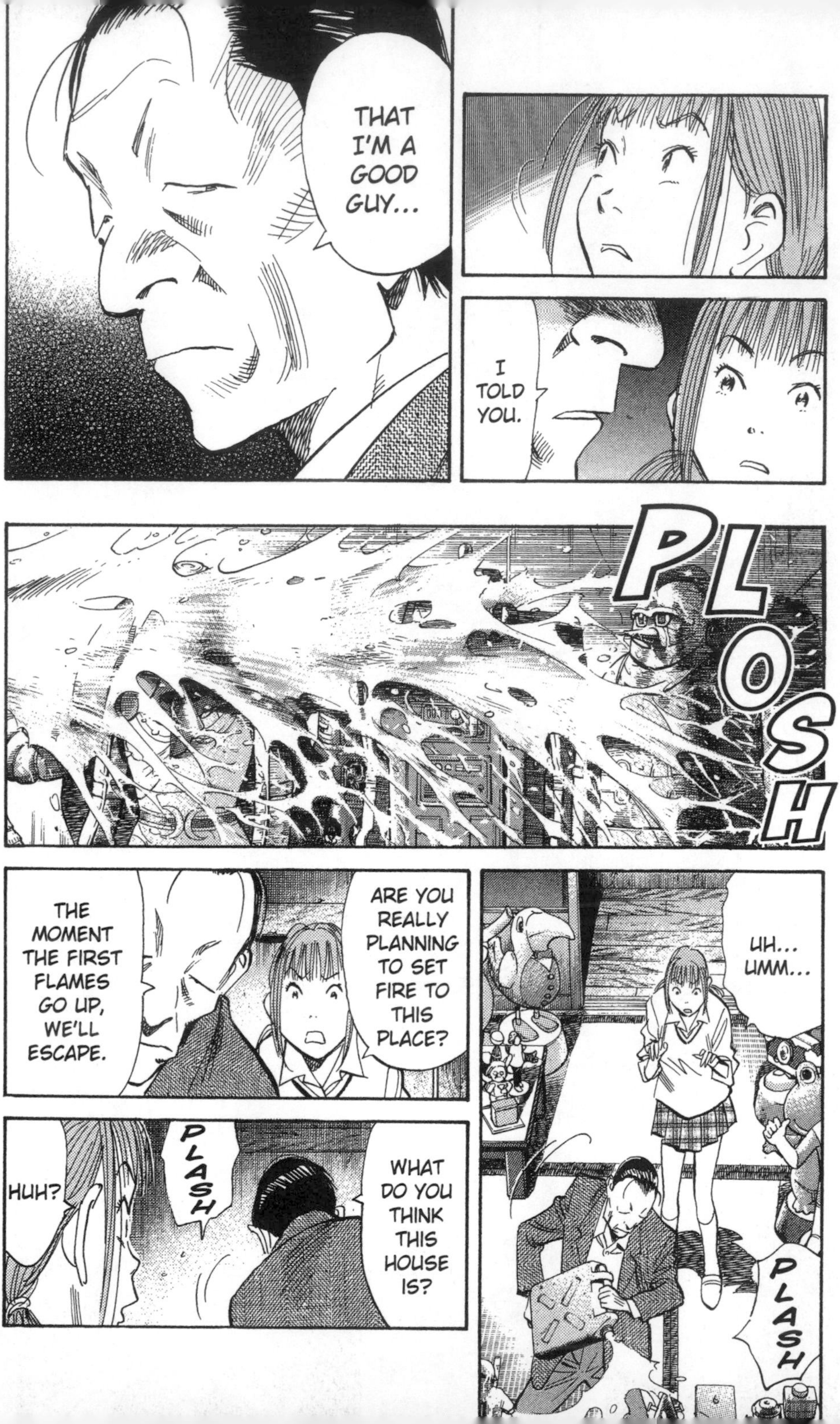

I TOLD YOU.
THAT I'M A GOOD GUY...
PLOSH
UH... UMM...
PLASH
ARE YOU REALLY PLANNING TO SET FIRE TO THIS PLACE?
THE MOMENT THE FIRST FLAMES GO UP, WE'LL ESCAPE.
WHAT DO YOU THINK THIS HOUSE IS?
PLASH
HUH?

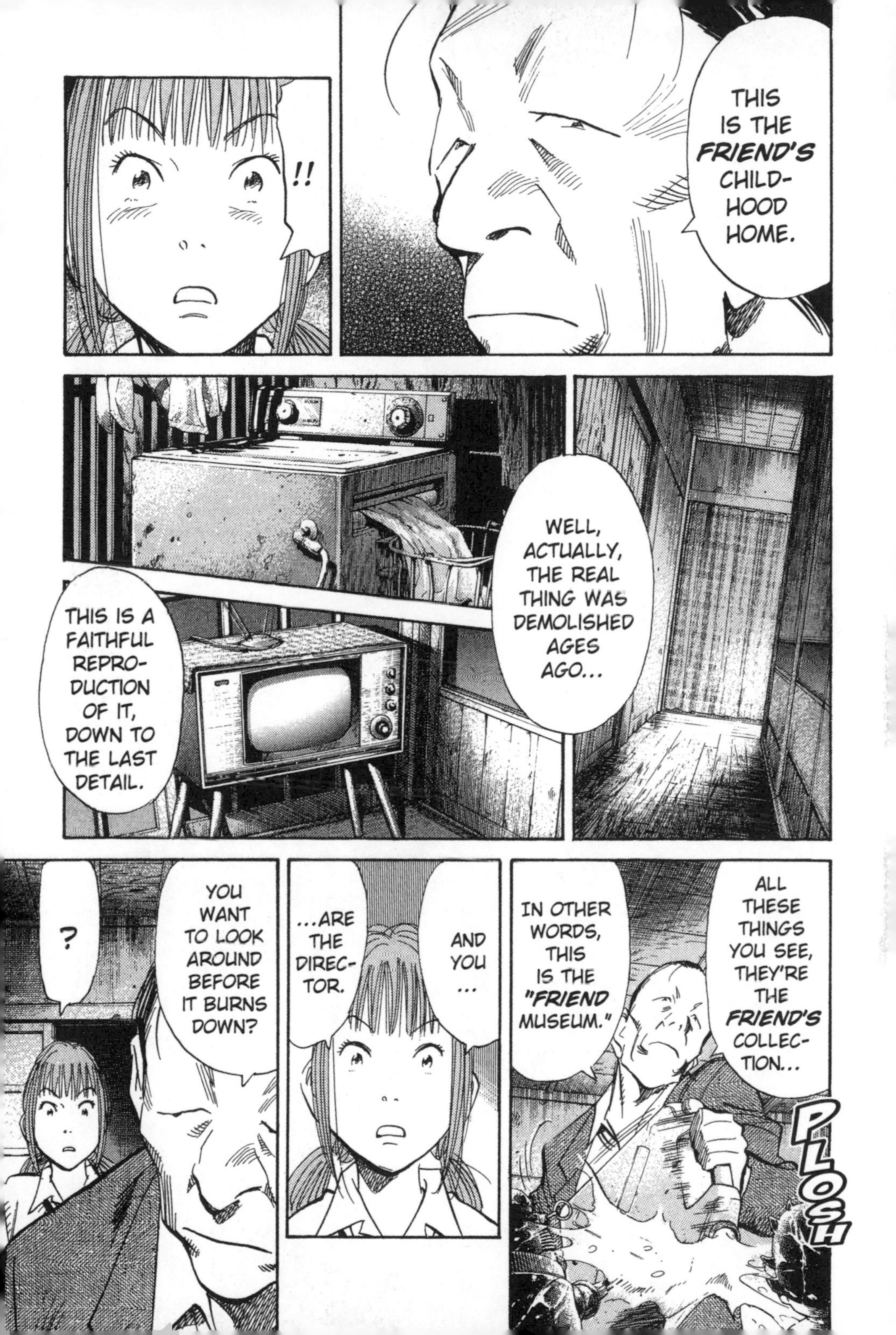
THIS IS THE FRIEND'S CHILDHOOD HOME.
!!
WELL, ACTUALLY, THE REAL THING WAS DEMOLISHED AGES AGO...
THIS IS A FAITHFUL REPRODUCTION OF IT, DOWN TO THE LAST DETAIL.
ALL THESE THINGS YOU SEE, THEY'RE THE FRIEND'S COLLECTION...
IN OTHER WORDS, THIS IS THE "FRIEND MUSEUM."
PLOSH
AND YOU ...
...ARE THE DIRECTOR.
YOU WANT TO LOOK AROUND BEFORE IT BURNS DOWN?
?

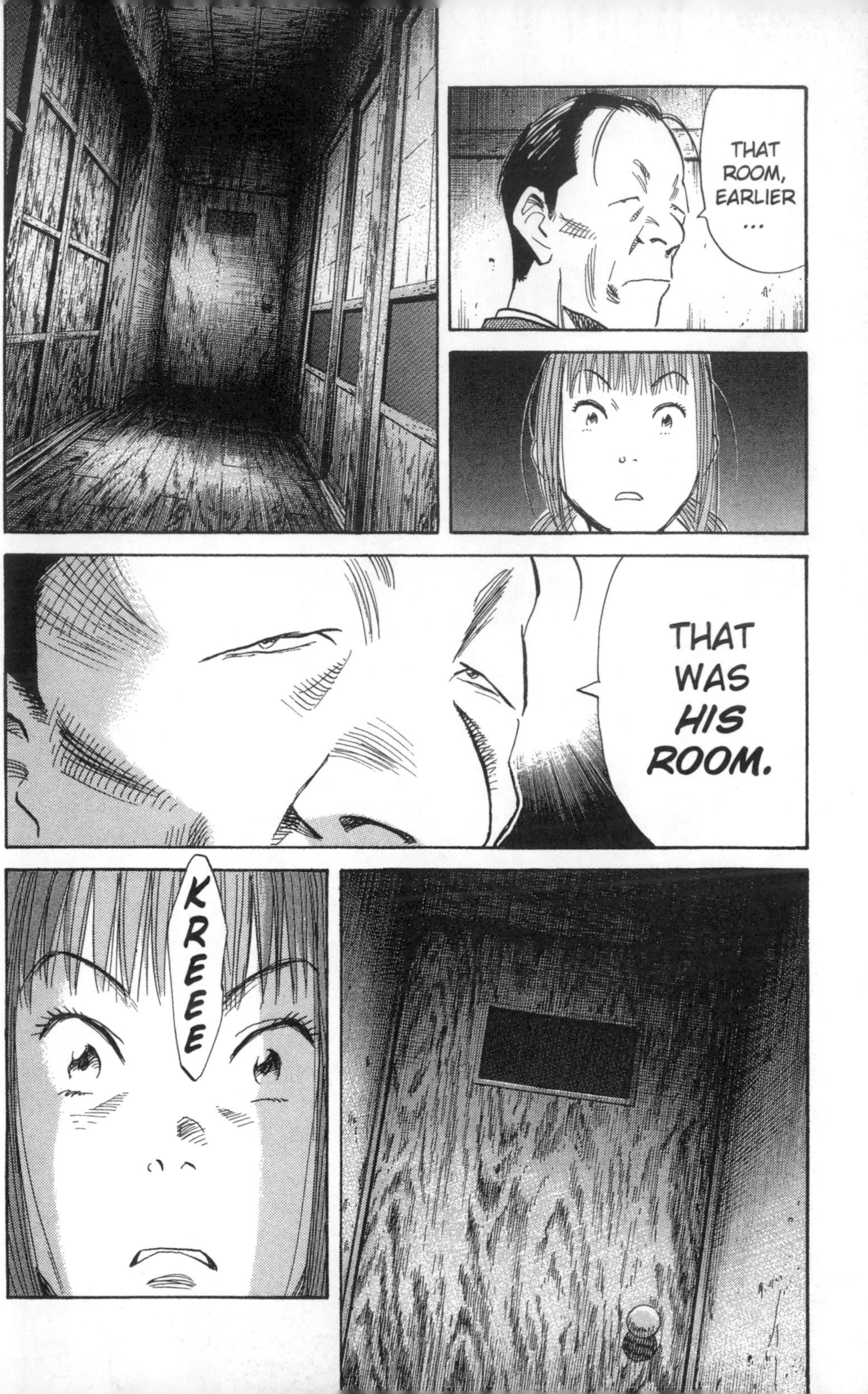
THAT ROOM, EARLIER ...
THAT WAS *HIS* ROOM.
KREEE

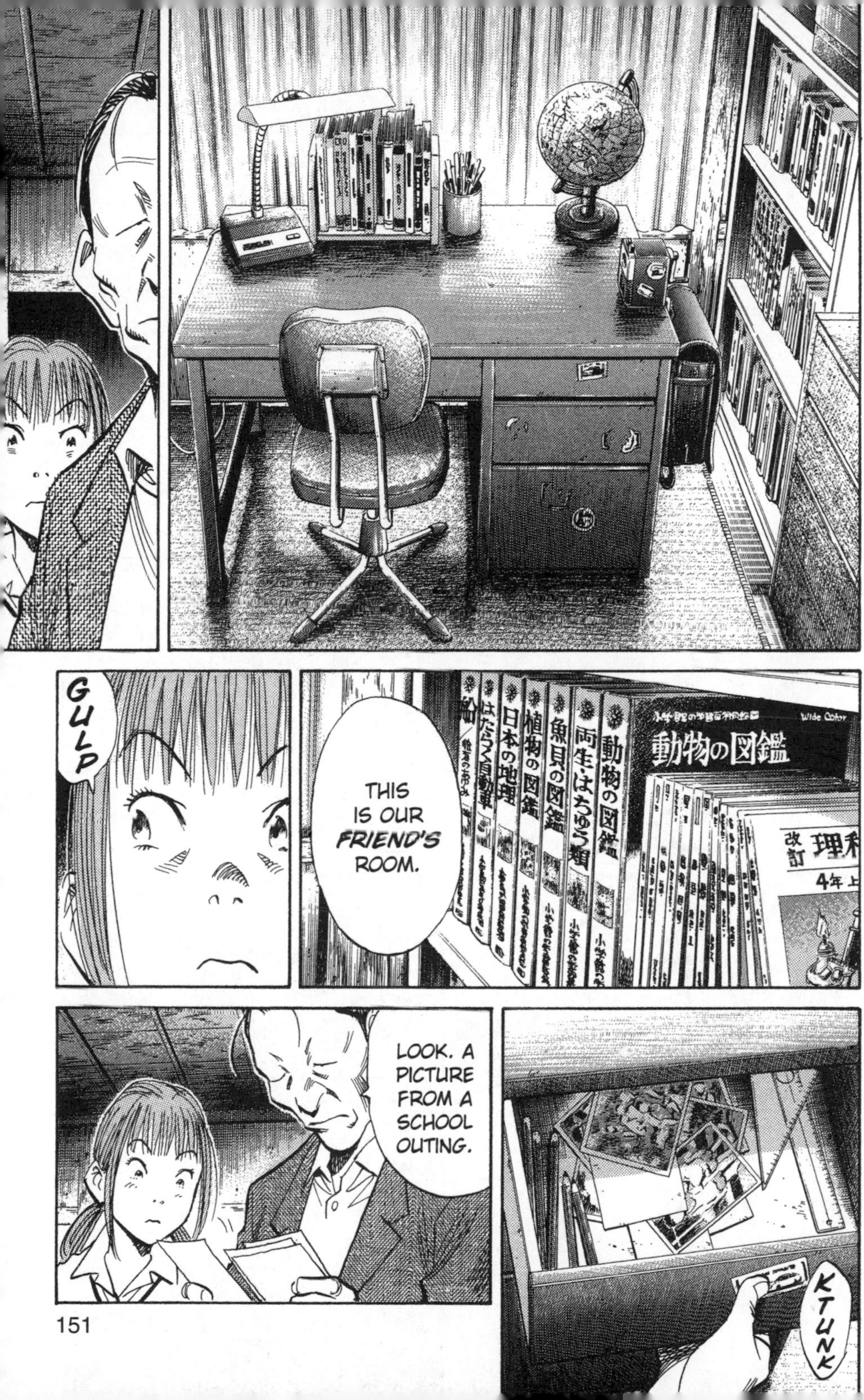
Wide Color
動物の図鑑
改訂 理科
4年上
動物の図鑑
両生・はちゅう類
魚貝の図鑑
植物の図鑑
日本の地理
はたらく自動車
THIS IS OUR *FRIEND'S* ROOM.
GULP
KTUNK
LOOK. A PICTURE FROM A SCHOOL OUTING.

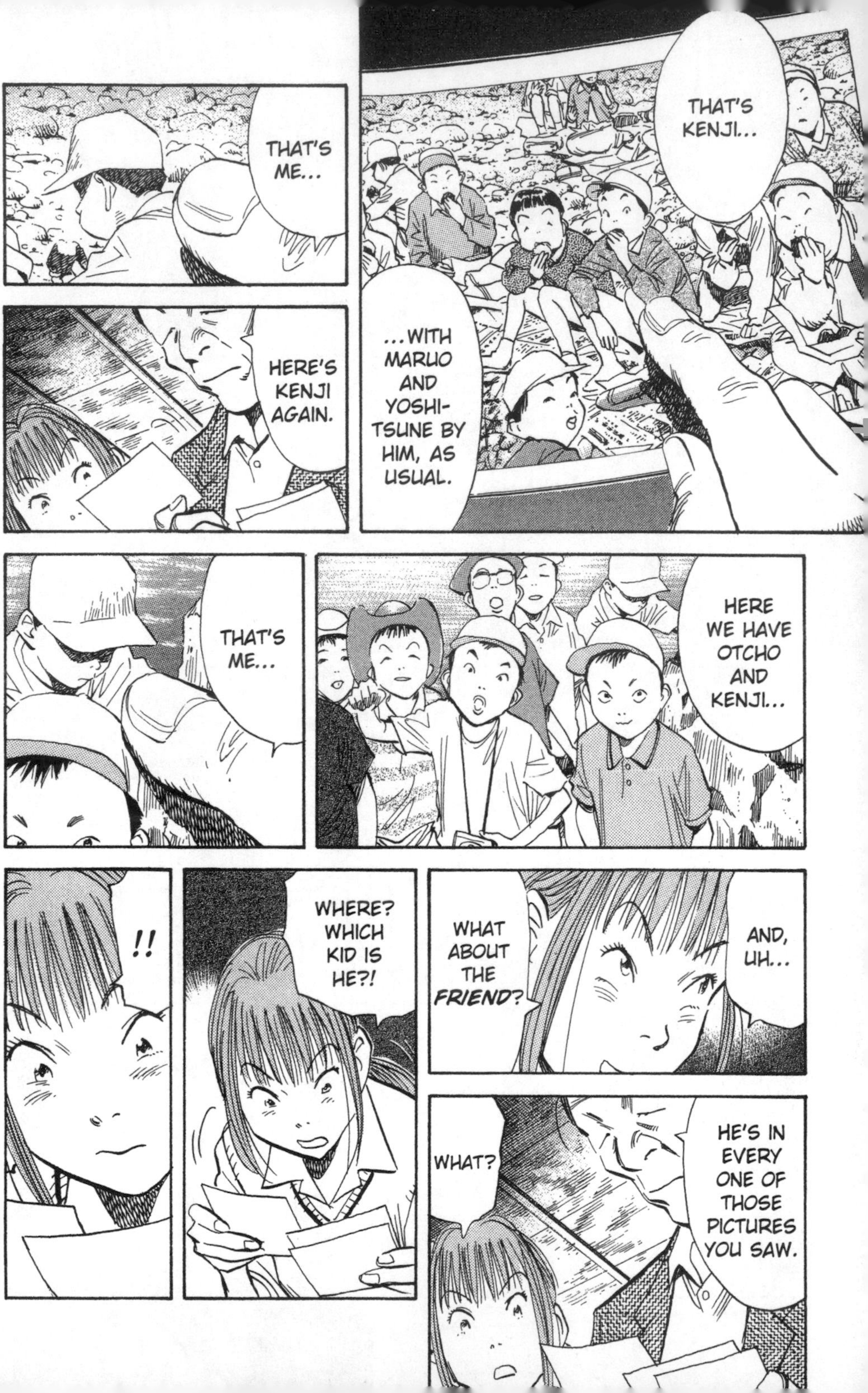
THAT'S KENJI...
...WITH MARUO AND YOSHI-TSUNE BY HIM, AS USUAL.
THAT'S ME...
HERE'S KENJI AGAIN.
HERE WE HAVE OTCHO AND KENJI...
THAT'S ME...
AND, UH...
WHAT ABOUT THE *FRIEND*?
HE'S IN EVERY ONE OF THOSE PICTURES YOU SAW.
WHAT?
WHERE? WHICH KID IS HE?!
!!

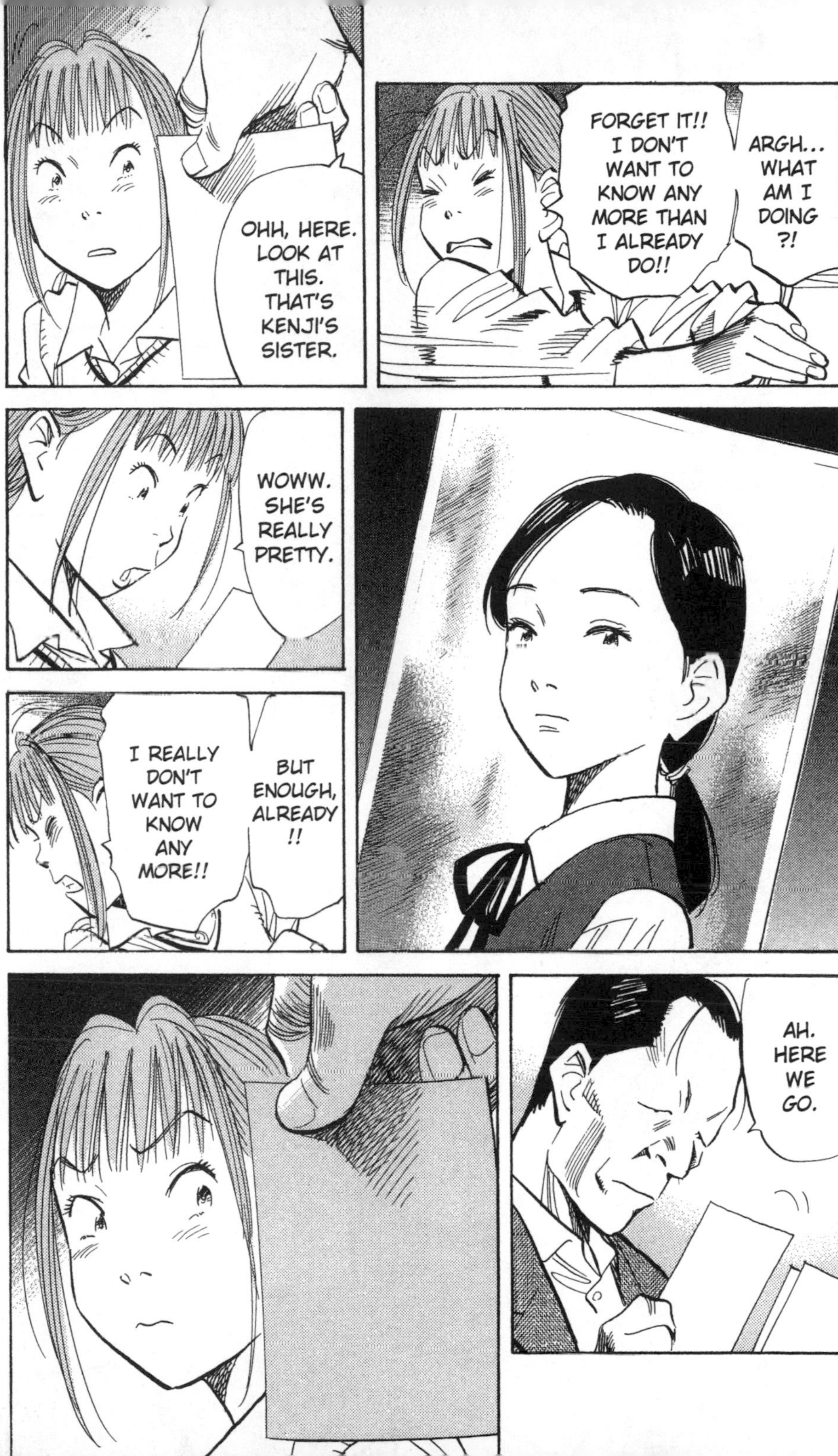
ARGH... WHAT AM I DOING ?!
FORGET IT!! I DON'T WANT TO KNOW ANY MORE THAN I ALREADY DO!!
OHH, HERE. LOOK AT THIS. THAT'S KENJI'S SISTER.
WOWW. SHE'S REALLY PRETTY.
BUT ENOUGH, ALREADY !!
I REALLY DON'T WANT TO KNOW ANY MORE!!
AH. HERE WE GO.

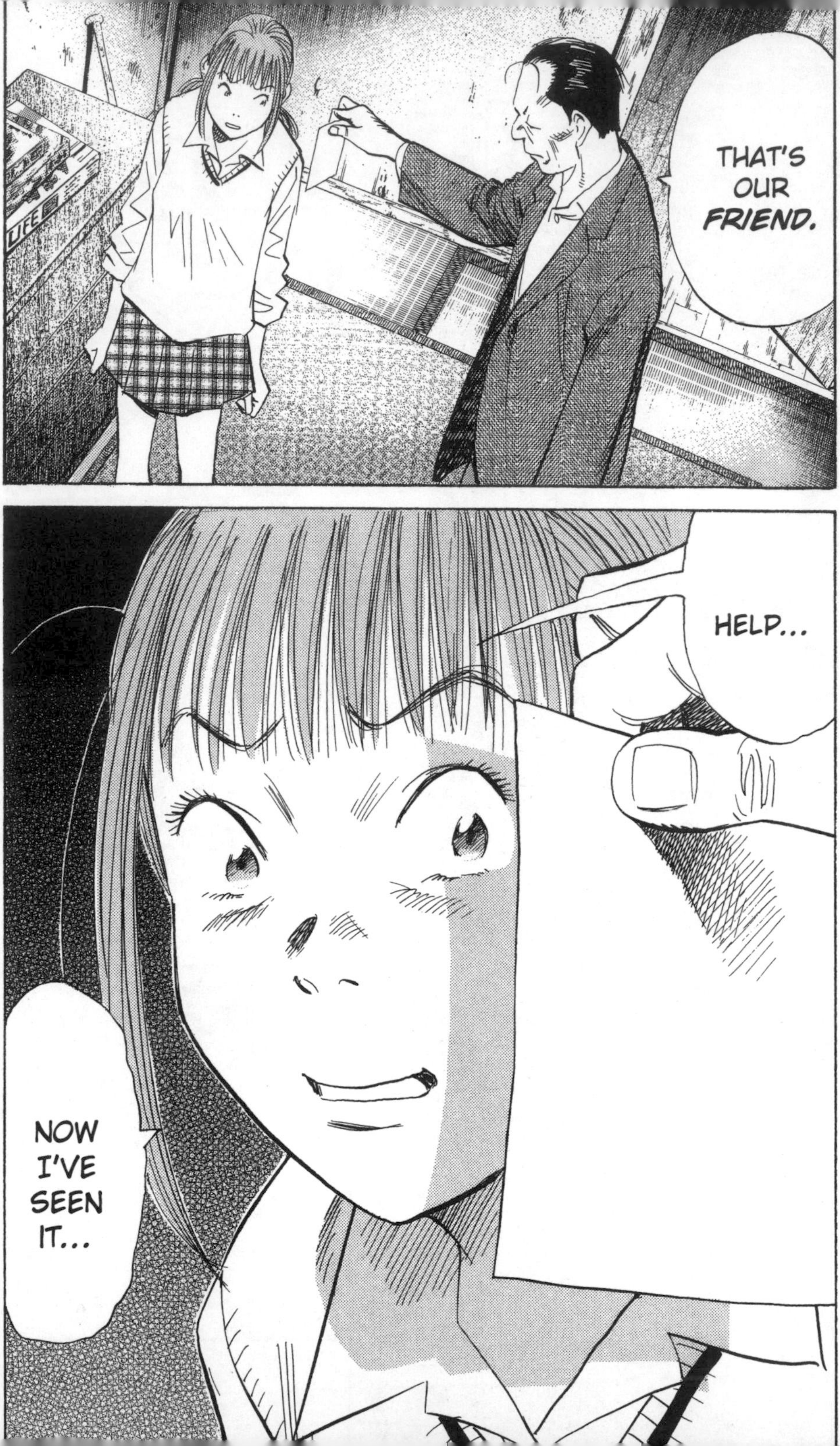
THAT'S OUR *FRIEND.*
HELP...
NOW I'VE SEEN IT...

Chapter 9 The Faceless Boy

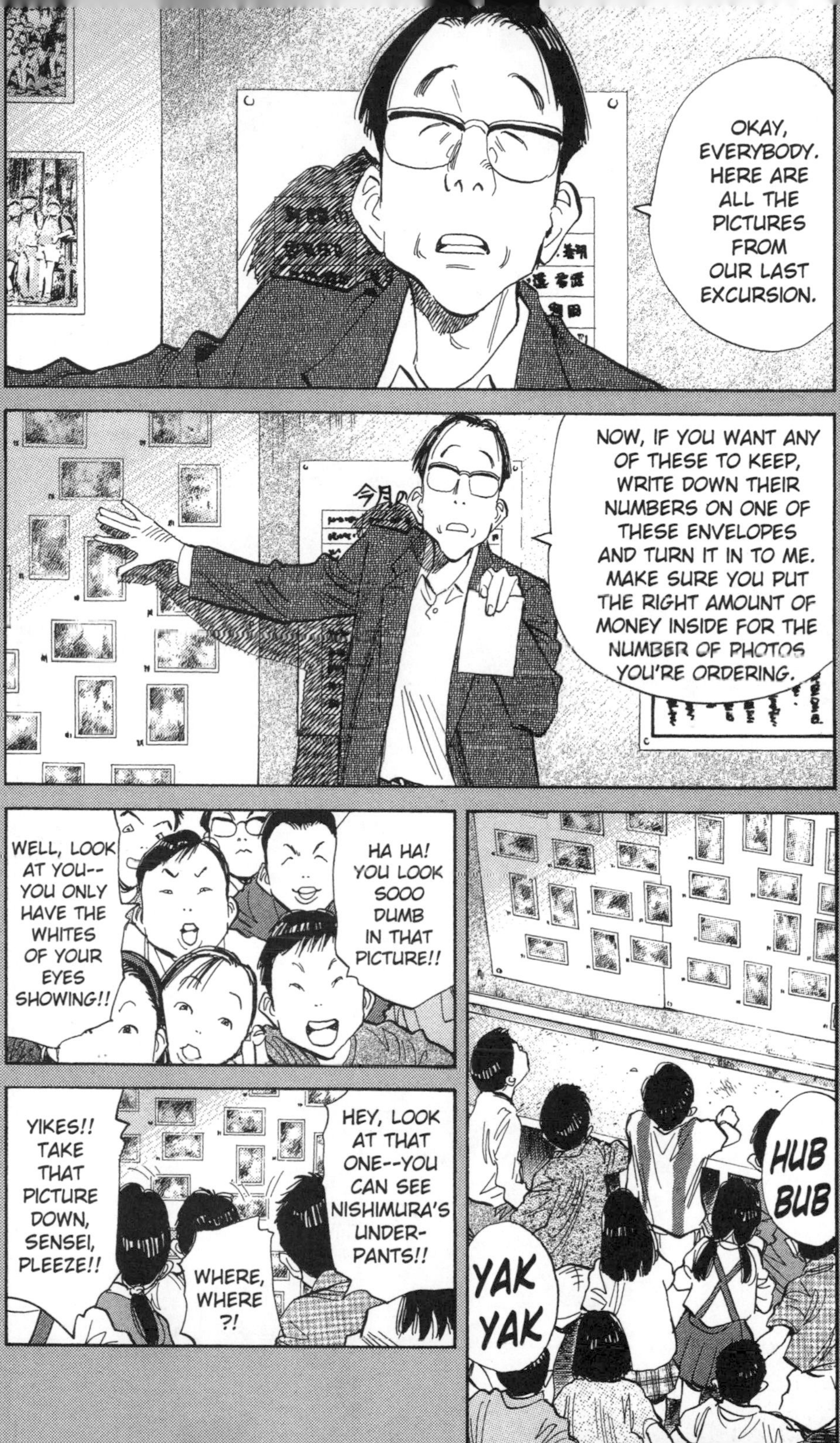
OKAY, EVERYBODY. HERE ARE ALL THE PICTURES FROM OUR LAST EXCURSION.
NOW, IF YOU WANT ANY OF THESE TO KEEP, WRITE DOWN THEIR NUMBERS ON ONE OF THESE ENVELOPES AND TURN IT IN TO ME. MAKE SURE YOU PUT THE RIGHT AMOUNT OF MONEY INSIDE FOR THE NUMBER OF PHOTOS YOU'RE ORDERING.
HUB BUB
YAK YAK
HA HA! YOU LOOK SOOO DUMB IN THAT PICTURE!!
WELL, LOOK AT YOU-- YOU ONLY HAVE THE WHITES OF YOUR EYES SHOWING!!
HEY, LOOK AT THAT ONE--YOU CAN SEE NISHIMURA'S UNDER-PANTS!!
WHERE, WHERE ?!
YIKES!! TAKE THAT PICTURE DOWN, SENSEI, PLEEZE!!

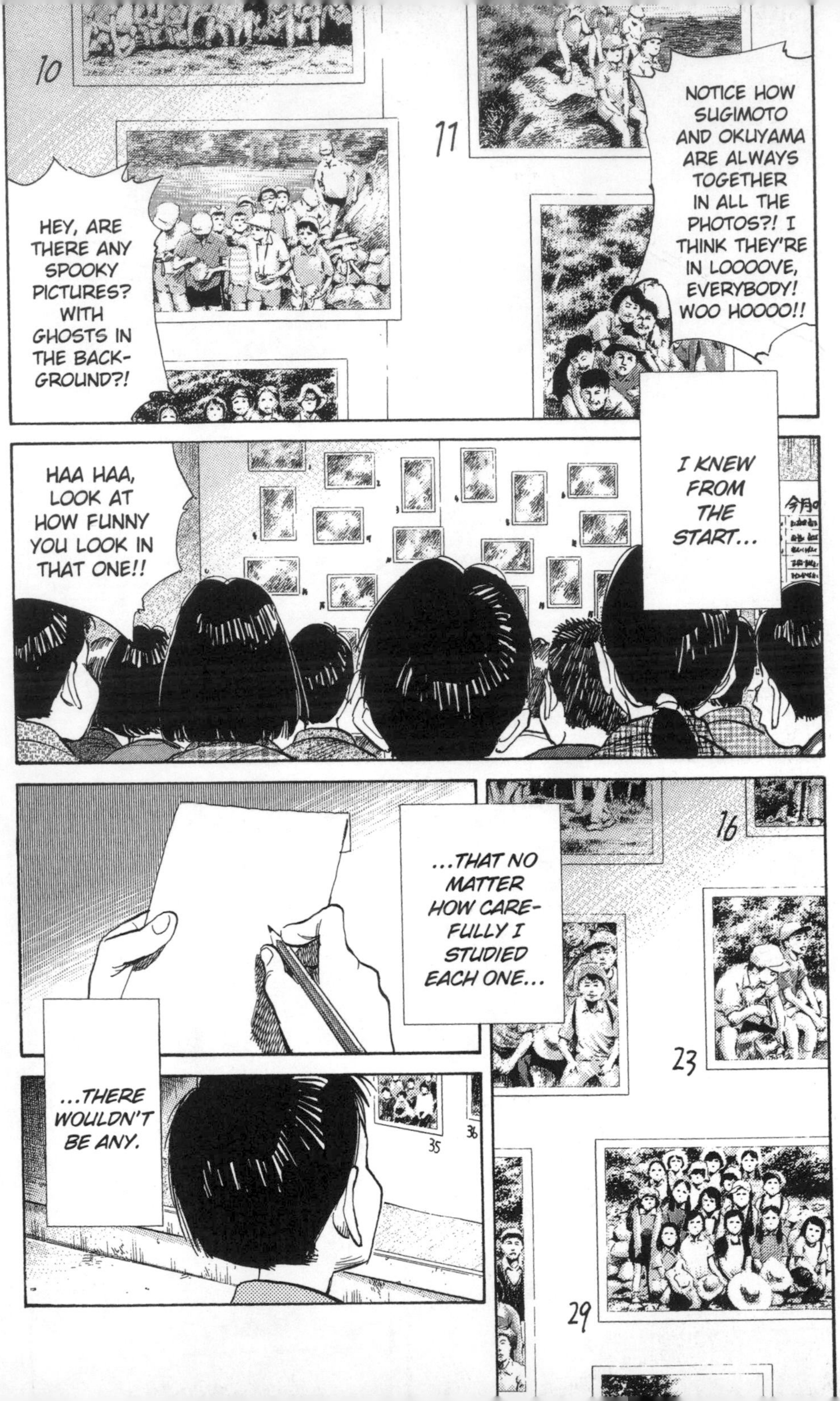
11
NOTICE HOW SUGIMOTO AND OKUYAMA ARE ALWAYS TOGETHER IN ALL THE PHOTOS?! I THINK THEY'RE IN LOOOOVE, EVERYBODY! WOO HOOOO!!
10
HEY, ARE THERE ANY SPOOKY PICTURES? WITH GHOSTS IN THE BACK-GROUND?!
I KNEW FROM THE START...
HAA HAA, LOOK AT HOW FUNNY YOU LOOK IN THAT ONE!!
16
23
29
...THAT NO MATTER HOW CARE-FULLY I STUDIED EACH ONE...
...THERE WOULDN'T BE ANY.
36
35

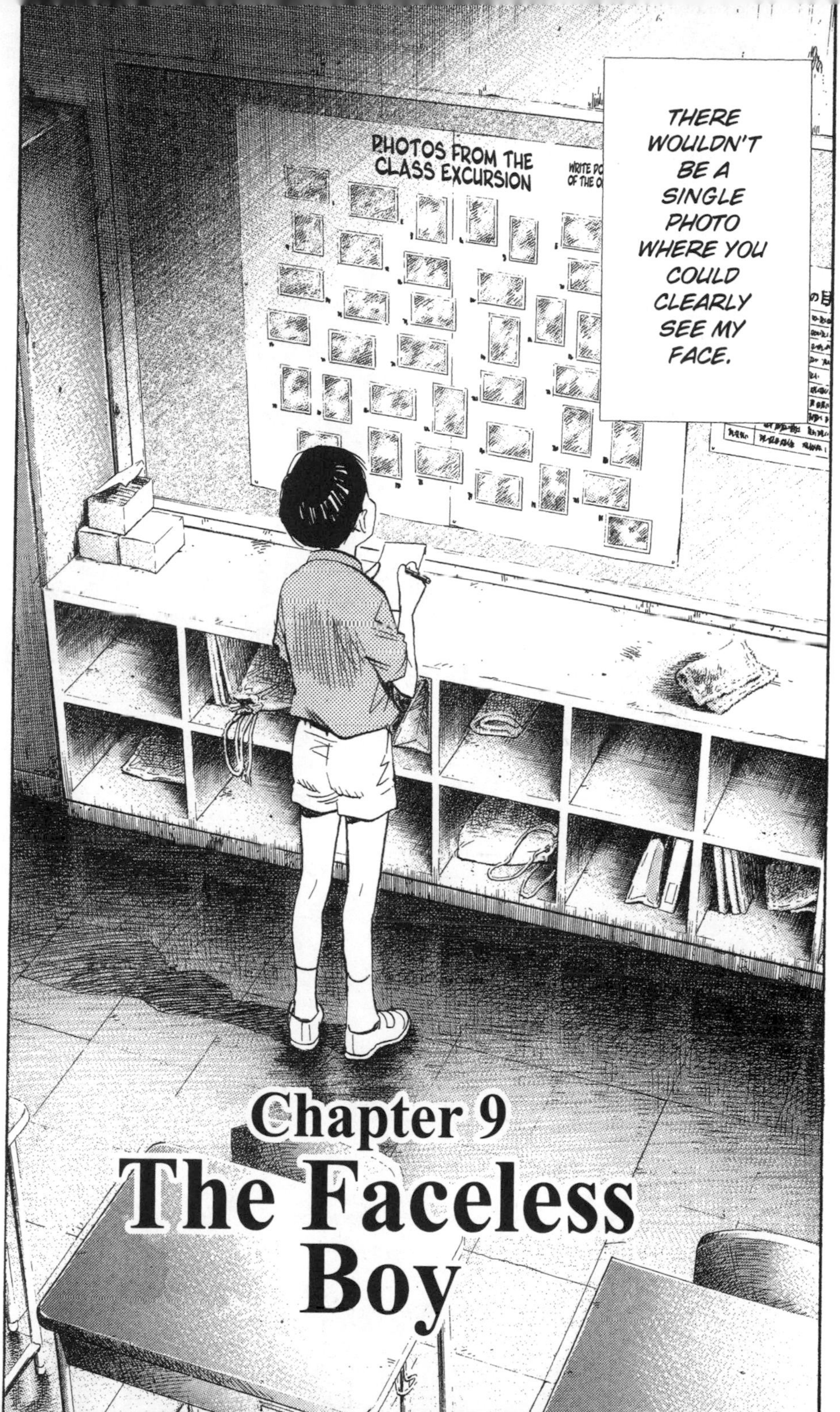
THERE WOULDN'T BE A SINGLE PHOTO WHERE YOU COULD CLEARLY SEE MY FACE.
PHOTOS FROM THE CLASS EXCURSION

Chapter 9
The Faceless Boy

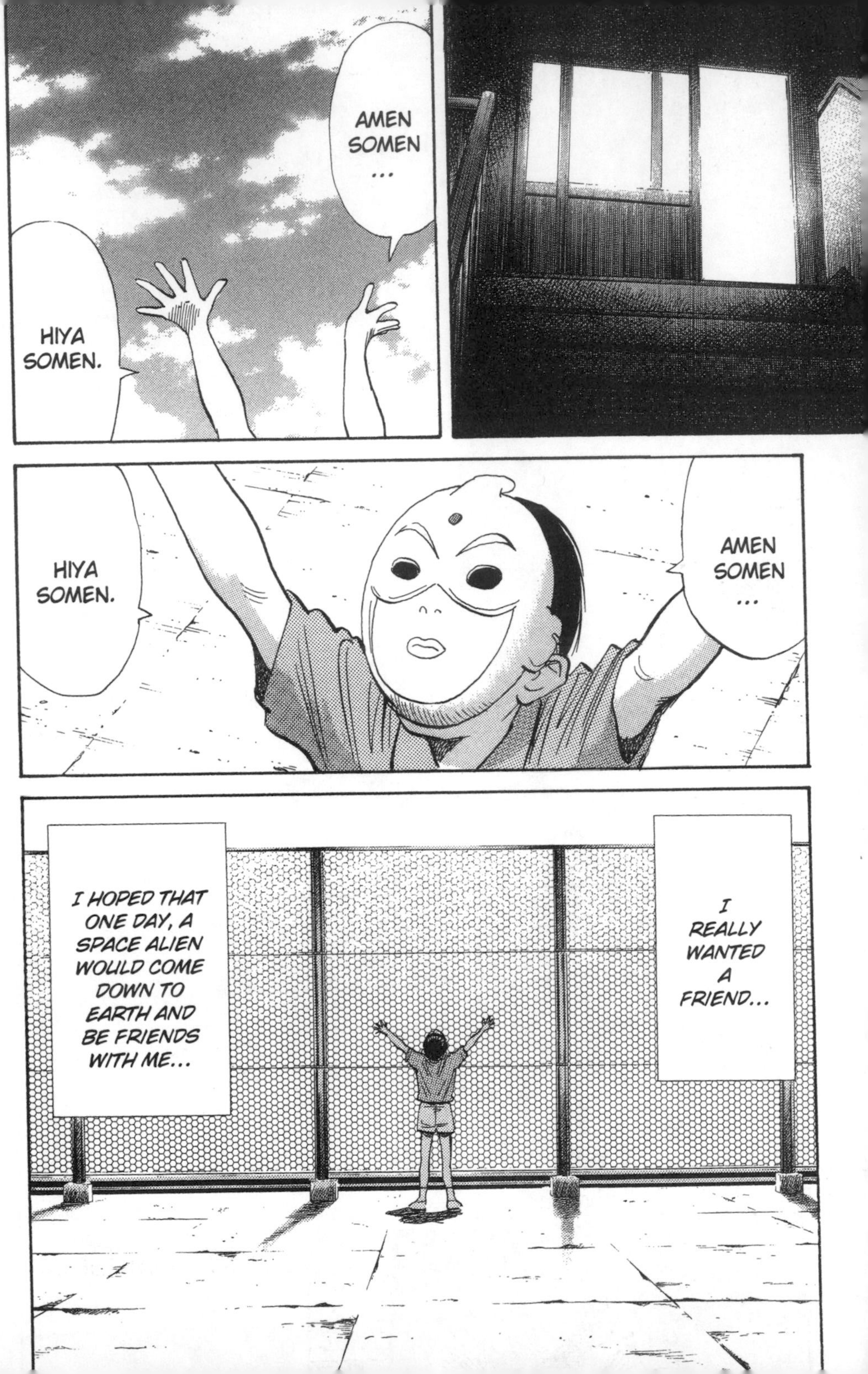
AMEN SOMEN ...
HIYA SOMEN.
AMEN SOMEN ...
HIYA SOMEN.
I REALLY WANTED A FRIEND...
I HOPED THAT ONE DAY, A SPACE ALIEN WOULD COME DOWN TO EARTH AND BE FRIENDS WITH ME...

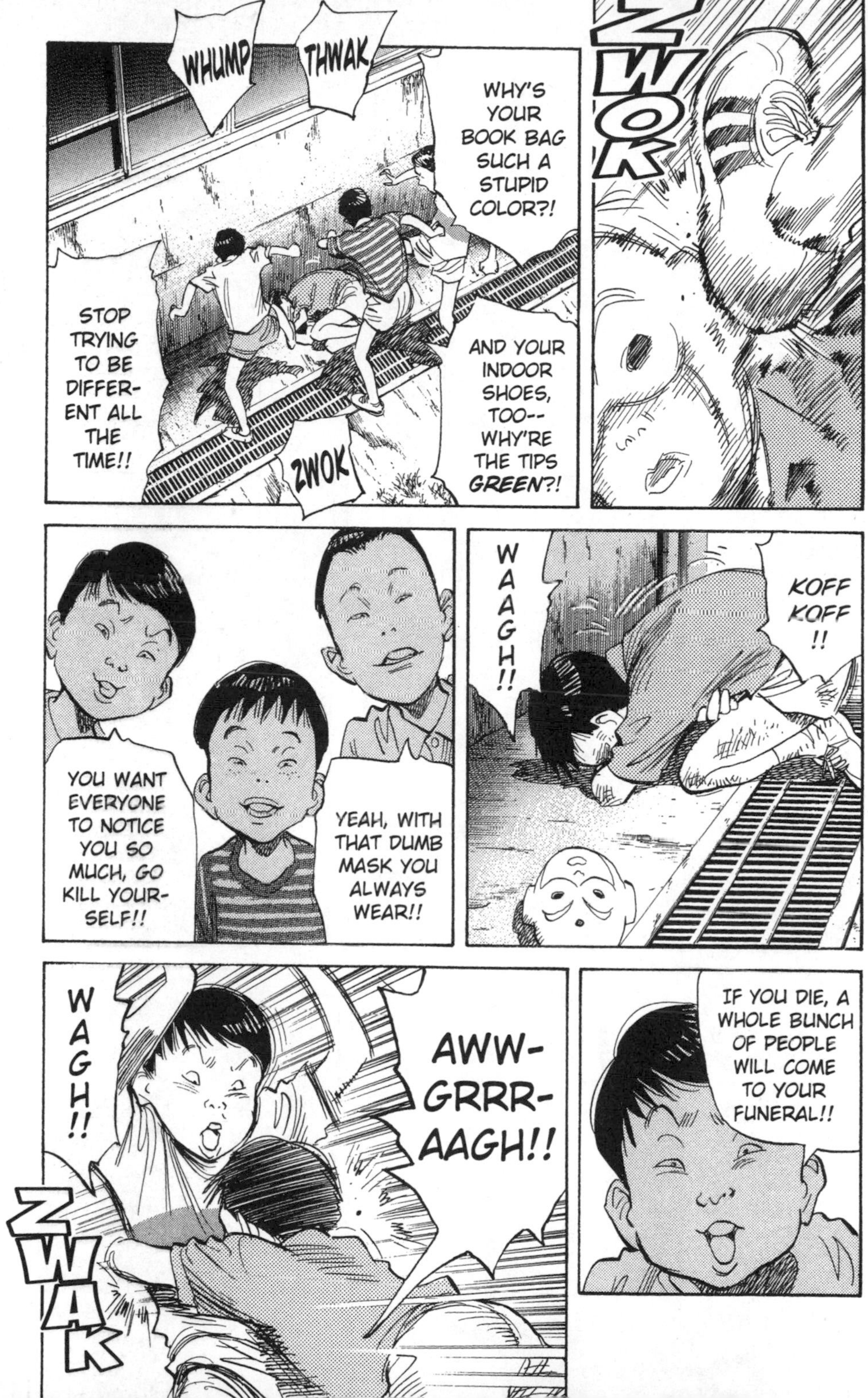
ZWOK
THWAK
WHUMP
WHY'S YOUR BOOK BAG SUCH A STUPID COLOR?!
AND YOUR INDOOR SHOES, TOO-- WHY'RE THE TIPS *GREEN*?!
STOP TRYING TO BE DIFFER-ENT ALL THE TIME!!
ZWOK
KOFF KOFF !!
WAAGH!!
YEAH, WITH THAT DUMB MASK YOU ALWAYS WEAR!!
YOU WANT EVERYONE TO NOTICE YOU SO MUCH, GO KILL YOUR-SELF!!
IF YOU DIE, A WHOLE BUNCH OF PEOPLE WILL COME TO YOUR FUNERAL!!
AWW-GRRR-AAGH!!
WAGH!!
ZWAK

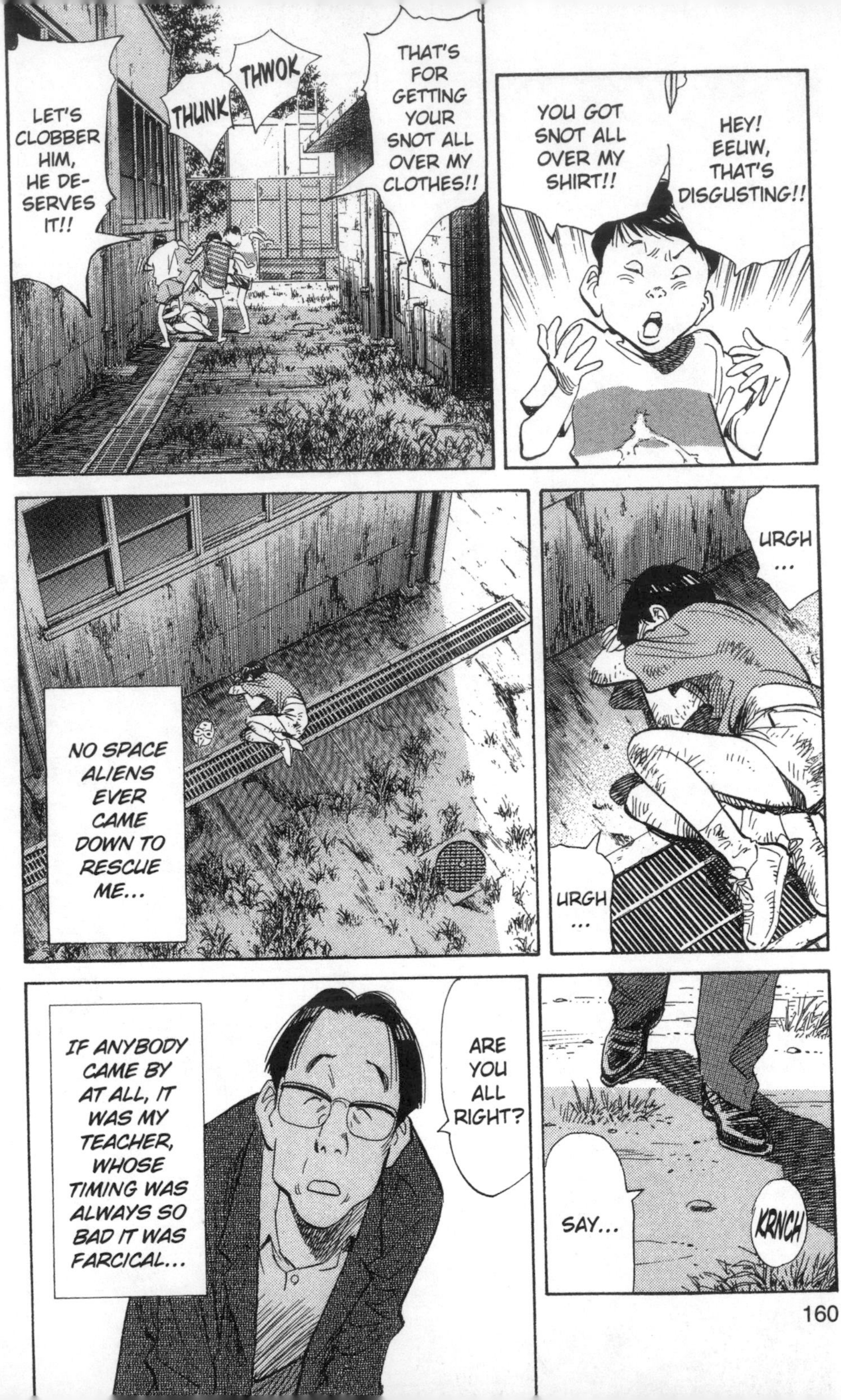
HEY! EEUW, THAT'S DISGUSTING!!
YOU GOT SNOT ALL OVER MY SHIRT!!
THAT'S FOR GETTING YOUR SNOT ALL OVER MY CLOTHES!!
THWOK
THUNK
LET'S CLOBBER HIM, HE DE-SERVES IT!!
URGH...
URGH...
NO SPACE ALIENS EVER CAME DOWN TO RESCUE ME...
SAY...
KRNCH
ARE YOU ALL RIGHT?
IF ANYBODY CAME BY AT ALL, IT WAS MY TEACHER, WHOSE TIMING WAS ALWAYS SO BAD IT WAS FARCICAL...

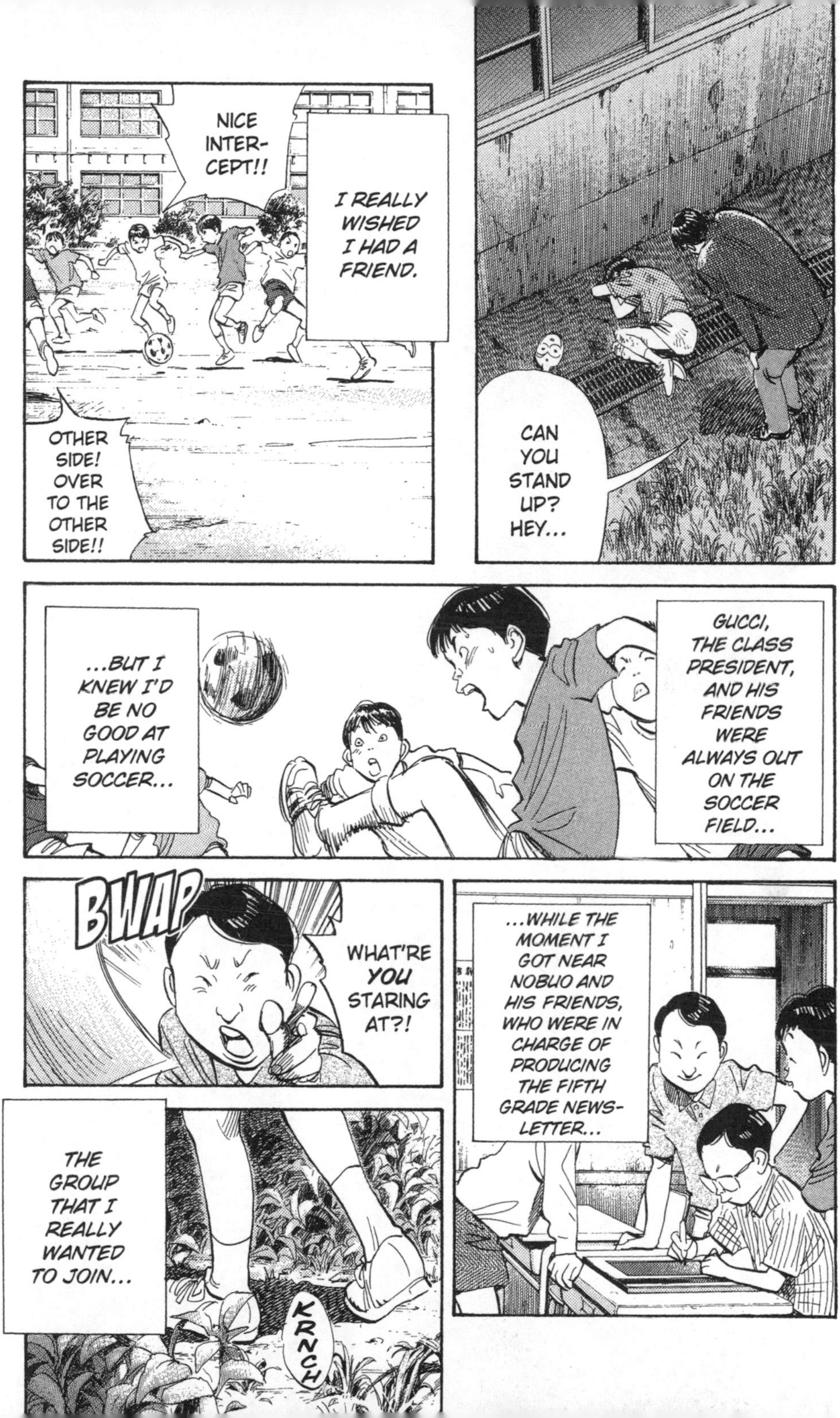

CAN YOU STAND UP? HEY...
I REALLY WISHED I HAD A FRIEND.
NICE INTERCEPT!!
OTHER SIDE! OVER TO THE OTHER SIDE!!
GUCCI, THE CLASS PRESIDENT, AND HIS FRIENDS WERE ALWAYS OUT ON THE SOCCER FIELD...
...BUT I KNEW I'D BE NO GOOD AT PLAYING SOCCER...
...WHILE THE MOMENT I GOT NEAR NOBUO AND HIS FRIENDS, WHO WERE IN CHARGE OF PRODUCING THE FIFTH GRADE NEWS-LETTER...
BWAP
WHAT'RE YOU STARING AT?!
THE GROUP THAT I REALLY WANTED TO JOIN...
KRNCH

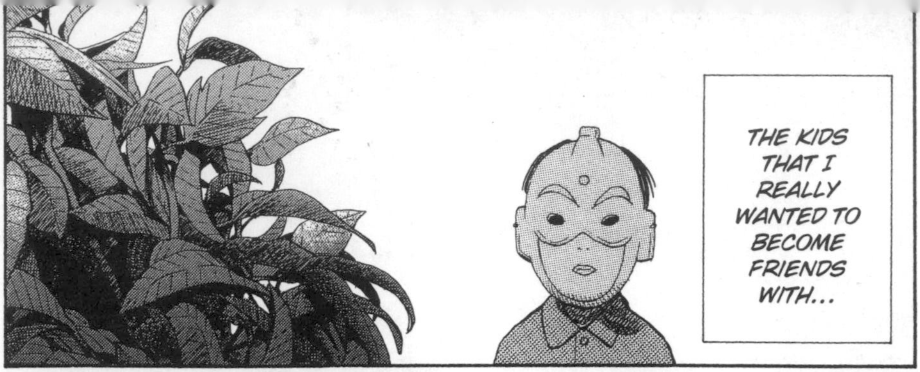
THE KIDS THAT I REALLY WANTED TO BECOME FRIENDS WITH...
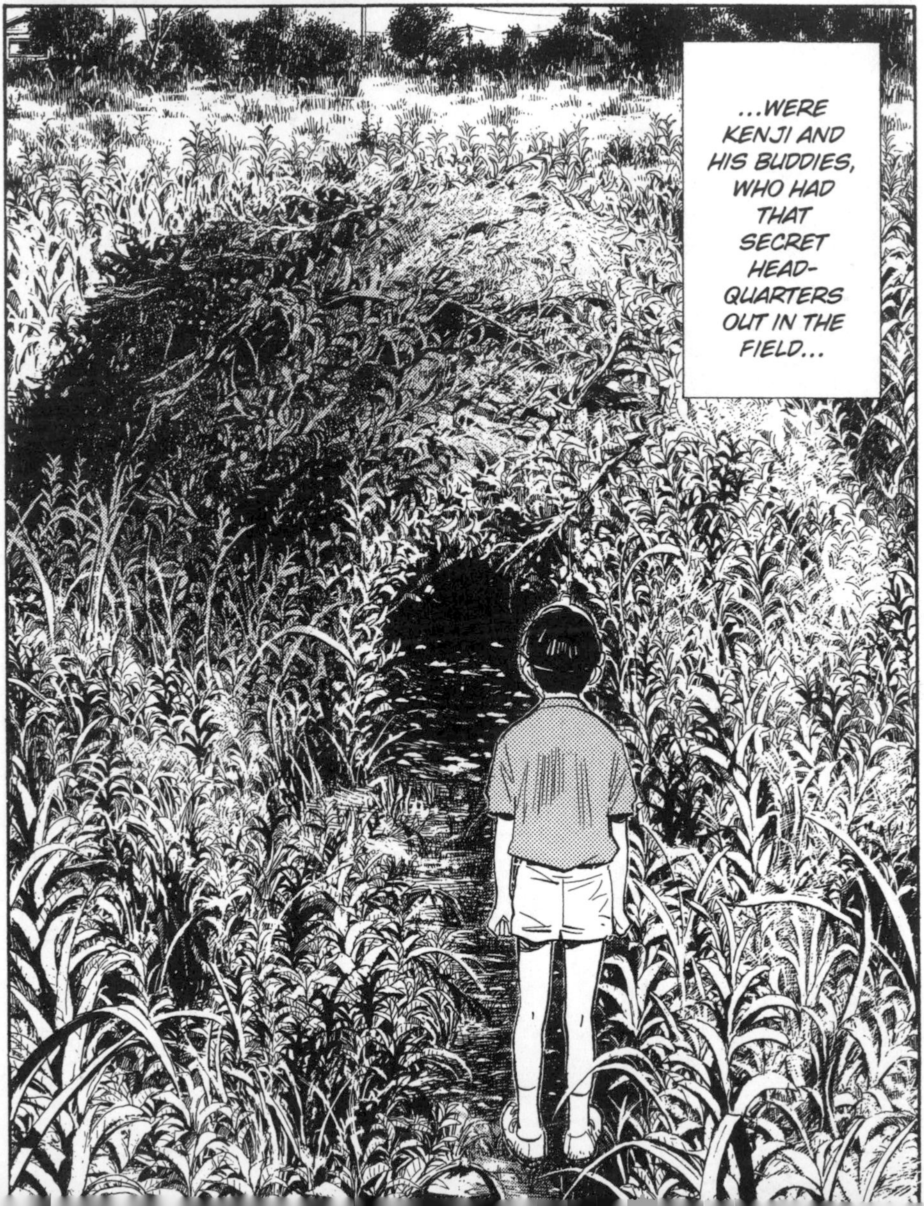
...WERE KENJI AND HIS BUDDIES, WHO HAD THAT SECRET HEAD-QUARTERS OUT IN THE FIELD...

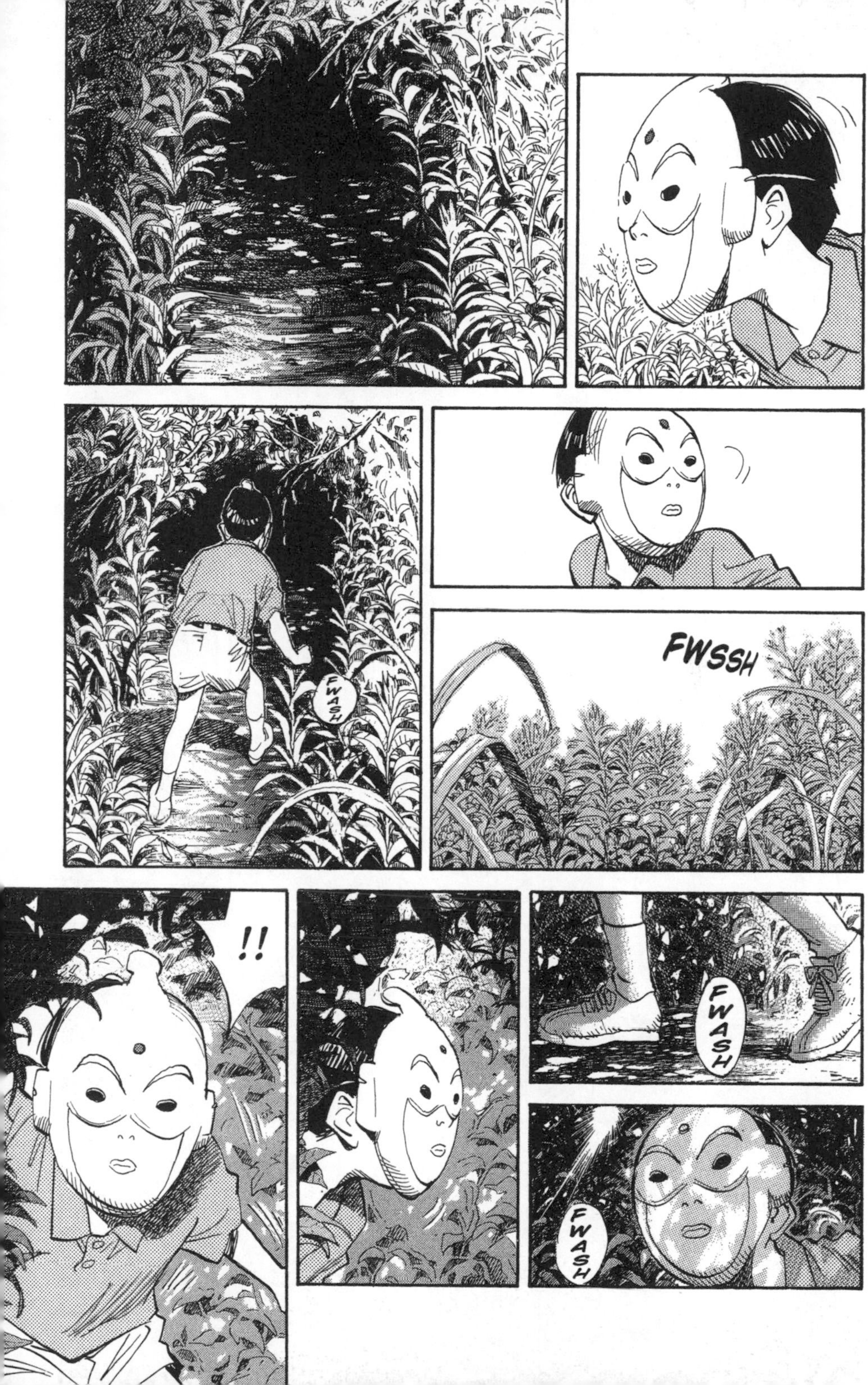
FWSSH
FWASH
FWASH
FWASH
!!

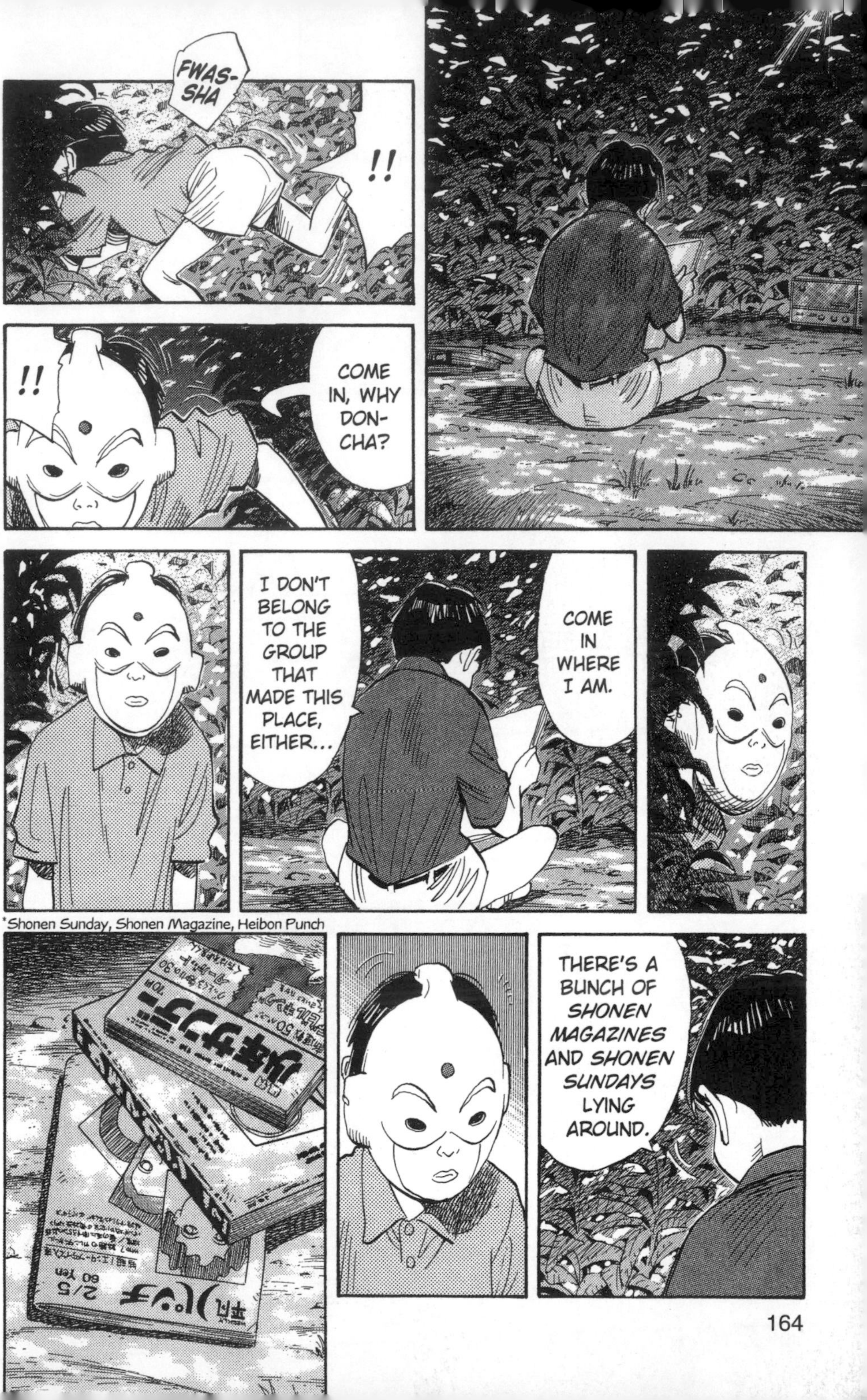
FWAS-SHA
!!
!!
COME IN, WHY DON-CHA?
COME IN WHERE I AM.
I DON'T BELONG TO THE GROUP THAT MADE THIS PLACE, EITHER...
THERE'S A BUNCH OF SHONEN MAGAZINES AND SHONEN SUNDAYS LYING AROUND.
2/5
80 Yen

*Shonen Sunday, Shonen Magazine, Heibon Punch

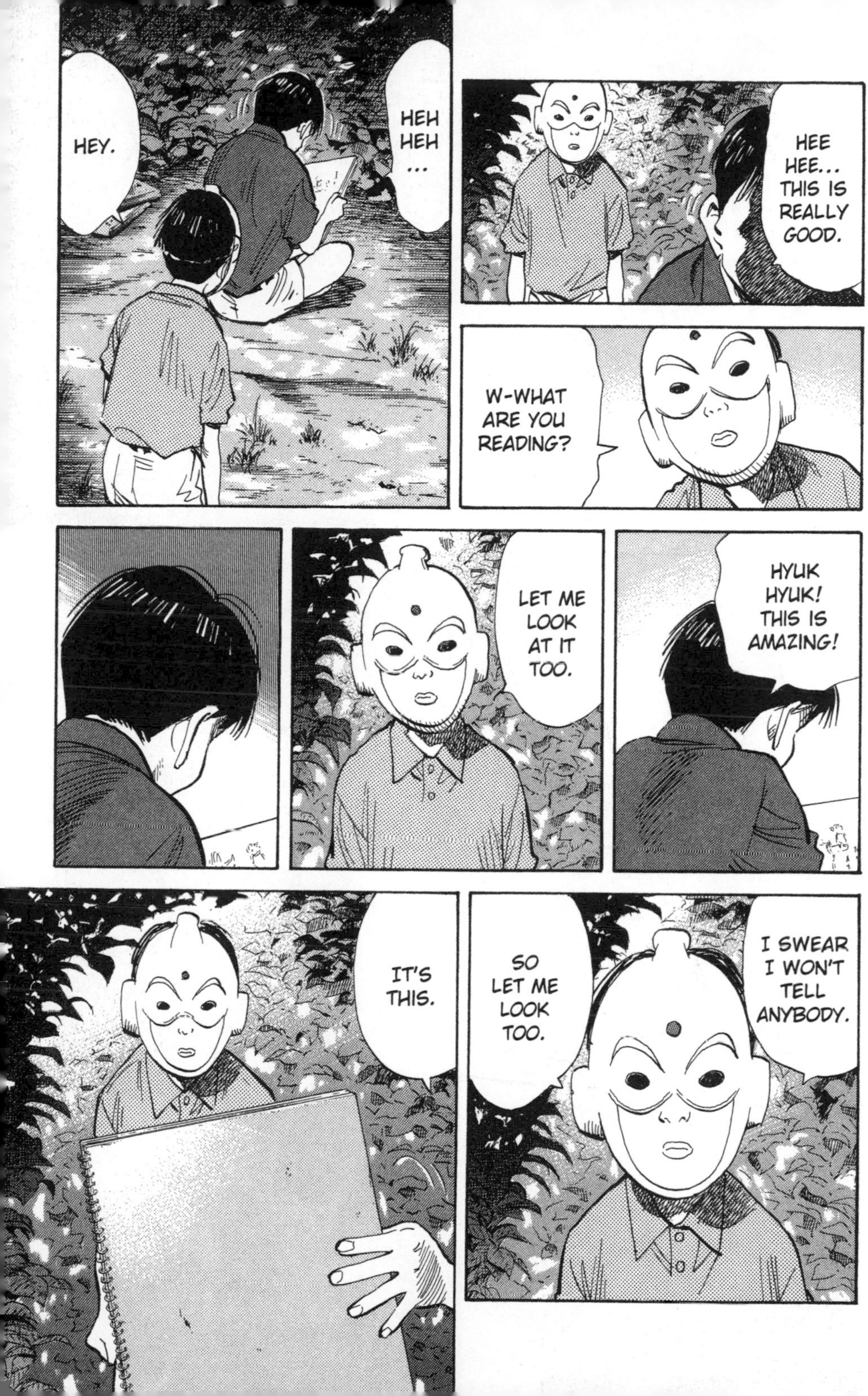
HEE HEE... THIS IS REALLY GOOD.
W-WHAT ARE YOU READING?
HEH HEH ...
HEY.
HYUK HYUK! THIS IS AMAZING!
LET ME LOOK AT IT TOO.
I SWEAR I WON'T TELL ANYBODY.
SO LET ME LOOK TOO.
IT'S THIS.

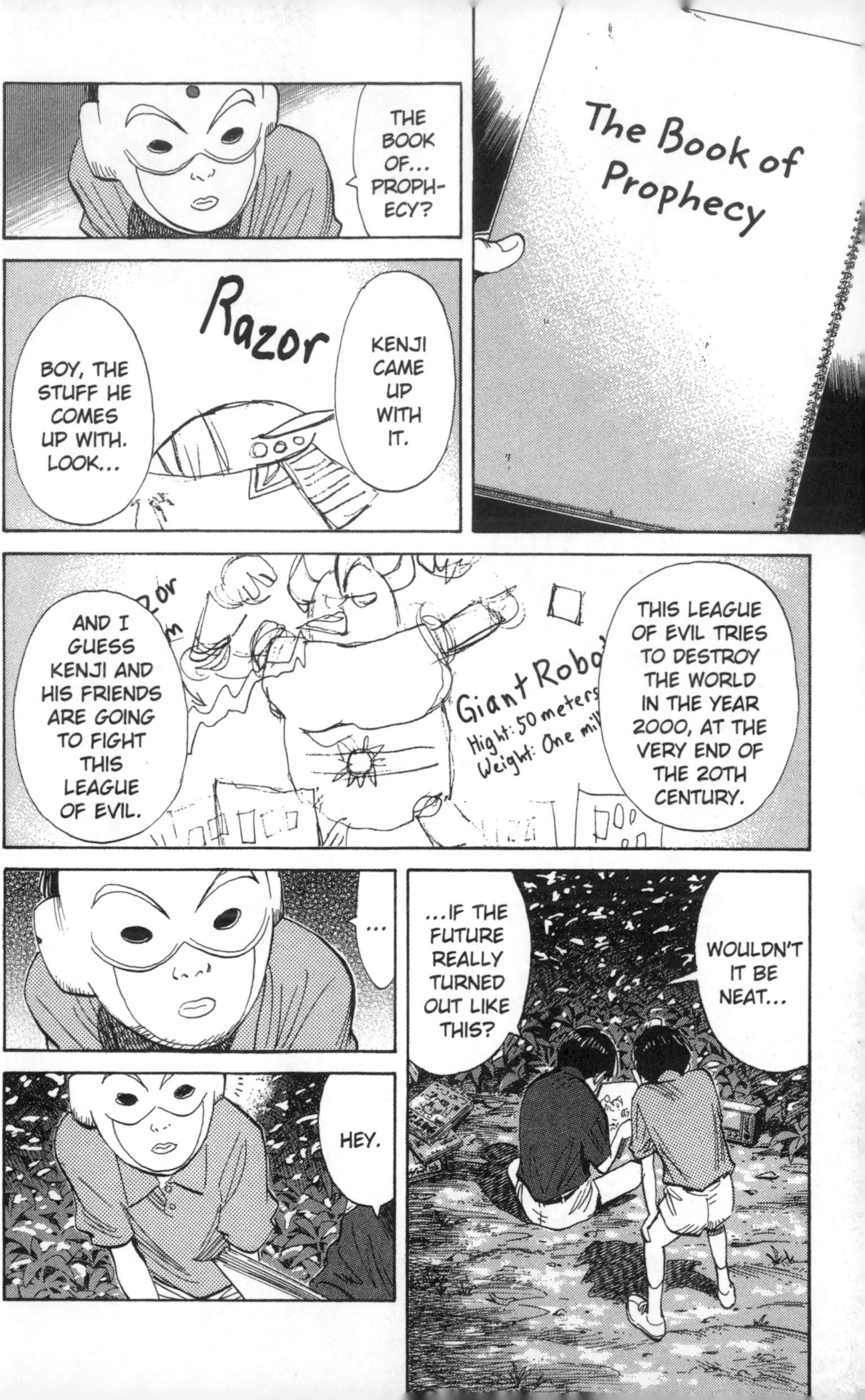
The Book of Prophecy
THE BOOK OF... PROPHECY?
KENJI CAME UP WITH IT.
Razor
BOY, THE STUFF HE COMES UP WITH. LOOK...
THIS LEAGUE OF EVIL TRIES TO DESTROY THE WORLD IN THE YEAR 2000, AT THE VERY END OF THE 20TH CENTURY.
AND I GUESS KENJI AND HIS FRIENDS ARE GOING TO FIGHT THIS LEAGUE OF EVIL.
WOULDN'T IT BE NEAT...
...IF THE FUTURE REALLY TURNED OUT LIKE THIS?
...
HEY.

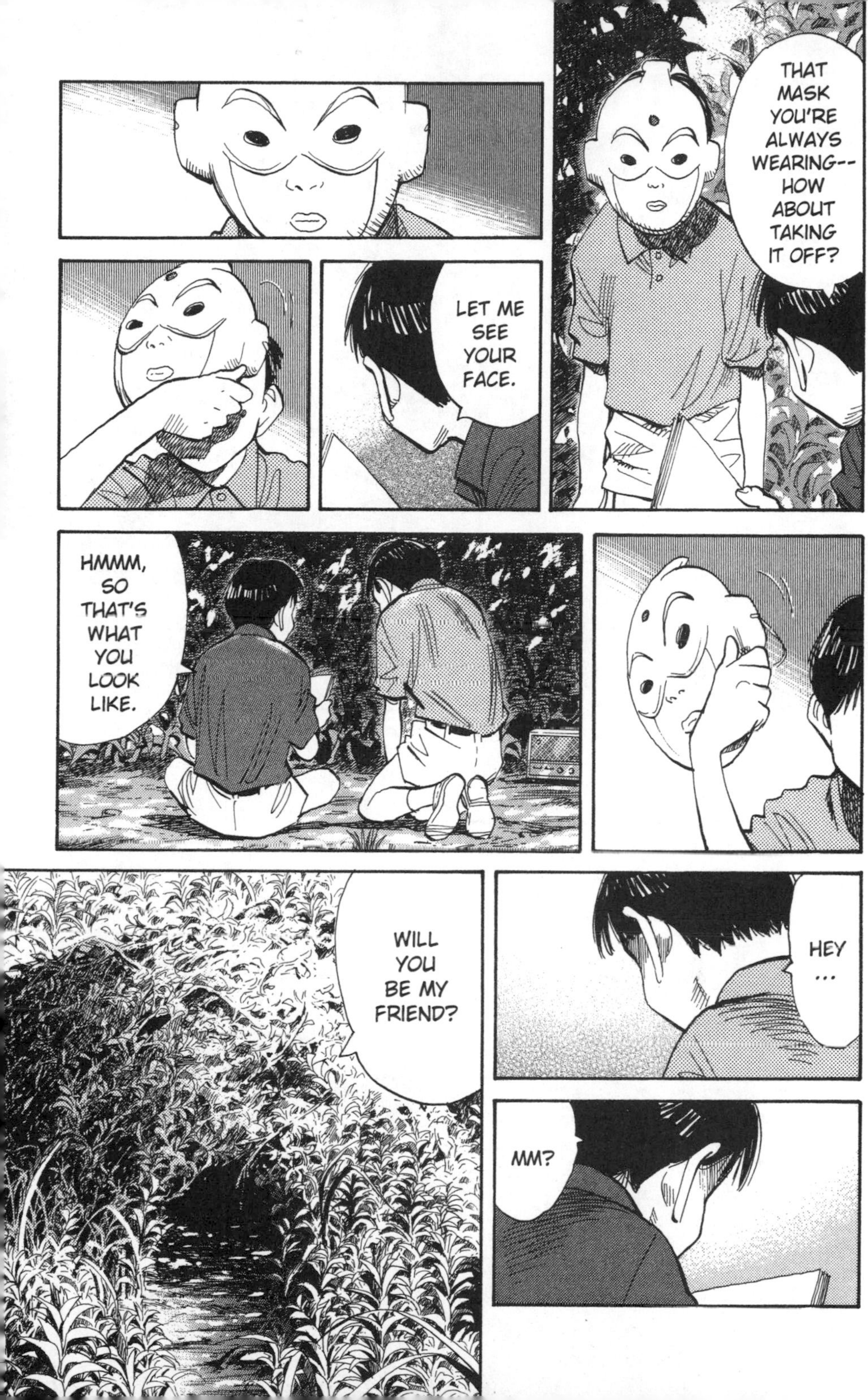
THAT MASK YOU'RE ALWAYS WEARING-- HOW ABOUT TAKING IT OFF?
LET ME SEE YOUR FACE.
HMMM, SO THAT'S WHAT YOU LOOK LIKE.
HEY ...
MM?
WILL YOU BE MY FRIEND?

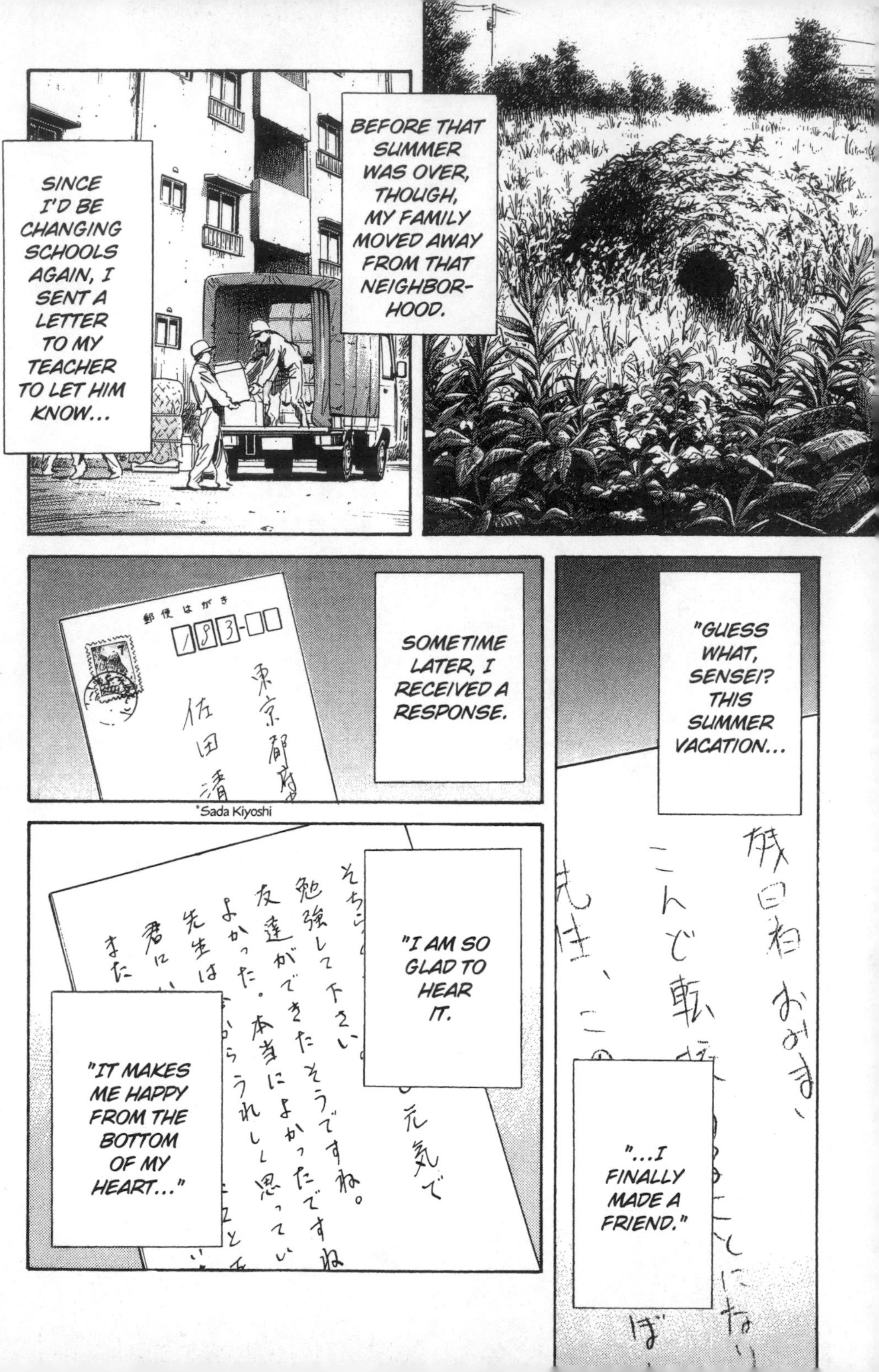
BEFORE THAT SUMMER WAS OVER, THOUGH, MY FAMILY MOVED AWAY FROM THAT NEIGHBOR-HOOD.
SINCE I'D BE CHANGING SCHOOLS AGAIN, I SENT A LETTER TO MY TEACHER TO LET HIM KNOW...
"GUESS WHAT, SENSEI? THIS SUMMER VACATION...
"...I FINALLY MADE A FRIEND."
SOMETIME LATER, I RECEIVED A RESPONSE.
郵便はがき
佐田清
*Sada Kiyoshi
"I AM SO GLAD TO HEAR IT.
"IT MAKES ME HAPPY FROM THE BOTTOM OF MY HEART..."

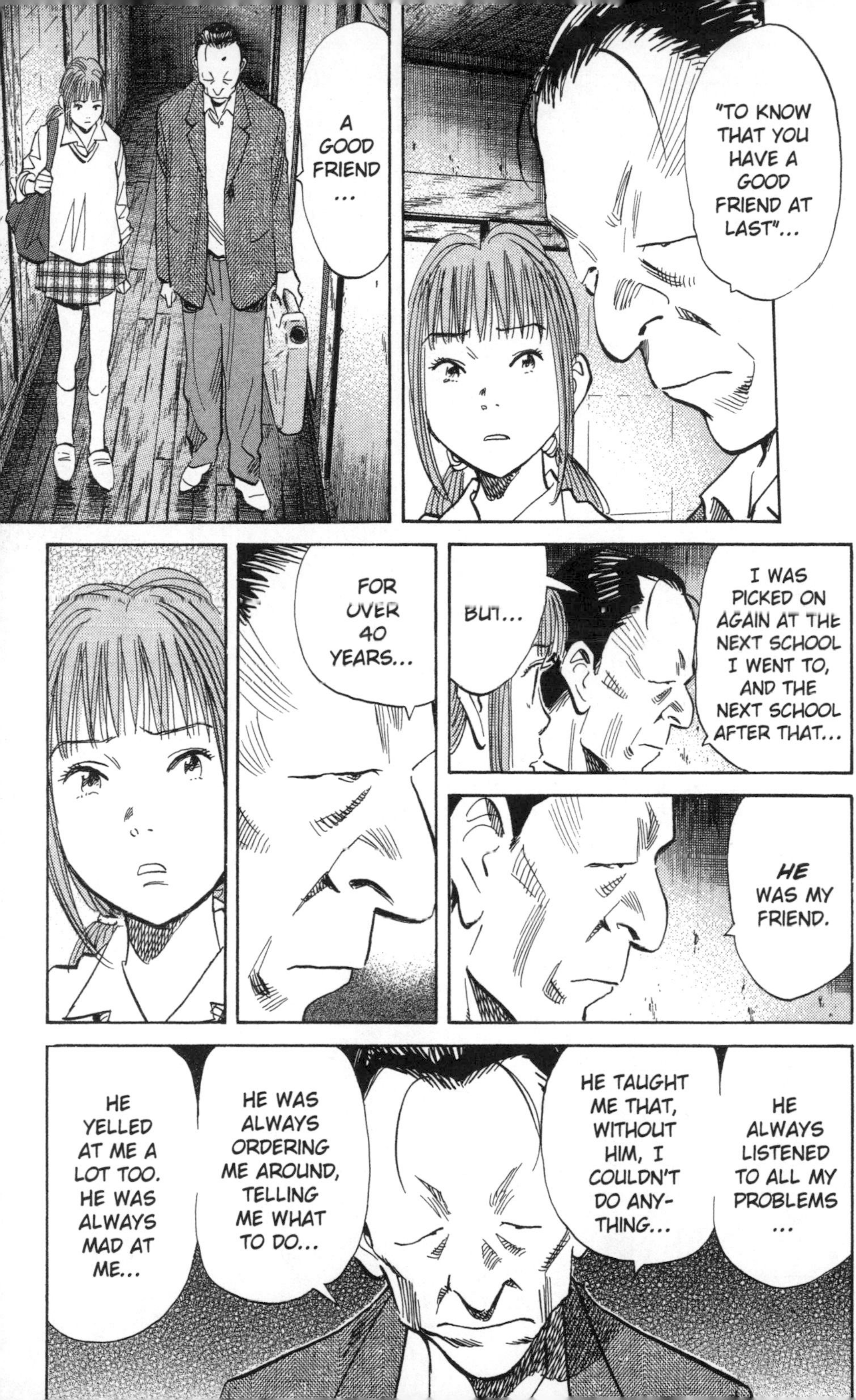
"TO KNOW THAT YOU HAVE A GOOD FRIEND AT LAST"...
A GOOD FRIEND ...
I WAS PICKED ON AGAIN AT THE NEXT SCHOOL I WENT TO, AND THE NEXT SCHOOL AFTER THAT...
BUT...
HE WAS MY FRIEND.
FOR OVER 40 YEARS...
HE ALWAYS LISTENED TO ALL MY PROBLEMS ...
HE TAUGHT ME THAT, WITHOUT HIM, I COULDN'T DO ANY-THING...
HE WAS ALWAYS ORDERING ME AROUND, TELLING ME WHAT TO DO...
HE YELLED AT ME A LOT TOO. HE WAS ALWAYS MAD AT ME...

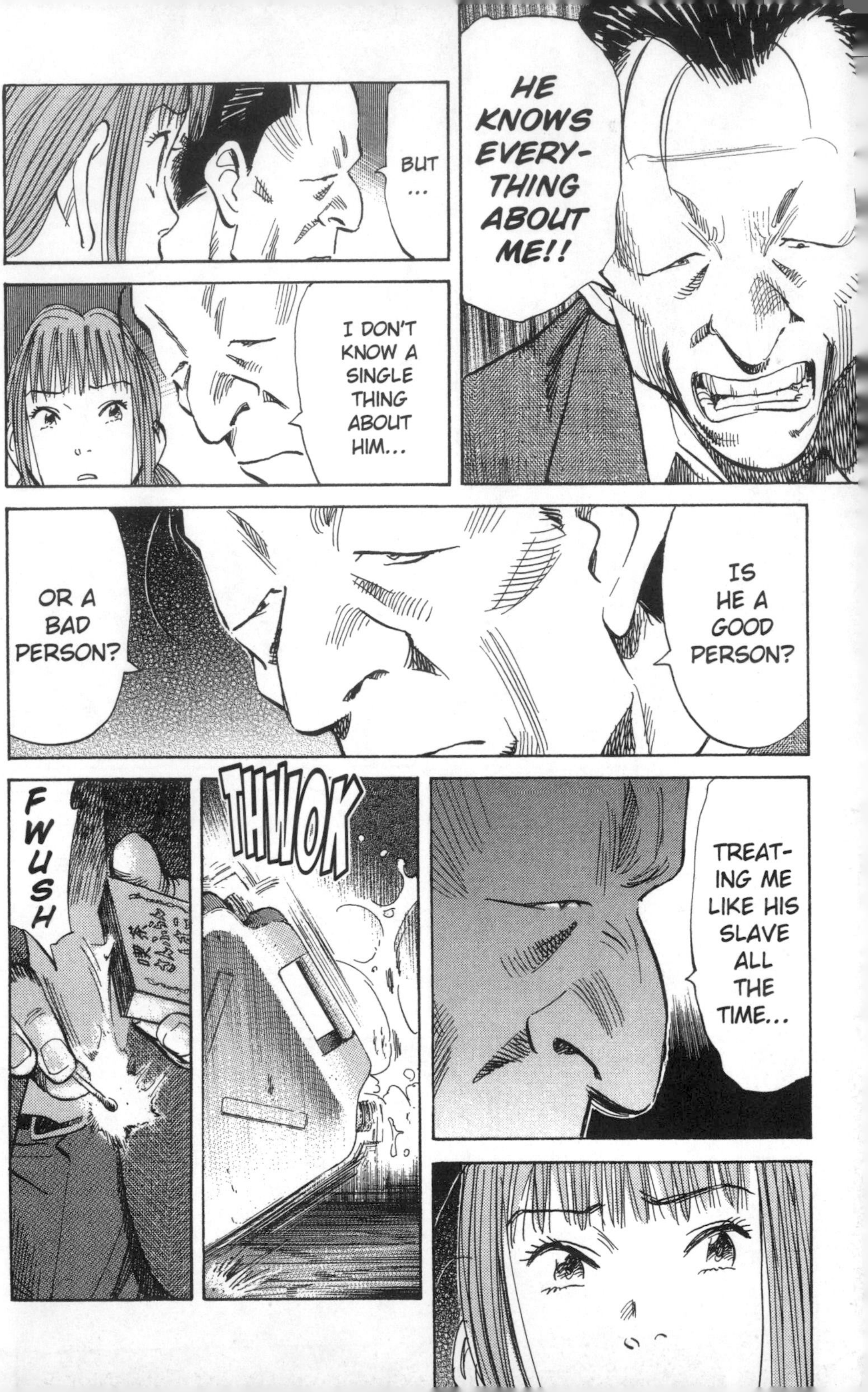
HE KNOWS EVERY-THING ABOUT ME!!
BUT ...
I DON'T KNOW A SINGLE THING ABOUT HIM...
IS HE A GOOD PERSON?
OR A BAD PERSON?
TREAT-ING ME LIKE HIS SLAVE ALL THE TIME...
THWOK
FWUSH

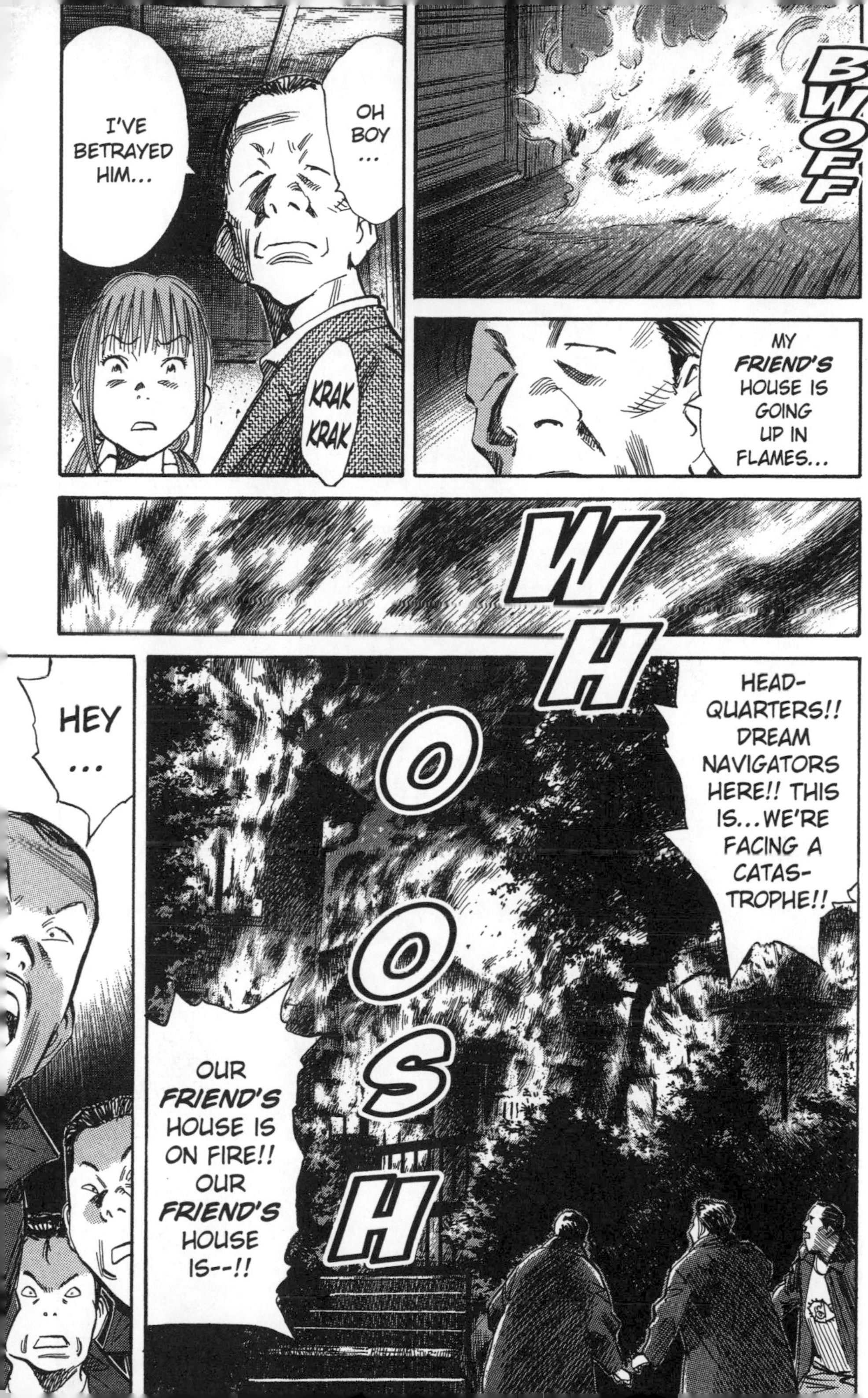
BWOFF
OH BOY...
I'VE BETRAYED HIM...
KRAK KRAK
MY FRIEND'S HOUSE IS GOING UP IN FLAMES...
HEADQUARTERS!! DREAM NAVIGATORS HERE!! THIS IS...WE'RE FACING A CATASTROPHE!!
WHOOSH
OUR FRIEND'S HOUSE IS ON FIRE!! OUR FRIEND'S HOUSE IS--!!
HEY...

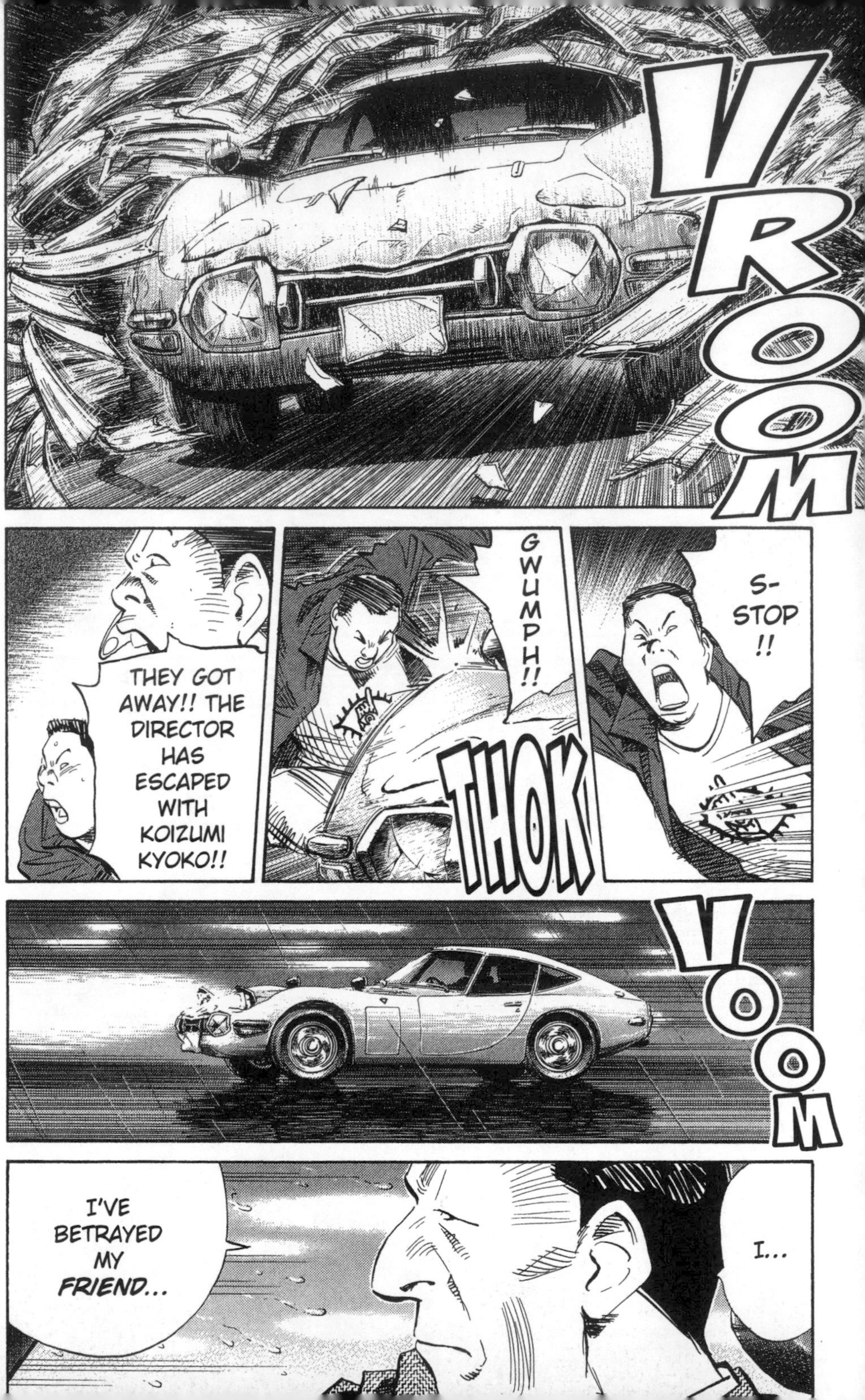
VROOM
S-STOP!!
GWUMPH!!
THOK
THEY GOT AWAY!! THE DIRECTOR HAS ESCAPED WITH KOIZUMI KYOKO!!
VOOOM
I...
I'VE BETRAYED MY *FRIEND*...

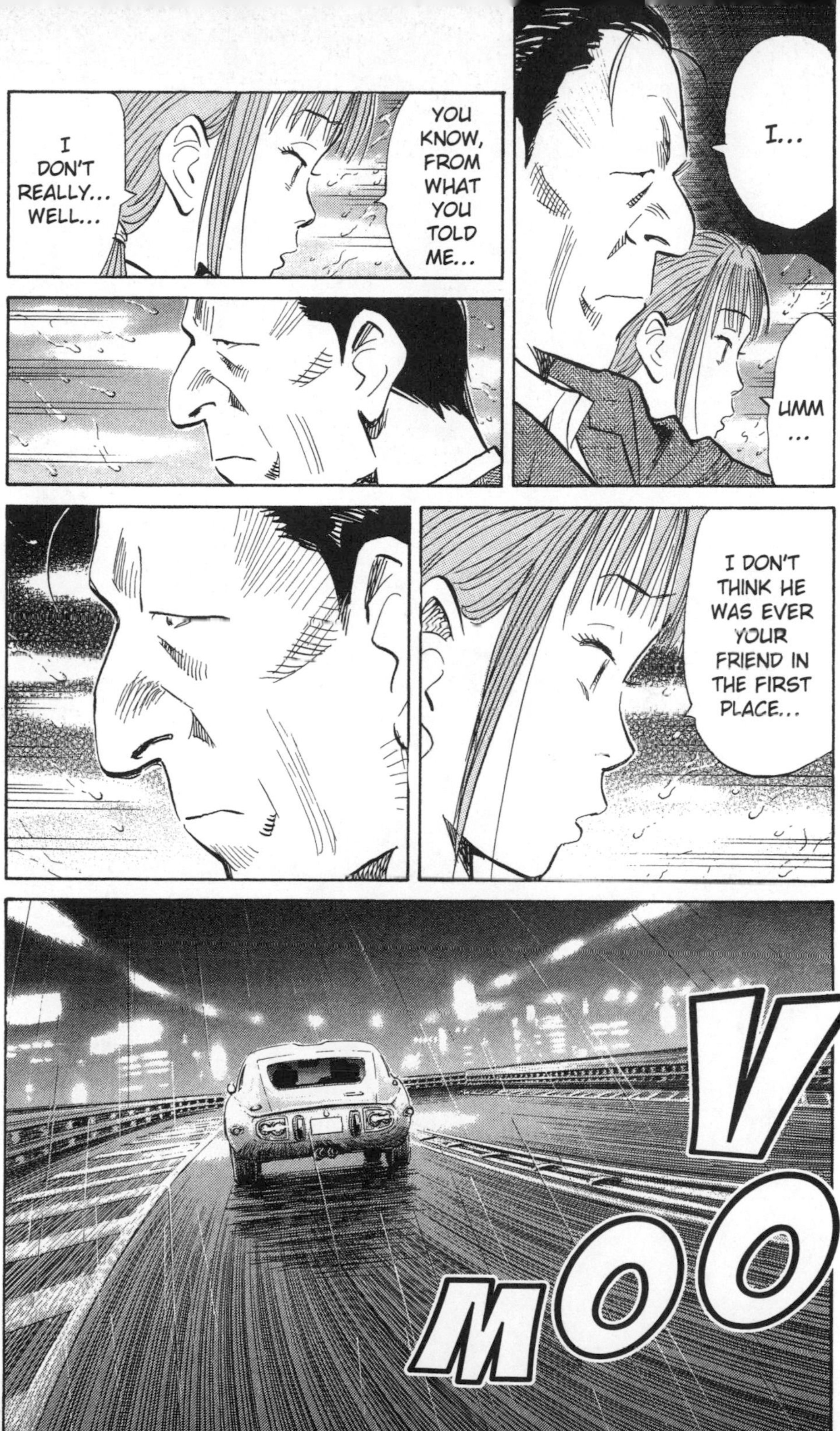
I...
UMM ...
YOU KNOW, FROM WHAT YOU TOLD ME...
I DON'T REALLY... WELL...
I DON'T THINK HE WAS EVER YOUR FRIEND IN THE FIRST PLACE...
VMOO

Chapter 10 Faceless No More

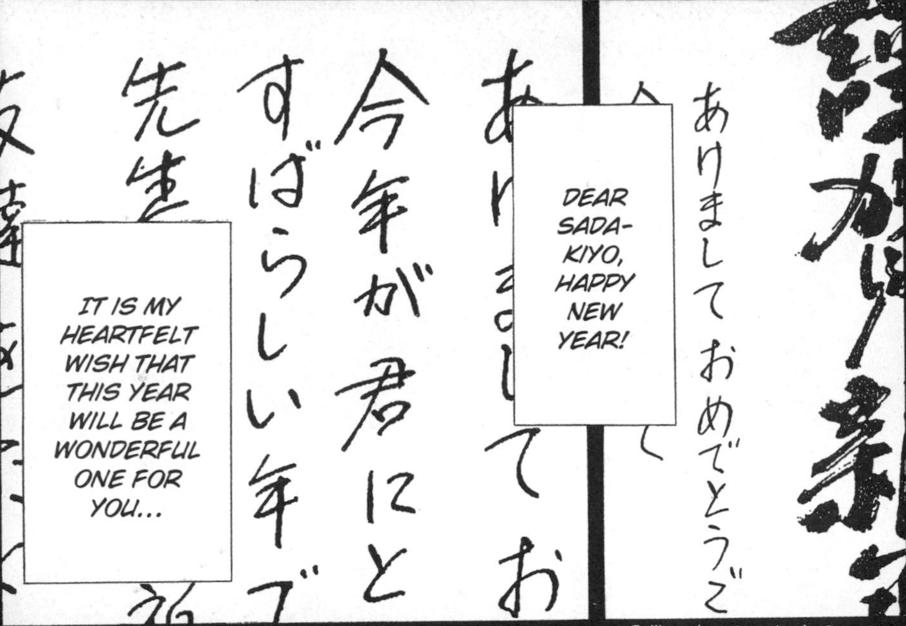
DEAR SADA-KIYO, HAPPY NEW YEAR!
IT IS MY HEARTFELT WISH THAT THIS YEAR WILL BE A WONDERFUL ONE FOR YOU...

Calligraphy: New Year's Greetings

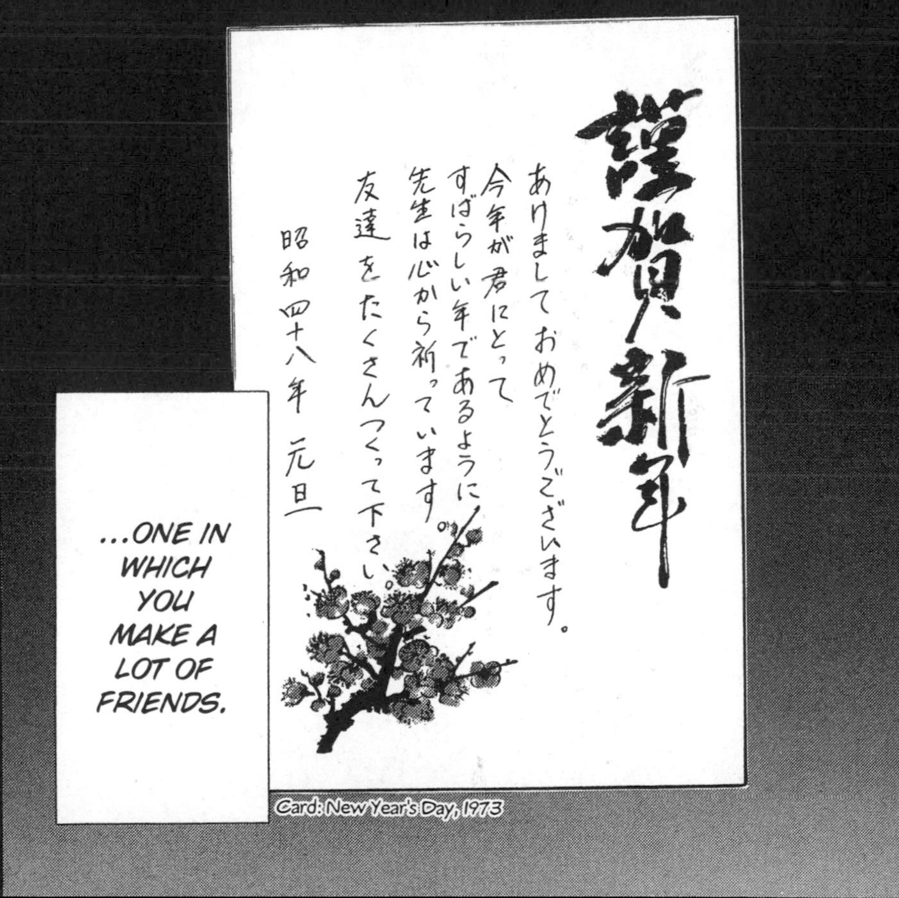
謹賀新年
ありましておめでとうございます。
今年が君にとって
すばらしい年であるように
先生は心から祈っています。
友達をたくさんつくって下さい。
昭和四十八年 元旦
...ONE IN WHICH YOU MAKE A LOT OF FRIENDS.

Card: New Year's Day, 1973

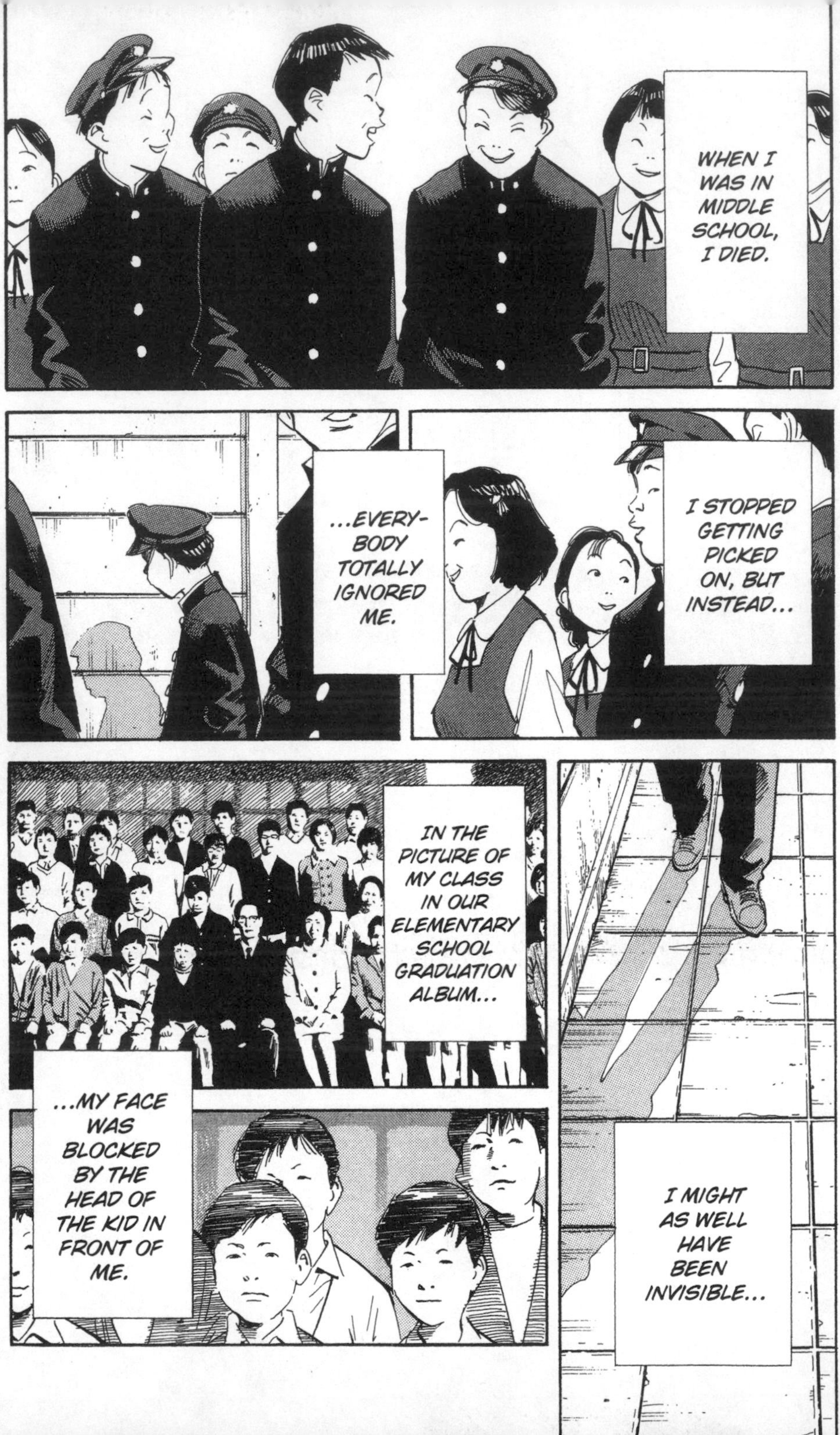
WHEN I WAS IN MIDDLE SCHOOL, I DIED.
I STOPPED GETTING PICKED ON, BUT INSTEAD...
...EVERY-BODY TOTALLY IGNORED ME.
I MIGHT AS WELL HAVE BEEN INVISIBLE...
IN THE PICTURE OF MY CLASS IN OUR ELEMENTARY SCHOOL GRADUATION ALBUM...
...MY FACE WAS BLOCKED BY THE HEAD OF THE KID IN FRONT OF ME.

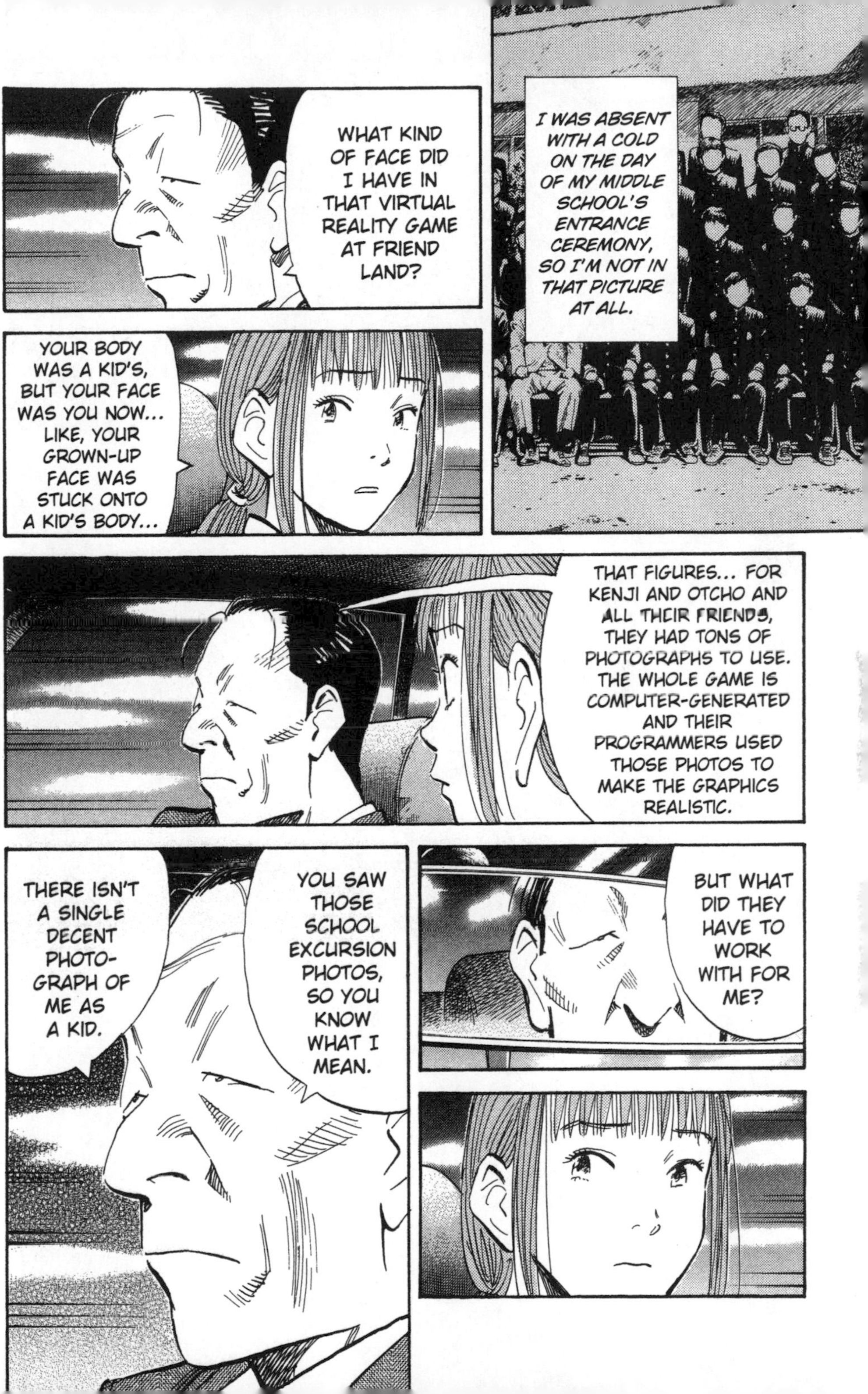
I WAS ABSENT WITH A COLD ON THE DAY OF MY MIDDLE SCHOOL'S ENTRANCE CEREMONY, SO I'M NOT IN THAT PICTURE AT ALL.
WHAT KIND OF FACE DID I HAVE IN THAT VIRTUAL REALITY GAME AT FRIEND LAND?
YOUR BODY WAS A KID'S, BUT YOUR FACE WAS YOU NOW... LIKE, YOUR GROWN-UP FACE WAS STUCK ONTO A KID'S BODY...
THAT FIGURES... FOR KENJI AND OTCHO AND ALL THEIR FRIENDS, THEY HAD TONS OF PHOTOGRAPHS TO USE. THE WHOLE GAME IS COMPUTER-GENERATED AND THEIR PROGRAMMERS USED THOSE PHOTOS TO MAKE THE GRAPHICS REALISTIC.
BUT WHAT DID THEY HAVE TO WORK WITH FOR ME?
YOU SAW THOSE SCHOOL EXCURSION PHOTOS, SO YOU KNOW WHAT I MEAN.
THERE ISN'T A SINGLE DECENT PHOTO-GRAPH OF ME AS A KID.

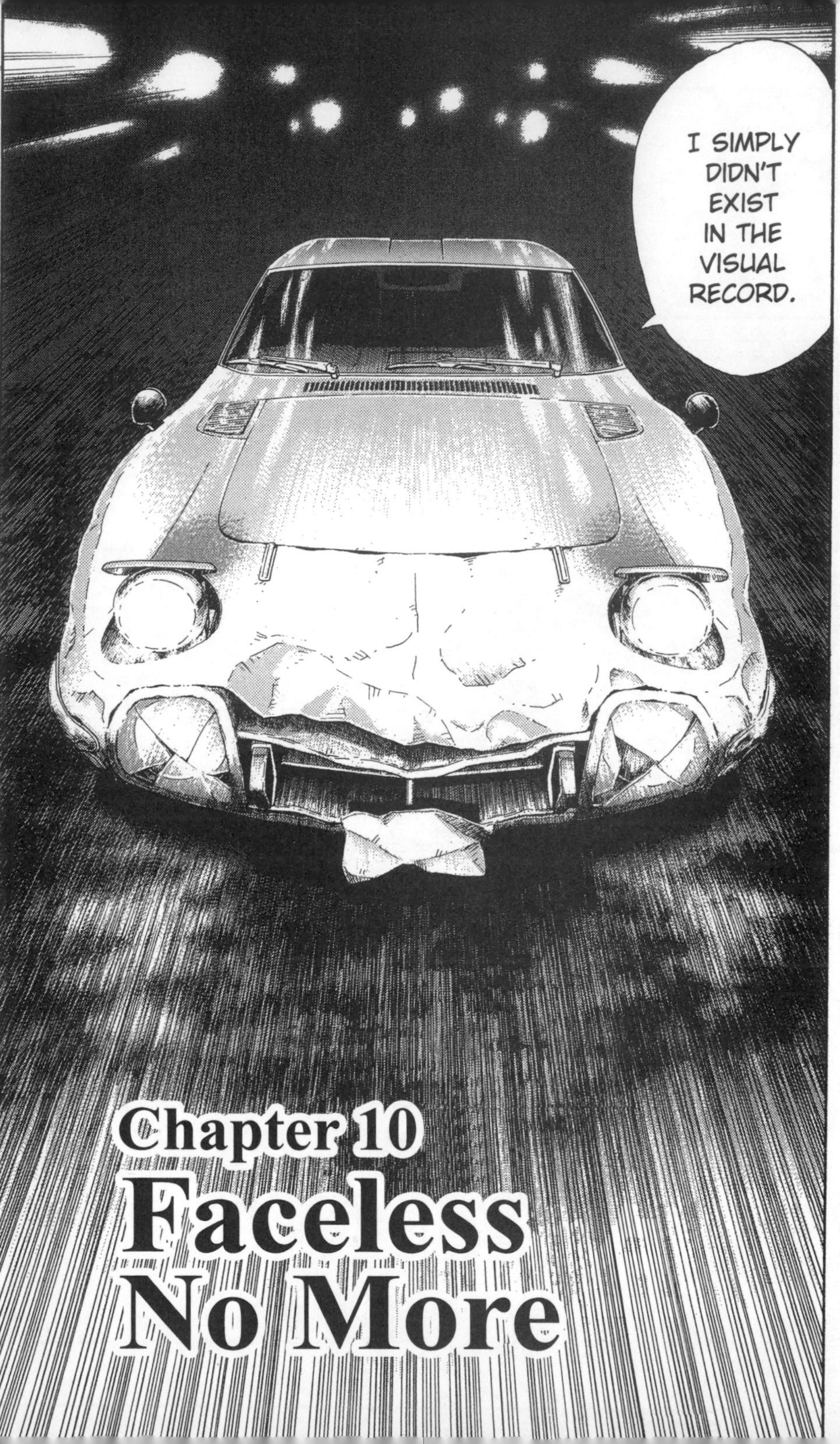
I SIMPLY DIDN'T EXIST IN THE VISUAL RECORD.
Chapter 10
Faceless No More

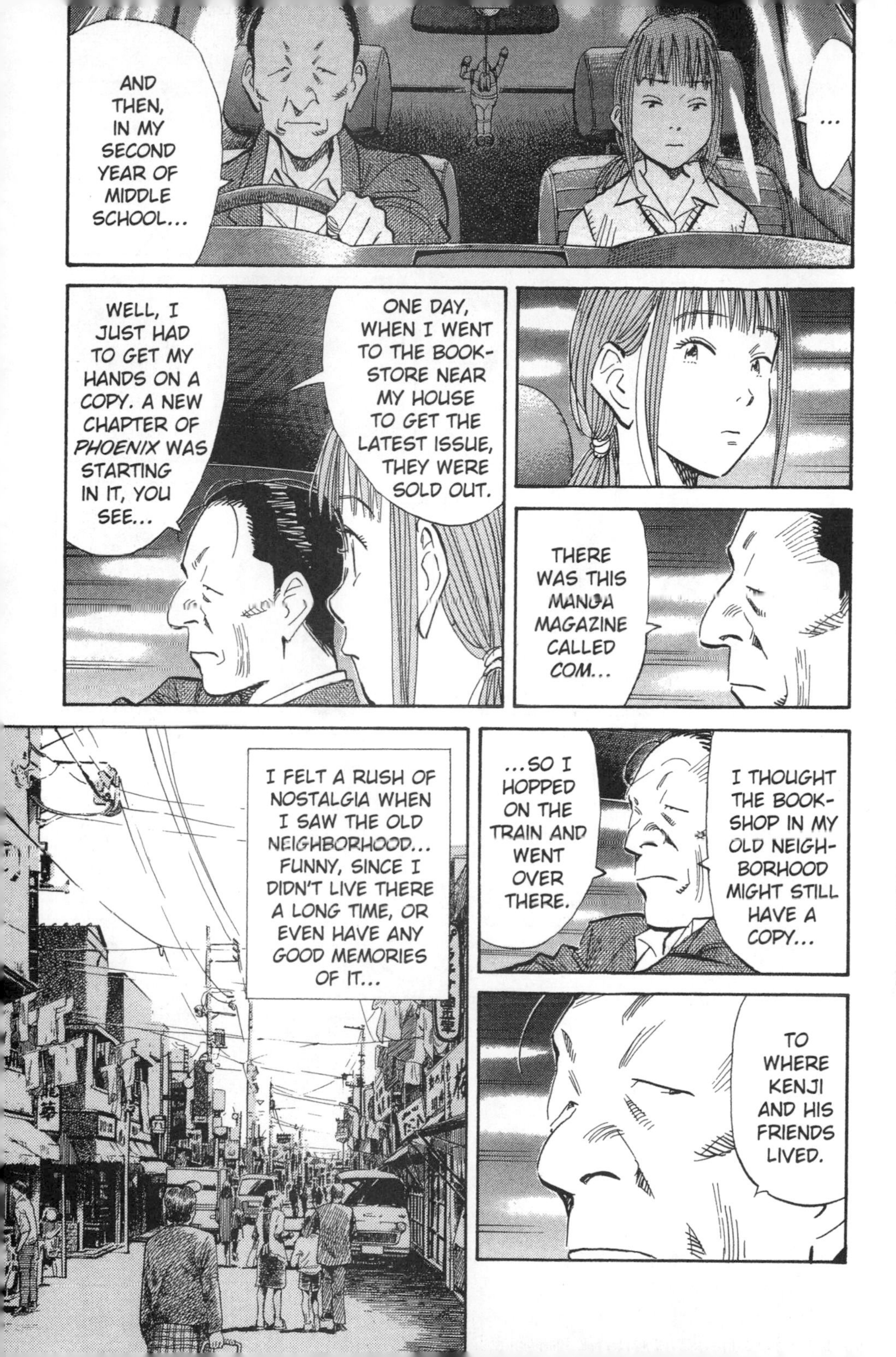
…
AND THEN, IN MY SECOND YEAR OF MIDDLE SCHOOL…
THERE WAS THIS MANGA MAGAZINE CALLED COM…
WELL, I JUST HAD TO GET MY HANDS ON A COPY. A NEW CHAPTER OF *PHOENIX* WAS STARTING IN IT, YOU SEE…
ONE DAY, WHEN I WENT TO THE BOOK-STORE NEAR MY HOUSE TO GET THE LATEST ISSUE, THEY WERE SOLD OUT.
I THOUGHT THE BOOK-SHOP IN MY OLD NEIGH-BORHOOD MIGHT STILL HAVE A COPY…
…SO I HOPPED ON THE TRAIN AND WENT OVER THERE.
TO WHERE KENJI AND HIS FRIENDS LIVED.
I FELT A RUSH OF NOSTALGIA WHEN I SAW THE OLD NEIGHBORHOOD… FUNNY, SINCE I DIDN'T LIVE THERE A LONG TIME, OR EVEN HAVE ANY GOOD MEMORIES OF IT…

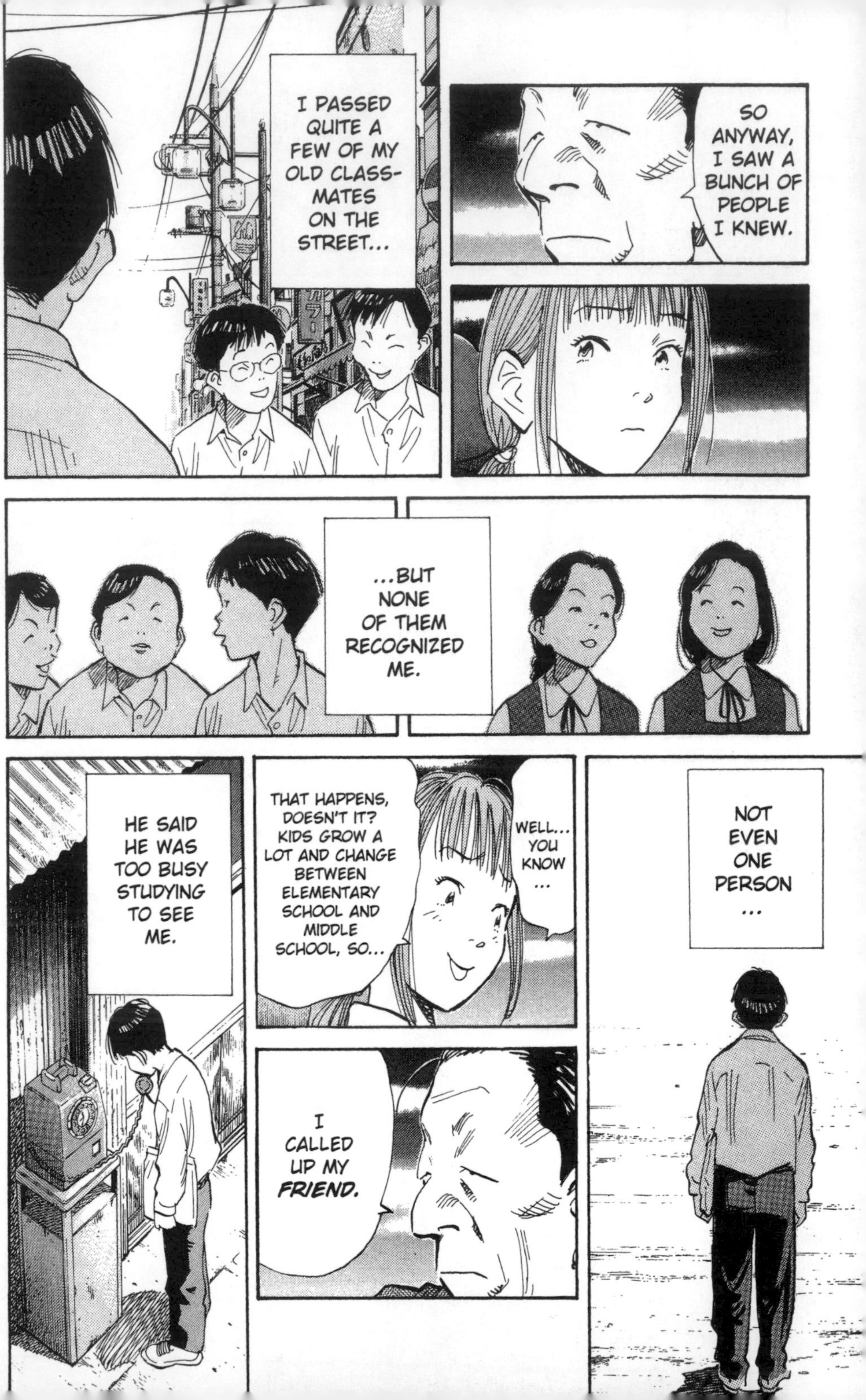
SO ANYWAY, I SAW A BUNCH OF PEOPLE I KNEW.
I PASSED QUITE A FEW OF MY OLD CLASS-MATES ON THE STREET...
...BUT NONE OF THEM RECOGNIZED ME.
NOT EVEN ONE PERSON...
WELL... YOU KNOW...
THAT HAPPENS, DOESN'T IT? KIDS GROW A LOT AND CHANGE BETWEEN ELEMENTARY SCHOOL AND MIDDLE SCHOOL, SO...
I CALLED UP MY *FRIEND.*
HE SAID HE WAS TOO BUSY STUDYING TO SEE ME.

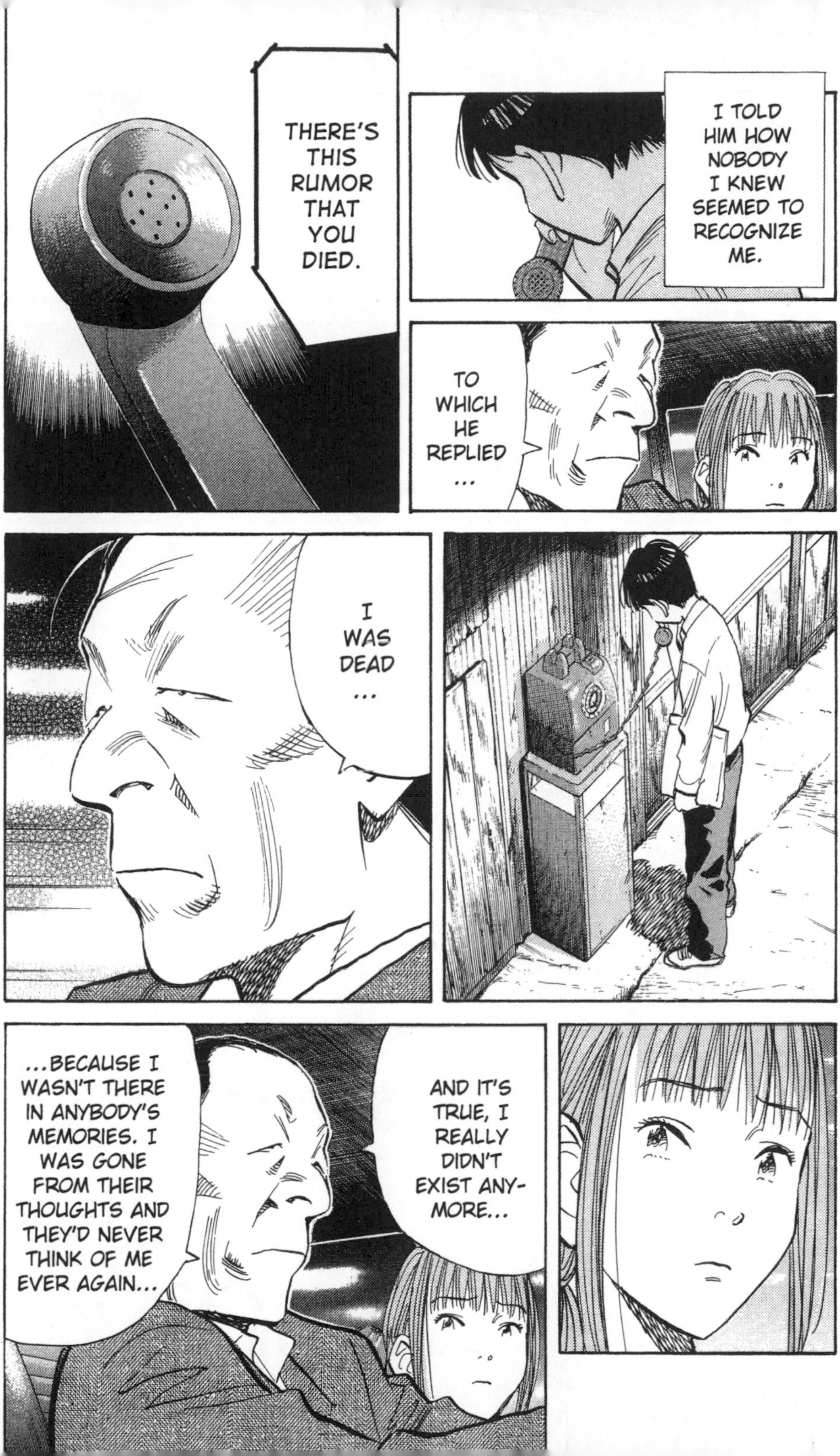
I TOLD HIM HOW NOBODY I KNEW SEEMED TO RECOGNIZE ME.
TO WHICH HE REPLIED ...
THERE'S THIS RUMOR THAT YOU DIED.
I WAS DEAD ...
...BECAUSE I WASN'T THERE IN ANYBODY'S MEMORIES. I WAS GONE FROM THEIR THOUGHTS AND THEY'D NEVER THINK OF ME EVER AGAIN...
AND IT'S TRUE, I REALLY DIDN'T EXIST ANY-MORE...

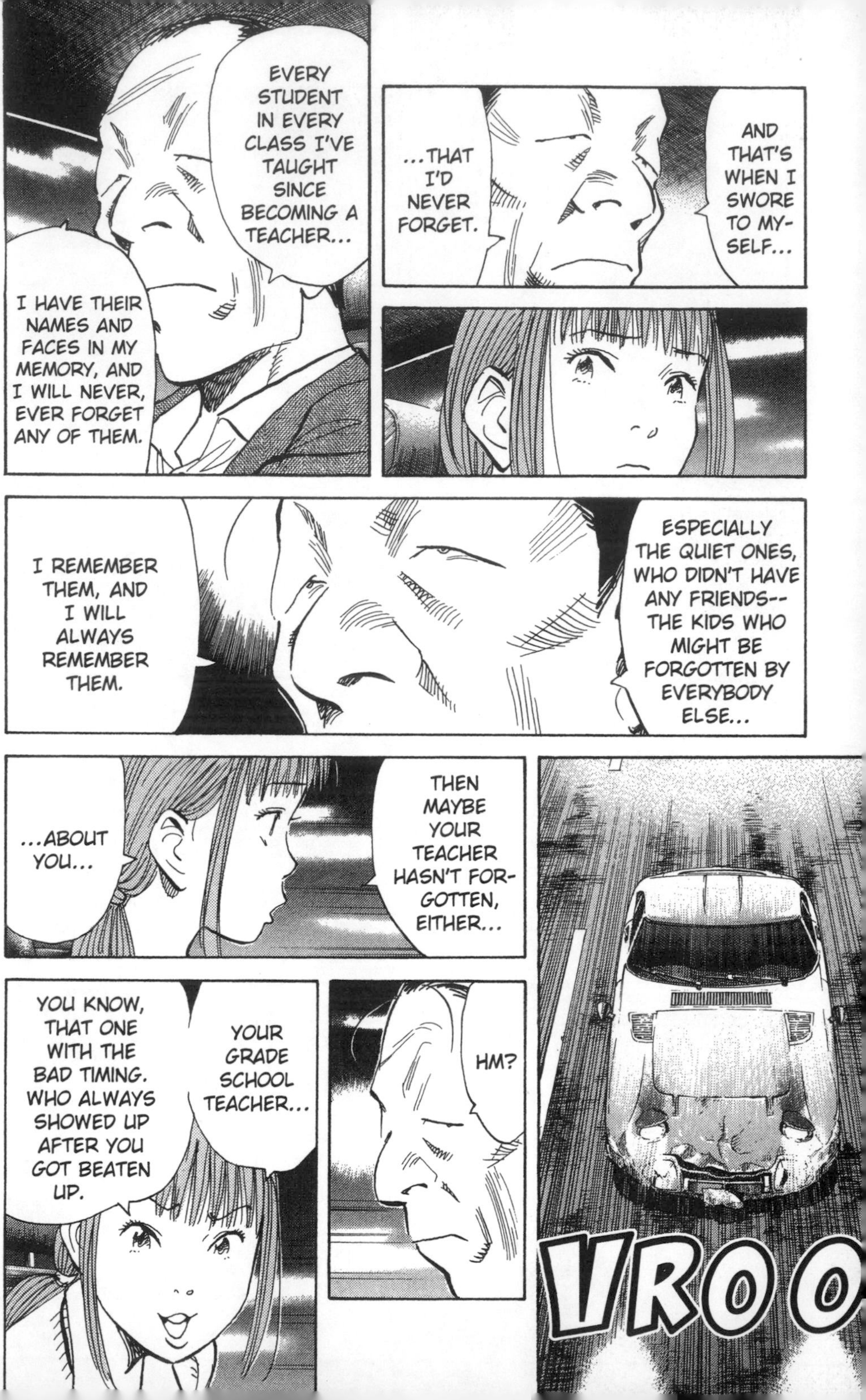
AND THAT'S WHEN I SWORE TO MY-SELF...
...THAT I'D NEVER FORGET.
EVERY STUDENT IN EVERY CLASS I'VE TAUGHT SINCE BECOMING A TEACHER...
I HAVE THEIR NAMES AND FACES IN MY MEMORY, AND I WILL NEVER, EVER FORGET ANY OF THEM.
ESPECIALLY THE QUIET ONES, WHO DIDN'T HAVE ANY FRIENDS-- THE KIDS WHO MIGHT BE FORGOTTEN BY EVERYBODY ELSE...
I REMEMBER THEM, AND I WILL ALWAYS REMEMBER THEM.
VROOO
THEN MAYBE YOUR TEACHER HASN'T FOR-GOTTEN, EITHER...
...ABOUT YOU...
HM?
YOUR GRADE SCHOOL TEACHER...
YOU KNOW, THAT ONE WITH THE BAD TIMING. WHO ALWAYS SHOWED UP AFTER YOU GOT BEATEN UP.

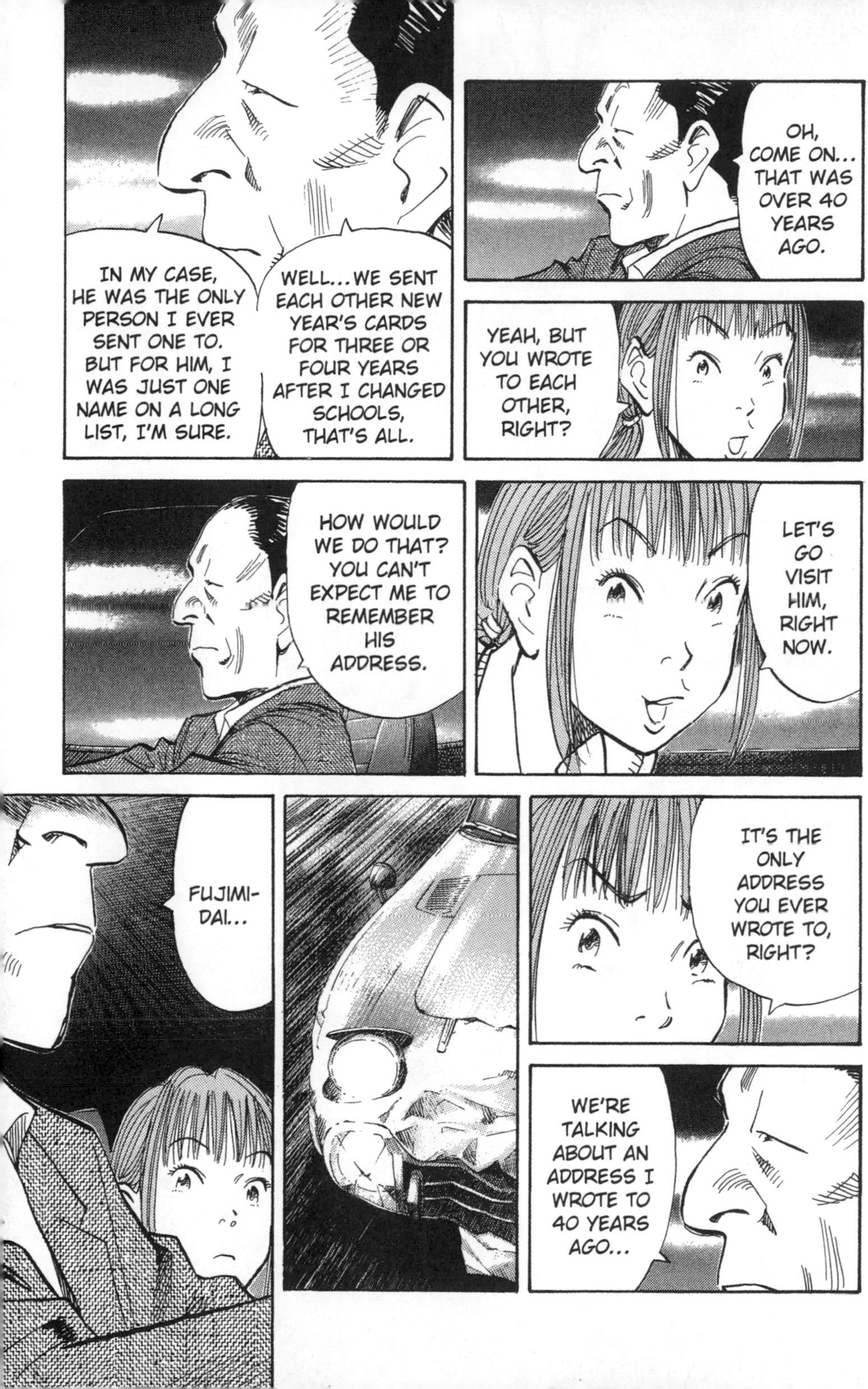
OH, COME ON... THAT WAS OVER 40 YEARS AGO.
YEAH, BUT YOU WROTE TO EACH OTHER, RIGHT?
WELL...WE SENT EACH OTHER NEW YEAR'S CARDS FOR THREE OR FOUR YEARS AFTER I CHANGED SCHOOLS, THAT'S ALL.
IN MY CASE, HE WAS THE ONLY PERSON I EVER SENT ONE TO. BUT FOR HIM, I WAS JUST ONE NAME ON A LONG LIST, I'M SURE.
LET'S GO VISIT HIM, RIGHT NOW.
HOW WOULD WE DO THAT? YOU CAN'T EXPECT ME TO REMEMBER HIS ADDRESS.
IT'S THE ONLY ADDRESS YOU EVER WROTE TO, RIGHT?
WE'RE TALKING ABOUT AN ADDRESS I WROTE TO 40 YEARS AGO...
FUJIMI-DAI...

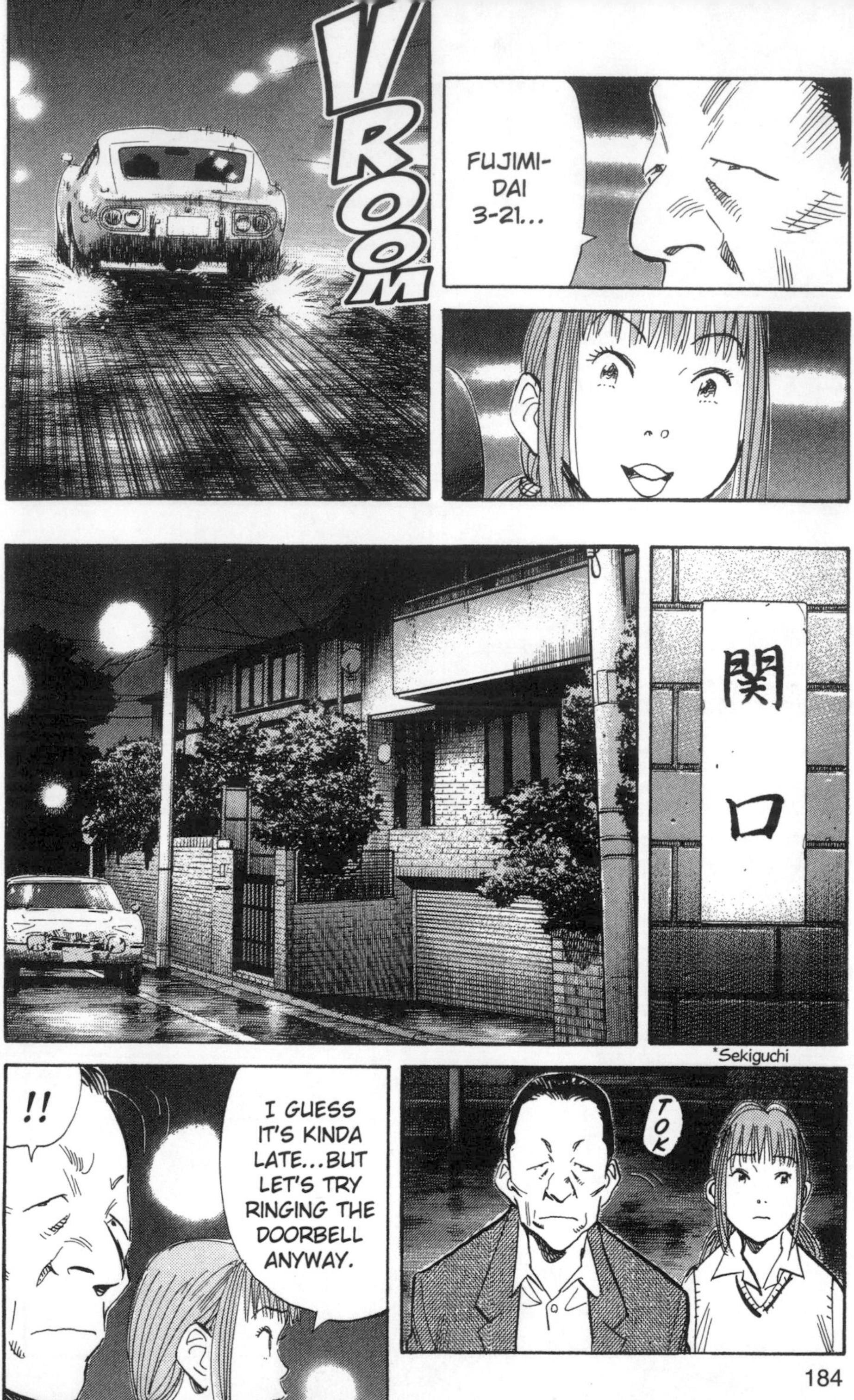
FUJIMI-DAI 3-21...
VROOM
関口
*Sekiguchi
TOK
!!
I GUESS IT'S KINDA LATE...BUT LET'S TRY RINGING THE DOORBELL ANYWAY.

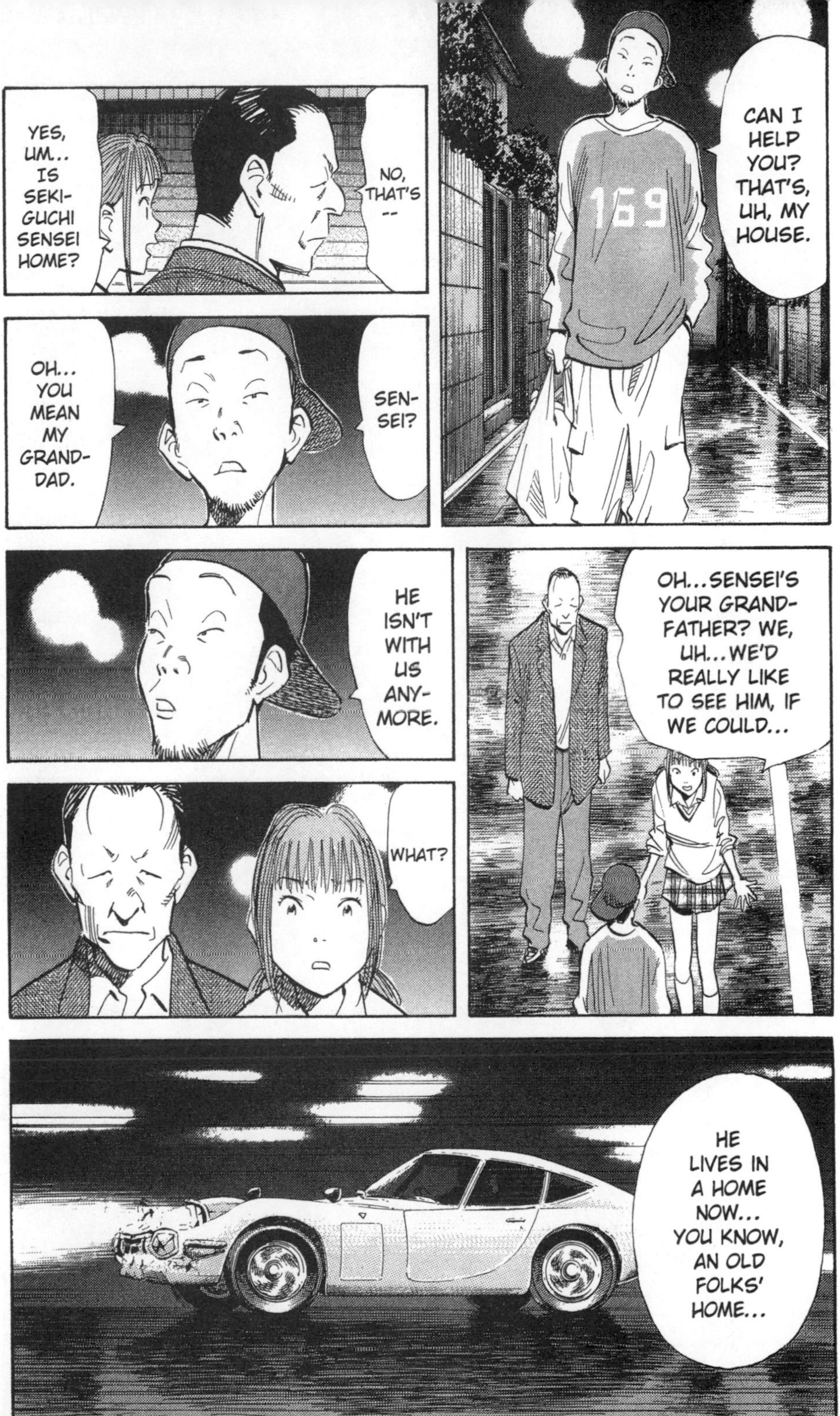
CAN I HELP YOU? THAT'S, UH, MY HOUSE.
NO, THAT'S --
YES, UM... IS SEKIGUCHI SENSEI HOME?
SENSEI?
OH... YOU MEAN MY GRANDDAD.
OH...SENSEI'S YOUR GRANDFATHER? WE, UH...WE'D REALLY LIKE TO SEE HIM, IF WE COULD...
HE ISN'T WITH US ANYMORE.
WHAT?
HE LIVES IN A HOME NOW... YOU KNOW, AN OLD FOLKS' HOME...

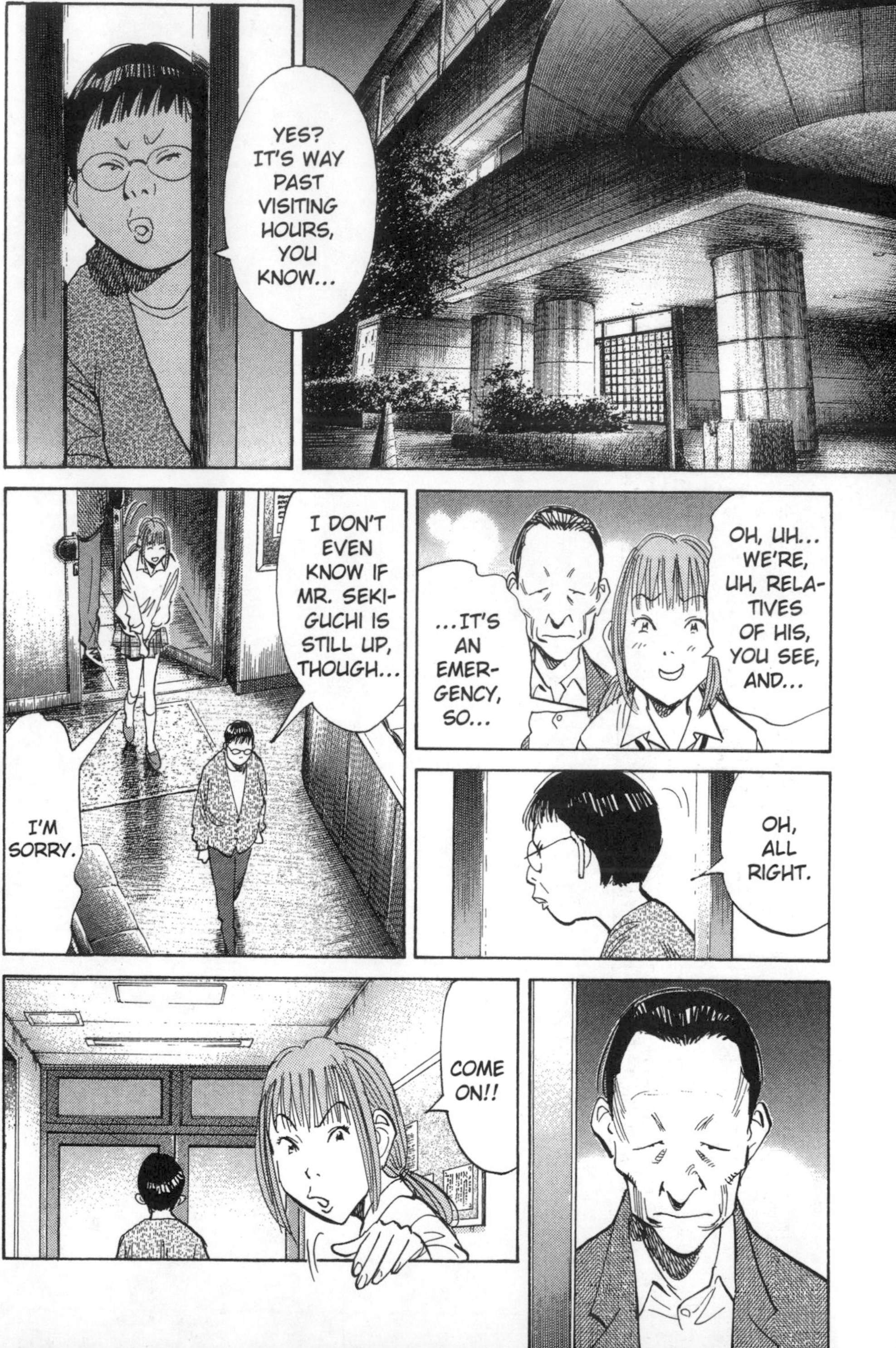
YES? IT'S WAY PAST VISITING HOURS, YOU KNOW...
OH, UH... WE'RE, UH, RELATIVES OF HIS, YOU SEE, AND...
...IT'S AN EMERGENCY, SO...
OH, ALL RIGHT.
I DON'T EVEN KNOW IF MR. SEKIGUCHI IS STILL UP, THOUGH...
I'M SORRY.
COME ON!!

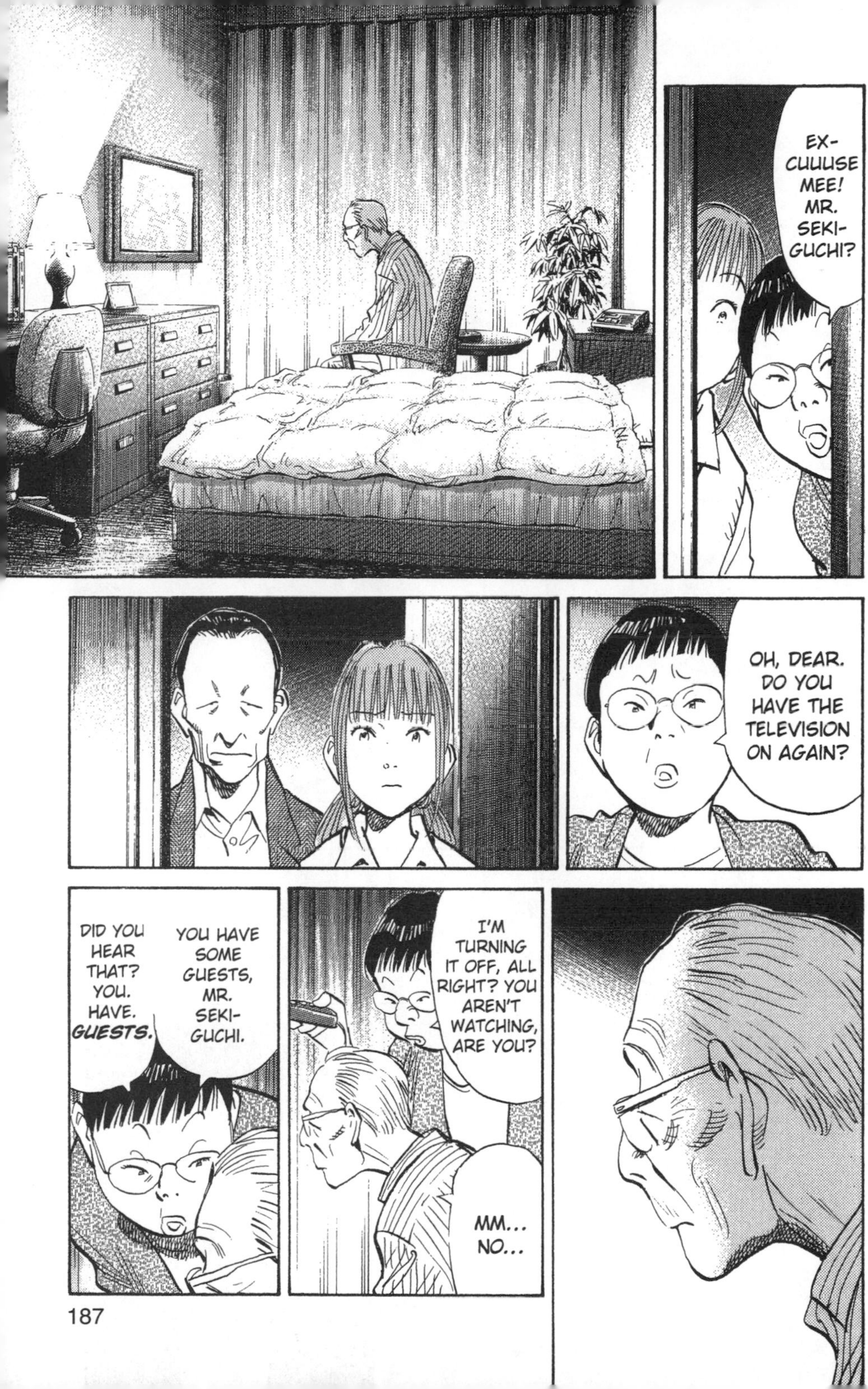
EX-CUUUSE MEE! MR. SEKI-GUCHI?
OH, DEAR. DO YOU HAVE THE TELEVISION ON AGAIN?
I'M TURNING IT OFF, ALL RIGHT? YOU AREN'T WATCHING, ARE YOU?
MM... NO...
YOU HAVE SOME GUESTS, MR. SEKI-GUCHI.
DID YOU HEAR THAT? YOU. HAVE. **GUESTS.**

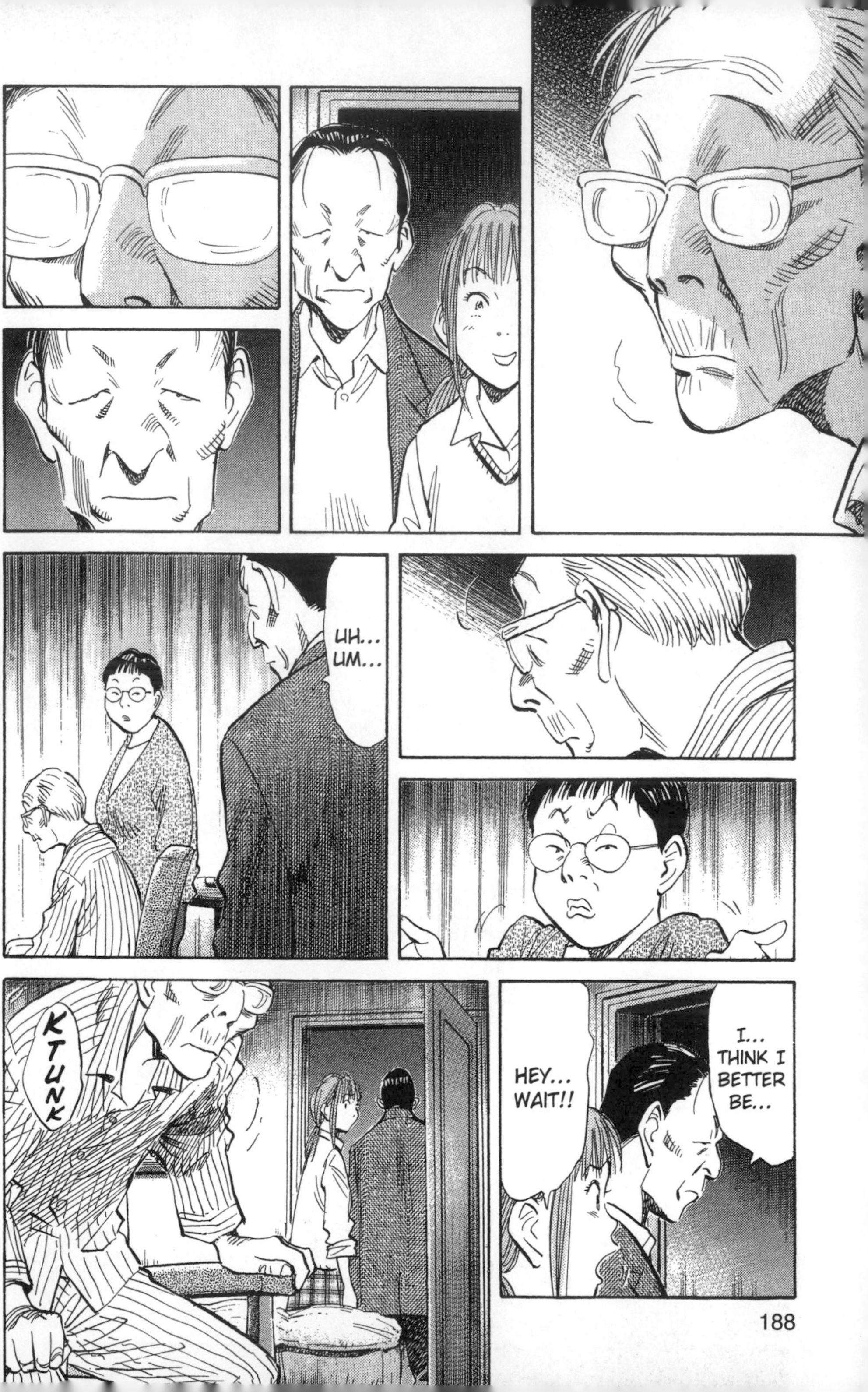
UH... UM...
I... THINK I BETTER BE...
HEY... WAIT!!
KTUNK

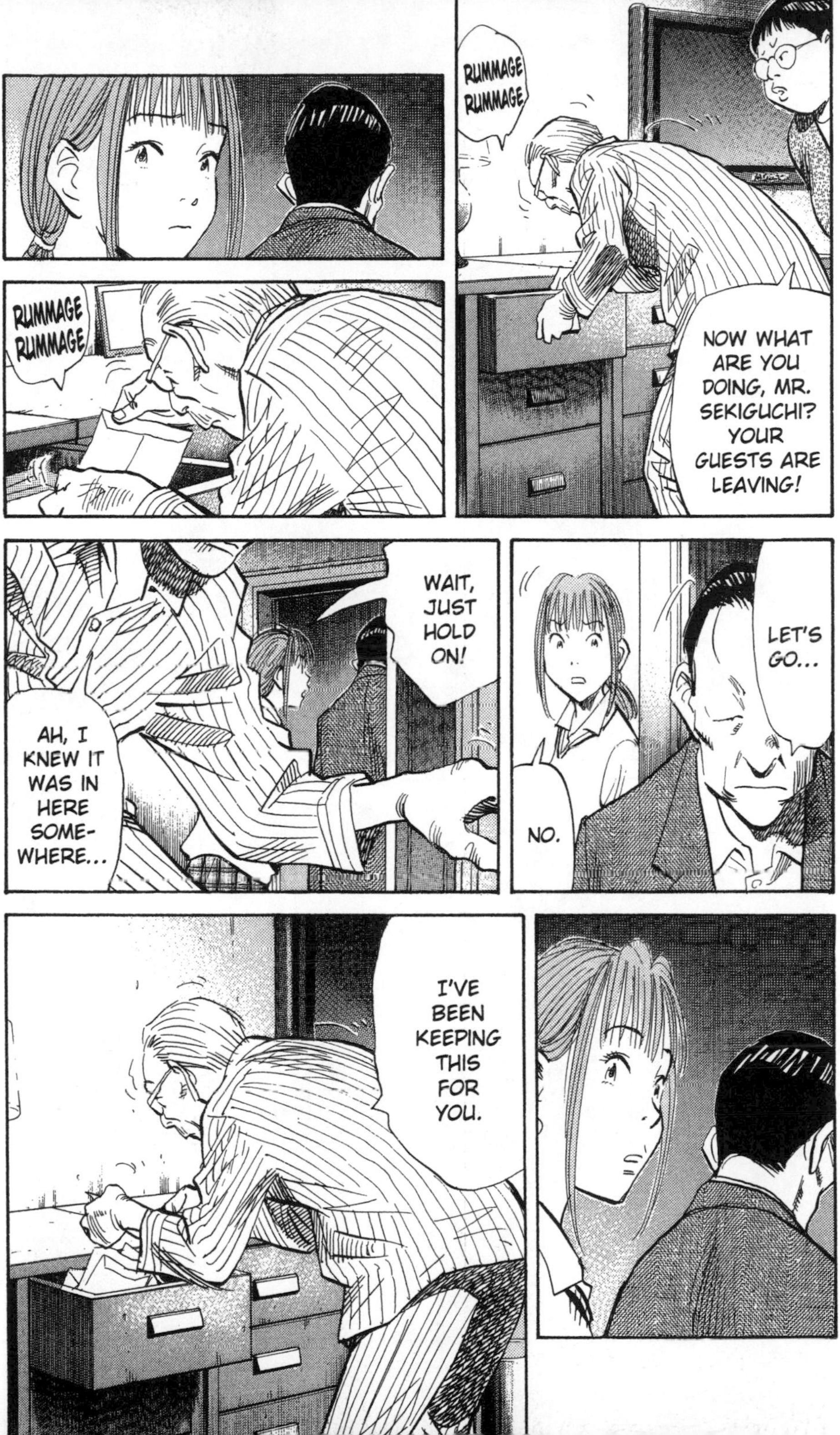
RUMMAGE RUMMAGE
NOW WHAT ARE YOU DOING, MR. SEKIGUCHI? YOUR GUESTS ARE LEAVING!
RUMMAGE RUMMAGE
LET'S GO...
NO.
WAIT, JUST HOLD ON!
AH, I KNEW IT WAS IN HERE SOMEWHERE...
I'VE BEEN KEEPING THIS FOR YOU.

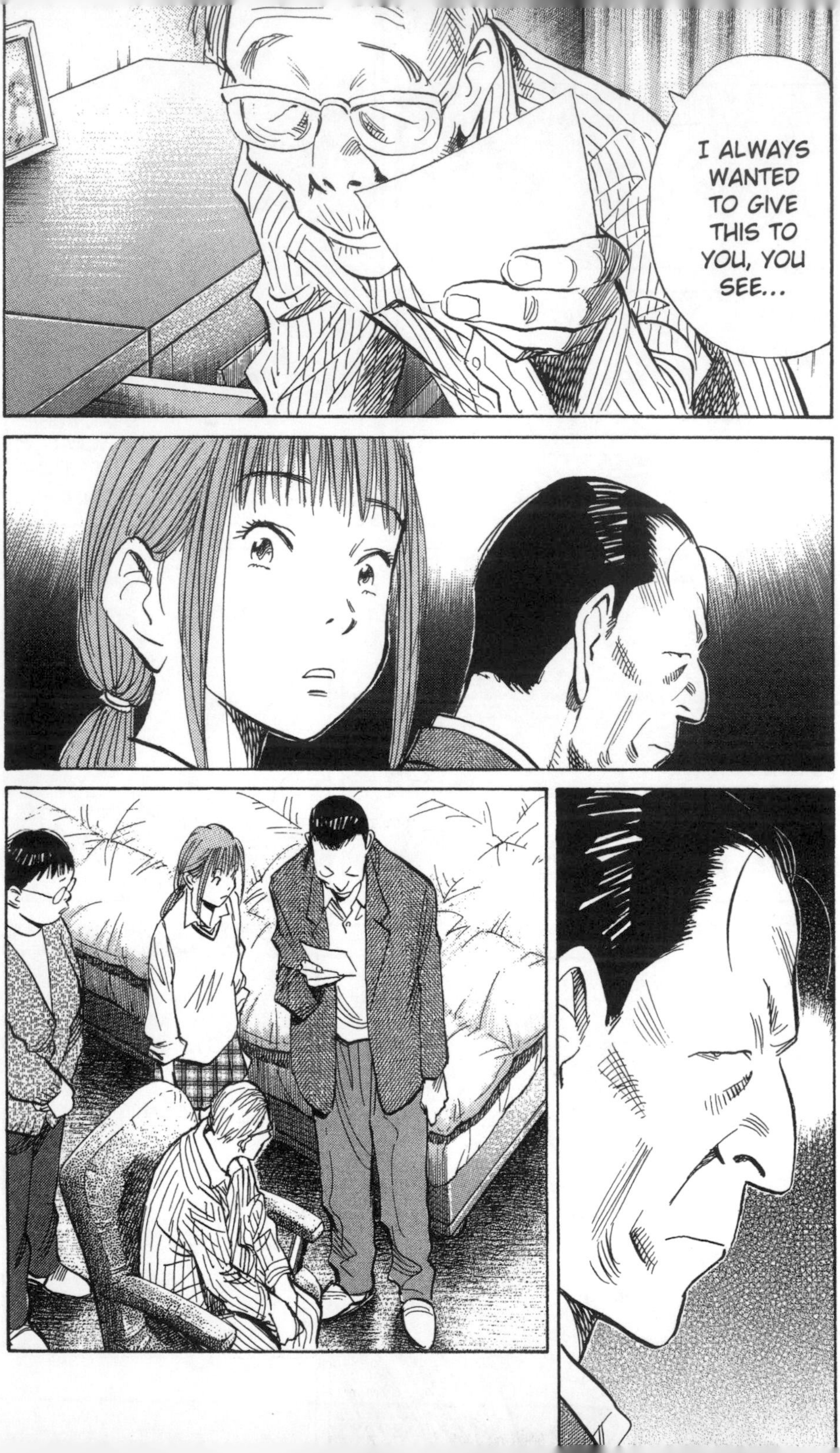
I ALWAYS WANTED TO GIVE THIS TO YOU, YOU SEE...

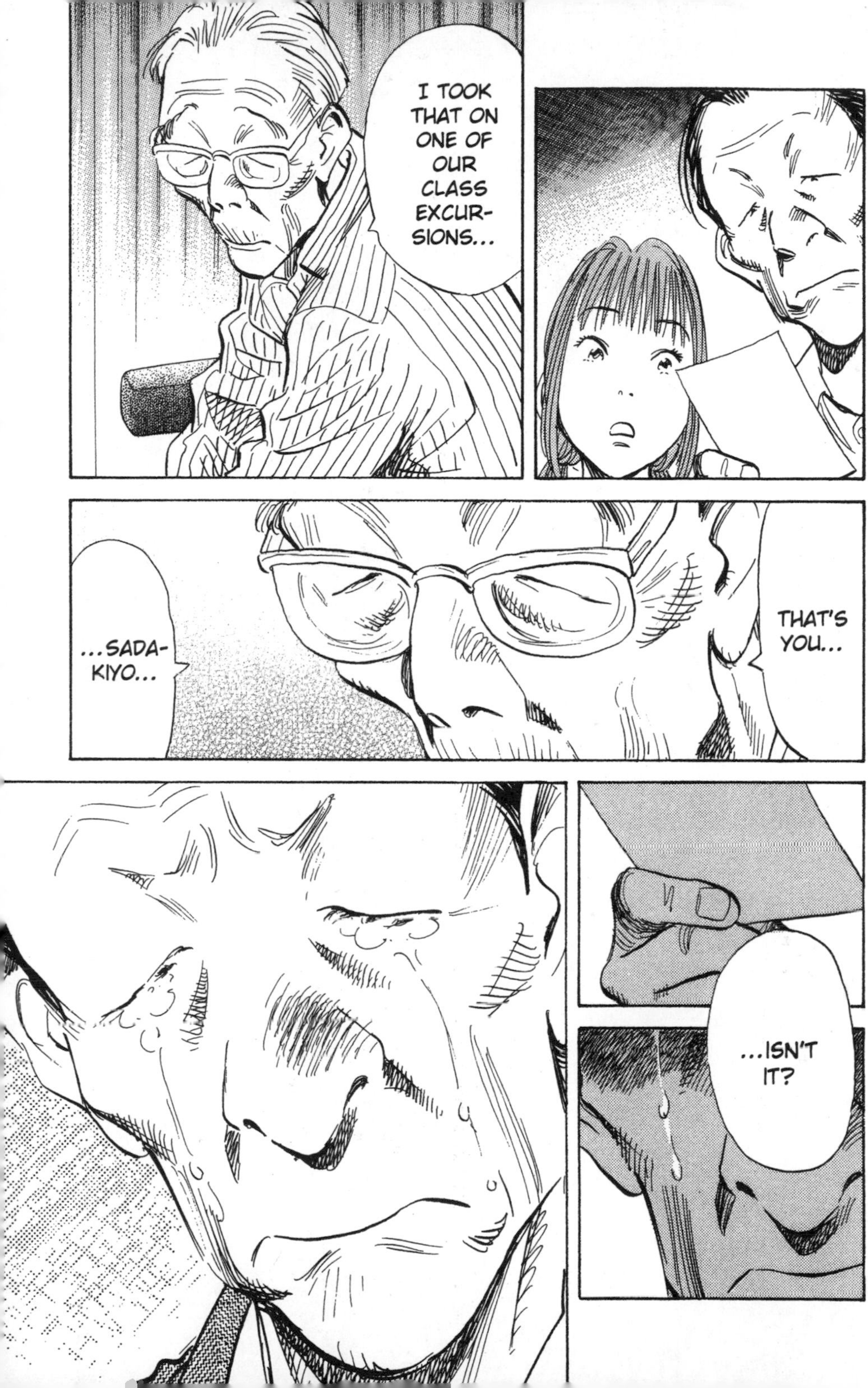
I TOOK THAT ON ONE OF OUR CLASS EXCURSIONS...
THAT'S YOU...
...SADAKIYO...
...ISN'T IT?

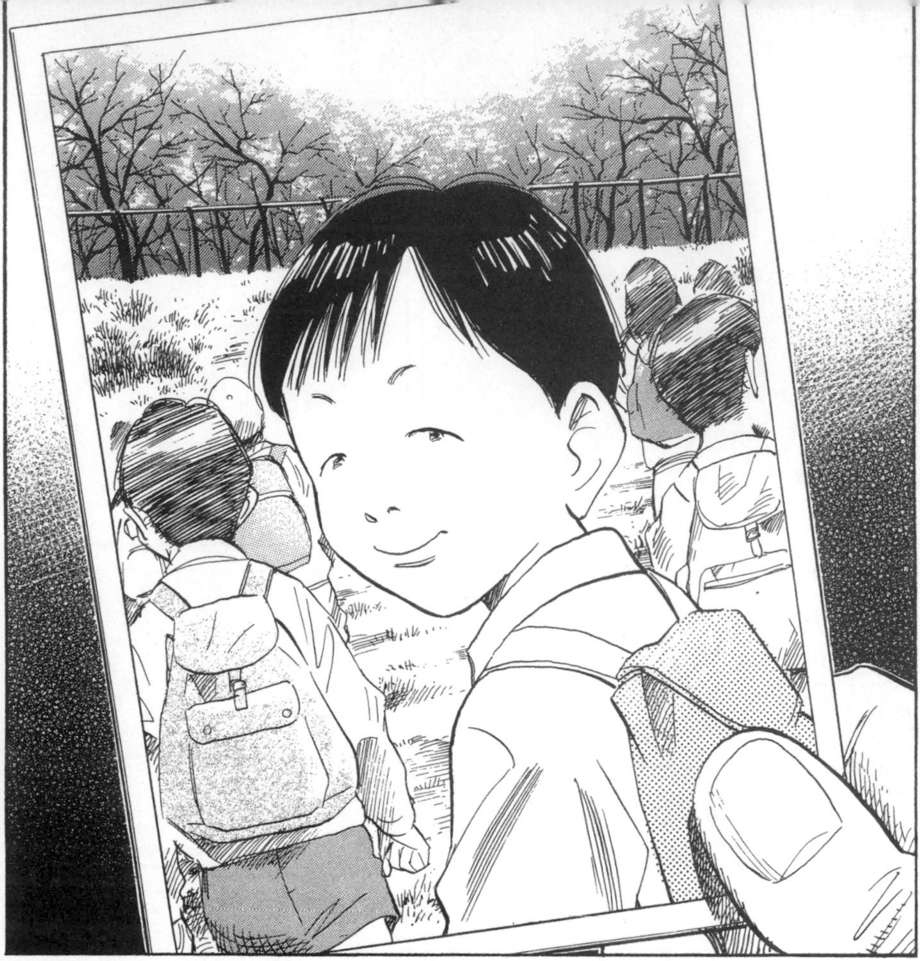
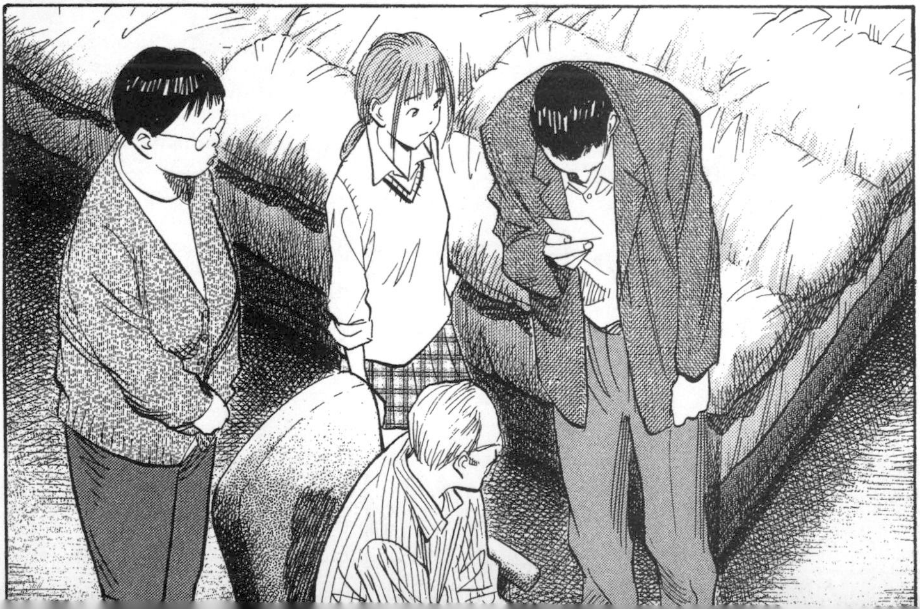

Chapter 11 Thunder

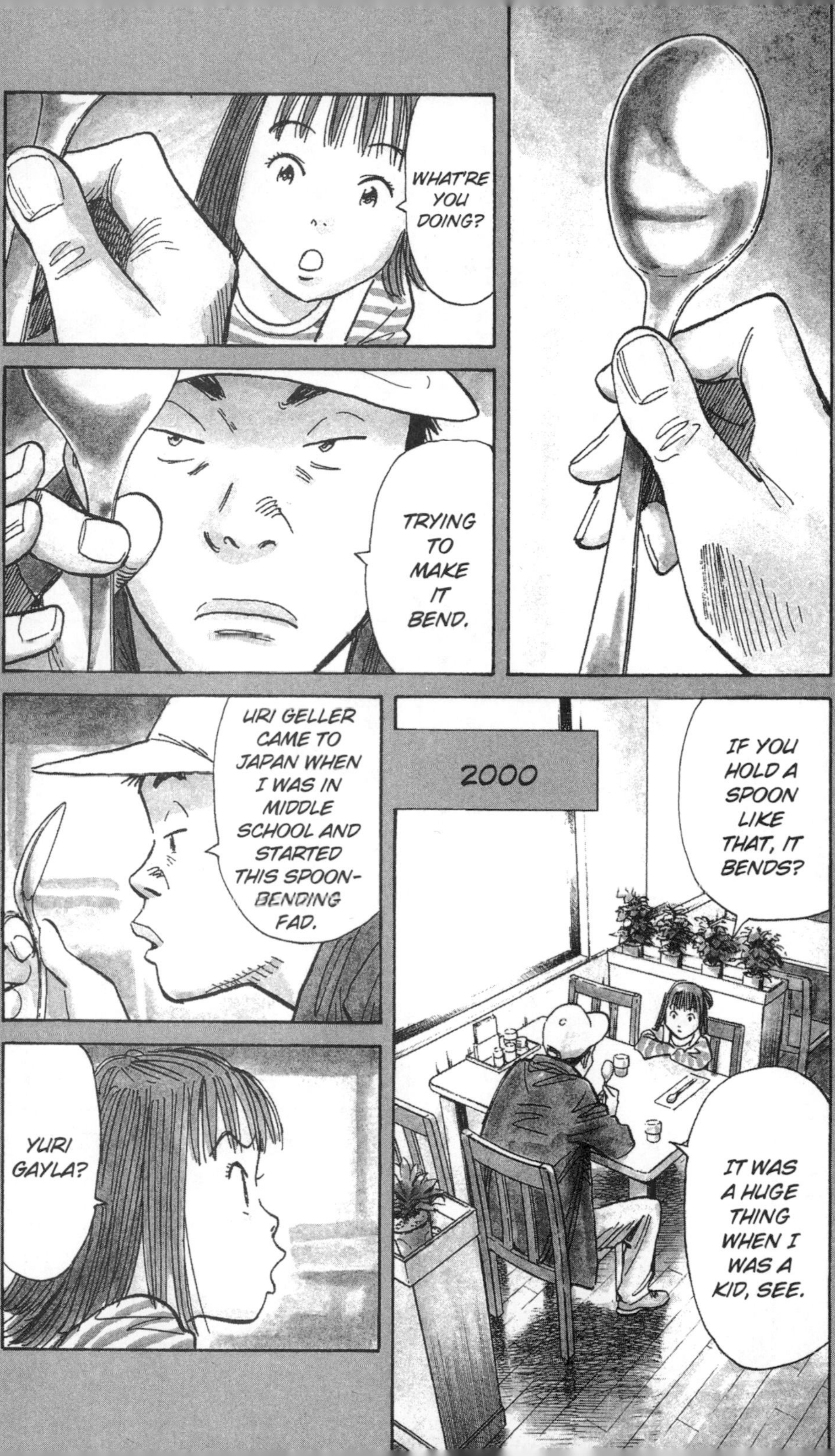
WHAT'RE YOU DOING?
TRYING TO MAKE IT BEND.
2000
IF YOU HOLD A SPOON LIKE THAT, IT BENDS?
IT WAS A HUGE THING WHEN I WAS A KID, SEE.
URI GELLER CAME TO JAPAN WHEN I WAS IN MIDDLE SCHOOL AND STARTED THIS SPOON-BENDING FAD.
YURI GAYLA?

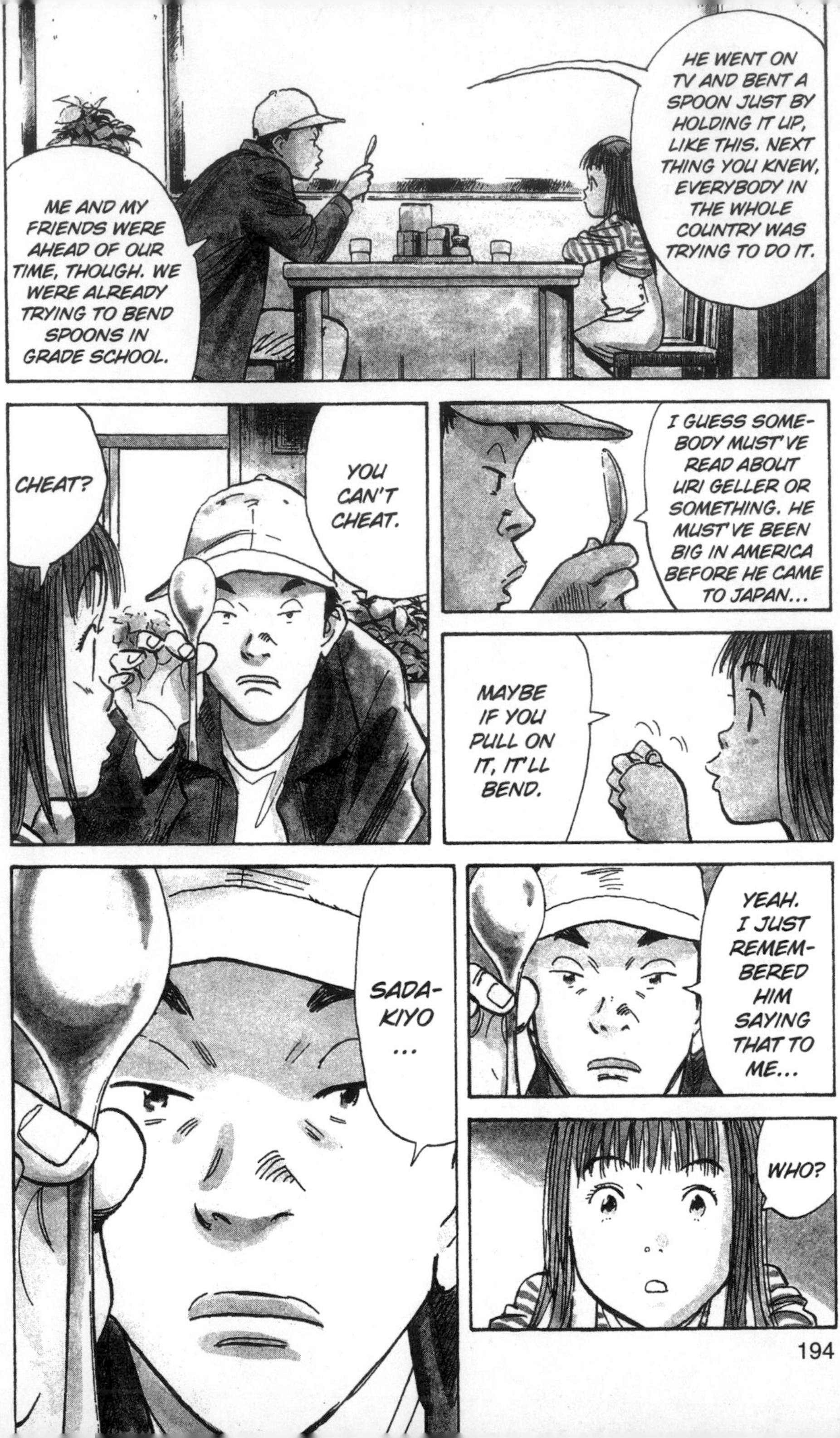
HE WENT ON TV AND BENT A SPOON JUST BY HOLDING IT UP, LIKE THIS. NEXT THING YOU KNEW, EVERYBODY IN THE WHOLE COUNTRY WAS TRYING TO DO IT.
ME AND MY FRIENDS WERE AHEAD OF OUR TIME, THOUGH. WE WERE ALREADY TRYING TO BEND SPOONS IN GRADE SCHOOL.
I GUESS SOME-BODY MUST'VE READ ABOUT URI GELLER OR SOMETHING. HE MUST'VE BEEN BIG IN AMERICA BEFORE HE CAME TO JAPAN...
MAYBE IF YOU PULL ON IT, IT'LL BEND.
YOU CAN'T CHEAT.
CHEAT?
YEAH. I JUST REMEM-BERED HIM SAYING THAT TO ME...
WHO?
SADA-KIYO ...

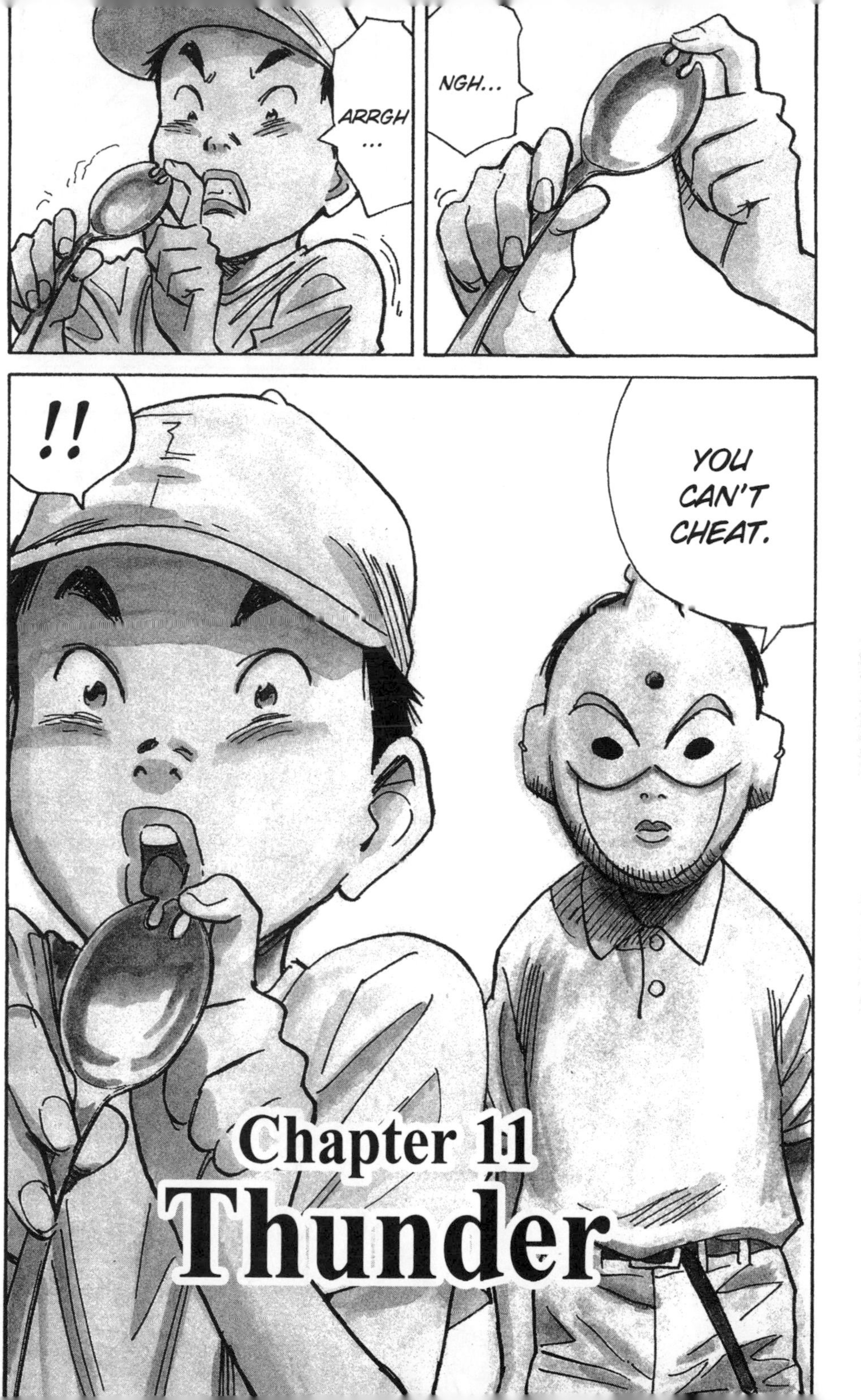
NGH...
ARRGH ...
YOU CAN'T CHEAT.
!!
Chapter 11
Thunder

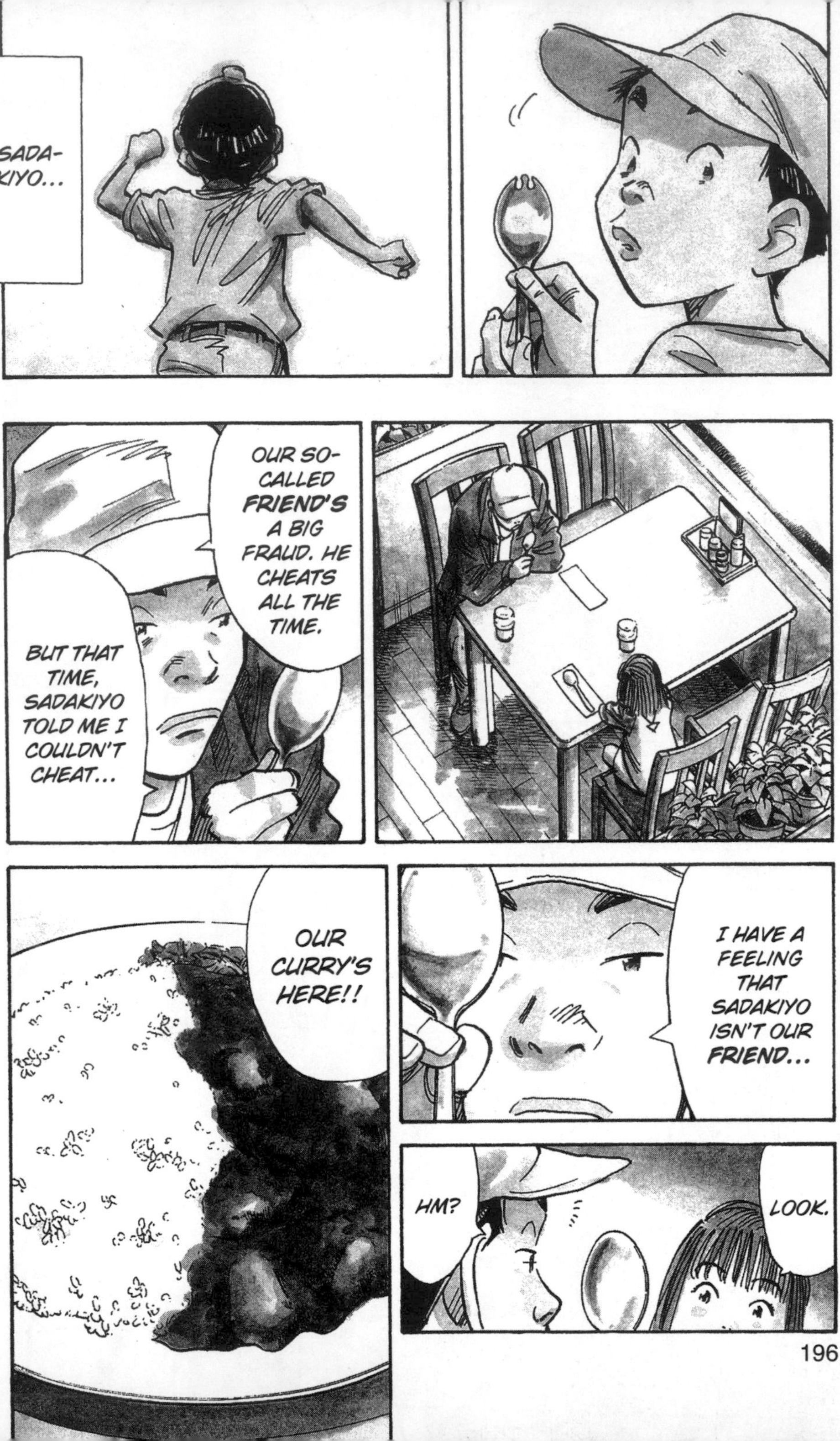
SADA-KIYO...
OUR SO-CALLED FRIEND'S A BIG FRAUD. HE CHEATS ALL THE TIME.
BUT THAT TIME, SADAKIYO TOLD ME I COULDN'T CHEAT...
I HAVE A FEELING THAT SADAKIYO ISN'T OUR FRIEND...
LOOK.
HM?
OUR CURRY'S HERE!!

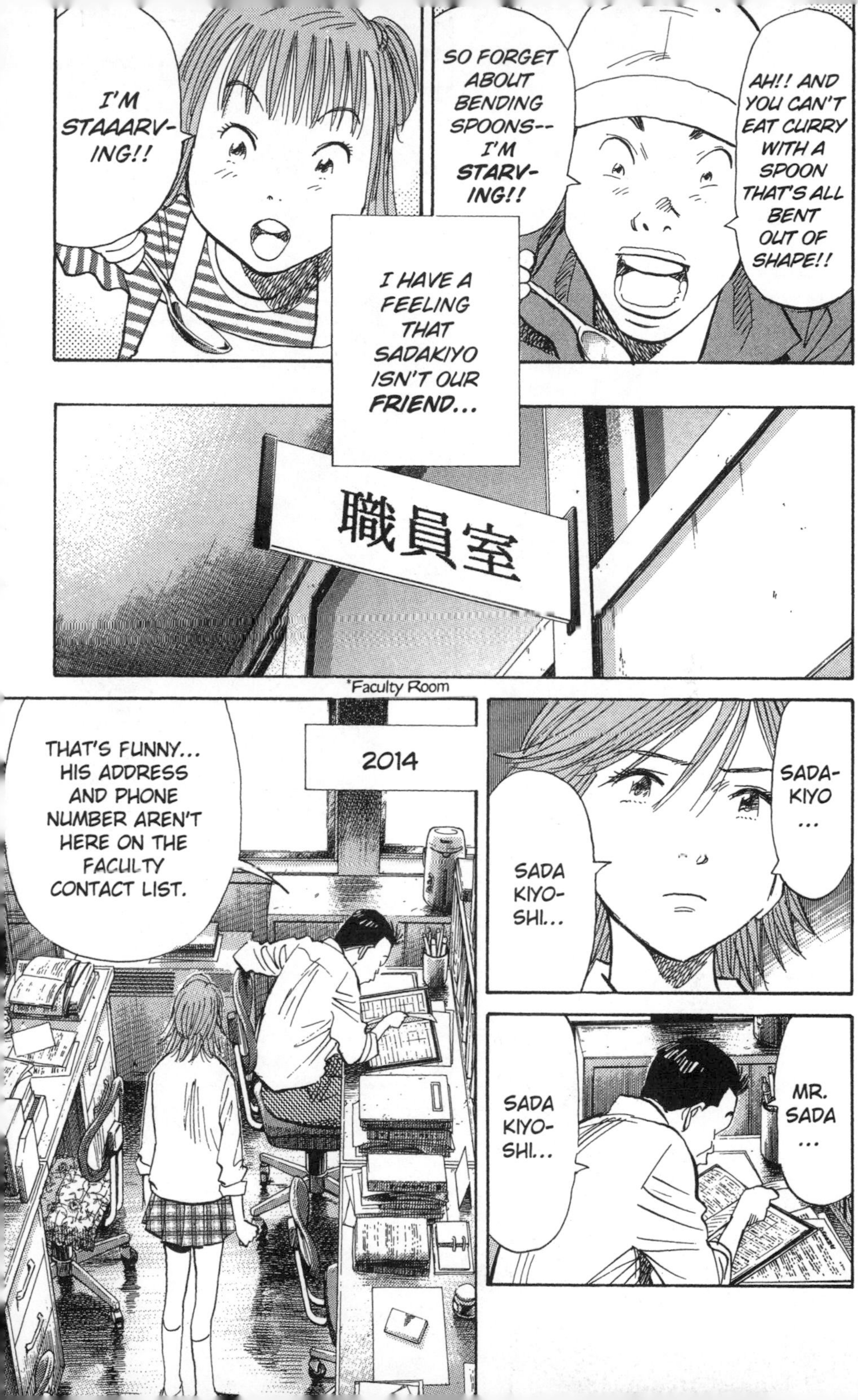
AH!! AND YOU CAN'T EAT CURRY WITH A SPOON THAT'S ALL BENT OUT OF SHAPE!!
SO FORGET ABOUT BENDING SPOONS-- I'M STARV-ING!!
I'M STAAARV-ING!!
I HAVE A FEELING THAT SADAKIYO ISN'T OUR FRIEND...
職員室
*Faculty Room
SADA-KIYO ...
SADA KIYO-SHI...
MR. SADA ...
SADA KIYO-SHI...
2014
THAT'S FUNNY... HIS ADDRESS AND PHONE NUMBER AREN'T HERE ON THE FACULTY CONTACT LIST.

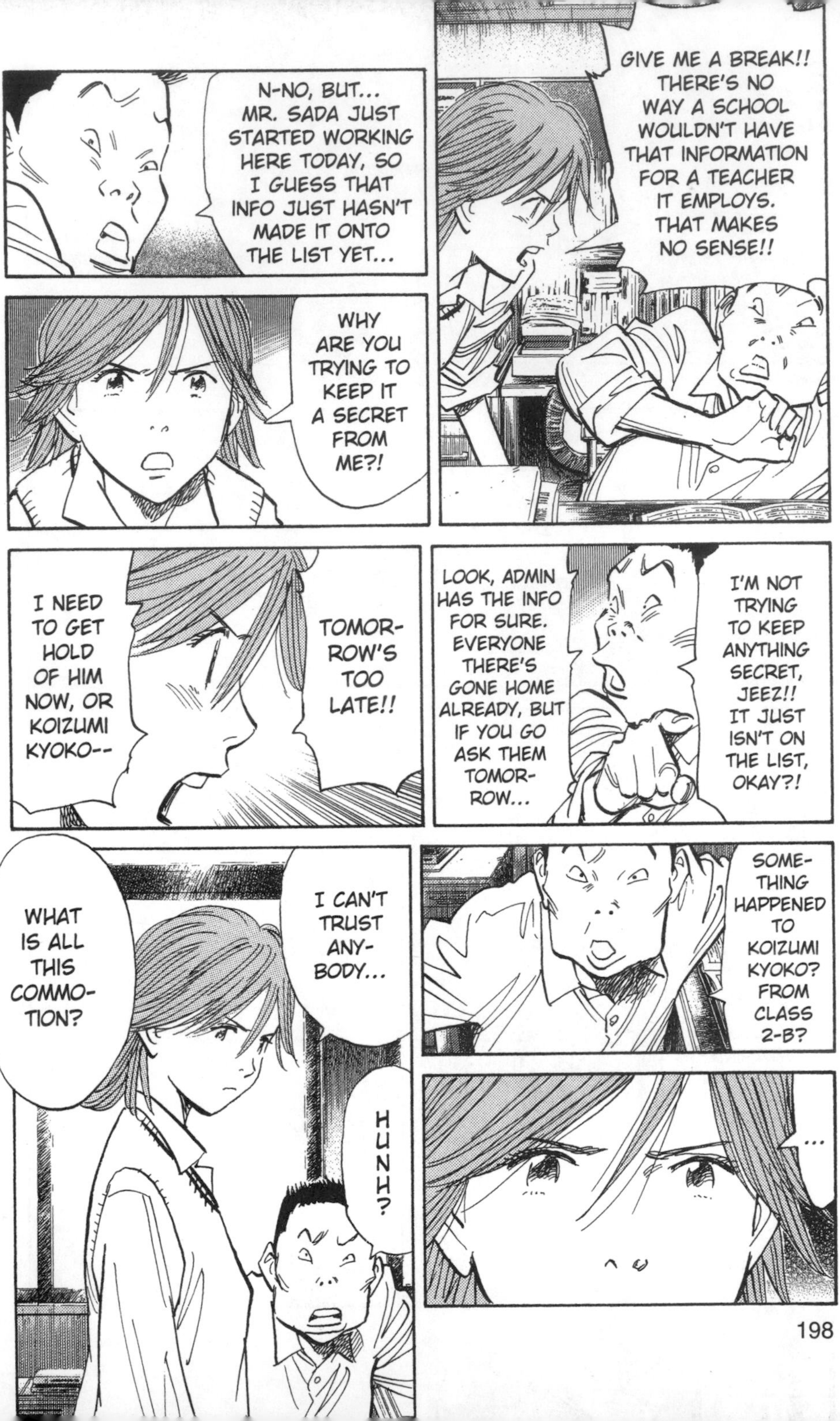
GIVE ME A BREAK!! THERE'S NO WAY A SCHOOL WOULDN'T HAVE THAT INFORMATION FOR A TEACHER IT EMPLOYS. THAT MAKES NO SENSE!!
N-NO, BUT... MR. SADA JUST STARTED WORKING HERE TODAY, SO I GUESS THAT INFO JUST HASN'T MADE IT ONTO THE LIST YET...
WHY ARE YOU TRYING TO KEEP IT A SECRET FROM ME?!
I'M NOT TRYING TO KEEP ANYTHING SECRET, JEEZ!! IT JUST ISN'T ON THE LIST, OKAY?!
LOOK, ADMIN HAS THE INFO FOR SURE. EVERYONE THERE'S GONE HOME ALREADY, BUT IF YOU GO ASK THEM TOMOR-ROW...
TOMOR-ROW'S TOO LATE!!
I NEED TO GET HOLD OF HIM NOW, OR KOIZUMI KYOKO--
SOME-THING HAPPENED TO KOIZUMI KYOKO? FROM CLASS 2-B?
...
I CAN'T TRUST ANY-BODY...
WHAT IS ALL THIS COMMO-TION?
HUNH?

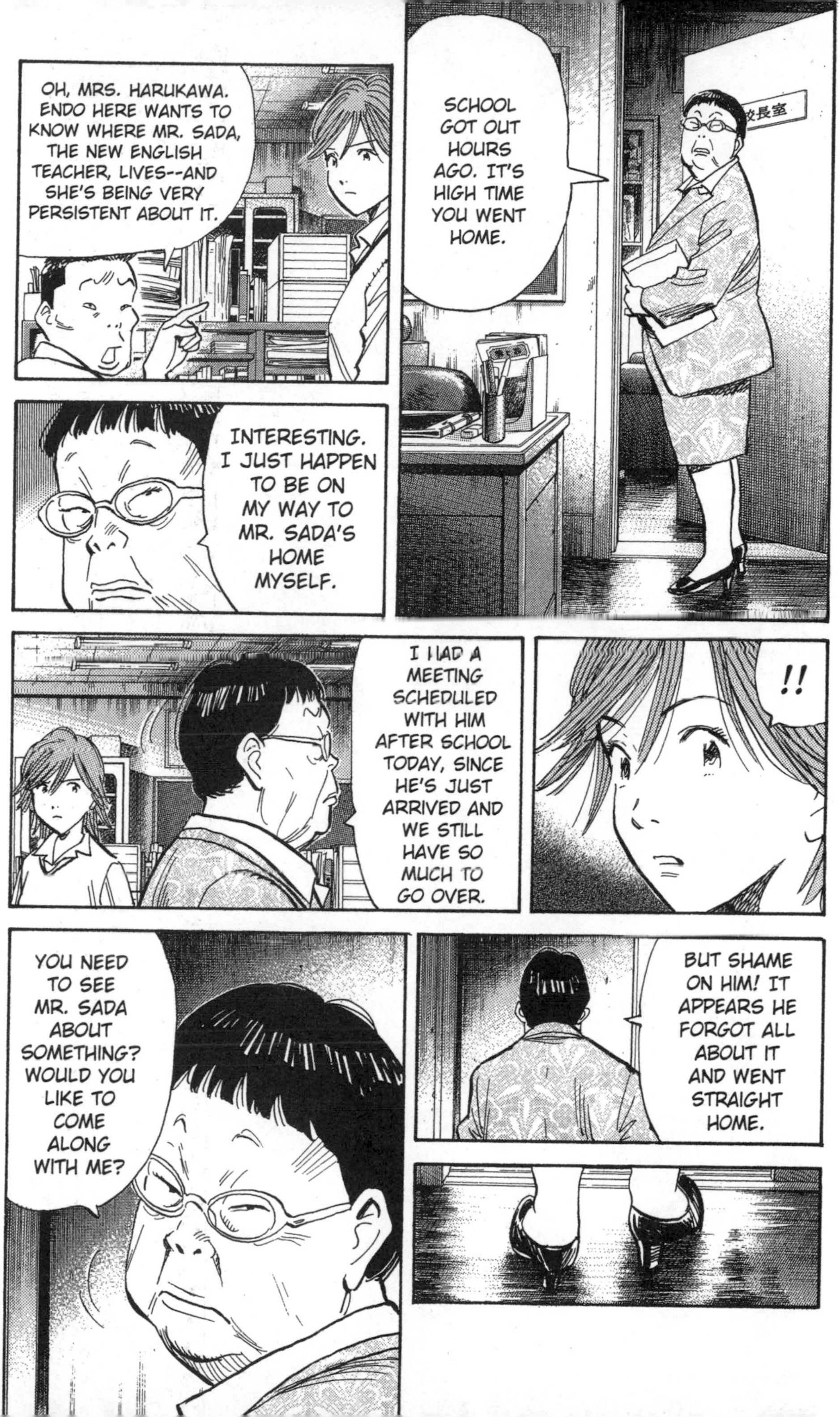
校長室
SCHOOL GOT OUT HOURS AGO. IT'S HIGH TIME YOU WENT HOME.
OH, MRS. HARUKAWA. ENDO HERE WANTS TO KNOW WHERE MR. SADA, THE NEW ENGLISH TEACHER, LIVES--AND SHE'S BEING VERY PERSISTENT ABOUT IT.
INTERESTING. I JUST HAPPEN TO BE ON MY WAY TO MR. SADA'S HOME MYSELF.
!!
I HAD A MEETING SCHEDULED WITH HIM AFTER SCHOOL TODAY, SINCE HE'S JUST ARRIVED AND WE STILL HAVE SO MUCH TO GO OVER.
BUT SHAME ON HIM! IT APPEARS HE FORGOT ALL ABOUT IT AND WENT STRAIGHT HOME.
YOU NEED TO SEE MR. SADA ABOUT SOMETHING? WOULD YOU LIKE TO COME ALONG WITH ME?

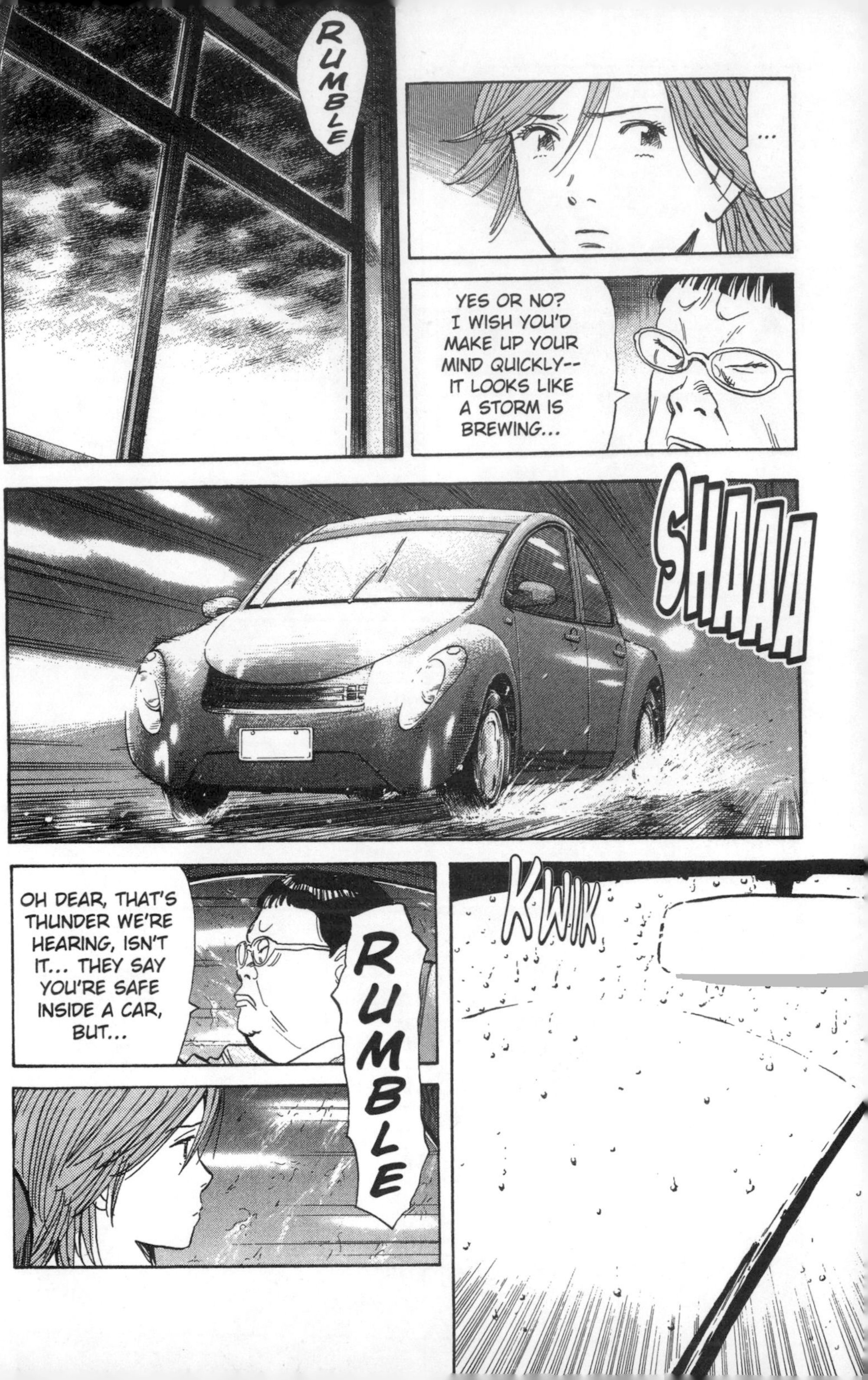
...
YES OR NO? I WISH YOU'D MAKE UP YOUR MIND QUICKLY-- IT LOOKS LIKE A STORM IS BREWING...
RUMBLE
SHAAA
KWIK
OH DEAR, THAT'S THUNDER WE'RE HEARING, ISN'T IT... THEY SAY YOU'RE SAFE INSIDE A CAR, BUT...
RUMBLE

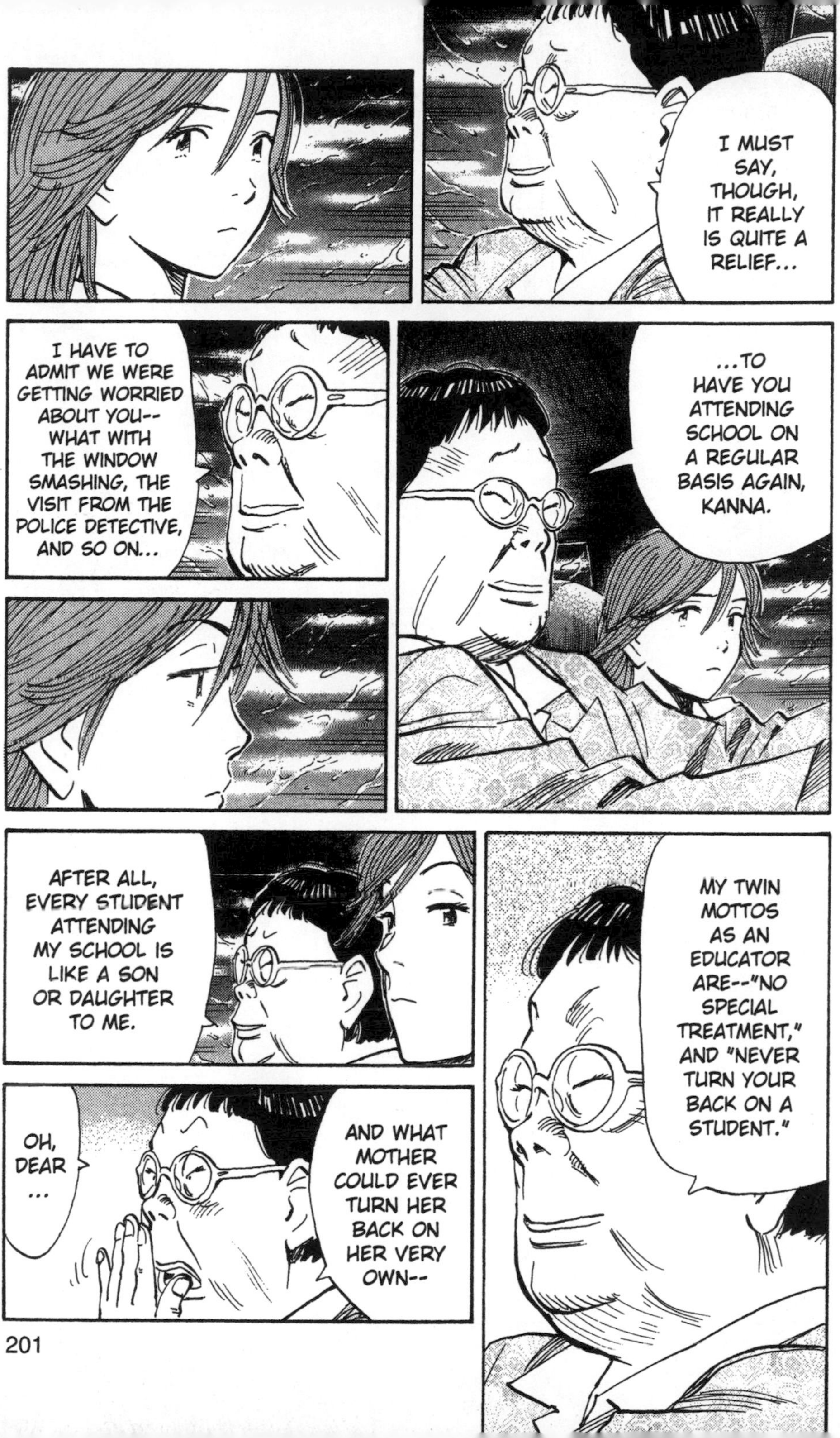
I MUST SAY, THOUGH, IT REALLY IS QUITE A RELIEF...
...TO HAVE YOU ATTENDING SCHOOL ON A REGULAR BASIS AGAIN, KANNA.
I HAVE TO ADMIT WE WERE GETTING WORRIED ABOUT YOU--WHAT WITH THE WINDOW SMASHING, THE VISIT FROM THE POLICE DETECTIVE, AND SO ON...
MY TWIN MOTTOS AS AN EDUCATOR ARE--"NO SPECIAL TREATMENT," AND "NEVER TURN YOUR BACK ON A STUDENT."
AFTER ALL, EVERY STUDENT ATTENDING MY SCHOOL IS LIKE A SON OR DAUGHTER TO ME.
AND WHAT MOTHER COULD EVER TURN HER BACK ON HER VERY OWN--
OH, DEAR...

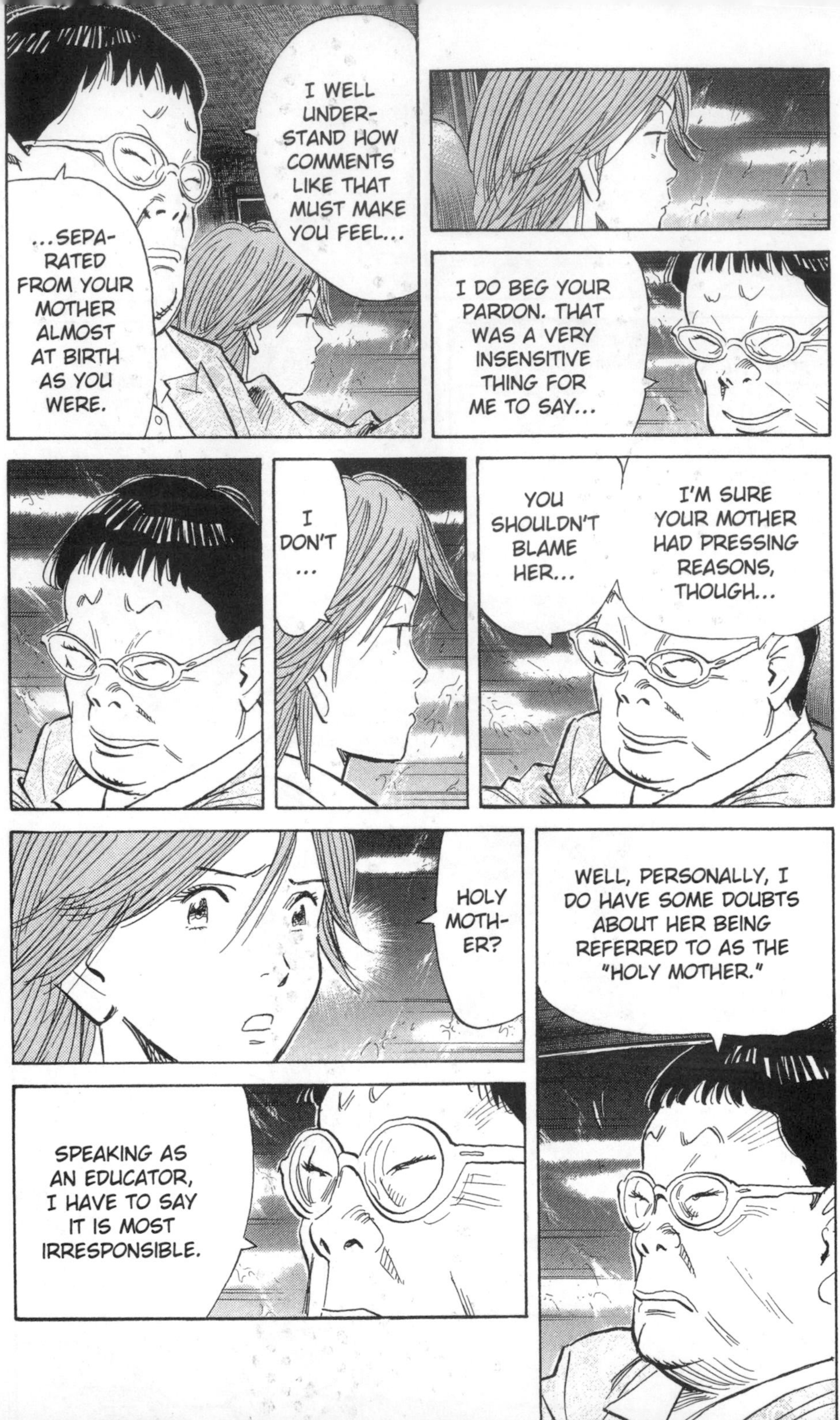

I DO BEG YOUR PARDON. THAT WAS A VERY INSENSITIVE THING FOR ME TO SAY...
I WELL UNDER-STAND HOW COMMENTS LIKE THAT MUST MAKE YOU FEEL...
...SEPA-RATED FROM YOUR MOTHER ALMOST AT BIRTH AS YOU WERE.
I'M SURE YOUR MOTHER HAD PRESSING REASONS, THOUGH...
YOU SHOULDN'T BLAME HER...
I DON'T ...
WELL, PERSONALLY, I DO HAVE SOME DOUBTS ABOUT HER BEING REFERRED TO AS THE "HOLY MOTHER."
HOLY MOTH-ER?
SPEAKING AS AN EDUCATOR, I HAVE TO SAY IT IS MOST IRRESPONSIBLE.

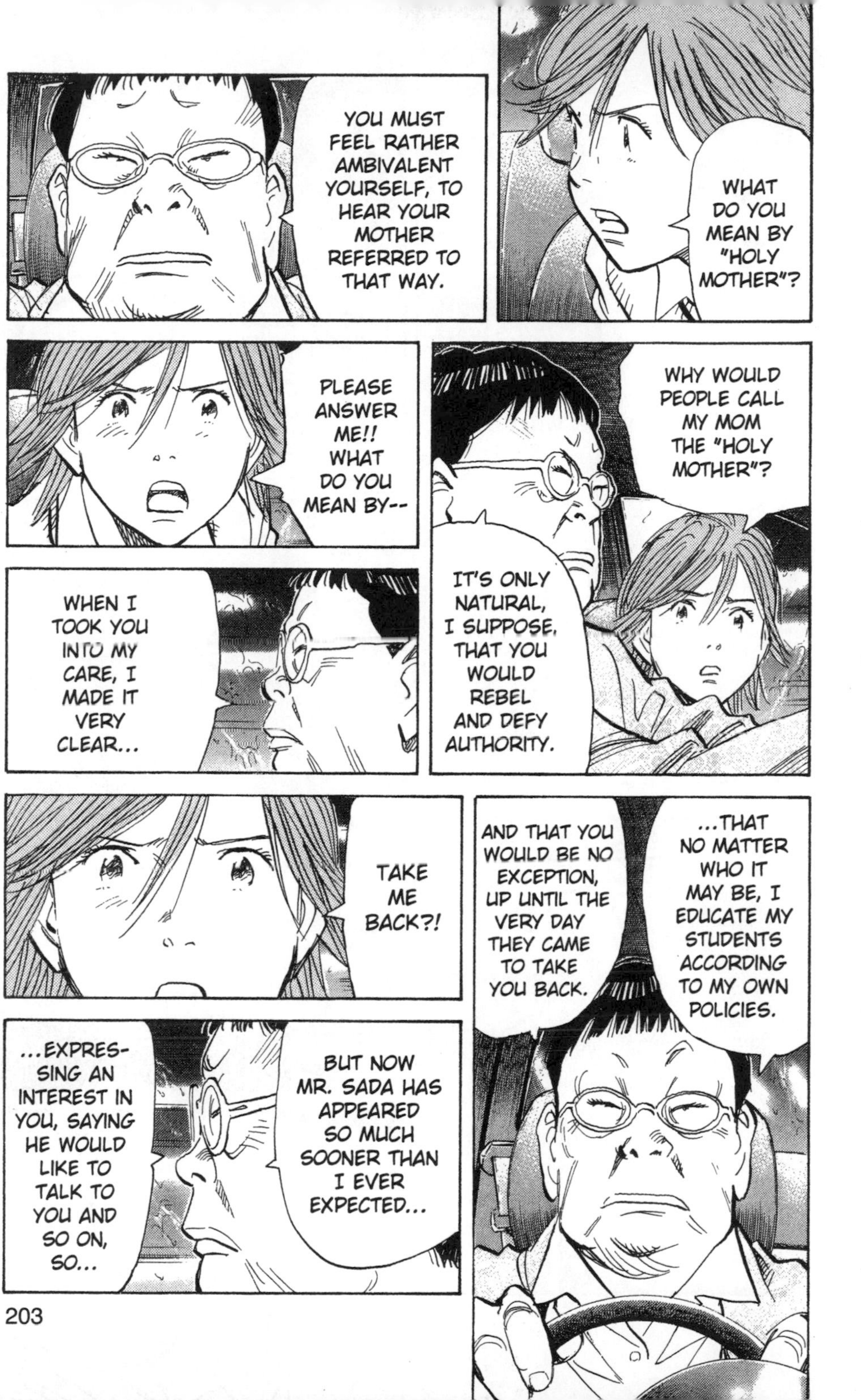
WHAT DO YOU MEAN BY "HOLY MOTHER"?
YOU MUST FEEL RATHER AMBIVALENT YOURSELF, TO HEAR YOUR MOTHER REFERRED TO THAT WAY.
WHY WOULD PEOPLE CALL MY MOM THE "HOLY MOTHER"?
IT'S ONLY NATURAL, I SUPPOSE, THAT YOU WOULD REBEL AND DEFY AUTHORITY.
PLEASE ANSWER ME!! WHAT DO YOU MEAN BY--
WHEN I TOOK YOU INTO MY CARE, I MADE IT VERY CLEAR...
...THAT NO MATTER WHO IT MAY BE, I EDUCATE MY STUDENTS ACCORDING TO MY OWN POLICIES.
AND THAT YOU WOULD BE NO EXCEPTION, UP UNTIL THE VERY DAY THEY CAME TO TAKE YOU BACK.
TAKE ME BACK?!
BUT NOW MR. SADA HAS APPEARED SO MUCH SOONER THAN I EVER EXPECTED...
...EXPRES-SING AN INTEREST IN YOU, SAYING HE WOULD LIKE TO TALK TO YOU AND SO ON, SO...

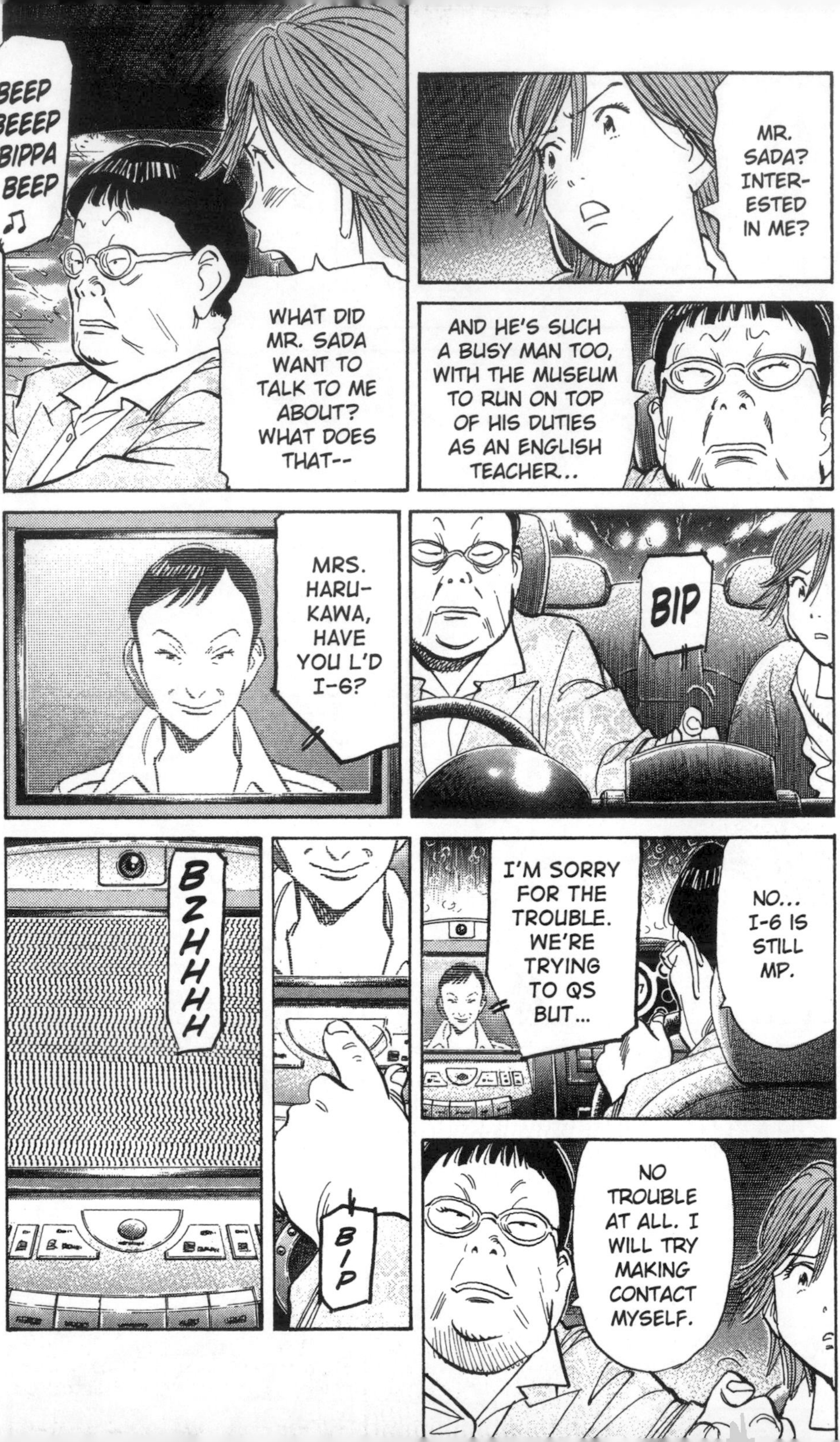
MR. SADA? INTERESTED IN ME?
AND HE'S SUCH A BUSY MAN TOO, WITH THE MUSEUM TO RUN ON TOP OF HIS DUTIES AS AN ENGLISH TEACHER...
BEEP BEEEP BIPPA BEEP ♫
WHAT DID MR. SADA WANT TO TALK TO ME ABOUT? WHAT DOES THAT--
BIP
MRS. HARUKAWA, HAVE YOU L'D I-6?
NO... I-6 IS STILL MP.
I'M SORRY FOR THE TROUBLE. WE'RE TRYING TO QS BUT...
NO TROUBLE AT ALL. I WILL TRY MAKING CONTACT MYSELF.
BIP
BZHHHHH

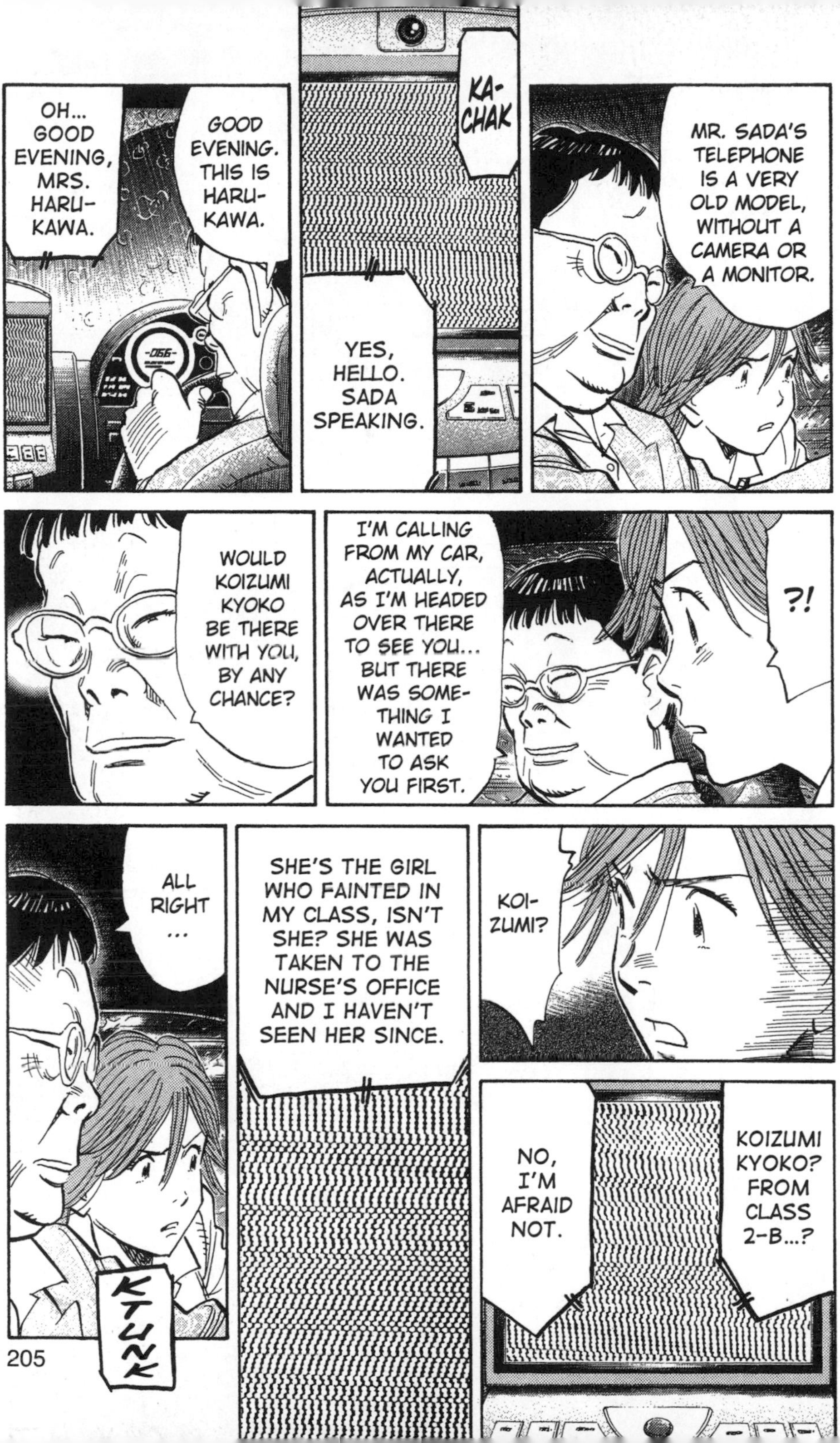
MR. SADA'S TELEPHONE IS A VERY OLD MODEL, WITHOUT A CAMERA OR A MONITOR.
KA-CHAK
YES, HELLO. SADA SPEAKING.
GOOD EVENING. THIS IS HARU-KAWA.
OH... GOOD EVENING, MRS. HARU-KAWA.
?!
I'M CALLING FROM MY CAR, ACTUALLY, AS I'M HEADED OVER THERE TO SEE YOU... BUT THERE WAS SOME-THING I WANTED TO ASK YOU FIRST.
WOULD KOIZUMI KYOKO BE THERE WITH YOU, BY ANY CHANCE?
KOI-ZUMI?
KOIZUMI KYOKO? FROM CLASS 2-B...?
NO, I'M AFRAID NOT.
SHE'S THE GIRL WHO FAINTED IN MY CLASS, ISN'T SHE? SHE WAS TAKEN TO THE NURSE'S OFFICE AND I HAVEN'T SEEN HER SINCE.
ALL RIGHT...
KTUNK

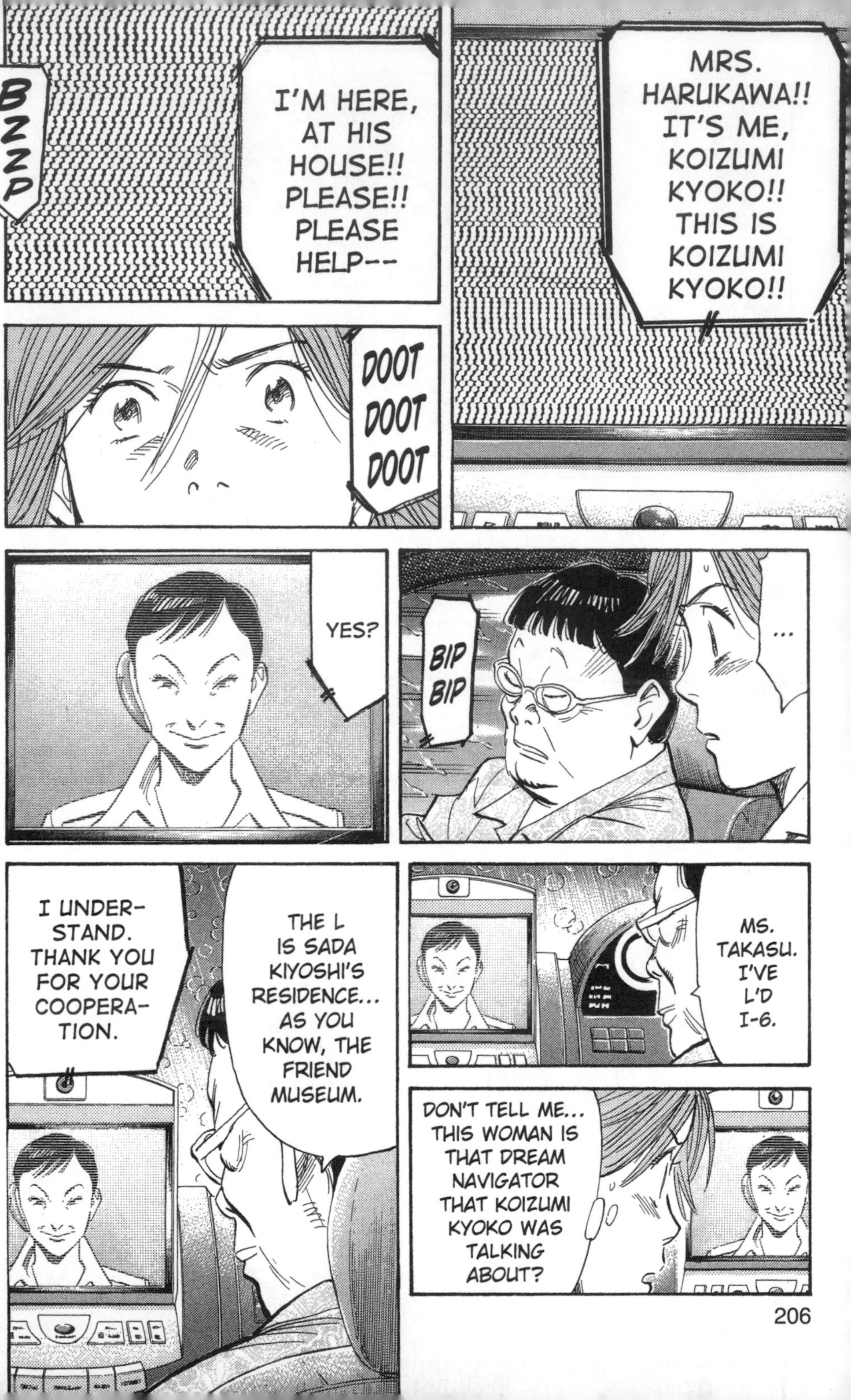
MRS. HARUKAWA!! IT'S ME, KOIZUMI KYOKO!! THIS IS KOIZUMI KYOKO!!
BZZP
I'M HERE, AT HIS HOUSE!! PLEASE!! PLEASE HELP--
DOOT DOOT DOOT
...
BIP BIP
YES?
MS. TAKASU. I'VE L'D I-6.
DON'T TELL ME... THIS WOMAN IS THAT DREAM NAVIGATOR THAT KOIZUMI KYOKO WAS TALKING ABOUT?
THE L IS SADA KIYOSHI'S RESIDENCE... AS YOU KNOW, THE FRIEND MUSEUM.
I UNDER-STAND. THANK YOU FOR YOUR COOPERA-TION.

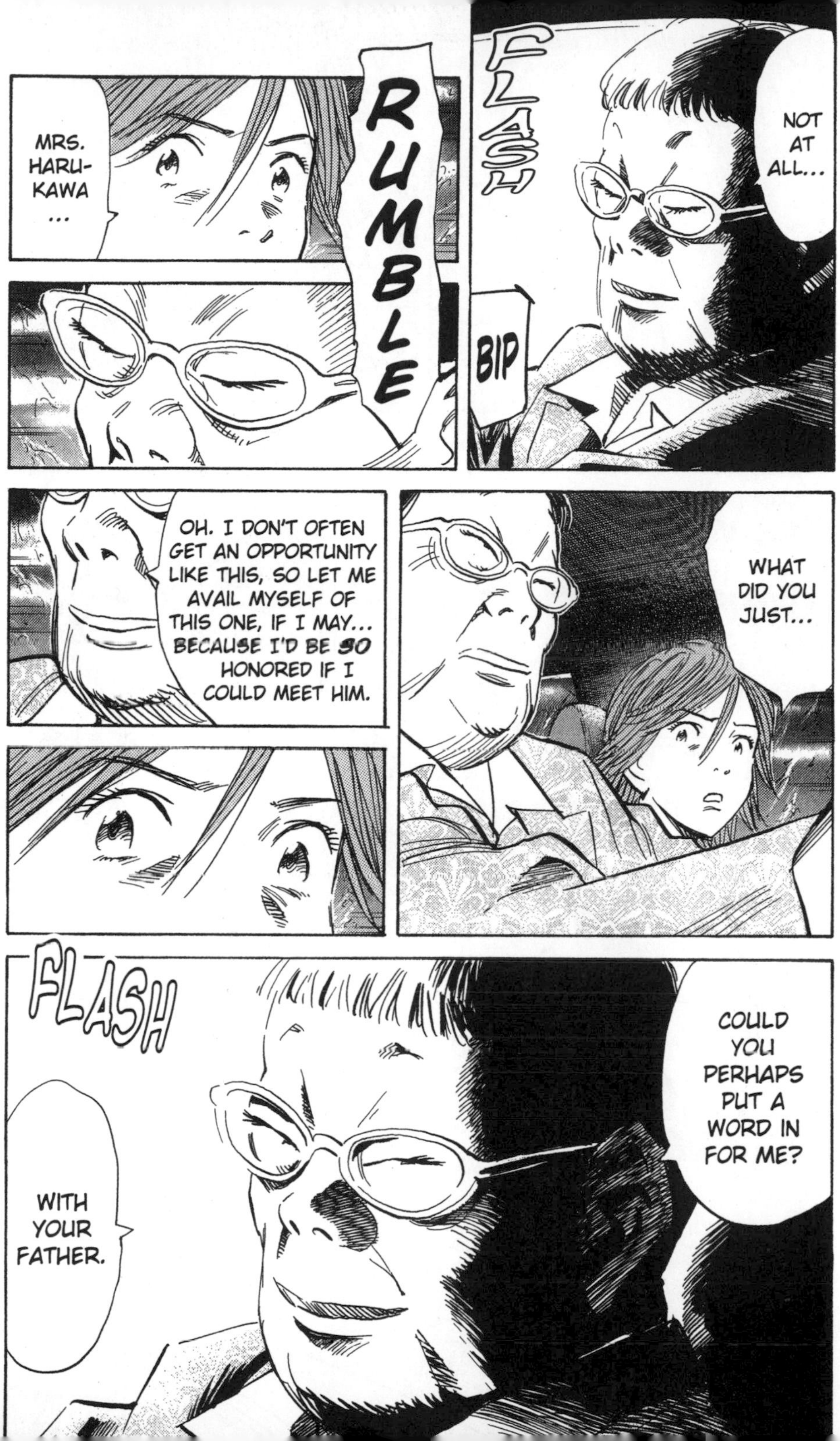
FLASH
NOT AT ALL...
BIP
RUMBLE
MRS. HARUKAWA...
WHAT DID YOU JUST...
OH. I DON'T OFTEN GET AN OPPORTUNITY LIKE THIS, SO LET ME AVAIL MYSELF OF THIS ONE, IF I MAY... BECAUSE I'D BE SO HONORED IF I COULD MEET HIM.
COULD YOU PERHAPS PUT A WORD IN FOR ME?
FLASH
WITH YOUR FATHER.

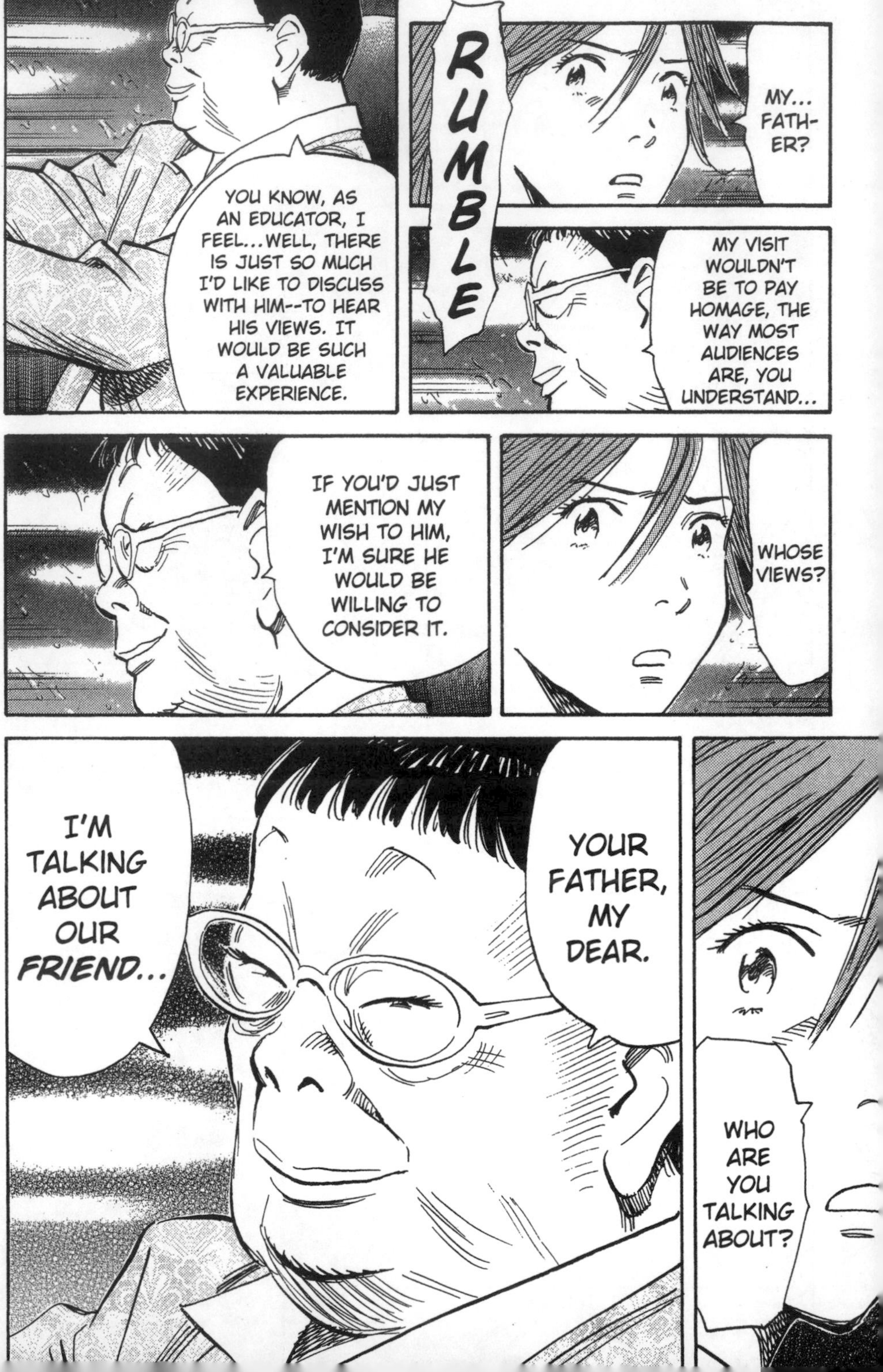
RUMBLE
MY... FATHER?
MY VISIT WOULDN'T BE TO PAY HOMAGE, THE WAY MOST AUDIENCES ARE, YOU UNDERSTAND...
YOU KNOW, AS AN EDUCATOR, I FEEL...WELL, THERE IS JUST SO MUCH I'D LIKE TO DISCUSS WITH HIM--TO HEAR HIS VIEWS. IT WOULD BE SUCH A VALUABLE EXPERIENCE.
WHOSE VIEWS?
IF YOU'D JUST MENTION MY WISH TO HIM, I'M SURE HE WOULD BE WILLING TO CONSIDER IT.
WHO ARE YOU TALKING ABOUT?
YOUR FATHER, MY DEAR.
I'M TALKING ABOUT OUR *FRIEND*...

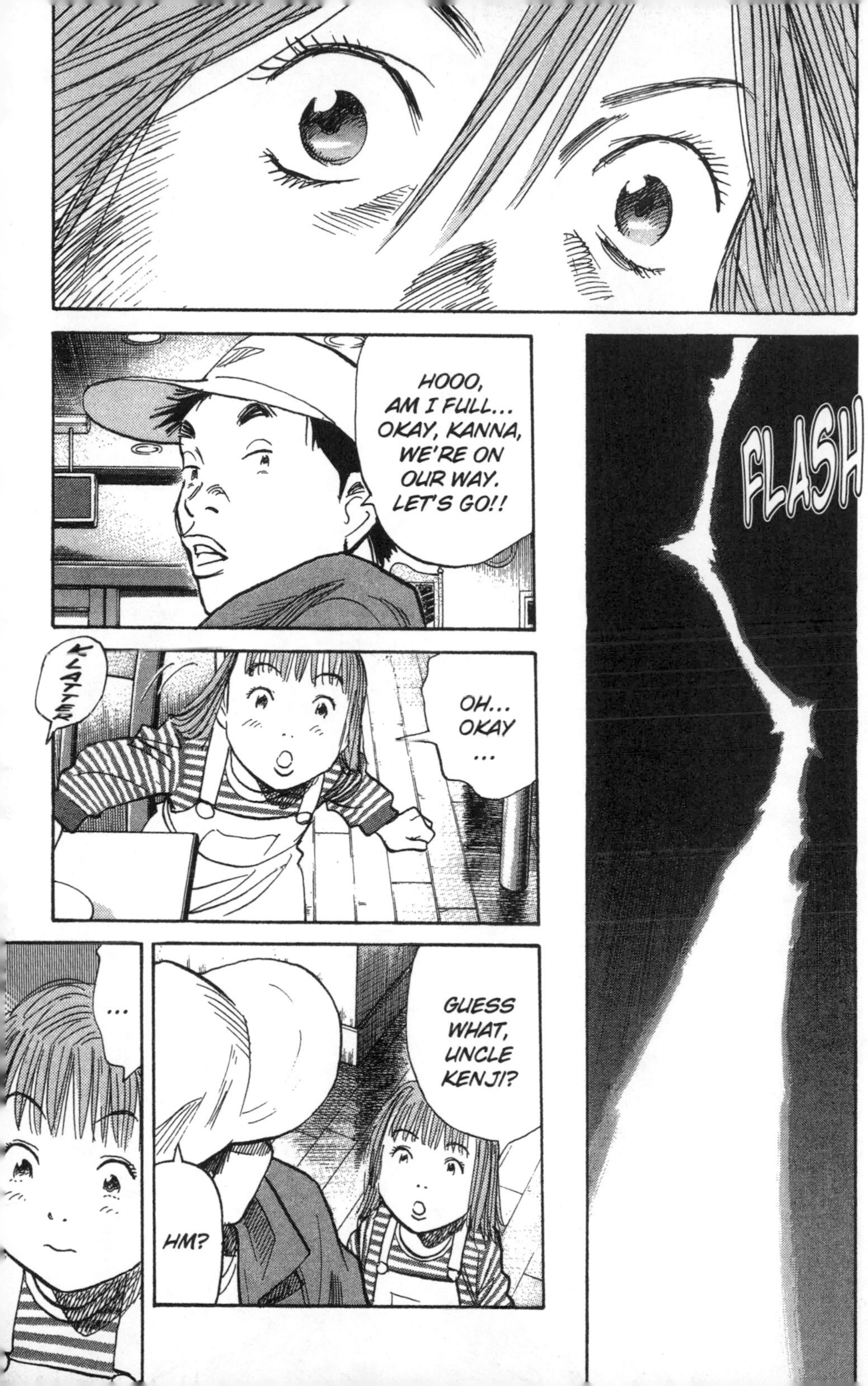
FLASH
HOOO, AM I FULL... OKAY, KANNA, WE'RE ON OUR WAY. LET'S GO!!
OH... OKAY ...
KYATTER
GUESS WHAT, UNCLE KENJI?
HM?
...

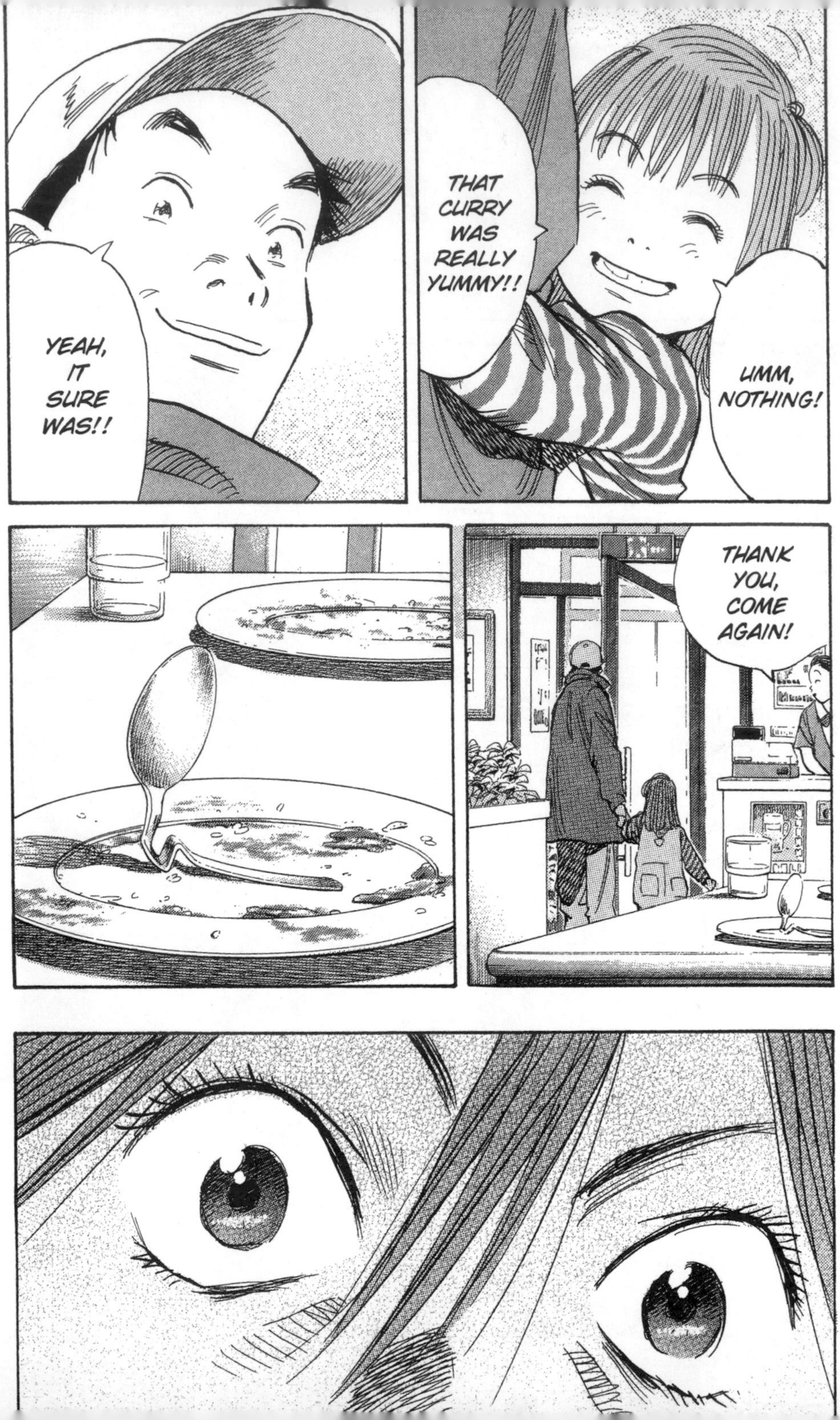
UMM, NOTHING!
THAT CURRY WAS REALLY YUMMY!!
YEAH, IT SURE WAS!!
THANK YOU, COME AGAIN!

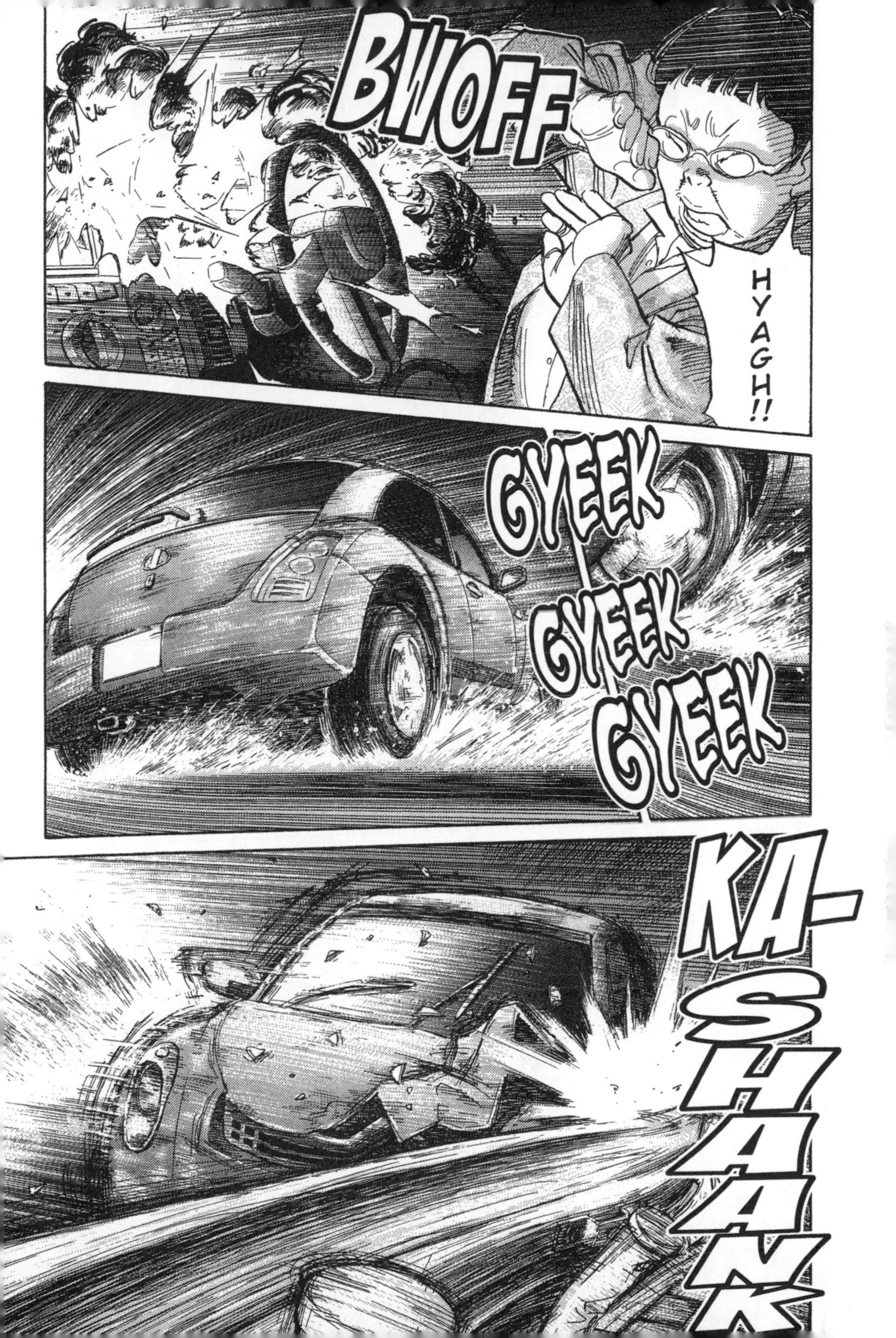
BWOFF
HYAGH!!
GYEEK GYEEK GYEEK
KA-SHAANK

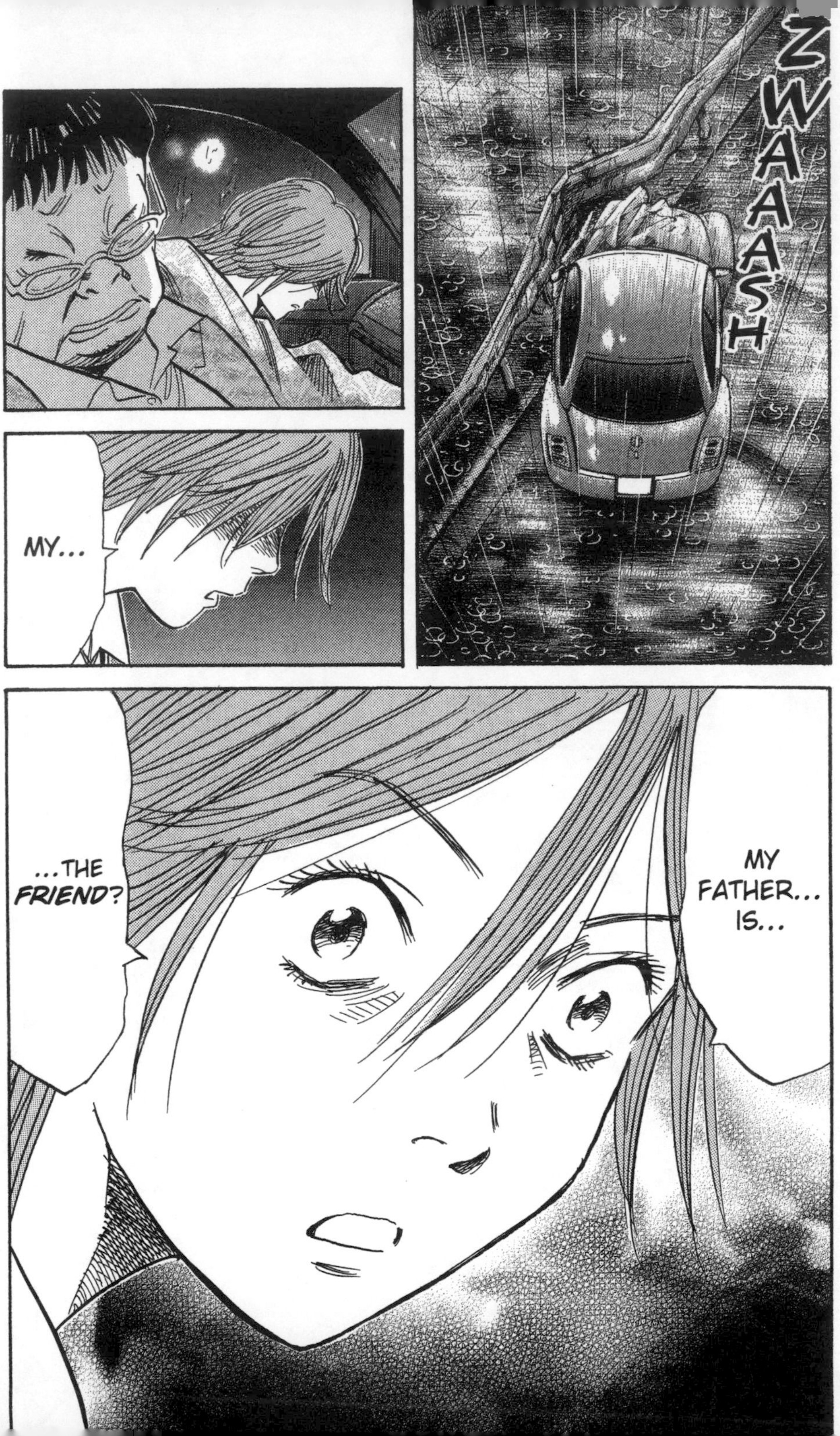
ZWAAAASH
MY...
MY FATHER... IS...
...THE FRIEND?

TO BE CONTINUED

NOTES FROM THE TRANSLATOR

This series follows the Japanese naming convention, with a character's family name followed by their given name. Honorifics such as -*san* and -*kun* are also preserved.

Page 113: *Mugi-cha* is roasted barley tea and is served cold in the summer. *Calpis* is a sweet, fermented milk beverage.

Page 132: Nagashima Shigeo, famed player for the Tokyo Yomiuri Giants. Also known in Japan as "Mr. Giants" and "Mr. Baseball."

Page 151: Books on shelf are Shogakukan encyclopedias for kids and are the kind that most middle-class children would own. From left: *Ships / Working Vehicles / Geography of Japan / Plants / Fish and Mollusks / Amphibians and Reptiles / Animals.*

Page 158: "Amen somen hiya somen" is a nonsensical chant that was popular among Japanese children in the 1970s.

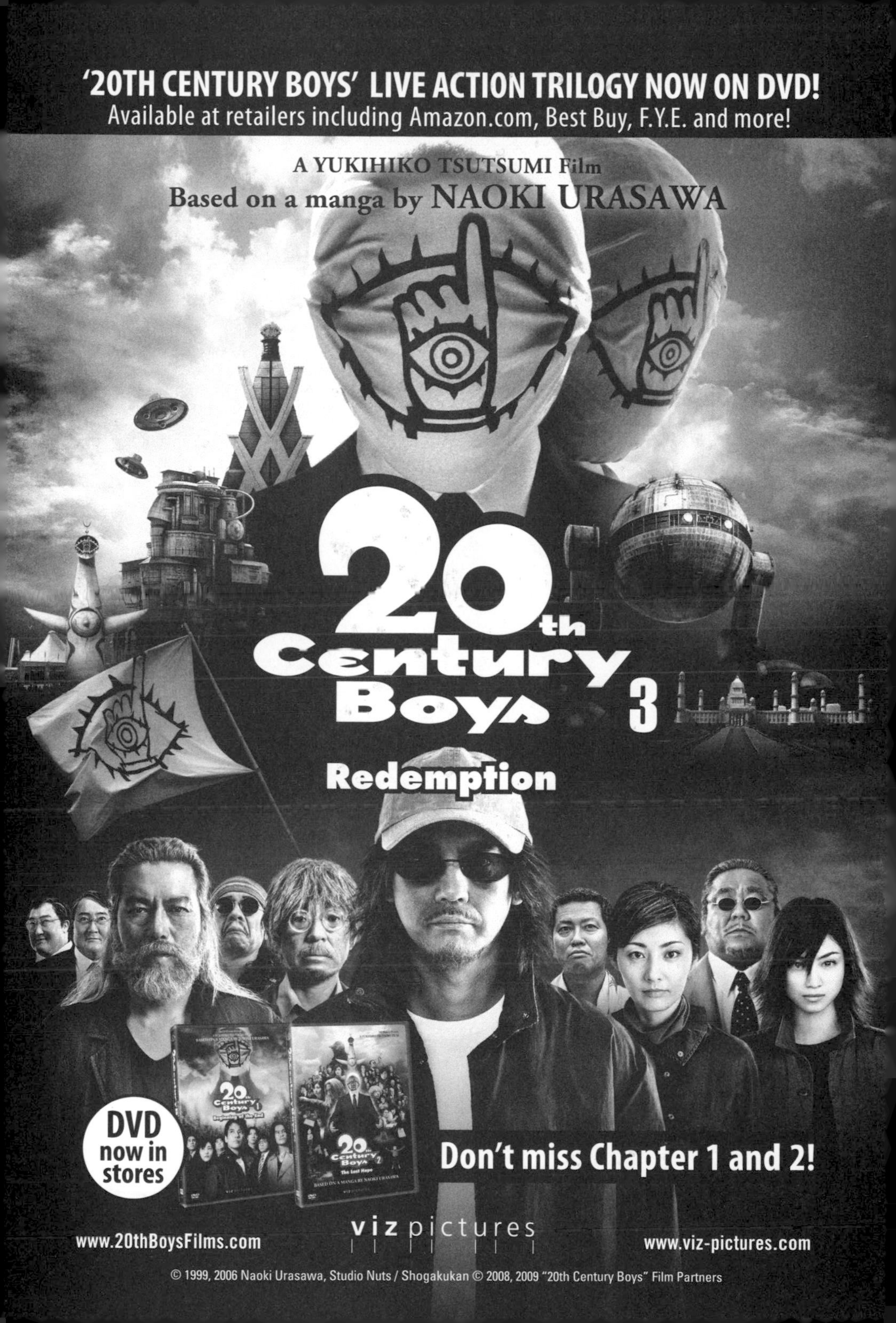
'20TH CENTURY BOYS' LIVE ACTION TRILOGY NOW ON DVD!
Available at retailers including Amazon.com, Best Buy, F.Y.E. and more!
A YUKIHIKO TSUTSUMI Film
Based on a manga by NAOKI URASAWA
20th Century Boys 3
Redemption
DVD now in stores
Don't miss Chapter 1 and 2!
viz pictures
www.20thBoysFilms.com
www.viz-pictures.com
© 1999, 2006 Naoki Urasawa, Studio Nuts / Shogakukan © 2008, 2009 "20th Century Boys" Film Partners